ENCYCLOPEDIA OF
CONFLICTS SINCE WORLD WAR II

ENCYCLOPEDIA OF
CONFLICTS SINCE WORLD WAR II

Volume 1: Afghanistan through Burundi

EDITOR
JAMES CIMENT
New School University

CONTRIBUTORS

KENNETH L. HILL   *La Salle University*

DAVID MacMICHAEL   *University of Oregon*

CARL SKUTSCH   *Baruch College, City University of New York*

SHARPE REFERENCE
an imprint of M.E. Sharpe, Inc.

SHARPE REFERENCE

Sharpe Reference is an imprint of M.E. Sharpe INC.

M.E. Sharpe INC.
80 Business Park Drive
Armonk, NY 10504

© 1999 by M.E. Sharpe INC.

Library of Congress Cataloging-in-Publication Data

Ciment, James.
Encyclopedia of conflicts since World War II / James Ciment.
p. cm.
Includes bibliographical references and index.
Summary: Discusses the roots of war, various alliances and summit meetings
meant to forestall conflict, and the background and events connected with
numerous specific conflicts in the second half of the twentieth century.
ISBN 0-7656-8004-1 (set : alk. paper)
1. World politics—1945– —Encyclopedias. 2. Military history,
Modern—20th century—Encyclopedias. 3. Summit meetings—Encyclopedias.
I. Ciment, James. II. Title.
D843.H49 1999
909.82—dc21
98-28374
CIP

Printed and bound in the United States of America

The paper used in this publication meets the minimum requirements of
American National Standard for Information Sciences—Permanence of
Paper for Printed Library Materials,
ANSI Z 39.48.1984.

BM (c) 10 9 8 7 6 5 4 3 2 1

Vice President and Publisher: Evelyn M. Fazio
Vice President and Production Director: Carmen P. Chetti
Production Editor: Wendy E. Muto
Editorial Coordinator: Aud Thiessen
Editorial Assistants: Esther Clark and Patricia Loo
Fact Checker: Monique Widyono
In-house Typesetter: Wilford Bryan Lammers
Consulting Project Manager: Michael Weber
Cartographer: Alice Thiede, Carto-Graphics
Photo Research: Ann Burns Images

CONTENTS

Volume 3

Volume 4

CONTENTS

Appendixes

Indexes

EDITOR

James Ciment
New School University
New York, New York

CONTRIBUTORS

Kenneth L. Hill
La Salle University
Philadelphia, Pennsylvania

David MacMichael
University of Oregon
Eugene, Oregon

Carl Skutsch
Baruch College
City University of New York
New York, New York

William H. Alexander
Norfolk State University
Norfolk, Virginia

Michael Andregg
Ground Zero
St. Paul, Minnesota

D. Elwood Dunn
University of the South
Sewanee, Tennessee

Steven Hoffman
Skidmore College
Saratoga Springs, New York

Mark Ungar
Brooklyn College
Brooklyn, NY

Ravi Kalia
City College
City University of New York
New York, New York

Gordon McCormick
Naval Post-Graduate School
Monterey, California

ACKNOWLEDGMENTS

With any project of this magnitude, there are numerous people to acknowledge for their contributions. First, I offer a much-deserved thank you to the publisher and editors at M.E. Sharpe for their professionalism, patience, and dedication to this project—including Evelyn Fazio, publisher; Wendy Muto, production editor; and Aud Thiessen, editorial coordinator. In addition, the very capable project manager, Michael Weber, made sense of the 180-plus entries swirling through cyberspace. Anne Burns, our photo researcher, is responsible for the many outstanding images found in these volumes. I also thank the librarians at New York University, the New York Public Library, and the Library of Congress for their tireless research and reference help.

Carl Skutsch would personally like to thank his wife, Kristin Marting, who supported, encouraged, and endured him during the project. He says he could not have done it without her. Dave MacMichael would personally like to thank Lawrence Birns and the Council on Hemispheric Affairs for access to their special collection of material on Latin American conflicts, as well as to the staff of the Fenwick Memorial Library at George Mason University for their assistance.

Finally, all the contributors to *Encyclopedia of Conflicts Since World War II* join together to dedicate these volumes to the tens of millions of civilians—men, women, and children alike—who have suffered in the conflicts chronicled in these pages.

INTRODUCTION

The Dawn of the Post–World War II Era

This encyclopedia covers every major international and civil conflict since the end of World War II. Its four volumes contain some 1,400 pages and more than 180 individual entries. That it takes all of this paper and ink to chronicle a mere fifty or so years of humanity's propensity to settle its differences through bloodshed is both depressing and disheartening. If, as American Civil War General William Tecumseh Sherman famously noted, "war is hell," then these volumes serve as a travel guide to a netherworld of recent human creation.

In 1945, the world emerged from a conflagration of epic proportions. With the broad exception of the Western Hemisphere, no part of the world lay untouched by World War II. Europe, Asia, Africa, and Oceania had all seen armies pass through and great battles fought. Much of the Soviet Union, Europe, North Africa, China, Japan, and the Pacific islands had been devastated by bombing, artillery, street-fighting, and tank battles. Humanity emerged from the war hungry, displaced, and shell shocked.

What would happen next? There was hope. Fascism—in its German, Italian, and Japanese forms—had been crushed. A new United Nations offered an international dispute-resolution forum that seemed to offer more promise than had the doomed League of Nations, which had emerged out of World War I. There was an alliance, however shaky and uneasy, between the two new great powers—the Soviet Union and the United States. For the peoples of Asia, Africa, and other colonized regions, the end of the war promised the possibility of independence, if only because the imperialist European powers had been left so wasted by the conflict. To paraphrase a popular World War II era song, the lights appeared to be coming on all over the world.

Sadly, however, they only flickered. The grand wartime alliance of the Soviet Union and the United States quickly degenerated into a chilly stand-off of disappointment, distrust, and blustering. The United Nations—enveloped in the smoth-ering ideological confrontation between East and West—proved nearly as impotent in settling disputes as the League.

The European powers, particularly France and Portugal, showed themselves unwilling to accept what British Prime Minister Harold Macmillan dubbed "the winds of change"—that is, decolonization. Moreover, these stubborn colonial powers were joined by settler states such as Israel and South Africa, where the population of European origin—seen as alien by their non-European co-inhabitants, but lacking a native land to return to—attacked and came under attack repeatedly.

Even where the Europeans did depart, longstanding indigenous disputes—made worse by imperialist policy and practice—erupted with a vengeance. The nearly one million Muslims and Hindus slaughtered in the partition of the Indian subcontinent did not bode well for the post-colonial order, as the seemingly endless conflicts that later engulfed Africa seemed to bear out.

Finally, hanging over the collective head of humankind was a new weapon—tried and proved on Japan near the end of World War II—that finally made world-ending Armageddon—a portentious element in nearly all the world's great faiths—a distinct possibility. The mushroom cloud and the specter of World War III had come to haunt the world's imagination.

World Wars III and IV?

Some have argued, however, that World War III is not a specter but a reality, having taken the form of a cold war between the superpowers that regularly turned hot in battlefields as far strewn as Angola, Hungary, and Vietnam, and as separate in time as Greece (1947), Laos (early 1960s), and Nicaragua (1980s). In other words, World War III began the moment World War II ended and ended with the collapse of the Soviet Union in 1991.

But what of the conflicts that have erupted since the end of the cold war? Despite predictions of history ending with the fall of communism and the universal "triumph" of Western-style free-market economies and political democracy, fighting and dying has continued on every single continent, with the possible exception of North America. Might the many wars in both the former communist and free worlds be the opening battles in a conflict that we might call World War IV?

A look at the evolution of war in the twentieth century might offer an answer. The world wars of the first half of the twentieth century evolved from the largely static, European-based World War I to the mobile, semi-global World War II. Moreover, the fronts of World War I—in Russia, France, and the Middle East—were hundreds of miles apart and involved largely the same adversaries. The fronts of World War II were thousands of miles apart and were fought by semi-related adversaries: largely Germany and the Soviet Union in Eastern Europe; Britain, Germany, and the United States in Western Europe and North Africa; and the United States, Japan, and China in Asia and the Pacific.

The "world wars" of the second half of the twentieth century have been transformed into truly global conflicts involving dozens of adversaries fighting along fronts that are entirely disconnected from one another. But World War II and the hypothetical World War III do have one thing in common: many of the adversaries were partly or fully integrated into grand alliances, even if the combatants fought their wars for a host of reasons unrelated to the power politics of the cold war. Moreover, as in World War II, many of the conflicts of World War III were charged with ideological differences. As for the even more hypothetical World War IV, any hint of grand alliances and ideology seem to have disappeared altogether. Now, it appears, wars are fought for entirely local reasons. Or are they?

As the proponents of the end-of-history thesis argue, the world has supposedly entered a post-ideological era, where new or ongoing conflicts merely involve a working-through of the problems on the road to Western values. In other words, conflicts since the end of the cold war are essentially non-ideological, unlike those that came before.

For example, the fascist warlords of Japan justified their aggression in World War II as a means to replace what they considered to be a European-biased imperialist order with a distinctly Asian order, led by Tokyo. Similarly, third-world communist revolutionaries—often backed, though rarely directed, by Moscow—reasoned that their attacks on the existing order were being made to supplant a Western and capitalist-dominated economic and political world order with a locally controlled socialist system.

Looking back, while we may agree or disagree with the aims of the Japanese militarists and third-world revolutionaries, we might also note that their appraisals of the inequities of the existing order were not entirely off the mark. Europe did dominate Asia in the first half of the twentieth century and the capitalist West did control much of the non-communist developing world in the second half.

Finally, just as the end of World War II spawned hope for a peaceful post-war order, so did the demise of the cold war. That neither fulfilled this hope is testament to the fact that the economic and political inequities that spawned those conflicts still lived in the eras that followed.

Absent an ideological framework, the conflicts of the post–cold war era seem to lack rhyme or reason, fought as they appear to be over such non-rational issues as ethnicity, tribe, and religion. But it can be argued that these issues are largely symbolic ones, useful handles for adversaries seeking to identify friend or foe in struggles over diminishing resources and wealth in the developing world—those diminishing resources and wealth being a symptom of the basic inequities of the world order in which the West continues to dominate.

So what is new in all of this? Perhaps nothing. Perhaps, the concept that the last hundred years are a history of four consecutive "world wars" is flawed. Rather than splitting history, it might be better to try lumping it together. Since the late fifteenth century, the capitalist order of Europe—and, later, a few of the more rapidly developing countries such as the United States and Japan—has been gradually extending its grip over the rest of the world, while the rest of the world has mounted a mighty, though often futile, resistance. Might not the various "world wars" of the twentieth century be seen as mere battles in a conflict which was half a millennium in the making?

This is, perhaps, too big a question for any single study to answer, especially one such as this—one that attempts to provide the details of dozens of wars that may or may not be manifestations of some grand, epoch-making conflict. Rather, the following entries attempt to define the differences, even as the accumulation of that detail hints at something bigger than the sum of the parts.

Organization—How to Use This Encyclopedia

Encyclopedia of Conflicts Since World War II is divided into three sections, plus two appendices.

Roots of War

The first section is called "Roots of War" and consists of eight entries outlining the major types of conflicts and the underlying causes of war in the post–World War II era. Each entry concludes with a bibliography.

"Cold War Confrontations" outlines how different historians interpret the roots of the cold war in Europe and the developing world. In addition, it discusses how the superpower struggle manifested itself in various developing world conflicts. "Anti-Colonialism" reveals the ways in which many of the conflicts of the past fifty years remain a legacy of the European imperialist order of past centuries. "People's Wars" examines the means by which peoples of the developing world have struggled to overcome the legacy of the imperialist order in a world divided ideologically between East and West. "Coups" explains why violent internal power struggles—usually involving various groups of elites in developing world countries—have been so ubiquitous over the past fifty years. "Invasions and Border Disputes" provides an examination of international conflicts within the context of international law and geopolitical power struggles. "Ethnic and Religious Conflicts" explains why and how these long-standing internal divisions can sometimes become the battlelines of civil conflicts. "Terrorism and International Inci-

dents" discusses the means and ends of perhaps the most desperate of tactics in modern warfare. Finally, "International Arms Trade" offers a study of how the largely politically neutral marketplace in weapons has served to exacerbate the conflicts of the post–World War II era.

Alliances and Treaties

This section deals with the ways various countries, regions, blocs of geographically and ideologically united or culturally related nations, or the international community as a whole, have dealt with threats to security, resolved conflicts, and maintained peace. In general, these efforts fall into two general areas: collective security arrangements in the form of alliances and blocs, and conflict resolution and international tension reduction through the United Nations and international summits. This section consists of twenty entries, arranged alphabetically. Each of the entries concludes with a "See Also" heading that directs the reader to related entries, and a Bibliography listing articles and books for further reading.

Conflicts

By far the longest section of this encyclopedia, "Conflicts" consists of some 151 entries. These entries are titled and arranged according to the most important country involved in the conflict. In some cases, the entries are titled alphabetically. For example, the India-Pakistan conflict of 1965 is listed under India simply because "I" comes before "P" in the dictionary. In the case of Israel's struggles with surrounding Arab nations, the conflicts are listed under Israel because it remains the key nation in these conflicts, fighting against a host of enemies.

After listing the most important country involved in the conflict, the entry heading indicates the type of conflict and the participants in the conflict. The type of conflict category correlates with the "Roots of War" essays. For example, if a conflict is listed as a cold war confrontation, the reader may turn to the appropriate essay in part one on this type of conflict to learn more about how that conflict fits into the larger context of the cold war.

Each "Conflicts" entry concludes with two items: a "See Also" heading that lists related conflict and alliances entries and a Bibliography listing books and articles for further reading.

Appendixes

Biographies

This section consists of brief biographies of the most significant individuals involved in the conflicts and diplomacy of the post–World War II era.

Glossary

This section offers definitions of key organizations, groups, and terms involved in the conflicts and diplomacy of the post–World War II era. It also offers a handy reference guide to the many abbreviations and acronyms listed in the "Alliances and Diplomacy" and "Conflicts" entries.

Bibliographies

In addition to the bibliographies in the individual entries, a general bibliography is presented here, offering reading suggestions on the general history and theory of warfare, as well as individual conflicts.

Indexes

Encyclopedia of Conflicts Since World War II contains three separate indexes: a general subject, a biographical and organizational name index, and a geographical index.

ROOTS OF WAR

Cold War Confrontations

Introduction

The cold war—a term coined by journalist and scholar Walter Lippman in 1947—refers to the forty-five-year-long confrontation between the United States and the Soviet Union that began at the end of World War II and ended with the collapse of communism in Eastern Europe and the Soviet Union at the end of the 1980s and beginning of the 1990s.

Though appropriate for the time and poetic enough to last the ages, the term cold war is something of a misnomer. Contrasted to a hot war—such as World War II—it implies a non-violent confrontation between the two great superpowers of the post–World War II era. Where hot wars produce invasions, power politics, and the application of violence, the cold war consisted of tense borders, ideological disputes, and an arms race—an unnerving and costly war, but essentially a bloodless one. Indeed, many American and Soviet apologists for the nuclear arms race that accompanied it say the cold war kept the peace.

This is roughly true in Europe, where the cold war began, but it is preposterous when applied to much of the rest of the world, particularly the developing world. There the cold war turned hot. The cold war only occasionally involved soldiers from the United States and the Soviet Union in significant numbers (Korea and Vietnam for the former; Afghanistan for the latter). Instead, the two superpowers armed their proxies, or substitutes, in Asia, Africa, and Latin America to do their fighting—and their dying—for them.

The cold war is also a misleading term for a less direct reason: both the United States and the Soviet Union tended to interpret most civil and international conflicts as part of the great ideological struggle between East and West. Indeed, policy-makers in both Washington and Moscow generally believed that their superpower opponent was behind every conflict. Both sides often failed to consider indigenous historical considerations in their assessment of why conflicts erupted and how conflicts could be resolved. Thus, in Vietnam, the United States ignored traditional Viet nationalism, while the Soviet Union underplayed clan strife and Islamic fundamentalism before intervening in Afghanistan.

This entry attempts to define the cold war in two ways. First, it examines the origins of the conflict—specifically, the different schools of thought concerning who started it and why. Second, the cold war is examined in its effects—how it played itself out in the developing world. Indeed, after the initial, largely non-violent confrontation over Europe in the late 1940s, the cold war's real battleground was in Asia, Africa, and Latin America. First, however, an account of the cold war is required.

Origins of the Cold War

If the cold war began shortly after World War II, its background can be found in the disaster of World War I. In March 1917, the czarist government of Russia collapsed, a victim of wartime shortages and anti-war sentiment as well as other, more longterm problems. The democratic government that replaced it insisted on keeping its wartime obligations to its allies France and England. This inspired more unrest in Russian cities, leading to a second uprising, spearheaded by the communist Bolsheviks under the leadership of Vladimir Lenin and implemented through local worker and peasant councils, known as "soviets." Promising "land, bread, and peace," the new Bolshevik government immediately pulled Russia (soon to be renamed the Soviet Union) out of World War I.

The revolution set off a civil war between Bolshevik and anti-Bolshevik, or "white" Russian forces—bolstered by small contingents of troops from Britain, France, Japan, Czechoslovakia, and elsewhere. The civil war ravaged the country for two years and resulted in the total victory of Lenin and the Bolsheviks. The United States, among other nations, severed diplomatic relations with the new government in Moscow, not reopening them until 1933.

Meanwhile, within the Soviet Union, a struggle emerged following the death of Lenin in 1924 between advocates of world revolution and proponents of "socialism in a single country." The latter, led by Joseph Stalin, triumphed. Stalin industrialized the economy rapidly. He did this by collectivizing agriculture, starving out the independent peasantry, and centralizing economic decision-making. In the process, millions of people died, but the Soviet Union made rapid strides in creating an industrial infrastructure, an achievement admired by many in the West who were dismayed by capitalism's failure in the Great Depression.

Indeed, it was that Great Depression that helped propel the rise to power of National Socialism—or Nazism—in Germany in 1933. Advocating renewed militarism and German racial superiority, Nazi Germany quickly rearmed and began its expansionist crusade.

Nazism and Soviet communism were bitterly opposed to each other, but for pragmatic reasons—each feared the other's power—they signed a non-aggression pact in August 1939. A month later, the Nazis invaded Poland, with the Soviets taking their own half of the defeated nation. England and France immediately declared war on Germany, and World War II began, with the Soviet Union largely neutral.

In June 1941, however, the Nazis tore up the non-aggression pact and sent a massive force into the Soviet Union in the greatest invasion in history. Within months, the Soviets had fallen back to the suburbs of Moscow, and it appeared as if the country might completely fall to the Nazis. Gradually, however, over the next year and a half, the Soviet Red Army would halt the invasion and begin to turn the tide.

Meanwhile, following Japan's attack on Pearl Harbor on December 7, 1941, the United States entered the war. (Japan, Germany, and Italy had formed an alliance called "the Axis." After Pearl Harbor, Germany and Italy declared war on the United States.) An alliance was quickly established between the three main anti-Axis powers—Great Britain, the Soviet Union, and the United States. There were strains in the alliance, however. Stalin, in particular, was angry at what he perceived to be delays in Anglo-American plans to open a second front against Nazi Germany in France. Still, the alliance held through the end of the European war in May 1945. By the war's final year, when it was apparent that it was only a matter of time until Germany was defeated, questions began to present themselves concerning the post-war order. There were essentially three important areas of dispute: the fate of Germany, the fate of Eastern Europe, and the ongoing war with Japan.

In February 1945, the leaders of the three great powers—Soviet Premier Stalin, British Prime Minister Winston Churchill, and U.S. President Franklin Roosevelt—had met at Yalta, in the Russian Crimea. There it was decided that Germany would be jointly occupied by the victors, East European nations would be permitted to decide their own destiny in popular elections (so long as they pursued a pro-Soviet foreign policy), and the Soviet Union would join the Anglo-American war against Japan ninety days after the surrender of Germany.

In July, the three powers met again at Potsdam, a suburb of Berlin, the former capital of the now-defeated Germany. There the three powers created a joint military administration (which now included France) for occupied Germany and agreed to move the borders of Poland westward. In mid-conference, however, the American delegation—headed by U.S. President Harry Truman, who had replaced Roosevelt upon the latter's death in April—received word that the atomic bomb had proved successful in tests in the New Mexico desert. The atomic bomb rendered Soviet help in the war against Japan unnecessary. By implication, this undermined Britain and America's need to offer concessions to the Soviet Union over Eastern Europe—consisting largely of pro-Soviet regimes. In early September, following two atomic bomb attacks against its cities, Hiroshima and Nagasaki, Japan formally surrendered and was occupied by the United States.

Post–World War II Crises

It did not take long for tensions to build between the former Allies. When the Soviet Union demanded access to the Dardanelles—linking the Black Sea to the Mediterranean—and Iran, with its oil reserves, the United States and Britain refused. Meanwhile, the Soviet Union refused to participate in the World Bank and International Monetary Fund, two institutions designed to revive the war-damaged capitalist economies of Europe and Asia. In Eastern Europe and the Balkans tensions were highest. With the Red Army occupying all of the former and much of the latter (the main exceptions being much of Yugoslavia and Greece), there appeared to be little the Allies could do to demand free elections, short of launching World War III. In 1946, former British Prime Minister Churchill warned of a Soviet-imposed "iron curtain" falling across Eastern Europe.

In Greece, however, a civil war between pro-Western and communist forces offered an opportunity. In 1947, the British government told Washington that it no longer had the resources to back the pro-Western elements there. This was part of Britain's overall retreat from much of the world, thus letting the United States assume the mantle of Western leadership. The American administration responded with the Truman Doctrine, effectively promising U.S. aid to any country attempting to fight off a communist insurgency. That same year, George Kennan, a State Department officer in America's Moscow embassy, enunciated a policy—known as the "containment" doctrine—which soon won the attention of the U.S. foreign policy establishment. The doctrine proposed that the Soviet Union's expansionist policies must be resisted by force if necessary, especially in those areas of vital interest to the United States.

Eastern Europe, it was soon decided, lay outside that area. Thus, as Stalin imposed pro-Soviet Communist regimes in these countries by force, the United States did little but complain. By the end of the 1940s, then, both Germany and Europe were divided into two spheres, with the western half of Germany and the continent (supported by the United States through the massive aid of the Marshall Plan) becoming democratic and capitalist and the eastern half (under the umbrella of the Soviet army) communist. Both sides soon organized military blocs to protect themselves against attacks by the other. In 1949, the United States established the North Atlantic Treaty Organization (NATO), followed six years later by the Warsaw Pact of Soviet-bloc countries. With the occasional confrontation over Berlin, the East-West confrontation in Europe soon settled into a status quo of peace, economic development, and nuclear tension (the Soviet Union having developed its own atomic bomb in 1949).

The Cold War Shifts to the Third World

By 1950, the battle lines between the capitalist and communist worlds had shifted to Asia. In 1949, the Communist Chinese had defeated the nationalists in a massive civil war. A year later, the Communist North Koreans invaded the non-Communist southern half of the peninsula. The United States—at the head of a United Nations force—rose to the latter's defense. The conflict became a three-year-long bloody stalemate following Communist China's entry into the war at the end of 1950. Meanwhile, in 1954, French colonial forces were defeated in Vietnam by Communist-led nationalists, leaving Vietnam divided between a Communist north and a non-Communist south.

Tensions between the Soviet Union and the United States eased a bit by the late 1950s. A more liberal Nikita Khrushchev had taken power in the Soviet Union following the death of Stalin in 1953. Khrushchev began to enunciate the doctrine of "peaceful co-

existence" with the West. Still, Khrushchev was determined to keep East European countries in the Soviet orbit, sending an invasion force into wavering Hungary in 1956. The United States and the West refused to intervene, revealing to many in Eastern Europe that there was little chance the West would help them rid the region of Soviet control. The decision not to intervene was part of Eisenhower's policy. After the war ended in Korea, he was not eager to engage U.S. forces in conflicts around the world. Instead, Eisenhower relied on covert action by the Central Intelligence Agency to overthrow developing world regimes deemed hostile to the West, while keeping the Soviets at bay through America's overwhelming nuclear superiority, which had been enhanced by the detonation of the first hydrogen bomb in 1953.

Increasingly, however, there was growing dissent to these policies in both the United States and Soviet Union. In America, many politicians, including 1960 presidential candidate John F. Kennedy, believed that America must develop a more flexible response to the varied types of Communist threat—from nuclear blustering by the Soviet Union to the brush-fire insurgencies of Asia, Africa, and Latin America. In 1961, President Kennedy approved an Eisenhower-era plan to launch a CIA-inspired invasion of Cuba, led by anti-Communist exiles. (Cuba had undergone a revolution in 1959 under the leadership of the Marxist-nationalist Fidel Castro). The invasion failed disastrously. A year later, the Soviets began placing nuclear missiles on the island. Confronted by the United States, Khrushchev was forced down. The humiliation led to his overthrow two years later by Leonid Brezhnev and other hard-liners in the Kremlin who believed that the Soviet Union should pursue its interests in the developing world more forcefully.

Meanwhile, Kennedy—fearful of being branded soft on communism by Republicans—began sending advisors to back the anti-Communist regime in South Vietnam, under siege from indigenous Communist forces. Following Kennedy's assassination in 1963, his successor Lyndon Johnson escalated U.S. involvement to the tune of 550,000 troops by 1968. The increasingly unpopular war led to Johnson's downfall and America's withdrawal in 1973. The rapid collapse of the South Vietnamese in 1975 embittered Americans toward direct involvement in international conflicts. This so-called Vietnam syndrome coincided with a period of Soviet expansionism. Having largely achieved nuclear parity with the United States by the mid-1970s, the Soviets embarked on a campaign to support Communist and pro-Communist regimes in Asia, Africa, and Latin America, largely through military aid and advisors. In Afghanistan, however, Moscow sent in tens of thousands of troops in 1979 to back the pro-Soviet regime there.

In the United States, political forces were gathering to challenge the legacy of Vietnam. By the end of the Carter administration, the United States had started supporting anti-Communist forces and governments from El Salvador to Afghanistan, while beginning a new arms build-up. This process was dramatically escalated during the presidency of Ronald Reagan, who also upped the level of anti-Soviet rhetoric.

By the mid-1980s, it was the Soviet Union's turn to feel the limits on its power. Bogged down in Afghanistan, the increasingly cumbersome centralized economy of the Soviet Union was going broke trying to match the latest arms build-up by the United States. Recognizing its plight, the ruling Politburo chose a young reformer named Mikhail Gorbachev to revamp the Soviet economy and ease tensions with the United States. Gorbachev quickly announced that as far as he was concerned the arms race with the United States was no longer relevant, and he moved to develop closer relations with Washington. At the same time, he opened up political debate at home and made it clear to East European governments that they could no longer expect Soviet aid in quelling domestic disturbances. This new doctrine allowed anti-Communist sentiment to come into the open across Eastern Europe, leading to the collapse of many of the Communist regimes there in 1989. Soviet troops were soon withdrawn from the region, and the Warsaw Pact dissolved.

Beset by a collapsing economy at home and apparent political chaos, the Soviet army decided to step in, launching a military coup in August 1991. The rapid collapse of the coup quickly led to the collapse of the Soviet Union. In December, Russian Federation President Boris Yeltsin officially dissolved the union, establishing the Commonwealth of Independent States in its place. With the Soviet Union gone and Eastern Europe no longer Communist, the cold war had come to a sudden end.

Theories About the Origins of the Cold War

Essentially, theories about the origins of the cold war—at least, among scholars in the United States specifically and the West generally—fit into three general categories: orthodox, revisionist, and realist. To simplify—or rather, to oversimplify—the arguments of these three schools of thought, it can be said that orthodox theorists blame the Soviet Union for starting the cold war, revisionist scholars say the United States was at fault, and the realists argue that both and neither powers were to blame. Instead, this latter group argues, the origins of the cold war were fixed in misconceptions by both sides and driven by forces of history beyond the command of policy-makers in both Washington and Moscow.

The orthodox theorists rose to predominance first. Largely products of the early years of the cold war themselves, the ideas of orthodox scholars reflected the thinking of policy-makers in Washington and London. The revisionists came next, responding to U.S. hegemony overseas in the 1950s and 1960s, especially during the course of the Vietnam War. The realist school somewhat overlapped the revisionists, but generally came to the fore in the 1970s and 1980s, at a time when both the United States and the Soviet Union were agressively pursuing their interests throughout the developing world.

Orthodox Theory

According to orthodox theorists, the United States was filled with good intentions as World War II came to a close. Hoping to build on the collective allied security principles of World War II, American policy-makers wanted to rely on the newly created United Nations and its Security Council to resolve international tensions. Moreover, the United States was willing to forego the advantage of its nuclear monopoly by turning over control of those weapons to an international monitoring agency. In Eastern Europe, says the orthodox school of thought, the United States was willing to meet the Soviet Union half way. As long as there were free elections, Moscow could insist that the foreign policy of the democratic states be pro-Soviet. Finally, the United States was willing to help the Soviet Union and Eastern Europe recover from the devastation of

World War II by participating in the massive aid program known as the Marshall Plan. According to the orthodox school, America had reached an understanding on these points with the Soviets at Yalta—agreements that the Soviet Union either never intended to honor or refused to honor later.

For all these benign intentions, however, American policy-makers were met by Soviet duplicity, intransigence and aggression, say orthodox theorists. Rather than agreeing to collective security, the Soviet Union engaged in unilateral measures to ensure its national interests. It refused to allow free elections in Eastern Europe; it ignored American offers for an internationally monitored atomic bomb and embarked on a nuclear weapons program of its own; and it contemptibly dismissed the Marshall Plan as a clandestine American plot to undermine its Communist system. The Soviet Union, says the orthodox school, was also responsible for putting the Communists in power in China and giving the go-ahead to North Korea for its invasion of the south.

There were, however, variations in the orthodox school as far as Soviet motivation went. Extreme hard-liners—many of whom were exiles from the Soviet Union—claimed that Moscow was primarily driven by Marxist ideology, which called for a worldwide anti-capitalist revolution. The implication of this interpretation of Soviet behavior was grim. Since any agreement would be torn up by the ideologically committed Soviets when it was convenient, negotiations with Moscow were worse than useless, they were dangerously naive. Moreover, the United States must adopt a policy of "liberating" Soviet-controlled countries or face an indefinite future of hostile aggression.

Others, especially the career diplomats and State Department officials such as Kennan, offered a less desperate view of Soviet motivations. Rather than being driven by ideological considerations, Moscow was merely trying to pursue its own national interests, just as the czarist government had done for centuries. Its efforts to dominate Eastern Europe were part of a centuries-old policy of using that territory to protect itself from aggressive West European states, a fear aggravated by twin German invasions in World War I and World War II. By this reasoning, the United States could best deal with Soviet expansionism by meeting it with selective force, the so-called containment doctrine. Moreover, since Soviet aims were based on national self-interest, it was possible to negotiate with Moscow.

Revisionist Theory

Like the orthodox school of thought, revisionist theory has many variants, though all are united by several basic premises. First, the United States generally took the lead in provoking cold war confrontations, whether by cutting off aid to the Soviet Union in the days following the end of World War II or making demands that ran counter to legitimate Soviet security interests in Eastern Europe. Secondly, the United States, with its overwhelming military and economic power in 1945, was, by necessity, the nation that should have offered conciliatory gestures. Third, the Soviet Union, having much of its industrial infrastructure destroyed in the war and having lost some 8 percent of its population, was in a far weaker position than the United States and was motivated to take the actions it did out of fear.

According to what might be called the moderate school of revisionism, the United States—by making demands for democratic governments in Eastern Europe, the key se-

curity zone for a Soviet Union recently invaded via that region—provoked the Soviet Union into setting up puppet regimes in Poland and overthrowing the democratically elected government in Czechoslovakia. Moreover, the overall weakness of the Soviet Union during the 1940s and 1950s dictated a cautious foreign policy. For example, Stalin only acted in those parts of Eastern Europe where he felt that he had a right to do so. He quickly backed down in the face of Western protests in Iran and Turkey in 1946 and agreed not to intervene to help the Greek Communists in 1947. Thus, despite the ideological bravado and bombastic anti-Western rhetoric, the Soviet Union acted carefully abroad and stuck to the letter of the agreements it signed.

Most moderate revisionists blame the Truman administration for the origins and onset of the cold war. Truman lacked the diplomatic finesse of Roosevelt. Instead of recognizing the Soviet Union's legitimate security concerns, Truman tried to bully Moscow. According to these revisionists, the dropping of two atomic bombs on Japan in 1945—despite evidence that Tokyo was about to surrender—was done to inform Moscow of U.S. possession of a nuclear arsenal and Washington's resolve to use those weapons. In other words, Truman practiced the age-old tactic of saber-rattling to force the Soviet Union to back down, interpreted Soviet moves to defend itself as acts of aggression, precipitously cut off aid to a desperate former ally, and launched a war of rhetoric intended to rally world opinion against Moscow. All of these moves, then, forced the defensive and fearful Soviet Union to react.

More radical revisionists dismissed the moderate revisionist argument as too personality-based. It did not matter, they said, who was in charge of American foreign policy, since that policy was driven by political, economic, and ideological forces beyond the control of any administration. Specifically, they argued that in the wake of Britain's collapse, the United States took up the mantle of Western leadership. This meant maintaining the West's centuries-long hegemony over the rest of the world. Moreover, U.S. policy-makers believed that a post-war depression could only be prevented through opening up the international marketplaces to U.S. products.

With the collapse of Nazism and Japanese imperialism in World War II, Soviet communism represented the only threat to Western hegemony, as witnessed by Moscow's successful efforts to re-orient the economies of Eastern Europe away from the West. Indeed, this desire to keep communism at bay—for fear of losing markets and Western control of the developing world, especially as the latter decolonized in the two decades following World War II—was the underlying motive behind American foreign policy throughout the cold war. In effect, then, radical revisionists agreed with official Soviet theories on the origins of the cold war. According to Moscow, America was driven not by a fear of the Soviet Union but a desire to capture world markets, since imperialist-capitalism depended on ever-greater access to markets and resources. Communism, by this reckoning, threatened those markets and resources and had to be stopped. And since the Soviet Union generally supported Communist movements in those countries, it had to be contained.

Realist Theory

The realist school mixed elements of the revisionists and orthodox theorists in its own assessment of the causes of the cold war. At the same time, it tried to mesh the actions of individuals with the forces of history. According to the realists, both sides hoped that wartime cooperation would continue after the war, though each expected this to happen on its own terms. The Soviets, pursuing what they considered their own legitimate security concerns in Eastern Europe, expected the United States to go along. While Washington, fearful that a collapsing international economy would set off a major depression at home, expected the Soviets to accept U.S. hegemony in much of the world outside the immediate Soviet orbit. Neither wanted to precipitate a confrontation. But in taking steps to pursue their own interests, each forced the other to take counter-measures, thereby setting off a vicious circle of fear and hostility on both sides. In short, the realists saw the cold war confrontation as a new version of an old-fashioned balance-of-power struggle.

The realists also argued that internal politics in the United States and even the Soviet Union played a role in the cold war confrontation. Because the Red Army occupied Eastern Europe toward the end of World War II, Roosevelt was forced to recognize Soviet hegemony there. He could not admit this to the country, however, especially since descendents of immigrants from that region were a key component of the New Deal coalition. Thus, when the reality of Soviet dominance became clear after the war, the American people felt that Roosevelt and the Democrats had betrayed the country, leading to a rise in anti-Communist hysteria at home. At the same time, they also believed that the Soviets had gone back on their word and could not be trusted.

Other realists cited contradictions within the Communist system. They note the great irony of the cold war's ideological struggle: specifically, that those countries under Soviet control—namely, Eastern Europe—were the most hostile to communism, while countries outside the Soviet orbit—including such countries as Italy, India, and Vietnam—were more amenable to communism. In a sense, then, Soviet foreign policy was driven by an effort to survive in the face of a hostile capitalist West by maintaining control over a restive East European sphere of influence while projecting influence into those parts of the world that were sympathetic to communism. Both of these policies served to further antagonize the West, leading to countermeasures that forced the Soviet Union into more aggressive action abroad.

Impact of the Cold War

The cold war, as noted above, was driven in part by an ideological struggle between East and West. Part of this struggle, of course, involved the best means to organize human society—that is, via capitalist democracy or communism. Aside from this basic split, however, there were many other underlying beliefs, beliefs that came to be accepted as unquestioned facts.

For Soviet leaders, there were several such truisms. One was that capitalism was doomed to collapse of its own contradictions. That is to say, that the exploitation of workers by capitalists was destined to intensify to a point in which the former would overthrow the latter. A second Soviet truism said that the only way this event could happen was through violent revolution. Third, capitalist powers, led by the United States, were determined to prevent this from happening by any means necessary. Since the Soviet Union offered a model for developing world countries to emulate—as well as concrete assistance to groups in those countries attempting to foment Communist revolution—the West felt compelled to contain Moscow, as part of its overall defense of capitalism worldwide.

Out of these beliefs gradually developed a Soviet policy in which virtually every nationalist rebellion or anti-Western government was seen as a potential Soviet ally, thereby deserving of help. In addition, any movement fighting against a pro-Western government fell into the same category. Thus, the Soviet Union found itself backing both legitimate Communist governments, as well as dictatorial governments that paid little more than lip service to the Communist cause.

This policy was mirrored by the United States, which also backed brutal dictatorships that were anti-Communist. American policy-makers had other truisms that were uniquely their own, leading to errors in policy. Such policy errors based on false truisms are not unique to the cold war. For example, at the 1938 Munich conference, Britain and France acceded to Hitler's demands as a means of appeasing the German dictator and preventing war. Because they failed to do either, the Munich agreements offered powerful lessons to Western policy-makers. Specifically, Munich confirmed the belief that bowing to a dictatorial government's demands only leads to further demands and eventually war. This experience offered a model for dealing with Soviet expansionism.

U.S. foreign policy during the cold war was equally misguided. It assumed that all efforts to overthrow pro-Western governments were Communist in origin and that all of them were directed by Moscow. The depth of this belief can be measured by the fact that it persisted among many U.S. policy-makers long after events revealed an increasingly hostile relationship between Moscow and Beijing—the two giants of the Communist world—in the early 1960s.

These truisms on both sides had fatal consequences. One, of course, was the arms race. Since both superpowers believed that the other was driven by ideology and self-interest to neutralize their antagonist, each side believed it had to defend itself by any means necessary. In a nuclear age, this meant building enough weapons to utterly destroy the other. This, then, created enormous constituencies in both countries—the military elite in the Soviet Union and the military-industrial complex in the United States—that demanded more weapons to counter advances made by the other side. Ultimately, the arms race would damage the American economy and destroy the Soviet one.

More importantly for the purposes of this book, the truisms of the cold war served to ensure that the United States and the Soviet Union involved themselves in many of the world's civil conflicts—conflicts that were often based on causes indigenous to each society. By offering money, weaponry, intelligence, military training, and, occasionally, advisors and soldiers, the United States and the Soviet Union exacerbated, extended, and exaggerated these conflicts. At the same time, the two sides cast the struggle in ideological terms, which made it impossible to seek out the true causes of the conflict. By setting up a kind of ideological force field, the cold war confrontation deflected potential negotiations and peaceful solutions to many conflicts.

Many developing world countries tried to evade the implications of these cold war truisms by advocating a middle course. In 1955, many of the leaders of the developing world met at Bandung, Indonesia, to establish the non-aligned group of nations. Somewhat successful in charting a third way for a number of developing countries, the movement faced enormous obstacles, perhaps the most important of which was the overall distrust in which Moscow and especially Washington held this movement. Much of the cold war policy of both the Soviet Union and the United States was driven by one basic rule of thumb: those who are not with us are against us. Membership in the non-aligned movement—though widespread—was often rendered meaningless by Soviet and American policy of interference.

Of course, the cold war had its ups and downs. From time to time, tensions between the Soviet Union and the United States eased. This usually resulted in a lessening of tensions, as well as the occasional trade agreement and nuclear weapons limitation treaty, but it rarely served to limit U.S. or Soviet interventionism in developing world conflicts. Indeed, the mid-1970s, the period of warmest détente, or friendship, between Moscow and Washington, was marked by an escalation of U.S. and Soviet interference in the conflicts of Africa.

Thus, despite moves toward reconciliation on arms and trade or the easing of tensions along the heavily armed European divide, the cold war never really lessened in the developing world. That should not seem too surprising since, with the advent of European peace in the late 1940s, it was the developing world that served as a battleground between East and West. This, too, is not surprising since the developing world remained the main prize sought by both sides in the cold war. In that sense, the cold war was little different than most of the major "hot wars" of the last several hundred years: It was a battle to control the vast resources and markets of the developing world. And like those hot wars, the cold war could not end until one side was defeated.

Legacy and Aftermath

Just as the two great struggles of the first half of the twentieth century—that is, World Wars I and II—left a legacy of troubled peace, so has the great cold war confrontation. As noted above, many of the conflicts that punctuated the cold war had origins that stretched to an era long before Yalta or even the Bolshevik revolution. Indeed, it could be argued that it was the era of European imperialism that planted the seeds for many of the bitterest and most long-lasting struggles of the post–World War II era, including the conflicts between Israel and Palestine, India and Pakistan, and even Vietnam. Clearly, the cold war fueled the fury of these wars, although in the case of the first war, it started long before the cold war began and has now outlasted it.

Yet, there are many other conflicts that, while rooted in the pre–cold war era, were intensified so greatly by Soviet and American involvement that they can be said to be legacies of the cold war. These conflicts include such ongoing struggles as the one in Angola between the government and Jonas Savimbi's rebels (Savimbi was backed by the United States; the government by the Soviet Union) or the continuing strife in Cambodia.

Moreover, the very collapse of the Communist order has triggered a number of conflicts in that part of the world, most notably in the former Yugoslavia. The impact of the cold war there is less certain. Clearly, communism contained ethnic strife in the former Yugoslavia. Its repressive political system—whether triggered by cold war fears or an inherent part of communism as it came to exist in Eastern Europe—prevented ethnic groups with both a long tradition of rivalry and a recent history of brutality (specifically, the struggle between fascist Croats and Communist Serbs during World War II) from cutting each other's throats. Whether the Communist system honestly reconciled these groups (if only temporarily), simply postponed the inevitable, or actually inflamed ethnic hatred by refusing to acknowledge it is uncertain.

One thing does seem certain, however. The legacy of the cold war is bound to inspire as many competing scholarly theories as its origins.

James Ciment

Bibliography

Ball, Simon J. *The Cold War: An International History, 1947–1991.* New York: St. Martin's Press, 1998.

Clough, Michael. *Free at Last? U.S. Policy Toward Africa and the End of the Cold War.* New York: Council on Foreign Relations, 1992.

Crockatt, Richard. *The Fifty Years War: The United States and the Soviet Union in World Politics, 1941–1991.* New York: Routledge, 1994.

Day, Richard B. *Cold War Capitalism: The View from Moscow, 1945–1975.* Armonk, NY: M.E. Sharpe, 1995.

Hunter, Allen, ed. *Rethinking the Cold War.* Philadelphia: Temple University Press, 1998.

Judge, Edward H., and John W. Langdon. *A Hard and Bitter Peace: A Global History of the Cold War.* Englewood Cliffs, NJ: Prentice Hall, 1996.

LaFeber, Walter. *America, Russia and the Cold War, 1945–1990,* 6th ed. New York: McGraw-Hill, 1991.

Leffler, Melvyn, ed. *Origins of the Cold War: An International History.* New York: Routledge, 1994.

Rodman, Peter W. *More Precious than Peace: The Cold War and the Struggle for the Third World.* New York: Charles Scribner's Sons, 1994.

Young, John W. *Cold War Europe, 1945–1989: A Political History.* New York: Routledge, 1991.

Anti-Colonialism

Roots of European Colonialism

Anti-colonialism grew in response to European colonial expansion, and its origins can be traced to the West itself, although it ultimately found its strongest expression in Africa, Asia, and Latin America. Fueled by the maturing of commercial capitalism at home, and in pursuit of gold, God, and glory, West Europeans in the fifteenth century began their great expansion overseas. What was different about commercial capitalism from earlier developments in the world was its inherently expansionist social order that stimulated the discovery of new lands overseas, the acquisitions of colonies globally, and the founding of economic theories and practices known as mercantilism. Simultaneously, Europe also experienced the emergence of the scientific revolution, which, together with mercantilist theories, was to usher in the age of capitalist civilization.

Rising population and increased output in agriculture, mining, fishing, and forestry stimulated economic growth in Europe, increasing the power and prestige of the European merchant, which was unmatched elsewhere in the world. The merchant, for example, was regarded as socially inferior in China and suffered several political restrictions in his native country. Significantly, just when merchants and their joint stock companies started to provide the capital to European monarchies to launch overseas expeditions, the Chinese expeditions, which predated the European efforts, were suddenly halted by imperial fiat in 1433.

The resulting European global expansion between the sixteenth and nineteenth centuries led to the development of mercantilism. Mercantilism by its inherent logic was aimed at enhancing and unifying the power of new monarchies. This was to be achieved by amassing gold to pay for the cost of the recurring wars and the proliferating bureaucracies. Maintaining a favorable balance of trade became a preoccupation of every European monarchy, and this was to be achieved by granting royal charters of monopoly privileges to joint stock companies in colonizing or trading in specified overseas territories.

The logic of monopoly privileges to overseas-trading, joint stock companies meant that these privileges had to be defended at every cost to prevent unwanted competition, which inevitably subordinated the interests of colonies to those of European nations. Consequently, colonies were to provide markets for manufacturers, to supply raw materials that could not be produced at home, to support a merchant marine that would be valuable in wartime, and to engender a large colonial population that would provide manpower. All West European nations followed these mercantilist practices, whether it was Portugal obtaining spices in the East Indies, Spain extracting gold and silver in the Americas, Holland developing a worldwide merchant marine, or Britain passing the Navigation Acts against Dutch trade and enforcing the British East India Company's tea monopoly, which culminated in the Boston Tea Party. What distinguished this new mass trade in necessities from the earlier traditional trade in luxury goods was its unprecedented volume that encompassed the globe, integrating countries and continents into the new international market economy in which each trading European nation was obligated to defend its monopoly. Defense of monopoly inevitably resulted in gaining political control of a colony. The Englishman W. W. Hunter best described the practice in the nineteenth century when he admitted in the case of India that the British, "true to our national character," had transformed themselves from "merchants" into "rulers."

Adam Smith, the astute Scottish economist of the late eighteenth century, perceived in his *The Wealth of Nations* that significance of the global trade when he noted that the overseas discoveries opened "a new and bottomless supply of customers for all European goods"—a market that encompassed "most of Asia, Africa and Americas." But he also noted the adverse effect of the global trade on the native populations: "By uniting, in some measure, the most distant parts of the world, by enabling them to relieve one another's wants, to increase one another's enjoyments, and to encourage one another's industry, their general tendency would seem to be beneficial. To the natives, however, both of the East and West Indies, all the commercial benefits which can have resulted from those events have been sunk and lost in the dreadful misfortunes which they have occasioned. . . . The savage injustice of the Europeans rendered an event, which ought to have been beneficial to all, ruinous and destructive to several of those unfortunate countries."

In assigning "dreadful misfortunes" to the "savage injustice of the Europeans," Adam Smith articulated perhaps one of the earliest anti-colonial sentiments and opened a debate on the effects of colonialism that persists to the present day. On the one hand, there are those who have supported Adam Smith's position, arguing that Western colonization resulted in the deprivation from which the third world still suffers. A more nuanced interpretation of this position has been provided by Edward Said, who in his polemical work *Orientalism* (1978) argued that European literature about the East could not be politically neutral because of the authors' colonial relationship. On the other hand, there are those who argue that pre-European overseas societies were not "moral" utopias, and that there was at least as much exploitation under native rulers and elites as later under European administrators and businessmen. A more brazen interpretation of this position has been provided by the Swiss-born French architect Charles-Edouard Jeanneret (popularly known as Le Corbusier), who called Western colonization to be a "force morale" for development. A recent re-assertion of this position was provided by the American columnist Patrick Buchanan, who remarked that Africa would not have had railways and all the other modern comforts were it not for European rule.

The remarkable thing about Western expansion after the fifteenth century is not that Europeans were able to colonize such large territories globally; rather, it is that Europeans in such small numbers were able to control and govern such disparate peoples in far-flung parts of the world for so long with relative ease. This could not have been possible without the collaboration of the native populations in administering European rule in colonies. The Europeans were obliged to teach Western education to at least enough natives to facilitate and sustain the effective administration of the territories recently brought under their vast new imperial umbrella. The alternative—training young Europeans to become fluent in native languages enough to carry on the daily chores of administrative collecting, spending, and punishing—was simply too expensive and intellectually unappealing. The impact of Western education, much like that of Christian missionary preaching, proved, at best, a mixed blessing to European rule. The shrewd Scot, Mountstuart Elphinstone, had known how dangerous Western education would prove to be when he had the courage to introduce it in Bombay in India; indeed, he called it "our highroad back to Europe." For introduction of Western education in colonies accelerated demands for the demise of European colonial rule by arming local elites with the words with which to call for it.

Beginnings of Decolonization

Much of the European mystique and position had been based on its historical establishment and control of a world system. By the early twentieth century, the fortunes of empire-building since the fifteenth century had given Europe influence in the hybrid New World societies it had created and control over Africa and much of Asia. Indeed, conscripts from the colonies joined forces with the metropolitan states during both world wars. But the wars weakened Europe just as they intensified the resolve of colonized peoples to direct their own destinies. Many in the colonies and beyond employed European socioeconomic doctrines and different elements of nationalism to challenge the structures of dominance; the post-war decades witnessed the self-assertion of the non-European world at the expense of the imperial systems.

At the end of World War I, U.S. President Woodrow Wilson and Soviet Premier Vladimir Lenin emerged as beacons of anticolonialism. In his Fourteen Points, Wilson's plan for a post-war order set the principles for peace settlements, calling for "adjustment of all colonial claims," insisting that "the interests of the populations concerned must have equal weight with the equitable claims of the government whose title is to be determined." The United States would be "intimate partners of all the governments and peoples associated together against the Imperialists." Notwithstanding the fact that Wilson did not have Asia and Africa in mind when he articulated these positions to colonized peoples, they were still a clarion call to independence and self-government.

Lenin had defined imperialism as "the highest stage of capitalism," which he hardily condemned. As leader of the Russian Revolution (1917) and heir to the Marxist doctrine advocating the end of oppression and the transformation of society, Lenin was poised to symbolize colonial struggles even though he paid little attention to the aspirations of the colonized in Asia and Africa. Lenin's communism, however, provided both critical theory and an ideology that was amazingly adaptable to colonial assertion. The Soviet-led Communist International (Comintern, 1919–1943) offered a vehicle for the export of revolution, although the late-twentieth-century events in Eastern Europe and the Soviet Union have proved nationalism to be a far more powerful force than International Communism.

The process of decolonization transformed colonies into nations that were often geopolitical constructs at variance with the traditions and allegiances of the societies involved. That ambiguous force known as nationalism obviously played a consequential role in these designs. Decolonization created independent political units, but it did not end the "cross-fertilization" existing between the European states and their former colonies: migrations and cultural and economic movements have kept the ties alive. Sometimes these relationships have perpetuated conditions of dominance (economic, cultural, and so on) by former European colonial powers, a phenomenon referred to as "neo-colonialism." When associated with earlier colonies (especially those in Latin America), these emergent states have been designated the "third world," a term that was coined after World War II to refer to countries that were not part of either NATO or the Warsaw Pact. The fortunes of third-world countries have run the gamut from positive non-alignment, founded in 1955 by Afro-Asian nations at the Bandung (Indonesia) Conference, to pawnship at the hands of the United States or the Soviet Union and their respective allies. China has offered a different response to European influences, albeit a curious blend of communist and capitalist principles, and a unique pattern of self-assertion against the Western world and the United States.

European society itself underwent major disruptions in the early part of the twentieth century that had startling repercussions for its global roles. The two world wars that emanated from traditional European power conflicts demonstrated the fragility of the European balance of power. While Europe's global dominance gradually came to be challenged by the United States and Japan, it became equally evident that, given the imperial system, a war among European states could scarcely be contained in that orbit. For the colonies, the wars displayed the vulnerabilities of the imperial powers, which during wartime were often forced to relax their controls over their charges. Hundreds of thousands of indigenes served in the war efforts under European banners and frequently on European battlefields. Many of those who remained in Europe after the wars became organizers of anti-colonial movements.

Amid the turmoil of war, Europe actually consolidated its colonial holdings and refined its techniques of rule. Colonial officials were trained more seriously, and indigenous elites were increasingly incorporated into authority structures as policies of indirect rule ("association" or trusteeship) were employed. The empires of England and France expanded after World War I with the transfer of German territories in Africa and the Pacific and the acquisition of mandates over former Turkish subjects in the Middle East.

Europeans provided colonized peoples with examples, traditions of resistance and doctrines, which could be used to transcend local disparities of language, religion, and allegiance, and provided rallying-points for common action. Such doctrines as socialism and nationalism were powerful ideologies, the effectiveness of which had been demonstrated in the European arena. Moreover, these ideologies were sufficiently flexible to allow for numerous interpretations, and they could be adapted to the needs of different societies. Nationalism and socialism were especially appropriate because of their popular appeals in the colonies. Religious kinship allegiances could be expanded to nationalistic fervor; forms of communalism and cooperation, important ingredients of socialism, were not alien to the colonized. Beyond these, populism suggested a folk orientation that could appeal to the primarily agrarian masses. But the element of modification is extremely important, for the colonized peoples had not shared in the experiences out of which the doctrines had originally emerged.

The challenge of employing European doctrines, even in modified forms, was complicated by the disparities between European and non-European (in this case, colonized) societies. The latter were primarily agrarian societies with traditional economic structures; the inhabitants had little secular education, were often extremely religious, and were the victims of a situation where history and development had largely been frozen by colonialism. They confronted representatives of modern, industrial peoples rather confident of their historical roles. For pre-modern societies to adopt the expressions of modern societies, when in fact that very modernization had contributed much to the plight of colonized peoples, considerable adjustment was required.

Decolonization and Third-World Nationalism

"Westernized" elites were the vanguard of the liberation movements in colonial regions. The colonized elites often matured in European or Europeanized school systems, a longstanding practice that had increased in the early twentieth century. The elements and background of the European doctrines were familiar to the elites, and these doctrines embodied a long tradition of challenge to authority in European countries. Also, the elites and many others in each colony could make common cause through their use of a single language, albeit the one imposed by the colonizers.

Given the arbitrariness that led to the establishment of many colonial geopolities, cutting across ethnic and linguistic divisions, one can only speculate whether colonized regions would have united in protesting their situation as effectively as they did, had they not availed themselves of European doctrines. These doctrines—particularly, nationalism—had much value as organizing themes, which charismatic leaders could use to wield discipline and commitment. In the

long run, though, it had been the practical needs of a movement rather than strict adherence to doctrinal subtleties that had determined its directions. The doctrines have been most important at the resistance and transitional stages; beyond this point pragmatism has taken hold.

As a political ideology, nationalism is based on the premise that nationality (not territory) is the proper organizing principle for a state, and that therefore the existence of a nation is enough justification for the existence of a state which is to exercise sovereignty only over that nation. Thus, as it emerged in Europe by the middle of the nineteenth century, political nationalism signified the extension of representative democracy and popular sovereignty to the international system under the slogan: "One nation, one state."

Imperial systems are always organized according to the territorial principle, and European empires were no exception. However, previous empires (including those of pre-nineteenth-century Europe) had to contend only with the resistance that normally meets conquest, but which, lacking in ideology as a rallying point, can be dealt with in a variety of ways. The new "imperialism" had to contend with what was essentially an anti-imperialist doctrine not amenable to "sensible modification." Nationalism holds that whether there is oppression or not, whether there are advantages or not, each nation must have separate statehood.

As long as the Great Powers held nationalism in check in Europe, it was also possible to rationalize imperial action. When self-determination for national groups became the ordering principle for post–World War I Europe, it became intellectually dishonest to defend colonial rule. The mandate system of the League of Nations acknowledged that territorial possessions would in time receive national independence.

There were other signs that the imperial armor had been seriously cracked. In 1931, the Statute of Westminster, passed by the British parliament, recognized the extent of this process among white-settler colonies by granting independence and Commonwealth status to Australia, New Zealand, Canada, South Africa, and Newfoundland. And Egypt received nominal independence in 1922, in part due to agitation from the Wafd party.

The colonies were hit hard by the economic crisis of the 1930s. Prices for tropical raw materials declined, and colonies felt their vulnerability as the imperialists became preoccupied with their own recovery. While many peasants migrated to urban areas, in general the output of the colonial peasant rose, reflecting a move toward self-sufficiency.

India, Indochina, and the Dutch East Indies are classic examples of the process of decolonization in Asia. These territories were pretty much within colonial orbits by 1870. The Dutch thrust into the East Indies (the fabled Spice Islands) dates from the seventeenth century; the British filled a power vacuum in India in the eighteenth; and France secured Indochina in the nineteenth. The impact of modernization affected the peoples of these lands in varying manners, but such elements as the construction of communications arteries and the use of a European language to facilitate contact among diverse linguistic groups did foster a tendency toward unification in each colony; yet it was World War II that entrained the decisive historical juncture, the transition from colonial territory to independent state.

The Hindu religious renaissance of the nineteenth century had stirred national pride in India. The first Indian national congress met in 1885, and the idea of a self-governing dominion within the Empire emerged around World War I. During the inter-war period the nationalist movement grew under the leadership of Mohandas Gandhi, with his program of passive resistance (*satyagraha*— literally, to hold fast to truth) and home rule (*swaraj*), while at the same time Muslim factions agitated for a separate Muslim state including states where Muslims were a majority. Soon after World War II an Indian independence bill passed by the British parliament became law (August 1947) and gave rise to the Dominion of India and the Dominion of Pakistan.

The nationalist movement in the Dutch East Indies emerged in the early twentieth century, supported by the formation of a Communist party in the 1920s. The nationalists reacted to the Japanese occupation of the territory in March 1942, and at the close of the war, the Japanese finally offered them independence in 1945. The Dutch attempt to reclaim Indonesia resulted in years of fighting, but pressures from the United Nations and the United States led to independence at the end of 1949 under the leadership of Sukarno. The Dutch held on to New Guinea through several years of protracted hostilities until they finally surrendered the area in 1962. Most of the Dutch had been expelled, and the movement was complete.

Indochina offers a somewhat more complicated story, yet the process was similar. Nationalist uprisings began around 1908; Ho Chi Minh emerged as a charismatic leader, founding the Communist party in 1931. Like Indonesia, Indochina was occupied by the Japanese (1941), and Japan also offered independence, with Tonkin, Annam, and Cochin China becoming the autonomous state of Vietnam under the emperor, Bao Dai. After a temporary Chinese-British occupation following the war, France attempted to resume its prewar colonial position and fought the nationalist Vietminh forces until the former were defeated in 1954. Later, the United States became embroiled in a long, protracted conflict in Vietnam. Finally, the states of Vietnam, Laos, and Cambodia emerged from French Indochina.

The Japanese takeover of most of Southeast Asia during World War II fatally weakened the position of the European colonial powers. Once Japan was defeated, independence in fact was a matter of time.

After World War II, there were only three independent states in Africa: Ethiopia, Liberia, and the Union of South Africa. Egypt, though technically independent since 1922, was still occupied by British troops. In 1945, the Sixth Pan-African Congress was held in Manchester, England. Significantly, unlike previous conferences, which had been organized by African Americans and West Indians, this one was dominated by Africans, who included Kwame Nkrumah, future president of Ghana, and Jomo Kenyatta, future president of Kenya. The congress, among other things, demanded complete independence for the colonial areas of Black Africa. Nationalist revolts broke out in Madagascar, a French colony, in 1947, and in Kenya, a British colony with a large white-settler population, in 1952 (the Mau-Mau Rebellion). Two years later, in 1954, the Algerian war of independence began.

In 1957, the Gold Coast was granted its independence by England. Renamed Ghana, after the great medieval state in the savannah region, it was the first sub-Saharan African colony to gain its independence from a European colonial power. In 1960, a total of seventeen African colonies, including Nigeria, Somalia, Senegal, and Côte d'Ivoire became

independent. However, in southern Africa, Portugal resisted the trend toward independence by its colonies; war broke out in Angola in 1961, Guinea in 1963, and Mozambique in 1964.

In 1963, at the Pan-African Congress Conference, meeting in Addis Ababa, Ethiopia, African leaders established the Organization of African Unity (OAU). Since its founding, the OAU has successfully arbitrated a number of inter-African disputes. It has also consistently opposed the continuation of white rule in the Republic of South Africa. In June 1977, the last major European colony in Africa, Djibouti (the former French Somaliland and, later, the French Territory of the Ifar and Issas) became independent.

Following World War II, England, France, the Netherlands, and Portugal no longer had the will or the means to control vast colonial empires. Cold war realities demanded at least the rhetoric of decolonization from the European states. The Atlantic Charter and the United Nations Trustee Council endorsed self-government, and the United States, having fulfilled its promise of independence for the Philippines in 1946, actively supported the self-rule of India, Pakistan, and Indonesia. The paths of decolonization after 1945 were varied and often bumpy, with peaceful transfers of power in Ghana and Ceylon (modern Sri Lanka) matched by protracted colonial wars in Algeria, the Belgian Congo, and Angola.

Decolonization and the Cold War

The cold war played an important role in shaping the world after 1945, but events in the 1990s marked a historical turning point. Nineteen-ninety-one ushered in the end of the cold war. Communism collapsed almost everywhere, lifting the fear of global nuclear war (it was to re-surface in 1998 with the nuclear tests by India and Pakistan). The Soviet Union, the last great colonial empire, dissolved into fledgling independent states, prompting Francis Fukuyama, a political analyst with the right-wing think tank Rand Corporation, to proclaim the "end of history." The 1990s also witnessed the dismantling of the apartheid system in South Africa, replacing the minority white rule with a multiracial government headed by the African political activist Nelson Mandela in 1994. (Southwest Africa, under United Nations guidance, made the transition to majority rule in 1990, as the country of Namibia.)

Neither World War II nor the collapse of the Soviet System and communism really resulted in the end of history. The rise of ethnic and nationalist conflicts in Eastern Europe and the former Soviet Union have made some Western political analysts to romanticize about the old cold war rivalry. And the third world, made up principally of former colonies, continues to face severe economic challenges, even though since 1945 global economic productivity has expanded more rapidly than at any time in the past. Consequently, anti-colonialism, which in the first half of the twentieth century was directed against European colonial rule, in the second half of the century came to be re-directed against Western political dominance and disproportionate control of global economic resources. The countries of Asia, Africa, and Latin America maintain that they continue to be exploited by the Western states. Apart from being exploited in international trade and finance, these countries argue, they are being subjected to the "media imperialism" of the West. In fact, the controversy over the control of global resources and the international flow of information has developed alongside a related north-south controversy: the demand for a New International Economic Order. Some third-world countries have organized themselves in the "Group of Seventy-Seven" (an organization named from the number of its original participants in 1964) in their efforts to gain economic leverage against the developed world and use the international forum of the United Nations and its many agencies to realize their demand of a fair share in world resources and communications, as these clearly affect their own economic and social development. Not surprisingly, Western countries, especially the United States of America, have not responded warmly.

Not all governments of the third world are hostile to the West, notwithstanding the political rhetoric used to gain popular support domestically. Third-world countries are well aware of the West's power in encouraging economic and social development and in maintaining political peace. What the third-world governments are complaining about is the West's disproportionate control of global resources and ethnocentric attitudes. The creation of a new world economic order in which the third world shares a proportionate representation will, in their view, eliminate the negative effects of the West's "predilection" for trivializing the developing countries. The West should recognize the fact that the development of third-world countries is not necessarily inimical to its own interests; it could make an important contribution to promoting a two-way flow of quality information, provided efforts are made by both the West and the third world to seek cooperation rather than confrontation. To get different viewpoints in a pluralistic world, we need different sources of information. These can only become available when, given the present monolithic information system, proportionate representation is given to the third-world countries.

Ravi Kalia and William H. Alexander

Bibliography

Chamberlain, Muriel Evelyn. *Decolonization: The Fall of the European Empires.* New York: B. Blackwell, 1985.

Childs, Peter. *An Introduction to Post-Colonial Theory.* New York: Prentice Hall, 1997.

Darwin, John. *Britain and Decolonisation: The Retreat from Empire in the Post-War World.* New York: St. Martin's Press, 1988.

Fanon, Frantz. *A Dying Colonialism.* New York: Grove Press, 1965.

Fredi, Frank. *Colonial Wars and the Politics of Third World Nationalism.* New York: I.B. Tauris, 1994.

Hintjens, Helen M. *Alternatives to Independence: Explorations in Post-Colonial Relations.* Brookfield, VT: Dartmouth, 1995.

James, Lawrence. *The Rise and Fall of the British Empire.* New York: St. Martin's Press, 1996.

Moore-Gilbert, B.J. *Postcolonial Theory: Contexts, Practices, Politics.* New York: Verso, 1997.

Said, Edward. *Orientalism.* New York: Vintage Books, 1948.

Smith, Adam. *An Inquiry into the Nature and Causes of the Wealth of Nations.* Hartford, CT: Cooke & Hall, 1818.

Urquhart, Brian. *Decolonization and World Peace.* Austin: University of Texas Press, 1989.

Williams, Patrick, and Laura Chrisman, eds. *Colonial Discourse and Post-Colonial Theory: A Reader.* New York: Columbia University Press, 1994.

People's Wars

What is meant by the term "people's war"? The concept can be defined both narrowly and broadly. Defined narrowly, the term is used to denote the body of strategic thought on "protracted war" developed by Mao Zedong in the 1930s and 1940s, during the period of the Chinese Civil War and the struggle against the Japanese. This definition is firmly rooted in the larger Marxist-Leninist theory of class struggle. Defined broadly, the concept of people's war is used generically to denote any form of guerrilla conflict or popular insurrection, regardless of its ideological roots. By this definition, the opening and middle stages of the Chinese Communist struggle against the Nationalist (Kuomintang) regime was an example of a people's war, as was the Afghan campaign against the Marxist regime in Kabul.

The definition of people's war used in this entry takes a middle course. The term, on the one hand, will be used to describe a body of ideas on population-based conflict or insurgency that goes beyond the specific concept of operations developed by Mao. At the same time, we will retain the ideological meaning of the term by referring to those forms of "popular warfare" based on the concept of class struggle. Defining the concept in this manner distinguishes it, on the one hand, from the type of conflict waged in Afghanistan, which would represent a more generalized form of guerrilla warfare, as well as from the type of class-based revolutionary conflict envisioned by Lenin, which was based primarily on political rather than military forms of struggle. While the last act of revolutionary takeover, in Lenin's view, would be carried out by a popular insurrection, the months and years leading up to the insurrection would be characterized by careful, behind-the-scenes political work, designed to place the revolutionary party in a position to catalyze a final uprising and seize power when the historical moment was deemed to be propitious. It would not be characterized by a period of revolutionary *war*, per se, in which the outcome of the struggle would be decided by a military interaction.

Although the concept of people's war, for definitional purposes, can be usefully distinguished from the larger concept of guerrilla warfare, we should not lose sight of the fact that the first is merely an ideological subset of the second. The defining operational problem, in each case, is the same: overcoming the conventional military superiority of the state (or occupying power) through an asymmetrical campaign based on the support (and resources) of a constituent population. While the leadership of a people's war will attempt to draw support from among a revolutionary class (classically, the peasantry), the non-Marxist insurgency will define its natural constituency along different lines (e.g., ethnicity, communal affiliation, or regional identity). Where the first defines its popular base "horizontally" (according to class) across national or ethnic lines, the second defines its base of support "vertically" (according to some other group identifier) without regard to its class affiliation.

The underlying organizational tasks facing the leadership of a people's war are similar to those faced by that of any insurgency. We can define these as (1) *penetration,* which speaks to the revolutionary organization's need to "get inside" targeted social groupings as a prelude to "turning" them to the service of the organization's political and military objectives, (2) *transformation,* which speaks to the insurgency's need to consolidate its control over the targeted group and redirect some percentage of its resources to the organization's goals, and (3) *application,* which refers to the ways in which these resources are used to further develop an insurgent infrastructure, undermine the competing infrastructure of the state, and, ultimately, extend the insurgent's zone of control. Collectively, these tasks define the process of social mobilization. Every insurgent organization must address each of these operational tasks if it is to pose a viable challenge to the state. The manner in which it does so will define its theory of victory.

Revolutions and people's wars in the twentieth century have virtually all imitated or tried to imitate earlier revolutions. These successful cases of the past establish operational models that are adopted by latter-day revolutionaries who hope to repeat the success of those that preceded them by replicating their experience. While such cases have generally addressed the question of "why" one should revolt, as well as what revolutionary changes should be carried out in society at such time as one actually wins, the principal influence has been over *how* an armed revolt should be prosecuted in the first place. For those who come to the problem of overthrowing a standing regime with high ambition but little practical experience, a revolutionary paradigm offers an immediate (if often stylized) recipe for action.

The tradition of people's war, for its part, has been dominated by two original paradigms: the model of protracted conflict de-

veloped by Mao and the *foco* concept of guerrilla warfare developed by Ernesto "Che" Guevara. Most revolutionary insurgencies since the end of World War II have sought to either directly apply or adapt and refine one or the other of these baseline concepts of operation to local circumstances. Each of these models can be usefully defined in contrast to the other. The concept of protracted conflict developed by Mao is designed to be prosecuted by a "low-profile" organization carrying out a "bottom-up" approach to insurgency. By contrast, it can be said that the theory of insurgency developed by Che Guevara is designed to be prosecuted by a "high-profile" organization from the "top down." In certain key respects, these two models represent operational opposites. In doing so, they bound the larger concept of people's war.

The Chinese Model of People's War

Mao's assessment of the operational problem facing the Chinese Communist Party during its early struggles in the 1920s and 1930s rested on two essential considerations that bear on the general study of people's war. The first of these was his assessment of the standing government's overwhelming material advantage over the Communist party. The second was the government's equally apparent political weakness. Deposing the old regime, in Mao's view, would require the party to overcome its material weaknesses by exploiting the opportunities provided by its comparative political advantage. As Mao observed at the time, "All guerrilla units start from nothing and grow." At the outset of this type of struggle, the standing regime represents a force in being. The guerrilla, by contrast, represents a force in development. The latter begins with little more than an idea. The guerrilla's one opening under these circumstances, according to the theory of class conflict, is provided by the inherent frailty of the regime's political base and the corresponding weakness of its institutional presence throughout the countryside. Exploiting this opening, Mao argued, will permit a guerrilla force to bridge the gap between its grand ends and limited means over the course of the struggle.

Time, Space, and Initiative

The strategy designed by Mao to square the circle between ends and means rested on the calculated use of time and space. Buying time, Mao argued, was essential if the regime's strengths were to be turned into weaknesses and the guerrilla weaknesses were to be turned into strengths. The struggle, in its most abstract form, was envisioned to be an institutional contest between the developing architecture of the "new state" on the one hand and the declining institutions of the "old state" on the other. Building the new and dismantling the old, Mao recognized, would be a protracted undertaking. As this process unfolds, however, the relative balance between the guerrilla and the government would gradually shift. This shift, furthermore, could be expected to take on a dynamic quality over time. Guerrilla successes, he argued, would tend to be self-reinforcing, just as the regime's growing record of failure would tend to lead to the further erosion of the state and its administrative organs. While this process would ebb and flow, over the long run the decline of the state could be expected to accelerate, eventually at an increasing rate. The guerrillas' principal operational challenge, in this view, was not to end the war quickly, but to keep it going.

Unlimited time, in this strategy, required unlimited space. Space, in Mao's view, would provide the guerrillas with the room for maneuvers to buy the time necessary to win. All space, in this sense, is not created equal. For practical purposes, a distinction was made between territory that, in the opening stages of the engagement, was under the effective control of the regime, and that which was not. If the guerrillas' evaluation of the political environment facing each side was accurate, the regime's administrative control throughout the countryside would be imperfect. To survive their weak beginning, the guerrillas would open the struggle in those areas of the country in which the regime was weak and avoid making a stand in those areas of comparative regime strength. In pursuing such a strategy, the insurgency would give itself the best opportunity to gain the time it required to establish an institutional counterweight to the state. Revolutionary organization, in turn, would further extend the guerrillas' ability to establish effective spatial control.

These ideas formed the basis of Mao's concept of protracted war. According to this formula, the war will evolve via the dual mechanisms of "destruction and construction"—through the step-by-step destruction of the state and the associated construction of the new counterstate. The two, in Mao's view, are mutually dependent and must proceed in tandem. The erosion of the government's administrative architecture at the margin of its control will open additional opportunities for the insurgents to expand their own institutional presence, just as the organization's earlier (if still limited) institutional base provided the springboard to open its campaign against the state in the first place. This can be expected to take on an iterative quality over time, as each new advance by the guerrillas lays the groundwork for the next. The speed with which this campaign unfolds will be regulated by the strength of the state (which will tend to increase as the opposition pushes forward from the periphery to the state's center of gravity), the nature of the government's counter-strategy, the level of local resistance to the guerrillas' efforts to establish their own institutional presence, and the natural time limits associated with building an alternative set of political and military forms.

Expressed in geographical terms, this progression is intended to slowly result in an extension of guerrilla authority from peripheral areas of the countryside (or political margin), where state control will be comparatively weak, toward the cities (or political center) of the country where the position of the regime is traditionally much stronger. This process can be described as one of protracted encirclement, in which the urban regions of the country are encircled and eventually detached from the interior. The dynamic quality of this strategy is manifest in several ways. First, it calls for the guerrillas to push into areas of marginal control, even as they are being pulled into these areas by the political vacuum created by the retreat of the state. Second, as the opposition gains ground, it will naturally acquire the means to gain strength by gradually expanding its base of popular support. The inverse process, meanwhile, is occurring with the state, which is losing ground in a zero-sum contest for territorial control with the guerrillas. The result, in theory, is a compound shift in the relative balance of advantage as the guerrillas become absolutely stronger and the regime grows absolutely weaker at a more or less equivalent rate.

The nature of this encirclement strategy is somewhat different from that which typi-

cally characterizes Western military thought. For Mao, encirclement is not achieved by means of development, but through a process of "strategic convergence." Encirclement in the first sense, as one commentator noted some years ago, refers to a process of "eccentric maneuver," in which the attacking force advances from a single point to surround and strike at the enemy's flanks. In the Maoist system, by contrast, encirclement has taken on a more subtle cast. It is not a single action, but a complex "concentric maneuver" in which semi-autonomous forces converge on their target from multiple points in a protracted series of coordinated moves. Such an approach, if successful, will complicate the task facing the regime, which will be forced to counteract the guerrillas on multiple fronts, while simplifying the task facing the insurgents, who will be able to reduce their profile (and hence their vulnerability) to the enemy by not placing all of their eggs in a single (easily targeted) basket.

The Evolution of the Armed Struggle

A centerpiece of this strategy is the development of a series of rural bases from which the insurgents will attempt to extend their areas of control. "Political mobilization," Mao observed, is a fundamental condition for winning the war. Mobilization, in turn, will only be translated into effective insurgent support if it results in the creation of a network of strategic areas that are able to service the guerrillas' material needs. The base area, in this sense, provides a "protective shell" that provides the guerrillas with the opportunity "to organize, equip, and train." It is formed by bringing a large number of points of influence together under a common administrative center. This process is achieved by establishing a local military advantage, displacing (or neutralizing) the residual presence of the old regime, and creating an alternative set of governing and administrative institutions. This progression, once again, is a dynamic one. According to Abimael Guzman, one of Mao's recent imitators, "Base development, the [concomitant] development of [a] popular guerrilla army, and the resulting extension of the people's war [can be expected to take on a] momentum of their own, leading to the greater unfolding of the revolutionary situation." One thing leads to the next.

In developing this view, Mao clearly distinguished between "guerrilla bases" and "guerrilla zones." The guerrilla base, as we have suggested, is a region that has already been incorporated into the emerging insurgent regime. While Mao acknowledged that there could be different types of bases, depending upon their location and relative vulnerability to government attack, each represents a guerrilla "stronghold." Such strongholds can be distinguished from guerrilla zones, which Mao defined as areas in which the insurgents were able to operate with relative freedom, but where the state still retained a meaningful political and military presence. The guerrilla zone, in this sense, is considered to be an area of transition (contested ground). The final conquest of the zone, according to Mao, will be achieved by using the established basing system as a springboard to converge on any remaining state presence within the target area. Bases, in this view, effectively "encircle" guerrilla zones, which, once captured, will be absorbed into an expanded base area.

The revolution, in Mao's concept, will unfold in a series of stages, moving from the "strategic defensive," through a period of "strategic equilibrium," on to the "strategic offensive." The initial defensive stage of the conflict can be characterized as a period of "preparation." The insurgents' overriding objective during this phase is to establish a secure political base in the interior from which they can subsequently branch out and expand their range of operations. This is a period of high vulnerability. Like a water course, the guerrillas must find their own level. Decisive battles, head-on engagements, and areas of regime strength must all be avoided as the opposition gradually lays down its roots. This view was summarized nicely by Mao in his argument that the "first principle of war is to preserve oneself, and destroy the enemy." The insurgents' primary concern during the defensive stage of the struggle, in this view, must be on preserving their core organization, from which the means to destroy the enemy will eventually develop. By the end of this period, much of the countryside will have been transformed into a political checkerboard. While the regime will still enjoy effective control at the center, large areas of the countryside will have been brought under guerrilla influence.

The second stage of the conflict, strategic equilibrium, will be reached when the insurgents feel they have achieved "equivalence" with the incumbent regime. Mao referred to this stage as a period of "stalemate." If the initial defensive struggle can be described as a period of preparation, this phase of the war can be characterized as one of "consolidation." While the overriding concern during phase one was to establish an initial series of base areas, the primary operational objective in stage two will be to geographically connect these bases in an effort to consolidate and further extend the guerrillas' zone of control. Over time, the regime's remaining positions of influence in the interior are to be restricted, isolated, and gradually disconnected from the center. The checkerboard or "jigsaw" pattern of influence that characterized the end of phase one will evolve into an increasingly continuous pattern of guerrilla control by the end of phase two. By the end of this period, the regime will find itself forced into a defensive posture, preoccupied with hanging on to what it has and decreasingly able to move offensively against the guerrillas.

In Maoist parlance, the final phase of a people's war is the period of "annihilation." It might also be thought of as a period of "exploitation," in which the institutional groundwork laid during the preparatory and consolidative phases of the struggle are brought to fruition. The guerrillas will enter this stage poised to transition to the strategic offensive. The early pattern of territorial dispersion that flagged the opening weakness of the guerrillas will have been transformed over time into a pattern of territorial control in which the insurgents will have surrounded all but the most important points of regime influence. This development, in Mao's view, should be matched by a reorganization of significant elements of the guerrilla "army," which can now be gradually reformed into units capable of carrying out fluid but increasingly conventional operations. Guerrilla warfare, according to Mao, is not a strategy of choice but of necessity, imposed by the initial material weakness of the opposition. Once the balance of advantage in the conflict has swung to the opposition, the guerrillas are in a position to come out of the shadows and confront the regime on its own terms.

The Cuban Model of People's War

The Cuban model of people's war, codified by Che Guevara, was based on a highly stylized (and often inaccurate) interpretation of the Cuban insurrection (1956–1959). The baseline document outlining the key features of this model was written by Che Guevara and published by the Cuban Ministry of the Armed Forces in 1960 under the title *Guerrilla Warfare*. It was Che Guevara's first and most influential book. Guevara opened the monograph with the following observation: "The victory of the Cuban people over the Batista dictatorship . . . showed plainly the capacity of the people to free themselves by means of guerrilla warfare from a government that oppresses them." Three "fundamental lessons," he argued, could be drawn from this experience: First, that "popular forces can win a war against the army"; second, that "it is not necessary to wait until all conditions for making [a] revolution exist, the insurrection can create them"; and, third, that "in underdeveloped America the countryside is the basic area of fighting." The model of action that emerged from these "lessons" would shape or otherwise influence revolutionary efforts over the next thirty years.

Guevara's concept of operations was developed without reference to Mao's earlier writings on protracted war or a close understanding of the experiences of the Chinese Revolution. Guevara and Fidel Castro both claimed to have only been introduced to Mao's work in 1958, after the key features of the Cuban insurrection were already well defined. In their view and the view of others, this proved to be fortuitous, freeing them from the temptation to apply revolutionary lessons from a time and place that may have little to do with the particular challenges (and opportunities) faced by the Cuban guerrillas. The "university of experience," in Guevara's view, was a more useful instructor "than a million volumes of books." This perspective was echoed by Régis Debray, one of the chief interpreters of the Cuban insurrection, who suggested that it was a "stroke of good fortune that Fidel had not read the writings of Mao Zedong before disembarking on the coast of Oriente: he could thus invent, on the spot and out of his own experience, principles of a military doctrine in conformity with the terrain."

Where Mao's concept of protracted conflict may have been an appropriate model for the Far East, the new doctrine of people's war that emerged from the experience of the Cuban insurrection, it was argued, was the model of choice for the unique circumstances found in Latin America. "Revolutionaries in Latin America," Debray observed, were "reading Fidel's speeches and Che Guevara's writings with eyes that have already read Mao on the anti-Japanese war, Giap, and certain texts of Lenin—and they think they recognize the latter in the former." This, he argued, was both a distorted and dangerous "superimposition." The popular struggle in Latin America, according to Debray, possessed "highly special and profoundly distinct conditions of development, which [could] only be discovered through a particular experience." Prior "theoretical works on people's war," accordingly, could "do as much harm as good." While such writings, he suggested, "have been called the grammar books of the war, . . . a foreign language is learned faster in a country where it is spoken than at home studying a language manual." The Cuban experience, in short, was believed to offer a new paradigm for action.

The *Foco*

The central instrument in Guevara's theory was the guerrilla *foco*. The foco or guerrilla band, in Guevara's view, was the nucleus of the insurrection. It would be comprised of a handful of dedicated men who would "jump start" the campaign to overthrow the standing government through the power of example. Over time, Guevara envisioned, the foco would naturally begin to attract recruits. As this occurred it would slowly grow until it reached some maximum (optimal) size, which Guevara defined as somewhere between thirty and fifty men. At this point, it would split in two, each foco working independently of the other to attract a following in different regions of the country. Over time, as this budding process continued, the number of operational guerrilla bands would grow until the insurgents would eventually become a force to be reckoned with in the countryside. In Guevara's view this process was similar to that of a beehive "when at a given moment it releases a new queen, who goes to another region with a part of the swarm." The "mother hive," in this case, "with the most notable guerrilla chief will stay in the less dangerous places, while the new columns will penetrate other enemy territory [and repeat the earlier] cycle."

Guevara's concept of operations, to be sure, shared certain features with the theory of protracted war formulated by Mao. First and foremost was the assumption that the guerrillas' natural base of support would be found among the peasantry. It followed, in turn, that the natural locus of the insurgency should also be in the countryside. While Guevara, at least in theory, did not completely dismiss the supporting role that could be played by an urban underground, he clearly relegated the struggle in the cities to a subordinate position. The insurrection would turn on the rural guerrilla. Those who, "following dogma," still believed that a revolutionary action could only be carried out by urban workers, underrated, in his view, both the revolutionary sentiment of the peasantry on the one hand and the difficulties associated with operating in an urban environment on the other. "Illegal workers' movements," Guevara argued, faced "enormous dangers" (which were not similarly faced by their rural counterparts) because of their greater proximity to the regime's center of influence. To offset this greater risk, "They must function secretly without arms." The rural guerrilla, by contrast, is able to operate "beyond the reach of the oppressive forces," and is thus able to sidestep the state's opening advantage.

Like Mao, Guevara also believed that the insurgent struggle would evolve in stages. The first stage of the conflict was the "nomadic" phase, in which the initial guerrilla nucleus must continually remain on the move in order to survive. As the foco's relationship with the peasantry began to stabilize, the guerrillas would move into the second, "semi-nomadic" phase, in which the guerrillas, while still retaining a high level of fluidity, would be able to establish the first permanent base areas. The final phase of the conflict, Guevara argued, was the stage of "suburban guerrilla warfare." In language reminiscent of Mao, Guevara wrote that this stage would finally enable the guerrillas to "encircle fortified bases," engage in "mass action," and confront the army in open battle and win. "The enemy will fall," he suggested, when "the process of partial victories becomes transformed into final victories, that is to say, when the [army] is brought to accept the battle in conditions imposed by the guerrilla band; there he is annihilated and his surrender compelled." This, in turn, would ultimately result in an uprising of popular sentiment against the standing regime, sweeping it from power.

The Heroic Guerrilla

While Guevara's writings on people's war share certain similarities to those of Mao, the strategic theory that underlies this work is, in the end, quite distinct. First, in contrast to Mao, Guevara gave primacy to what he referred to as the "subjective" rather than "objective" conditions for victory. A successful insurrection, in this view, did not require that the peasantry be already primed to revolt; the conditions for revolution could often be engineered by the guerrilla band. While Guevara gave at least passing reference to the necessary preconditions for revolution in his initial discussion of the problem in *Guerrilla Warfare,* this caveat was increasingly relaxed over time. Guerrilla conflicts, he argued in a later article, could be successfully prosecuted throughout Latin America. Once set in motion, the revolution would "make itself." While the "initial conditions" did not exist everywhere in the orthodox sense of the term, the desire for revolutionary change lay just below the surface of the popular consciousness. It was only necessary to define, release, and finally channel these sentiments.

In contrast to Mao, Guevara's theory of victory ultimately relied heavily on the spontaneity of the insurgent's natural allies to provide the guerrilla foco with the critical mass it required to win. Guevara assumed, implicitly, that Latin-American society was in an inherently unstable equilibrium. The task facing the guerrilla nucleus was to aggravate the tension that he believed defined every Latin-American society, kick out the props that held up the old regime, and stand back while the target government was overcome in a popular uprising. Once set in motion, the guerrillas would not so much control this event as ride it into power. What was required under these circumstances was not a grassroots, step-by-step program of local contact, indoctrination, and organization, but an action-oriented program designed to capture the popular imagination and inspire the peasantry "from above." The foco's operational challenge, in this respect, was to sharpen and accelerate the natural process of social polarization, raise the peasants' political consciousness, and embolden them to join the revolution.

While the Chinese model of people's war considered political organization to be a necessary precondition for social mobilization, the Cuban model argued that a high-profile "guerrilla outbreak" could be used to effectively bypass the organizational requirement and proceed directly to mobilization. The basis of the insurgency, in the first case, rests with the vitality of the guerrillas' interlocking, village-based associations. Collectively, these represent an institutional counterweight to the state and the foundation of the insurgency's political and military position. The basis of the insurgency, in the second case, rests squarely on the shoulders of the guerrilla combatant, and through him, the guerrilla foco. Success or failure in this case depends on the power of their example. The guerrilla, for his part, must be a "fighter-teacher," who "need know little more than what is required of a good man or soldier." The guerrilla foco, for its part, must be an "armed nucleus," able to employ its limited resources to move its would-be followers to action. Creating this effect would not depend on organization, but on courage, discipline, and a willingness to act.

As this discussion suggests, the Cuban model placed great importance on the psychological dimensions of a guerrilla conflict. The guerrilla combatant, we are told, must never lose faith. He must "see reasons for a favorable decision even in moments when the analysis of the adverse and favorable conditions does not show an appreciable positive balance." It is particularly important to continually generate the impression of impending victory. This can be achieved initially in small ways that have big effects. A small guerrilla force can enhance its offensive punch, for example, by "striking like a tornado" to "sow panic" within the enemy's ranks. The cumulative effects of small victories won in such a fashion can, in turn, have higher-order effects on the general morale (and, hence, effectiveness) of the regime's military and political base, imbuing them with a sense of imminent doom. As these perceptions begin to take hold, the "objective conditions" of the conflict will gradually begin to shift to the insurgents' advantage, making it increasingly easy to sustain this momentum over time. The guerrillas will win when the enemy has finally come to believe that their own defeat is inevitable.

The theory of guerrilla warfare advanced by Che Guevara, in the end, had an uneven relationship to the underlying dynamics of the Cuban insurrection. Many aspects of the Cuban experience that proved to be critical to the ultimate success of the July 26 revolutionary movement were either left out or significantly downplayed in Guevara's concept of operations. Several of these should be noted here. First and foremost, perhaps, was Guevara's increasingly unrealistic view of the "revolutionary readiness" of Latin-American society. As noted above, Guevara gave little attention to the particular preconditions that must exist to bring even the best-laid plan to seize power in a popular insurgency to fruition. Revolution for Che Guevara could effectively be created out of whole cloth. What was of critical importance was not the particular state of society, or even the competing institutional strength of the opposition, but the courage, fortitude, and determination of the guerrilla fighter. Winning, in his view, boiled down to an act of will. Weak, pre-existing objective conditions could be offset by the individual guerrilla's grim refusal to accept defeat.

Second, in focusing on the *rural* guerrilla, Guevara ignored the decisive role played by the urban underground during the Cuban insurrection. The latter provided significant assistance to Fidel's rural operations. During the early days of the war, in particular, support from the July 26 movement's pre-existing urban networks was critical to the very survival of the rural foco. Throughout the course of the war, the actions of the urban underground—often carried out in a coordinated and simultaneous manner across the country—served as a major source of distraction, providing the guerrillas with the breathing space they required to stay in the game. The army was continually faced with the need to divide its efforts between the countryside and the cities, which made it difficult to concentrate on finding, fixing, and finally destroying Fidel's small group of rural combatants. In these and other ways, the cities proved to be a key variable in the outcome of the war. Despite this fact, the role of the urban underground was effectively dismissed in Guevara's writings in favor of his naturally heroic country cousin.

Finally, as much as Guevara appreciated the inherently dynamic, interactive nature of warfare, in attempting to generalize from the Cuban experience he imposed a post facto order and associated determinism on the course of the Cuban insurrection that it did not possess. Under the best of circumstances, combat is an uncertain process. There is often a high level of uncertainty surrounding the thousands of individual events that might make up a battle, and the hundreds of battles that might make up a war, which will often prove to be decisive in determining who is left standing at the end of the day. This was certainly the case in the Cuban insurrection, where except for happy chance, the guerrillas could have been defeated on any number of occasions during the course of the struggle. As the Duke of Wellington said of the Battle of Waterloo, "it was a close run thing." And yet, the problematic character of the conflict (and guerrilla warfare in general) is missing in Guevara's interpretive mode. The inherent uncertainty surrounding the problem of revolutionary action, in this case, is effectively replaced by a discussion of the guerrilla's fighting spirit. The guerrilla, in Guevara's view, will dominate events because of his superior determination.

The limits of this last assumption were demonstrated once and for all in Guevara's final action in Bolivia (1966-1967), where he was captured and killed attempting to put his theory into practice, one last time. The dramatic nature of his defeat proved to be the death knell for his model of guerrilla warfare. While the heroic quality of his death served to inspire those who came after him, subsequent guerrilla operations in Latin America would be defined by their efforts to correct the weaknesses inherent in his voluntarist theory of people's war.

Summary: Two Models of Guerrilla Warfare

The Chinese and Cuban models of people's war represent competing views of the structure and dynamics of guerrilla warfare. While both theories acknowledge that the underlying basis of revolutionary change ultimately rests on long-run historical forces, the operational guidance given to revolutionary hopefuls attempting to tap into and harness these forces, in each case, is distinct. For the Maoist, this is ultimately a problem of organization. Organization, in this sense, means building a grassroots, village-based alternative to the state. It follows that the chief measure of performance—which in this case is provided not by the scope or intensity of one's military actions, but the scope, depth, and vitality of one's organizational forms. The guerrilla's ability to pose a political and military challenge to the state is believed to be a by-product of his slowly developing institutional base. There is nothing "willful," in this view, about revolutionary outcomes. Strength of character and a pure heart are not considered to be effective substitutes for building an institutional counterweight to the state.

The opposite point of view, in many respects, defines the Cuban model of insurgency. Guerrilla actions, in this theory, are not a manifestation of popular support, but the source of such support in the first place. The target population, in this respect, is not "organized" but "impressed." Popular mobilization is less an iterative *process* than a catalytic *event*, in which the insurgents' natural constituency, spurred by the dramatic character of guerrilla actions, discovers its revolutionary identity and joins the rebellion. This shift, as noted, is expected to occur with little or no organizational investment by the insurgents. It will occur not as a result of a prior shift in local control, but in the wake of a general change in the sentiment of the revolutionary class. The guerrillas' primary task, then, is not institutional but psychological. Their goal is to capture the popular imagination in the expectation of generating a popular uprising against the state. Will, rather than numbers, can be expected to carry the day.

These two models of people's war, then, can be defined by a simple dichotomy. The Chinese model represents a bottom-up, low-profile approach to guerrilla conflict. For the low-profile challenger, insurgency is considered to be an institutional contest. The conflict will be pursued by undermining the institutional architecture of the state and replacing it with the guerrillas' own institutional alternative. Popular support is mobilized at the grassroots level (from the bottom up) in a staged process of organization building. The Cuban model, by contrast, can be defined as a top-down, high-profile approach to insurgency. For the high-profile challenger, a guerrilla conflict will not be prosecuted by undermining the state's institutional forms, but by attacking its perceptual foundations. The regime will not be slowly dismantled and replaced, but effectively taken by storm (from the top down) in a psychological convergence of popular sentiment away from the old regime and in favor of the opposition. The guerrilla's operational challenge is, first, to provide the spark that sets the conflict in motion and, second, to serve as a conduit to channel the population's revolutionary sentiments.

Gordon H. McCormick

Bibliography

Boorman, Scott A. *The Protracted Game: A Wei-chi Interpretation of Maoist Revolutionary Strategy.* London: Oxford University Press, 1969.

Childs, Matt D. "An Historical Critique of the Emergence and Evolution of Ernesto Che Guevara's *Foco* Theory." *Journal of Latin American Studies* (October 1995).

Connor, Walker. *The National Question in Marxist-Leninist Theory and Strategy.* Princeton: Princeton University Press, 1984.

Debray, Régis. *Revolution in the Revolution?* Westport: Greenwood Press, 1980.

Dunn, John. *Modern Revolutions.* Cambridge: Cambridge University Press, 1972.

Guevara, Che. *Guerrilla Warfare.* Lincoln: University of Nebraska Press, 1985.

———. "Guerrilla Warfare: A Method." In *Venceremos! The Speeches and Writings of Ernesto (Che) Guevara,* ed. John Gerassi. New York: Macmillan, 1968.

———. "Interview with Laura Berquist" (No. 1). In *Che: Selected Works of Ernesto Guevara,* ed. Rolando E. Bonachea and Nelson P. Valdés. Cambridge: MIT Press, 1969.

Guzman, Abimael. "Interview." *El Diario,* July 24, 1988.

Johnson, Chalmers. *Autopsy on People's War.* Berkeley: University of California Press, 1973.

Katzenbach, Edward L., Jr., and Gene Hanrahan. "The Revolutionary Strategy of Mao Tse-tung." *Political Science Quarterly* (September 1955).

Mao Zedong (Mao Tse-tung). "Guerrilla Warfare." In *Mao Tse-tung on Guerrilla Warfare,* trans. and ed.

Samuel B. Griffith II. Baltimore: Nautical and Aviation Publishing Company of America, 1992.

———. "On Protracted War." In *Selected Military Writings of Mao Tse-tung.* Beijing: Foreign Languages Press, 1967.

———. "Problems of Strategy in Guerrilla War Against Japan." In *Selected Military Writings of Mao Tse-tung.* Beijing: Foreign Languages Press, 1967.

McCormick, Gordon H. "Che Guevara's Revolutionary Odyssey." *Queen's Quarterly* (Summer 1998).

———. *Peruvian Maoism: The Shining Path and the Theory of People's War.* Santa Monica: RAND, 1992.

———. *Sharp Dressed Men: Peru's Tupac Amaru Revolutionary Movement.* Santa Monica: RAND, 1993.

Tucker, Robert C. *The Marxian Revolutionary Idea.* New York: W.W. Norton, 1969.

Coups

The Causes of Coups

The most common form of change in government since World War II has been the coup d'état. A coup is a quick, violent, and illegal overthrow of a government by a faction of the armed forces or other powerful sector in society. There are many specific kinds of coups. One type, a *putsch,* occurs during or immediately following a war, in which a segment of the military forms an alternative leadership as a first step toward creating a new government. Other unconstitutional changes are not considered coups, such as a "palace revolution" in which government insiders manipulate or replace the leader. The practice goes as far back as government itself, ever since Absalom conspired with leaders of ancient Israel's tribes to try to depose his father, King David. Such overthrows began to be called "coups d'état" in the late seventeenth century, as the rise of the modern state and its professional militaries— along with the nationalist tumult set in motion by the French Revolution—made them both feasible and common. Latin America's first century of independence, for example, was characterized by frequent coups, often in the form of the *pronunciamiento,* in which the military used its constitutional position as the defender of the national interest to conduct a ritualized process of consultations prior to bringing down a weak government. The proliferation of new nations and ideologies in the twentieth century—combined with the superpower rivalry of the cold war—led to an exponential increase in coups around the world after 1945. Nearly every Latin American country, and a majority of African and Asian countries, suffered successful and unsuccessful overthrows in this era. There were an estimated 380 successful coups and coup attempts between 1945 and 1967. There were at least 50 successful and 150 unsuccessful coups in Africa alone between 1955 and 1985.

Although coups are usually facilitated by external support and internal upheaval, the need for secret planning precludes inclusion in the planning by large sectors of the armed forces or population. All that is needed by a small group of plotters is the existence of a state bureaucratic apparatus. When that bureaucracy is filled with people who are linked to the political leaders through ethnic or other loyalties, as in countries such as imperial China and contemporary Saudi Arabia, clandestine infiltration and sudden action is exceedingly difficult. But in the political development of most countries, fewer state employees are connected with the leaders, the state bureaucracy becomes the foundation of governmental control and societal interaction, and the military and police forces become more hierarchal and professional. Under such conditions, it is far easier to have a sudden seizure of the state and removal of the government officials who run it.

Coups themselves encourage further coups, since each one sets a legal and political precedent that weakens civilian rule and makes its overthrow even more legitimate and practical. Constitutional executives under the threat of a coup feel pressed to maintain popular support through patronage and rash short-term policies, which end up undermining both the government and popular support for democracy. When combined with ethnic, political, or other societal divisions, such patterns lead to what political scientist Samuel Huntington calls "praetorian politics," in which every sector becomes more mobilized, less willing to compromise with other groups, and more likely to clamor for the "ultimate" resolution to domestic ruptures: a coup. In the process, the framework of democracy—accountable state agencies, meaningful elections, and a rule of law—becomes even more debilitated. Legitimization also comes through official or de facto recognition by other countries. The Wilson-Tobar Doctrine prohibits international recognition of a regime that seizes power by force, at least until it has demonstrated public support. This and related international standards, however, have no legal binding and in any case are obviated by the fact that states give de facto recognition to new governments by simply *not* making any declarations.

Although modern political developments have made coups common, the causes of each coup are rooted primarily in the particular conditions of the country in which it takes place. A country's own political, economic, and social conditions often lead to demands for a change in government, and the existence of a state structure, combined with meddling from other countries, makes coups the easiest and quickest way to fulfill such demands. An understanding of coups in the post–World War II era, therefore, requires a look not just at American and Soviet actions, but at their underlying national and regional causes and at the motives of those carrying them out.

Most generally, coups are caused by the inability of political parties and governments to enact effective policy and to keep societal divisions in check. Most coups, in fact, occur in the wake of an economic downturn or a bout of political conflict, as manifest social discontent and waves of mobilization compel the military and its allies to intervene. Many coup leaders cite economic mismanagement and fault the deposed government's inability to control spending, maintain citizens' standard of living, or avoid painful austerity measures. An economic decline not only undermines the government's legitimacy, but undercuts support from key sectors such as the middle class. Such scenarios are often rooted in "relative deprivation," which is the difference between the population's expectations of entitlements and its capabilities to attain them. When those capabilities decrease or the expectations increase without a corresponding change in the other, the result is often mass protest in the forms of strikes, looting, and rebellion. When the military also suffers from relative deprivation, the likelihood of a coup increases dramatically. While six of Africa's wealthiest countries experienced coups, in fact, thirteen of the continent's poorest countries have also experienced them.

The frequency and causes of coups are also determined by regional characteristics. Latin America has the longest tradition of coups, rooted in a history of civil strife, political instability, the military's institutional and legal power, and, since the beginning of the twentieth century, the battle against socialism and communism. In East Asia, agitation by communist and nationalist forces during the cold war was one of the main causes of that region's coups. In the Middle East, independence and cold war geopolitics brought out the deep-seated tensions between traditional and modernizing sectors, which coups tried to reconcile, often in the name of Islam and pan-Arabism. Even greater levels of economic underdevelopment and institutional weakness in sub-Saharan Africa combined with ethnic rivalry and the chaos of decolonization to give that region the greatest frequency of coups in the post–World War II period.

Motives and Justifications of Coupmakers

Underlying and often contradicting the causes of a coup, however, are its motives and justifications. Motives are the coupmakers' specific judgments, assessments, and personal and collective ambitions. While causes set the stage for a coup, motives make it happen. Ethnic and class differences cause coups, for example, but only when the military and its allies deem them serious enough. Amid Africa's prevalent ethnic strife, some successfully integrated militaries have launched coups in an attempt to control violence in society. Other armed forces mirror their societies' ethnic division, spurring coups when one group seizes power in its rivalry with the others. Only about one-third of Africa's armies have a stable ethnic balance, in fact, and threats to a particular ethnic group was at least one of the causes in most of the continent's coups. Class interests are the another motive of coupmakers. Most military officers come from the middle classes—mainly from the middle and upper-middle classes in Asia and Latin America and mainly from the lower-middle classes in Africa and Asia—and so often represent and speak for the interests of those classes.

Justifications, which are usually but not necessarily in line with the motives, are public stances designed to maximize political support for the coup leaders. Divulged in the new government's first public statements, justifications usually focus on the actions of the previous government, such as over-centralizing power, suppressing political opposition, indulging in nepotism, curtailing constitutional rights, fomenting ethnic rivalry, or inviting condemnation by the international community. Most new leaders point to the specific shortfalls of their predecessors, who they claim are too incompetent, too greedy, and too absorbed in personal rivalries to run a government that promotes the nation's interests. In all too many cases, the difference between justifications and motives becomes clear as the new regime repeats practices it had criticized.

Another common set of justifications is the military's self-proclaimed responsibility to act on behalf of the "national interest" in times of internal disorder, threats to national institutions, or foreign intervention. Such justifications usually mask motives of resentment against the government's interference in military affairs, its unwillingness to cooperate with the military, or its tarnishing of the military's honor. It is often the process of asserting that control, rather than the control itself, that breeds coup plots. A government asserting little control is unlikely to be offensive to the military, and most governments that already have control are capable of preventing coups altogether. A government makes itself vulnerable by trying to alter recruitment and dismissal policies, change training and education, or place its own officials in the military's top ranks. Another provocative move by the government is to establish security forces separate from the military, such as presidential or party militias. Prior to his 1971 coup in Uganda, for example, Major General Idi Amin criticized President Milton Obote for establishing an elite security force. Even military "professionalism" does not inoculate governments against coups. While some argue that the professional military's national loyalty, social responsibility, and attention to procedure make them less disposed to coups, others counter that such assumptions all hinge on the military's "principle of civil supremacy" and point to the many "professional" armies that have launched coups.

Even though it is carried out by a small group, a coup in itself does not imply any political orientation. While most coups since 1945 have been headed by conservative elements against leftist or moderate governments, many other coupmakers have been leftist or progressive because they remove oligarchal structures blocking needed reform and often align themselves with workers and peasants. Coupmakers' ideology, in fact, is often formed in opposition to that of the existing government. According to Huntington, "In the world of oligarchy, the soldier is a radical; in the middle-class world he is a participant and arbiter; as the mass-society looms on the horizon he becomes the conservative guardian of the existing order." In Venezuela, for example, the military intervened on behalf of the progressive Acción Democrática party in 1945 and 1958, but against it in 1948.

While coup leaders often portray their action as a temporary measure to restore order, democracy, or the "legitimate" government, they often have a long-term agenda that is revealed gradually and "requires" them to stay in power in order to carry it out. The 1968 coup in Peru, for example, enacted a radically new and extensive economic program, including re-nationalizations. Such continuation is supported through violent repression or legitimizing means such as new constitutions or elections, or, as in most cases, a combination of the two. Augusto Pinochet in Chile (1973–1989) and Sani Abacha in Nigeria (1993–1998) were two presidents who have used such a combination.

Sometimes junior officers are the ones who carry out a coup, overriding superiors who are regarded as part of the existing government. While most older officers gained their positions through traditional routes and were trained by the colonial power, junior officers are often educated with a very different set of principles and often suffer from inadequate or irregularly paid salaries. Without some involvement by top military leaders, though, such attempts usually fall short— intentionally or unintentionally—of a complete takeover. Junior officers arrested their superiors in Ethiopia but did not attempt to bring down the government in 1964, for example, while in Venezuela junior officials were responsible for two failed coup attempts in 1992. On the other hand, a coup based solely on the personal ambitions or grievances of a top military officer is rare. Even in extreme examples of personal ambition, such as Jean Bedel Bokassa's takeover of the Central African Republic on December 31, 1965, the coup leader must be able to exploit some flaw in the government and to convince other officers to help depose it.

Coups and the Cold War

Since 1945, all of these causes and motives played themselves out in a world where the cold war between the United States and the Soviet Union pervaded nearly every country and had at least some connection to nearly every coup. Rarely did the superpowers intervene directly, however, but instead armed and encouraged military factions or revolutionary groups, bringing a country's own political polarizations to the boiling point and providing a justification for the government's overthrow. Coups were also set off by regional "contagions," in which military factions acted out of fear of being pulled into neighbors' moves into the Communist or Western camp.

For the Soviet Union, coups were often the best way to install Communist or otherwise friendly regimes. With the Red Army occupying Eastern and Central Europe at the end of World War II, coups were unnecessary in countries such as Poland and Hungary, or in countries with strong indigenous Communist movements, such as Yugoslavia and Albania. But in Czechoslovakia, despite the fact that the Communists won a larger share of the vote than any other party in the post-war elections, the 1948 coup was needed to give them complete power.

Because the Soviet Union had weak ideological links to the third world and little to offer it in terms of long-term economic development, coups were also the usual way pro-Soviet governments came into power in Asia, Africa, and Latin America. Prior to the 1960s, the Soviets optimistically predicted that decolonization and rejection of the West would alone bring about pro-Soviet coups around the world. By the time of the fall of Premier Nikita Khrushchev, however, this optimism had been deflated by reality. There had been thirteen pro-Soviet coups, but many of them were unstable or more closely connected with religious or other ideologies than with Soviet communism. (Such coups include those in Egypt in 1952; Iraq in 1958 and 1968; Syria in 1966; Peru and Republic of Congo-Brazzaville in 1968; Somalia, Sudan, and Libya in 1969; Benin in 1972; Ethiopia in 1974 and 1977; South Yemen and Afghanistan in 1978; Grenada in 1979; and Suriname in 1980.) Many of them, in addition, soon fell to pro-Western forces.

While it still continued to encourage coups among military factions, the Kremlin broadened its strategy by also promoting "vanguard" parties that would bolster Marxist governments' defenses against military plots. This approach had several notable successes, in countries such as Angola, Mozambique, and South Yemen. With generous military assistance and the provision of Cuban, East German, or Soviet advisors to "protect" these governments, furthermore, chances of a counter-coup were minimized. In many countries the presence of Cubans was less offensive and imperialistic than that of Russians; Cuban advisors helped put down coup attempts against pro-Soviet Presidents Massamba-Debat of Congo-Brazzaville in 1966 and Agostinho Neto of Angola in 1977. (In some cases, however, Cuban and Soviet interests diverged, as in Grenada in 1983, when a radical Marxist pro-USSR faction overthrew President Maurice Bishop, a close ally of Cuba. In other cases, East German advisors helped prevent coups, such as the 1980 attempt against pro-Soviet Libyan leader Muammar Qaddafi.)

The United States was more successful in encouraging, engineering, or suppressing coups. (Coups in Africa that replaced pro-Soviet governments with pro-American ones include those in Algeria in 1965, Ghana in 1966, Mali in 1968, Sudan in 1971, and Equatorial Guinea in 1979.) While it never formulated an explicit policy on coups, U.S. action could be divided into two approaches. In the first, the United States directly fomented and organized coups by military factions or armed opposition groups in countries of vital geopolitical importance. In 1953, the United States and Great Britain feared a turn toward communism in Iran under that country's nationalist and popular prime minister, Mohammed Mossadegh. It then carried out an elaborate plan in which the Shah replaced Mossadegh amid demonstrations whipped up in the capital of Teheran. A year later, the U.S. Central Intelligence Agency used similar tactics to oust reformist President Jacobo Arbenz of Guatemala, orchestrating a fake invasion that forced the army and the population to lose faith in Arbenz and force him out. In 1963, as Vietnam became a central concern of U.S. foreign policy, the Kennedy administration worked with disgruntled military factions to overthrow the increasingly corrupt and repressive South Vietnamese regime of Ngo Dinh Diem.

As its operations came under more criticism, its logistic maneuverability tightened, and its support was becoming a liability for its allies, the United States shifted to using economic aid and more covert actions that avoided direct participation. This approach had mixed success. It supported successful coups against João Goulart in Brazil in 1964 and against Cambodian Prince Norodom Sihanouk in 1970 and helped stave off coups against friendly regimes in Egypt and the Dominican Republic. But it failed in Iran in 1979 and in Libya during the 1980s, and neglected the seriousness of threats to several friendly regimes, such as that of Haile Selassie in Ethiopia in 1974, which ended in anti-American coups.

The United States and the Soviet Union, though, were not the only powers using coups as an instrument of foreign policy. Eager to maintain influence in their former colonies and to ensure supplies of raw materials, Great Britain and France used military assistance and economic aid to encourage and suppress coups throughout Africa and Asia. If circumstances called for it, they did not flinch from direct intervention. (Of-

ficers trained by the French are said to have less respect for their civilian leaders than do those trained by the British.) The British were becoming annoyed with Ugandan President Milton Obote, for example, and inexplicably delayed his flight back from a 1971 Commonwealth meeting when Idi Amin seized power, and then quickly recognized the Amin government. Unlike other powers, France has been unapologetic about using the military option to help out its friends. It has been on the scene during unstable times in Benin, Burundi, Zaire, Togo, Chad, and Congo-Brazzaville. Though its exact role is often unclear, on some occasions it has used its own troops to prevent coups, such as its February 1964 effort to save Gabon President Léon M'Ba.

Most coups in the post–World War II era, in sum, have been the result of internal conflicts and weaknesses, motivated by military factions and cold war tensions. Three case studies, each from a different region, demonstrate how a particular set of causes and motives combined with international politics to lead to coups.

Argentina, 1976

An ever-growing communist menace aggravated Latin America's predilection toward coups, especially after the Cuban Revolution in 1959. While countries such as Mexico and Colombia escaped this pattern, a rash of coups that hit Central and South America brought in regimes far more durable than those in the past. Chile had been South America's most democratic country, for example, until the 1973 coup brought on seventeen repressive years of military rule. But the most brutal military regime in the region was the one that seized power in Argentina in 1976. Carried out against a weak civilian government unable to suppress leftist guerrillas, the coup appeared as just another casualty of cold war tensions, but it was rooted in a national history of civil strife and authoritarianism that extended back to the colonial era.

After declaring independence in 1816, Argentina plunged into sixty years of civil war between the Unitarians of the powerful Buenos Aires province and the Federalists from outlying provinces. The violence was brought under control only by increasing power by the military and the executive. A series of coups beginning in 1828 eventually led to the rule of Juan Manuel de Rosas, who used populist appeal to create a highly centralized, paternalistic, and repressive state that maintained continuing dominance over the economy by an agriculture and industrial oligarchy. Political strife re-emerged at the turn of the century amid growing immigration and trade union activism. In 1912, a progressive government introduced democratic and electoral reforms, which were continued through the 1920s under President Hipólito Yrigoyen of the Radical party. Along with these policies, Yrigoyen's own concentration of power rankled the conservative sectors, who supported his overthrow by the military in 1930. Legitimizing the new regime as legal, however it had been established, the Supreme Court set a pattern of legal justification that would be used over the next fifty years to justify military takeovers. The military regime repealed the democratic reforms, carried out widespread arrests, dismissed judges, and annulled local elections. Amid worsening economic problems, a military faction called the Group of United Officers (GOU) overthrew it in 1943. Disunity in that junta led to the rise of General Juan Perón, who quickly came to dominate a divided society that could not accept its own diversity.

As president, Perón purged the judiciary, created a monopolistic government-backed union, and enacted a constitution that gave him authority to impose a "state of internal war."

The military faction that overthrew Perón in 1955 promised a timely return to "the rule of law" and "an authentic democracy." With the Peronists banned, fresh elections brought in two weak Radical presidencies, but the party's stint in power was abruptly ended in June 1966 by the "Argentine Revolution," a military junta that made no pretense of being "provisional." It promptly dissolved Congress and the Supreme Court, prohibited political activity, awarded itself full executive and legislative authority, governed by decree, and demoted the constitution to third place behind the "Revolutionary Objectives" and the "Statute of the Argentine Revolution." Growing internal violence by armed groups such as the left-wing pro-Peronist *Montoneros* guerrillas, led to even harsher measures, such as the creation of special courts for insurrectionists.

The exiled Perón returned to power in 1973, but his government was riven by both factionalism and unrealistic popular expectations. Upon his death in 1974, Perón was succeeded by his widow and vice president, Isabel. Her incompetent government was no match for the increasing leftist violence and two years later was overthrown by a military junta that ruled the country for the next seven years. As before, the Supreme Court recognized the new regime by citing the need to end internal instability, which the regime did by dismantling the constitution, subjecting civilians to military tribunals, and "disappearing" nearly 30,000 people suspected of sympathizing with the left. So while the battle with communism was the declared motive and justification for the 1976 coup, of course, its causes stemmed from historical patterns of internal violence, political division, and the power of the military and the executive.

Ghana, 1966

While Latin America already had a long history of coups by 1945, the many newly independent nations of Africa hoped to have a different start. Most hope was pinned on countries with buoyant economies and highly developed political structures, such as Ghana. But the 1966 coup that overthrew Ghanaian President Kwame Nkrumah revealed the pervasive lack of immunity to coups in cold war Africa.

When Ghana became the first sub-Saharan African colony to gain independence in 1957, Nkrumah's Convention People's Party (CPP) had already become the dominant political force during the 1951–1957 period of internal self-government. Although many traditional leaders did not accept the CPP and although distrust continued among the country's main ethnic groups, Nkrumah's charisma and anti-colonial populism succeeded in uniting the country. The CPP distributed patronage widely, furthermore, and the Ghanaian military was thoroughly steeped in the British apolitical tradition. The immense expectations accompanying independence, however, generated increasing political pressure and opposition from all sides, including regional movements, the Muslim minority, and farmers who complained that their cocoa crop was subsidizing the poorer southern regions. National institutions were too fragile to accommodate these growing divisions, and political organizations began resorting to violence and electoral fraud. Nkrumah began restricting regional governments, deporting political leaders, enacting preventive detention laws, and stepping up anti-Western

rhetoric. As the regime became more personalistic and corrupt, it lost touch with the people and its own grassroots base. The 1960 parliamentary elections were suspended, and a 1964 referendum officially made the country a one-party state. On the economic front, the president began instituting a policy of "socialism from above," with measures such as agricultural collectivization. Although these policies increased state controls and strengthened the CPP, they soon collapsed into runaway unemployment and inflation. Along with a fall in cocoa prices, this failure obliged the government to turn to loans and aid from the Communist bloc.

It was Nkrumah's pan-African interventions in countries such as Democratic Republic of the Congo (formerly Zaire) that, in addition to further harming the economy, raised the ire of the 14,000-man military. The armed forces had a strong personal affinity with the British, who educated, trained, and equipped them, and so reacted strongly when Nkrumah began purchasing arms from the Soviet Union and sending recruits there for training. Antagonism deepened when the president formed a Russian-trained Presidential Guard, cut the military's budget, neglected to implement military plans, and increased his interference in activities ranging from officer selection to troop exercises. The military resented the CPP's attempts at closer ties with it. Confident that it would have Western support, a group of military officers overthrew the Nkrumah regime on February 24, 1966, to coincide with a presidential trip to Beijing and Hanoi.

Iraq, 1963

Coups in the Middle East were rooted less in institutional or economic weakness than in tension between supporters of tradition and advocates of modernization. As one of the most economically and politically developed Arab states, and with a pivotal role in the superpower rivalry in the region, Iraq illustrated how this tension interacted with cold war politics. As a British mandate after World War I, the country adopted Western democratic institutions such as a parliament, judiciary, and civil service. This transplant was eased through the leadership of King Faisal I, who was trusted by both the modernizing elite and traditional sectors. After becoming independent in 1932, however, the system fell apart. Faisal unexpectedly died in 1933, generating a period of upheaval with the army constantly replacing unpopular governments or taking power itself. This praetorian pattern was halted only with the revolution of 1958. A new generation of intellectuals and professionals, unaccepted by the elite, had begun to grow in importance and numbers and to ally themselves with a growing number of military officers who themselves were also becoming convinced that progress required a radical change in leadership and policy. These "Free Officers" created a Central Organization in the mid-1950s and were bound with the intellectuals by nationalism and Ba'athism, a pan-Arabist movement begun in Syria in 1940. On July 14, 1958, Brigadier Abd al-Karim Qasim, leader of the Free Officers, successfully overthrew the government and killed the royal family.

Qasim, however, continued old practices of centralization and repression. He aligned the country with the Soviet Union, but his increasingly unpopular policies and his military forays, such as resurrecting claims to Kuwait and an internal war with the Kurds, reduced Soviet influence in the region.

Meanwhile, the Free Officers split into pro-Communist and pro-Ba'athist factions, adding to the growing assertiveness by both the Communist and Ba'athist parties. On February 8, 1963, an army faction supported by the Ba'athists overthrew Qasim, once again trying to stop the cycle of praetorianism with an appeal to Islam and Arab nationalism.

Mark Ungar

Bibliography

Andrews, William George. *The Politics of the Coup d'Etat: Five Case Studies.* New York: Van Nostrand Reinhold, 1969.

Ciria, Alberto. *Parties and Power in Modern Argentina (1940-1946).* Buenos Aires: Editorial Universitaria de Buenos Aires, 1964.

David, Steven R. *Third World Coups d'Etat and International Security.* Baltimore: Johns Hopkins University Press, 1987.

Farcau, Bruce W. *The Coup: Tactics in the Seizure of Power.* Westport, CT: Praeger, 1994.

Finer, S.E. *The Man on Horseback.* London: Pall Mall Press, 1962.

Gurr, Ted Robert. *Why Men Rebel.* Princeton: Princeton University Press, 1970.

Huntington, Samuel. *Political Order in Changing Societies.* New Haven: Yale University Press, 1968.

Kraus, John. "Ghana, 1966." In *The Politics of the Coup D'tat,* ed. William G. Andrews and Uri Ra'anan. New York: Van Nostrand Reinhold, 1969.

Luttwak, Edward. *Coup d'Etat: A Practical Handbook.* New York: Knopf, 1969.

Malaparte, Curzio. *Coup d'Etat: The Technique of Revolution.* New York: E.P. Dutton, 1932.

Nordlinger, Eric. *Soldiers in Politics.* Englewood Cliffs, NJ: Prentice-Hall, 1977.

O'Kane, Rosemary H.T. *The Likelihood of Coups.* Brookfield, VT: Avebury, 1987.

Tullock, Gordon. *The Social Dilemma: The Economics of War and Revolution.* Blacksburg, VA: University Publications, 1974.

Wheatcroft, Andrew. *The World Atlas of Revolution.* New York: Simon and Schuster, 1983.

Woddis, Jack. *Armies and Politics.* New York: International, 1978.

Invasions and Border Disputes

Introduction

The twentieth century has seen more change in war than the previous 3,000 years. The development of weapons of mass destruction is one obvious expression of this change, as is the transition from mostly military casualties early in the century to mostly civilian casualties at the end, or the institution of permanent, million-man standing armies. Less obvious has been the transition from interstate wars to intra-state wars, or from classical wars to civil wars. A generation ago, most wars were between armies of nation-states. Today, almost all wars are civil wars between factions within nation-states. This has many implications for the world. This chapter reviews those conflicts categorized as "invasions and border disputes," which imply the existence of nation-states and some level of agreement about what the borders were before they were altered, or at least violated, by invasion.

This highlights an often overlooked dimension of war, its legal status. Initially, invasions are almost always illegal unless preceded by a formal declaration of war (a rarity after World War II). That legal status can change overnight when treaties are signed, or almost imperceptibly as the world becomes accustomed to what once was a tragic crime. For example, the invasion of Tibet by the forces of Communist China in October 1950 was widely condemned. But decades of patient diplomacy have done lit-

tle to change this "fact on the ground," and on the maps published around the world. Tibetan partisans point out grotesque conditions that continue, resulting in very high death rates for ethnic Tibetans who are being slowly replaced by Han Chinese. Most of the capitals of the world observe discreetly, however, because their calculations favor the government in Beijing.

Technical students of war sometimes refer to border disputes as "irredentist" disputes. More narrowly, irredenta refer to territories historically or ethnically related to one political unit, but presently subject to another. There are many. A global history of wars and of mass migrations of refugees fleeing war or persecution has left many irredenta that can serve as flashpoints for future war. Other than its use here, the term "irredentist" will be replaced with the word "border."

Border Disputes Versus General Roots of War

The causes of "invasions and border disputes" are not significantly different from the causes of wars in general, except for the fact that disputes over borders can reflect especially arcane bits of history. For example, most people know that the Persian Gulf War of 1990–1991 between Iraq, Kuwait, and the United States and its allies began with an invasion of Kuwait by Iraq on August 2, 1990. Almost everyone knows that control of oil supplies was more important than details of the border. Very few people in the Western world, however, know the seminal role played seventy-three years earlier by Sir Percy Cox in this war. Cox was a British diplomat based in Baghdad who drew the line between what would become Iraq and Kuwait, as part of the Sykes-Picot agreement of 1916 between Britain and France. He deliberately separated one tiny village, which became Kuwait City, and a large area of oil-rich desert from what would become modern Iraq. This was more than merely an expression of the principle of divide and rule applied to British interests in controlling oil supplies in the region. They were quite concerned with Turkish power allied with Germany during World War I and had to balance claims by dozens of tribes and clans in the region with British and French "spheres of influence." The important point to note is that borders drawn for reasons long past, all but forgotten by most, can serve as flashpoints for war today or tomorrow. The subsequent Balfour Declaration by the British Cabinet of November 2, 1917, had even greater consequences, most notably laying the groundwork for the partition of what would be called Palestine, and then Israel. Wars over borders have been quite frequent here.

Several wars in Africa near the close of the twentieth century reflect similar echoes of diplomatic map-makers from the colonial period, who carved up African lands according to European concerns, which were relatively indifferent to local ethnic geography. It is fashionable in some circles to blame all African problems on colonialism, old or new. That can be overdone, and there is no need here to replicate a review of colonial wars. Countries with conflicts such as Sudan should be noted, however. Sudan has suffered about one million dead in a long-running civil war between fundamentalist Islamic Arabs in the North, who control the central government, and animist or Christian Nubians and other black Africans in the South. The central political issue is the imposition of strict Sharia (Islamic law) on the whole nation. But this would not be an issue if colonial map-makers had not created a cultural artifact called "Sudan," which puts two very different peoples into the same formal nation-state.

The general causes of war include: competition for resources and power, population pressure, corruption of governance, authoritarian politics and militant religions, inequalities of wealth within and between nations, the hubris and demagoguery of scapegoating politicians and the desire of fickle followers for an enemy to blame all problems on, and a hundred other items. People who list causes of wars can create very long lists, because the fundamental truth about war is that it results from social decisions usually involving more than one key leader and supporting populations—who may go to war for just about any reason their hearts desire.

The lack of effective "international conflict resolution systems" is another important root of organized, armed conflict in the modern world, albeit harder to discern. Americans have managed to control most local violence at lower levels of social organization. Who could imagine, for example, Minnesota going to war with North Dakota over rights to the Red River water? Killing a neighbor because of a disagreement regarding city boundaries is considered murder all around the world. But an eight-year war that killed about a million people was started by Iraq's Saddam Hussein in September 1980, when he asserted a historic claim to the Shatt el Arab waterway, which divides Iraq from Iran. No higher authority existed to restrain him, and the international community had not matured enough yet to recognize that murder by nation-states over ownership of waterways is not philosophically different from murder between neighbors in a city over where the proper boundaries lie.

Another great complication for those who study why wars start is called "transmutability of cause," which means that causes can shift and blend such that no one can say for sure which cause is the "most important." For example, one can say that Iraqi leader Saddam Hussein's subsequent invasion of Kuwait was motivated by historic border disputes (as he did) and recent insults like Kuwait poaching oil from across the border by slant drilling (which, indeed, it was). Or one can say that history had nothing to do with this; it was a simple struggle over oil. Or money. What is the difference between oil and money, or between ancient history and current disputes? Well, there are some significant differences, and there were other significant financial disputes between debtor Iraq and creditor Kuwait (including huge debts from the preceding war between Iraq and Iran). The most important complication that "transmutability" presents is that no one can find a truly "objective" way to determine which of these, or twenty other putative causes of that war, were the most important factors underlying the ultimate decisions by both the leaders and the people to wage it.

Invasions are easier to discern precisely because of borders; someone left their border and moved to the other side by force of arms. But even then the question of who was the aggressor can be difficult to answer because of the history of provocations that often precedes the invasion—for example, intelligence organizations may stage bogus events to pre-

cipitate the crisis. The dark arts of psychological operations, in which propaganda is used to play with the minds of the enemy, and covert action were much enhanced by the cold war between the superpowers, which led to interventions nearly everywhere on earth.

The Cold War and Its Aftermath

The cold war between the United States and the Soviet Union and their respective allies thoroughly dominated the period from 1947 to 1991, when the Soviet Union disintegrated into fifteen independent states. Many proxy wars in third world locales resulted from the very conscious decision to do everything possible to avoid nuclear warfare between what came to be called the superpowers. This reasoning concluded that regular combat forces of the United States and the Soviet Union should never fight each other publicly, lest enraged populations insist on full-scale nuclear war. But the contest between capitalism and communism was fierce, so proxy wars erupted around the world as the United States and the Soviet Union took opposite sides in scores of local disputes. This section will focus only on how the end of the cold war started five or six smaller wars at the periphery of the Soviet empire, many over borders or the related issue of sovereignty, and ended several other civil wars in other parts of the world.

First, it should be noted that the collapse of the Soviet Union was preceded by their dramatic failure in Afghanistan, which they invaded in December 1979. Many called it their "Vietnam," because there were so many parallels with the U.S. experience in Southeast Asia. As per the protocols developed earlier, the United States shipped billions of dollars in weapons to the Afghans and provided much other financial and intelligence support. Once the battle was defined, however, the United States scrupulously avoided deploying American combat troops so that United States and Soviet Union combat forces would not kill each other directly. In the end, after a couple of million Afghans and many tens of thousands of Soviet soldiers died, the Soviet Union retreated, just as Americans had from the second Indochina war. The Soviet Union's image, its treasury, and its domestic cohesion were so damaged that most observers think this contributed substantially to its subsequent collapse. The Soviet invasion was preceded by substantial internal conflict among Afghan factions, and unfortunately, Afghanistan has endured nearly continuous civil war thereafter. But that is now a matter of internal borders rather than invasion from outside.

Shortly after the breakup of the Soviet Union, several small wars began at the edges of the Soviet empire: In Moldavia, between 830 and 930 persons died in a brief but fierce dispute in 1991 and 1992; in the Ingush Republic, about 350 died when Slavic North Ossetians battled Muslim Ingush over who would rule; in Georgia, latent ethnic tensions between dominant Georgians and minority Abkhazians in one area and South Ossetians in another led to a three-front civil war from 1989 to 1994; in Tajikistan, at least 20,000 people died during another civil war over succession to power; and in Azerbaijan, ethnic Armenians in a disputed enclave called Nagorno-Karabakh joined forces with Armenians from the homeland (formerly, another Soviet republic, now an independent state) to battle the Azeris over this territory. Approximately 20,000 people died there from 1991 to 1994. Of course, all such casualty estimates are rough when central order breaks down, and private vengeance competes with political purpose. The greatest ca-

sualties among these splinter wars occurred in Chechnya, where an "invasion" by Russian troops on December 11, 1994, led to a minimum of 40,000 dead including several thousand Russian troops.

Unlike Moldavia, Georgia, Tajikistan, or Azerbaijan, which were "republics" under the former Soviet system, Chechnya was never recognized as an even marginally independent part of the Soviet Union. It was considered part of Russia ever since it was overrun by czarist troops in the nineteenth century. The Chechens declared independence in 1991, under the leadership of former Soviet air force general Dzhokhar Dudayev. This highlights the political dilemma of labels. Should this be called a "civil war" within territorial Russia, or an invasion of independent Chechnya by Russian troops? The answer to that, in practical terms, depends mainly on how many other governments choose to recognize the independence of the disputed territory.

Meanwhile, elsewhere in the world, rapidly declining Russian support for previous clients in their many proxy wars with U.S. interests led to eventual resolution of several civil wars. Examples included El Salvador, Guatemala, Mozambique and for a while, Angola. In Angola, like many other civil wars, the situation was far more complicated. Peace was achieved, with U.N. help, between the formerly Soviet-sponsored central government in Luanda and the main insurgent group backed by the United States (UNITA). But it was UNITA's Jonas Savimbi who restarted this war in 1992 when he lost the U.N.-sponsored election.

So, even longstanding clients in the superpower cold war could, and often did, deny their nominal masters. One thing that the cold war almost always accomplished was a massive transfusion of weapons and political money into combat zones around the world. For example, Mohammed Siad Barre of Somalia in Northeast Africa played off the United States and the Soviet Union alternately accepting support from each. When he finally left the scene in 1991, the money was gone, but vast stocks of light arms were available for the many militias that arose to fight over the borders. An abortive peacekeeping effort in 1992–1994 by the United Nations managed to save many people from starvation, but utterly failed to stop the fighting and was ultimately driven out of the capital city, Mogadishu. As of 1998, no recognizable central government existed in Somalia.

About sixty countries around the world attracted major covert operations during the cold war, many with large-scale lethal consequences. Everywhere the CIA was, the KGB (Soviet intelligence) was also. Some of these wars would have occurred in any event, because many arguments had local roots. Other proxy wars would never have occurred without the "assistance" of the superpowers who were eager to play out their competition on foreign soils without engaging United States or Soviet Union combat units. But almost all of the proxy wars and many civil wars that attracted support by the superpowers went on longer and were far more lethal than otherwise would have been possible because of the relatively unlimited supplies of small arms, and financial support, available to those who would be clients of the superpowers.

Why Latin America Is Different

Although there are many theories on this, the most likely is that Latin America has been so thoroughly dominated by the United States, its patron to the north, that many disputes have been suppressed, or at least settled short of large-scale, lethal conflict. So the armies of this region have turned instead to persecuting their own peoples, in the name of stability and order, rather than planning invasions of their neighbors which all know would be quickly, and if need be ruthlessly, suppressed by the United States. Certainly a long history of "gunboat diplomacy" in this area, familiar to every Latin American if not to every North American, would support that point of view.

In the post–World War II period, examples of that "diplomacy" include the Bay of Pigs invasion of Cuba (1961) and the secret war that followed, armed intervention in the Dominican Republic (1965), invasions of Granada (1983) and Panama (1989), and the long "secret" war against Nicaragua, staged from Honduras and Costa Rica (1982–1990).

Other civil wars in Central America involved the superpowers, like El Salvador and Guatemala, but while some involved invasions and borders (especially the "contra" war in Nicaragua), these were mainly local disputes between rich and poor enflamed by the cold war competition between superpowers using third-world battlegrounds. The dirty war in Argentina (1976–1979) and its analogs in Uruguay, Bolivia, Chile, Brazil, and elsewhere, while killing many thousands of often innocent people, reflected the same forces and very seldom involved crossing borders. This leaves five cases with other dynamics or unambiguous border-crossings by armed forces: the "secret war" between America and Cuba known to spies as Operation Mongoose during the mid-1960s (preceded by the invasion of the Bay of Pigs); the "soccer war" of 1969 between El Salvador and Honduras; the semi-annual border "war" between Ecuador and Peru, which killed few but grows with global competition for resources; the Falklands war of 1982 between Argentina and Britain; and the invasion of Panama by U.S. forces on December 20, 1989.

Unknown to most North Americans, but very well known to Cubans, the United States conducted an extensive covert war against Cuba after the Cuban missile crisis of October 1962. That crisis brought the superpowers as close to nuclear holocaust as they have come, and its resolution evoked a promise from President John F. Kennedy never to invade Cuba again in return for the removal of Soviet nuclear missiles from that island nation. However, the CIA was still flush from its great successes in the covert war in Guatemala (1954), Iran (1953), and elsewhere, so it was determined to proceed with covert paramilitary operations against Cuba using expatriate Cubans based mainly in Miami and the Florida Keys. The CIA's Miami station became the largest station in the world. Hundreds of Cuban enemies of Fidel Castro were trained in paramilitary commando tactics and armed with various weapons. In addition to blowing up oil installations and several assassination attempts against Castro (twenty-eight according to Cuba), a large variety of unconventional attacks were launched including the use of biological weapons against Cuban crops and pigs.

The "soccer war" of 1969 is simpler, but no less bizarre. The nominal cause of this brief war between Honduras and El Salvador was a disputed call in a soccer game, hence the name. But this war began for another, more fundamental reason. That problem was illegal immigration from desperately crowded and poor El Salvador into much less crowded but no less poor Honduras. Honduras expelled about 11,000 Salvadoran "settlers" (of between 200,000 and 300,000 estimated in that country). El Salvador's army invaded Hon-

duras to protect their settlers. Honduras responded to protect its territory. Both claimed to be protecting the honor of World Cup Soccer, and about 5,000 people died before it was over. In many countries, soccer matches have nearly as potent political meaning. The Organization of American States intervened diplomatically, and the point was made without leading to further bloodshed as the regional powers, and common sense, stopped the fighting.

Peru has disputed the location of a jungle border with Ecuador since its creation in 1821. (Ecuador declared its independence from Spain on August 10, 1809.) For most of this time, there was nothing really to fight about since the jungle in question is extremely dense, waterlogged, and virtually uninhabited. However, for many years there have been annual border clashes over three disputed areas between the respective forces during the few months when travel of any kind is practical there. These skirmishes are becoming more severe as oil companies explore the region, which highlights again the eternal cause of so many wars—competition for resources.

Similarly, the dispute between Great Britain, which claims the Falkland Islands, and Argentina, which calls them the Islas Malvinas, has endured for almost 150 years. These barren rocks in the South Atlantic are home to about 2,000 people and 50,000 sheep, which are their main export. Subsequent international law has made such islands far more important economically due to exclusive economic zones defined by the "Law of the Sea" treaty. But the Falkland Islands War (which the British won) is more illustrative of "scapegoating," the so-called "Simmel effect," so named for an Austrian sociologist who first discussed this in print.

Simply put, foreign wars distract domestic discontent. Argentine President Leopoldo Galtieri was losing domestic support prior to an election, partly due to the fact that this general was blamed for bad economics and lots of dead Argentines after the dirty war from 1976 to 1979, when about 15,000 mostly young people died at the hands of secret police. Galtieri sought support in a time-honored way, by resurrecting an ancient land claim to the Malvinas and making it a cause of the people. The Argentine navy and army invaded the islands, whose virtually unarmed people and sheep promptly surrendered.

They did, however, call London and beg for help. The British prime minister, Margaret Thatcher, was not about to take the "Great" out of Great Britain and faced political opposition of her own. The "Iron Lady" of Britain had already prevailed over many pushy men and had a larger army with genuine global experience if declining reach, including nuclear submarines, which sank an Argentine troop ship, resulting in the largest casualties of the conflict. Britain won the war, and Thatcher was re-elected, while Galtieri was not. A little over 1,000 people died in this political exercise.

The invasion of Panama by U.S. forces in the early morning of December 20, 1989, was called Operation Just Cause, which merely shows the degree to which public relations has informed the art of naming battles in this world. No one will ever know the true number of casualties. The official U.S. count is 516 Panamanian deaths and 24 Americans, while local estimates run to at least 4,000. Almost a year after the event, American news organizations documented several mass graves, which the Pentagon had denied existed, leading to an estimate of 1,500 killed in this invasion. The nominal causes of this war were the need to remove dictator Manuel Noriega, to stop drug running through Panama, to safeguard American citizens there, and to "restore democracy." Other than disobedience by Noriega, none of these official "just causes" was likely a real cause for this war.

Far more important was the desire to reassert American control over Panamanian politics and to send an unambiguous message to Nicaragua, which was facing an election in two months that could end the long-running contra war, also backed by the United States. Noriega was later convicted in U.S. courts of drug trafficking (as many Latin American governments and military officers are suspected to be). Nevertheless, the CIA recruited Manuel Noriega from a military academy at the age of seventeen. The problem was that he was becoming uncontrollable, building an independent base of support among the poor and his Panamanian defense forces, and had refused to allow Panama to become a staging area for the U.S.-backed contras, unlike Nicaragua's more compliant neighbors, Honduras and Costa Rica. So he was removed, by force of arms. His Panamanian defense forces were decimated, and his base of support among the poor was served notice by the complete destruction of a neighborhood called Chorrillo. Casualty counts were manipulated by traditional means combined with the most extensive control of media in America's history to that time, guided by the able efforts of Fort Bragg's 4th Psychological Operations Group.

"Psychological operations" are propaganda elevated to a science, with subdisciplines ranging from how to hoodwink entire populations to how to drive a single man insane. It has been deeply informed by the advertising industry, which sells millions of products every day, and by decades of intense and often highly classified research during the cold war on every conceivable method of mind control.

We should not overdo discussion of the secret side of military operations in this world; they are not responsible for every conflict. But those who ignore the covert side of military affairs, or the darker side of real politics, do so at great risk. Why? Because propaganda is a pervasive feature of war, and because the nominal causes of wars are seldom the real causes of wars. The secret forces of the superpowers and various other powers in this world have become quite adept at their psychological operations. For example, some believe that Israel's Mossad (foreign intelligence) also had a hand in both the drug trade and the clandestine weapons trade in Central America at this time. It has been written about by former Mossad agent Ari Ben Menashi, and another former Mossad agent, Michael Harari, was security advisor to Manuel Noriega at the time. At times, Harari, Noriega, and sometimes CIA officers were allegedly present for the arrival of several aircraft that brought narcotics into Panama. After the invasion, Noriega was replaced by a former Panamanian banker, Guillermo Endara, who was flown from the United States to Albrook Air Force Base in Panama, the same base where Harari and the others had welcomed incoming drug traffic. Whatever the balance of power in Panama now, the drug trade certainly continues unabated and had nothing directly to do with Operation Just Cause.

All that said, Latin America has fewer wars than any other major region on earth. This is probably because it is so thoroughly dominated by the United States, which has no rival in "its neighborhood" for now. Balance-of-power theory suggests that this will change, but that is a concern for the future.

Colonial Maps and African Conflicts

In the twentieth century, Africa, by contrast, has had more wars than any other continent and more bloodshed by most counts. Most have not been invasions from without, or disputes over recognized borders, but civil wars among factions within the nation-states, the great majority of which resulted from the great decolonization of Africa following World War II. Many of those retreats by Western powers were preceded by wars of national liberation. As of 1998, the list of wars includes: Algeria (4 wars), Angola (2), Burundi (2), Cameroon, Chad (2), Congo (then Zaire, now the Democratic Republic of Congo, 3 wars), Ethiopia (2), Ghana (2), Guinea-Bissau, Kenya (2), Liberia (2), Libya, Madagascar, Morocco, Mozambique (2), Namibia, Nigeria (4), Rwanda (3), Sierra Leone (1), Somalia (1), South Africa (2), Sudan (2), Tunisia, Uganda (4), Western Sahara (1), Zambia (1), and Zimbabwe (formerly Rhodesia, 3). At least 9 million people have died in these wars or by related famine, as in Sudan, where denial of food is used as a weapon against the south, or Biafra in Nigeria before that, or in Angola or Somalia at various times.

The most obvious problem in Africa is the history of colonization and all that represented. But an equally important problem today is the tendency by some African leaders and people to blame all problems on the Europeans, which often becomes an excuse not to solve them. Not solving problems has led to many subsequent wars. Inexperience in large-scale government has played a role, though that is changing, and meddling by outsiders is easier when rulers are new. Poverty has obviously and gravely exacerbated many ethnic conflicts, and no one doubts that the correlation between political boundaries in Africa and distributions of ethnic groups is very poor. The OAU (Organization of African Unity), confronting this dilemma at its founding, determined that if border disputes were to be allowed as a legitimate cause of war, there would be endless wars in ethnically very diverse Africa. Nigeria alone has about 400 linguistic groups, with three very large tribes dominant in their respective areas and a dozen other major tribes, with very deep disputes among Muslims, Christians, and animist, or nature-based, religious groups.

So, colonial history and mixed ethnicity are pervasive in Africa, as well as poverty and meddling by the superpowers. What else applies to Africa? (1) A long history of armed nomadic groups, relatively indifferent to geopolitical boundaries. (2) A short history of governance by Western methods, which has led to hatred of elites but also to inflated expectations when elections finally come, soon to be dashed by corruption of governance that is inevitable even in allegedly advanced Western democracies. (3) Crushing debts to international institutions, many of which sincerely tried to help during the post-colonial period but did not really know how to do this effectively (grants, not loans), others of which just wanted to replace the old, military-based colonization with new, improved, banker-managed predatory capitalism via debt. (4) Very high birth rates, which, aside from the obvious contribution to competition for resources, also result in skewed age distributions where half the population is under the age of twenty, sometimes under fifteen years old.

Very large numbers of teenage males in conditions of desperate poverty with low confidence in existing governments and even lower prospects for long-term jobs, watching the minority of very wealthy elites connected to foreign financial powers maneuver to include their clans while excluding others, is an explosive mix. Add plenty of arms left over from the cold war, and you have a very explosive mix. Add an AIDS epidemic that has infected 10 percent to as high as 20 percent of the young adults of far too many African nations, and you have the kind of despair that leads to all sorts of conflict including invasions and border disputes.

A single case will exemplify this: Rwanda had the bloodiest war on earth in 1994, when something like 500,000 to 1,000,000 mostly ethnic Tutsi were slaughtered with small arms and machetes by the majority Hutu in that country. The most commonly cited estimate is 800,000 killed, in a period of just about three months. Rwanda also had a long colonial history where the Belgians manipulated these ethnic differences, the French manipulated economic and military interests, and complex internal politics made moderate Hutus in the political elite the primary target for the Hutu special forces when the killing began. Ironically, a Tutsi-led army based in Uganda (the Rwandan Patriotic Front) ultimately won this war, and drove the hardline Hutu out. Rwanda also had the highest birth rate in Africa when the killing began, yielding a growth rate of 3.8 percent per year. At that rate, the population would double in just over eighteen years, with half the population under the age of fifteen. This means that even an extremely fertile country like Rwanda will become deforested, and crowded, and that any ethnic conflicts that existed before will be further enflamed as places to hide, or even places to make a living, become scarce.

Do not forget that every single conflict listed in Africa has its own history, distinct people and political personalities, and different economies and prospects for the future.

To remember a much more hopeful example, in 1980 very few observers would have predicted that South Africans would successfully end their brutal civil war among nine distinct tribal and linguistic groups (two white, seven black), to forge a multi-ethnic nation with a relatively wealthy and stable economy. Also, Tanzania has avoided most of these problems and certainly war, due largely to enlightened leadership and industrious peoples. For many centuries, Europe was the center of conflict, but not since World War II. Nevertheless, all is not dismal in Africa.

Asian Agonies

Any discussion of Asia and war properly begins with China, the imperial power of its region. Since World War II, when it was occupied by Japan, and then overrun by the Communist movement led by Chairman Mao Zedong, China has been involved in invasions or border disputes with at least five countries: Tibet (1950–1951); Korea (1950–1953); India (1962); the Soviet Union (1969); and Vietnam (1979 and 1987).

The vast second Indochina war between Vietnam and America also involved invasions of Cambodia and Laos by both North Vietnamese regular forces and by special forces from America along with more bombs than were used during World War II. The aggregate death toll was estimated to be at least 2 million Vietnamese, 58,000 to 60,000 Americans depending on the status of 2,000 still missing from that war, and uncounted numbers of Cambodians and Laotians caught in the crossfire. It is likely that at least 3 million died directly from this war. This was part of the epic struggle of the cold war, which echoed for twenty-three more years as a civil war in Cambodia (1975–1998). Pol Pot,

supported by the Chinese, took power in 1975 as leader of the Khmer Rouge, then killed or "caused to die" roughly a million of his fellow Cambodians, forcing radical social change. Vietnam invaded Cambodia in 1978, allegedly to stop the slaughter and at least to stop the waves of refugees into destitute Vietnam, and installed a client of their own named Hun Sen. Civil war of various degrees was the norm for many years, between these two groups and one other "royal" faction aligned with the Sihanouk family (supported by China as well sometimes). That civil conflict probably ended with the death of Pol Pot in 1998, and the virtual elimination of the Khmer Rouge.

Back to China. There is no doubt that the invasion of Tibet was a disaster for that thinly populated country with a long history of prior wars with (e.g., in 1912 and 1918) and domination by China. Today, the land of Buddhist temples and its people are being slowly digested. Tibet's remoteness from Western capitals made it something of an internal affair, as the Chinese claimed. That political judgment makes all the difference in the legalities of war.

If you kill people of another country, this is murder, or war. There must be an "invasion." If you kill people in a "province" that you "own," then it is just police action. Brutal, perhaps, but nothing unusual in the affairs of many nation-states. The forces of Saddam Hussein, for example, killed about 100,000 Kurds in Iraq during a 1988 operation called the "anfal." World response was muted even when the use of chemical weapons against 4,000 to 5,000 civilians in a single village became known. Halabja's Kurds had helped the Iranians, it was said, and their deaths were generally considered an "internal affair."

Korea, unlike Tibet, was much closer to

Western interests such as Japan and had already been partitioned after World War II, the north dominated by Soviets entering late in the war as Japan declined, and the south dominated by Americans. Just who crossed the border first in 1950 is now in some dispute, but there is no doubt that once it started the north invaded the south massively, and it became a contest between communism and capitalism in Asia. The Chinese got involved when American victories were pushing close to their border. Massive attacks by China almost pushed the Americans into the sea, but increased Western support allowed them to gain the upper hand. The final division was determined by armistice, very close to the original starting lines. Another 3 million people died in that conflict.

In 1975, Indonesia was consolidating power under Suharto, who had deposed his predecessor (Sukarno) ten years earlier at a cost of about 650,000 lives. Indonesia is a vast nation encompassing hundreds of islands. While the world's attention in Southeast Asia was on ending the Vietnam War, Suharto decided to remove a minor irritant by invading and annexing the free half of one island called Timor. Unknown to most of the world, the island had been divided for almost 500 years between Dutch and Portuguese colonists. But the age of colonies was over. Indonesia already controlled the western half. Suharto thought the East Timorese would surrender quickly, and that no one would care about the new ruler due to larger issues in the region. Suharto was right that few cared, and he got permission from U.S. President Gerald Ford and Secretary of State Henry Kissinger just days before the invasion. He was wrong about resistance. By the time the Indonesian army was done, about one-third of the population of 600,000 was dead. A massacre of about 250 demonstra-

tors in the capital Dili occurred as recently as 1991. The fighting has continued sporadically since.

Many smaller ethnic groups on smaller islands in Indonesia, the Philippines, Malaysia, and elsewhere in the world have been overwhelmed by others who did not consider themselves invaders; they were merely extending the central government's rule to "rural areas." Such is the fate of many minority populations in this world. Either they accept the terms and definitions of the central government with the bigger guns, or they pass the way of indigenous peoples of many places and times, like the Iroquois long gone from North America, or the Yanomami of Brazil today, who are disappearing fast.

A minority in Sri Lanka has been getting squeezed by similar forces for some time. Whether you call this an invasion of "Tamil Elam," as the Hindu Tamil Tigers like to call it, or recovery of control over rural areas by the majority Buddhist Sinhalese, depends upon your loyalties. Most of the world calls Sri Lanka one country and recognizes only one government. In cases like this, diplomatic support can be extremely important.

India and Pakistan are much larger countries in the area and have fought three wars since they were born by partition in 1947. Most of the bloodshed has been over a bit of that territory, which began as a "princely state" called Kashmir. The original partition was determined mainly by whether majority populations were Muslim or Hindu, the former joining together as Pakistan, the latter comprising India. However, as inevitably occurs with partitions, there were some places where both mixed quite thoroughly and where political loyalty was stronger to local rulers, in this case the prince, than to either emerging nation. The difficulty is compounded when, in lands of poverty, the state in question is among the most beautiful and fertile, as is Kashmir.

In Pakistan and India, two populations differ, ethnically, religiously, and culturally. They grow on a finite resource base, so competition for resources is not about mere luxury. Who controls fertile ground can be the difference between life and death when harvests are slim. They have historical frictions, some quite recent, some extending back centuries or millennia (in this case, to the Aryan invasions of West India in ca. 1500 B.C.E.). In 1997, over 3,000 people died from political violence in Kashmir, as has occurred almost every recent year, as insurrection, Indian police action, and covert flows of aid from Pakistan continue. It is an endless border dispute. As of May 1998, India had tested five nuclear weapons to great dismay among other (often nuclear) powers. So pressure on Pakistan to demonstrate their clandestine nuclear weapons was intense. In 1998, following renewed testing in India, Pakistan exploded five nuclear devices. China has had nuclear weapons for years and border disputes of its own, including the seizure of some Himalayan territory from India in 1962, and the lesson of Tibet lies right on India's border.

The Balkans: Another Ancient Battleground with Great Potential for World Wars

World War I nominally began when a militant Serb in Sarajevo named Gavrilo Princip murdered an obscure Austrian archduke, Franz Ferdinand, on June 28, 1914. Within a few weeks, all of Europe was at war. Within years the United States and others would join in, and before it was done, one-tenth of all young European men were dead.

During World War II, the Nazis never really conquered the Balkans, although they surely tried to. They supported the Croatian faction there, whose Ustashe security force helped kill Chetnik Serbs, Bosnian Muslims, and pesky communist partisans of many ethnicities, led by a man named Josip Broz Tito. About a million died in these partly internecine conflicts, which set the stage for the largest war in Europe during the post–World War II period, as Yugoslavia disintegrated into at least seven provinces during three wars.

There were other invasions in Eastern Europe during this period also. Soviet soldiers invaded Hungary in 1956 and Czechoslovakia in 1968. But since Soviet soldiers already occupied these nominally independent nations, these actions were not generally called wars even when large numbers of civilians died.

Which brings us to post-Tito Yugoslavia. Field Marshal Josip Broz Tito ruled a communist, but genuinely independent, Yugoslavia created out of the ruins of World War II. A Croatian Catholic by birth, he married a Serbian woman, and having led the dominant partisans during the downfall of Nazi Germany, he was in a position to establish the Yugoslav Republic and to stifle ethnic dissent during his time. He was ruthless in the beginning, more benign near his end. Unfortunately, the ethnic peace he had imposed began to unravel shortly after his death, with mysterious, but calculated, hate campaigns dominated by the Serbs and a former Communist official named Slobodan Milosevic who still rules what is left of Serbia in 1998. For ten years, the center held in Yugoslavia, with a rotating presidency designed to keep the republics working together. But tensions grew, especially between the prosperous north (e.g., Slovenia and Croatia) and the poorer, but militarily stronger, south. Most of former Yugoslavia has seceded from Serbia, or would prefer to, due to the highly visible consequences of Serbian nationalism.

Slovenia declared independence on June 25, 1991, along with Croatia. On June 27, Yugoslav army units dominated by Serbs briefly invaded the richest province of the former Yugoslav Republic. This invasion was a tentative effort, however, and was quickly repulsed, since the Yugoslav army still had reservations about killing civilians, met determined resistance, and was far from its central supplies. Another province, Macedonia, declared independence in September 1991, but invasion never occurred there partly because the West—fearing that war in Macedonia would inevitably involve Greece, and then Turkey, which NATO would not allow—was much quicker to respond with on-the-ground, dedicated peacekeeping troops. War with Croatia began in the fall of 1991 with a full-scale invasion by Serb troops. Bosnia-Herzegovina declared independence on October 15, 1991. By April 1992, when Serb snipers opened fire on a large peace demonstration in the Bosnian capital, Sarajevo, tens of thousands had died in Croatia from the destruction of Vukovar and Dubrovnik in the far northeast and southwest. Hundreds of thousands would die in Bosnia before the "ethnic cleansing" in the region was over.

One can tease out historic roots of this conflict forever. Devotion to historic grievances and excessive nationalism are the main causes, but opinions on details will always differ. In early 1998, another province called Kosovo began to heat up, with 150 dead due to Serbian police actions in a province that is 90 percent Albanian and holds religious significance for the Serbs, who lost a major battle with the Ottoman Empire there in 1389.

But it is true for people everywhere that, if they search out every detail of their past, they can find ancestors who were killed by someone else's ancestors long ago. If everyone used this as an excuse for fighting today, it is said, no one would be safe.

One can speculate about the insanity of leaders, for which there is much evidence on many sides of the complex Yugoslav conflict. One of the craziest Serbs was a psychiatrist who ordered people in his own mental institution killed (Radovan Karadzik) along with thousands of his neighbors, while the leader of the Croats (Franjo Tudjman) was an officer in the pro-Nazi Ustashe regime during World War II. Milosevic himself was a demagogic politician, who built his fortune on promoting hatred of others, even as his country fell to ruin.

One can speculate about religion, since the three main factions in this region represent Eastern Orthodox Christianity (Serbs), Roman Catholic Christianity (Croats), and Islam (most Bosnians). But most observers doubt that religion plays any role larger than moral cloth over butchery. Who can say it is holy to slaughter your neighbors?

All these factors play some role, and probably the fall of the Soviet Union played some role as well, since it nearly coincided with the disintegration of the Yugoslav Republic. At the very least, the idea of national or ethnic independence from formerly dominant Slavs was in the air in Eastern Europe during the critical year of 1991.

The combination of all these factors, especially history and religion, make the Balkans a rare triple point where civilizations collide. The importance of triple points where civilizations mix is that they make the possible permutations of ethnic conflict more complex, and they generally occur in areas where trade converges over centuries. That, in turn, provides many opportunities for historic insult, and many connections to other powers, thereby increasing the risks that small conflicts may escalate into large ones, as did World War I. The other dramatic triple point on our globe, with an unparalleled history of armed conflict, is the Middle East.

The Middle East: One Big Border Dispute with Ultra-Ancient Roots

First Judaism, then Christianity, then Islam, and finally a resurgent Judaism gathered from physical diaspora and the psychic ashes of the Holocaust—these are the civilizations that converged in the tiny land called Israel today, and which mingle there now in various levels of physical tension and spiritual disharmony. Paradoxically, there are faithful of all these religions working hard for peace in the midst of bitter conflict. The entire area remains one big dispute over borders. Every square centimeter is claimed by at least two parties, and there have been many invasions there since World War II.

It is important to emphasize at the onset, that views about responsibility for these invasions are highly polarized. Of the five wars involving Israel, hard-liners among both Arab and Jewish populations blame every one on the other. Moderate Jews may allow Israeli responsibility for attacking in 1956, and moderate Arabs may accept blame for attacking Israel in the 1973 Yom Kippur War. But many blame each other for everything, citing atrocity by the other side as the beginning of the current conflict. Parallel realities among polarized enemies like this can result in cycles of war without apparent end. And cycles of revenge provide many opportunities for each side to set starting points that blame the "other."

In 1948, the first invasion by the Arab League occurred on the day the British left the newly created state of Israel. There had been much fighting before, including Jewish terrorism and Arab (and British) reprisals. When the Israeli Jews won the first rounds of the 1948–1949 war, they in turn killed some and expelled very large numbers of Palestinians (about 700,000) who became a refugee population with their own diaspora. But many Palestinians also stayed, reducing their ranks to about 20 percent of the remaining population instead of 45 percent. The United Nations intervened, and things stabilized for a while in 1949. In 1956, the Suez crisis erupted as Egypt attempted to nationalize its biggest resource, the Suez Canal, in order to fund the Aswan Dam project. One result was further war between Egypt and Israel, which coordinated an attack on Egypt by the British and the French. In 1967, the Israelis started what came to be known as the Six-Day War, by bombing Egyptian air bases at dawn (they felt the war was inevitable, calling this a "pre-emptive strike"). Although pre-emptive strikes often start wars, they did have reasons for concern, and who is to say for sure which side actually precipitated the crisis? Crises are usually preceded by long periods of mutual animosity where both sides provoke. In any event, the 1967 war resulted in substantial territorial losses to all Arab states involved: The Sinai Peninsula was lost by Egypt; the West Bank and East Jerusalem were lost by Jordan; the Golan Heights were lost by Syria; and, later, a ten-mile security strip was installed across the Lebanon-Israel border, patrolled by friendly militias.

This was so unpalatable to the Arabs that President Gamal Abdel Nasser of Egypt almost immediately began a smaller but longer series of border skirmishes along the Suez Canal, which came to be known as the War of Attrition and lasted until 1970. In 1973, the Yom Kippur War began, but this time the United Nations reported that Egypt and Syria began hostilities. Fighting was intense for several weeks, until the threatened use of "clandestine" nuclear weapons helped American and Soviet Union diplomatic efforts to broker another U.N. cease-fire. Nevertheless, the near defeat was very sobering to the Israeli side (6,000 dead and economic costs of nearly $7 billion, equal to a year of Israel's GNP) and eventually led to the Camp David Accords involving U.S. President Jimmy Carter, Egypt's Anwar Sadat, and Israel's Menachem Begin.

In 1974, there was a much smaller invasion of the island of Cyprus, not far off the Israeli and Syrian coasts, by Turkey's army in a dispute between Turkish and Greek Cypriotes. The invasion divided the island into separate ethnic enclaves, which remain to this day. To the world, it was not very important (and nuclear weapons were not threatened). But to the Cypriotes, it divided a beautiful and prosperous island into two bitter enclaves, each much poorer by far.

During this time, and continuing to this day, there were also large numbers of armed actions involving ethnic Kurds seeking independence from the four countries they straddle: Turkey, Iran, Iraq, and Syria. No other nation recognizes "Kurdistan," so these many operations do not count as border wars, even though each of the four named countries has sent troops past national boundaries in pursuit of Kurdish rebels. Turkey, in particular, has killed thousands of Kurds across their border with Iraq, and Iraq has killed far more.

In 1982, Israel invaded Lebanon again, this time in a bid to rid themselves of Palestinian terrorists forever, or at least those who had taken root in Lebanon to organize their ef-

forts. The Israelis were undoubtedly provoked by many rocket attacks from Lebanese positions and commando raids across their border—hundreds of episodes overall, in thirty-six years. So in 1982, Israeli armored divisions drove all the way to Beirut, occupied a third of Lebanon along the way, and did indeed destroy the Palestinian governmental structures there. Of course, the Palestinian people still had no permanent land and harbored even more bitter grudges. So despite the ten-mile buffer strip in southern Lebanon, and despite a virtually permanent United Nations presence feeding Palestinian refugees there, commando raids across the Israeli border or terrorist bombings continue from time to time, and bombing raids or artillery attacks from Israel enter Lebanon to strike at Palestinian targets. Syria also occupied the Lebanese Bekaa Valley in 1982, with a mandate from the Arab League to restore order and protect what was left from the Israelis. Syria remains to this day, protecting the Bekaa Valley and its lucrative marijuana and opium crops, because there is no central government in Lebanon strong enough to repel them.

In 1998, peace talks were ongoing but had been stalled for two years, since Prime Minister Yitzhak Rabin was assassinated by an ultra-conservative Israeli Jew named Yigal Amir, explicitly to derail the peace process. A map of the disputed West Bank of the Jordan River looks like a patient with measles or chicken pox, because there are so many administrative districts. Israeli Jews and Palestinian Arabs continue to argue bitterly over how to share power in a tiny area, which both would like to own outright. The boundaries are Byzantine. If border disputes are a cause of war, there will be plenty of angles to argue here. The situation is similar to the Balkans, where once benign pluralism has degenerated into fiercely ethnic nationalism mixed with militant religion.

Recall the eternal causes of wars: competition for resources and power, population pressure, authoritarian political systems and militant religions, corruption of governance, inequalities of wealth within and between nations, the lack of effective international conflict resolution systems, the hubris of political leaders and especially demagogic leaders who thrive on the hatred of some other, and the folly of the people who follow them. One can find all these things in both the Balkans and the Middle East. Of these causes, only corruption of governance does not apply often to invasions and border disputes, because this cause is most common to civil wars while invasions and border disputes are usually matters between sovereign states.

Michael Andregg

Bibliography

Anderson, Malcolm. *Frontiers: Territory and State Formation in the Modern World.* New York: Blackwell, 1996.

Boggs, Samuel Whittemore. *International Boundaries: A Study of Boundary Functions and Problems.* New York: AMS Press, 1966.

Prescott, J.R.V. *The Geography of Frontiers and Boundaries.* Chicago: Aldine, 1965.

Schofield, Clive H., ed. *Global Boundaries.* New York: Routledge, 1994.

Wilson, Thomas, and Hastings Donnan, eds. *Border Identities: Nation and State at International Frontiers.* New York: Cambridge University Press, 1998.

Ethnic and Religious Conflicts

Introduction

While inter-ethnic competition, some with religious overtones, can be traced to biblical times, it has been a noted characteristic of the post–World War II era. More than 300 of these struggles have occurred in the past half-century, and though the trend has accelerated since the 1960s, it was the demise of the cold war that brought international recognition to the phenomenon. Communal conflicts have devastated the former Yugoslavia, threatened, even overwhelmed, the stability of most of the former republics of the Soviet Union, brought about state collapse in a variety of African countries, exacerbated prolonged disputes in the Middle East and Southeast Asia, and are in the ascendant even in a number of Western industrialized countries. Together, such conflicts bear serious implications for international peace and security.

The domestic instabilities and collapses, and their consequent impact on global security, have spawned a sharp rise in refugees and the internally displaced, and triggered some fifty episodes of genocide and mass murder directed at more than seventy ethnic and religious minorities, and resulting in between 9 million and 20 million civilian fatalities. Such developments, troubling as they are, are accompanied by a proliferation of both conventional and nuclear arms, the latter dramatically underscored in May 1998 by the competitive explosions of nuclear devices by the governments of India and Pakistan, events with implications far beyond the Indian subcontinent.

Perhaps a natural consequence of these unsettling facts is an alarmist interpretation that some analysts have advanced about post–cold war "global chaos," unrestrained "international disorder," or global "pandemonium," as suggested by the title of U.S. Senator Daniel Patrick Moynihan's 1995 book. Professor Samuel Huntington has even elaborated a thesis about "cleavage among civilizations," positing that a "cultural" curtain has replaced the "iron" curtain that ideologically divided the world, and that religion (a crucial component of culture) provides the fuel for conflict as it inspires intolerance and irreconcilable images of "identity" and loyalty among civilizations in competition.

Yet ethnoreligious conflicts are not necessarily the harbingers of global chaos, for most seem amenable to some form of management or resolution. Most minorities, often the subject of ethnopolitical conflicts, sought "voice" or "access" within existing societies, not "exit" or adjustment of international borders. Thus, in the midst of the troubling realities of an alarming number of ethnic and religious conflicts devastating peoples and threatening global peace stands a mitigating reality that all types and locales of communal conflicts have in fact been limited by some form of political settlement.

Defining the Problem

What is an ethnic group? What is a religious group? How do they become politically salient within or beyond the nation-state? What is it that gives rise to groups' protests and rebellions or their demands for voice, access within, or exit from the societies of which they are a part? These are some of the pertinent questions that might provide insight into the phenomenon of ethnoreligious conflicts as they have manifested themselves since the end of World War II, but particularly since the end of the cold war.

Max Weber, the great German sociologist, defines an ethnic group as a people holding "a subjective belief in their common descent." There is a "presumed," "artificial," "accidental" identity that may be associated with such characteristics as physical appearance, customs, common memories, language, religion, and so on. Many scholars are in agreement about these "ethnic criteria," loose as they are, and point out that the strength of ethnic groups lies in the bonds of culture and not in those of association.

Questions remain regarding the context of those "bonds of culture" and how might one explain the religious component? Usually, conflict is occasioned by the recognition of discrimination and politically channeled collective grievance within a society, as well as the authorities' resistance to such demands. Ethnic conflicts are thus "conflicts in groups that define themselves using ethnic or national criteria," and on this basis claims are made on behalf of collective group interests against political actors, including the state.

Ethnic conflicts also bear a correlation with religious belief in that ethnicity's subjective belief in a common descent carries with it a "sacred" focus of group attention, the idea of a "chosen people," a "providential mission." Though normally a force for peace and harmony espousing universalistic ideals that accept all people's rights, religion is also a catalyst for "holy wars." And it is in this latter vein that, according to sociologists of religion, it becomes a source of conflict and war once particularistic and intolerant outlooks are adopted. What is crucial here is the joining of the religious and the ethnic. Muslims in the Middle East or Protestants and Catholic Christians in Northern Ireland represent communal groups who define themselves in terms of religious beliefs. Hence, religious differences add a special intensity to, or reinforce, ethnic conflicts that are themselves rooted in nationality and class differences.

The fact that religious cleavages are contributing factors to communal conflicts, but seldom the root cause, is borne out by a study by Ted Robert Gurr in which only 8 of 49 militant minority sects were defined solely or mainly by religious beliefs. The Shiites of Lebanon and Iraq have goals of political recognition, not faith propagation, and the sectarian minorities represented by Catholics in Northern Ireland and Turks in Germany have clear political (not religious) agendas, as do the Kurds and Palestinians of the Middle East.

It has been suggested that co-existing with (or existing within) most or all modern states are five important politically active ethnic groups: ethnonationalists (independent identities seeking to re-establish their own state); indigenous peoples (primarily concerned with protecting their traditional lands, resources, and culture); communal contenders (one among a number of culturally distinct groups in plural societies that compete for a share of political power); ethnoclasses (desirous of equal rights and opportunities to overcome effects of discrimination resulting from their immigration and minority status); and militant sects (politicized minority peoples defined wholly or substantially by religious beliefs).

Ethnonationalists include Corsicans and Bretons in France, Basques in Spain, French Canadians, Palestinians and Kurds in the Middle East, Slovenes, Latvians, and Armenians. Since 1991, in excess of a dozen new ones have emerged from the boundaries of the Soviet and Yugoslavia successor states. Usually equipped with an organized leadership and occupying substantial territory, these groups or movements may straddle internationally recognized borders and thus their activities spill over such borders with consequences for international peace and security.

Indigenous peoples are descendants of the original inhabitants of conquered or colonialized regions. A major impetus for their development of a common identity of purpose is their discrimination and exploitation by peoples with advanced technology. Examples of indigenous peoples include the natives of the Americas (36 million or 5 percent of the population of the Western Hemisphere, though in Bolivia, Guatemala, and Peru they constitute one-half of the populations), the Aborigines of Australia, the Maori of New Zealand, and the Masai of East Africa. For a long time, these groups have resisted discrimination in uncoordinated uprisings. The League of Nations was petitioned, with little effect, by a number of North American indigenes and the Maori of New Zealand. Since the creation of the United Nations, however, a number of measures have been taken to address the problems of indigenous peoples. They include the creation in 1975 of a World Council of Indig-

enous Peoples, a non-governmental organization that provides a forum for discussion, publicity, and concerted planning; the 1992 U.N.-sponsored conference in Brazil, which issued an Indigenous Peoples Earth Charter, a document that outlines a comprehensive set of cultural and environmental demands; and the U.N. Working Group on Indigenous Populations, which assembles 200 groups at annual meetings in Geneva, Switzerland. The latter has prepared a draft Universal Declaration of Indigenous Rights, which many hope will become a part of the corpus of international law.

The third category of ethnic groups coexisting with the state is the communal contender. Communal contenders are ethnic groups within national societies more interested in acquiring access to power than in instigating exit from the state. Such contenders include the Maronite Christians, and the Druze, Sunni, and Shiite Muslims of Lebanon; the South Sudanese; and the Igbos of Nigeria. The context for struggle involving this group is usually an arrangement where government political power is based on coalition among traditional or modern leaders of ethnic groups. Failure to establish or maintain multiethnic coalitions or otherwise manage cleavage conflicts may lead to wars of secession such as the Biafran attempt to secede from Nigeria in the late 1960s and the current conflict in the Sudan, which essentially pits two culturally and religiously dissimilar groups, one having the advantage of control of the government. The distinction between communal contenders and ethnonationalists is not a rigid one, for a communal group, once interested in secession, may be persuaded to enter a power-sharing arrangement at the political center. Settlement efforts in the Sudan have this in view, as was the restoration in the 1960s of the breakaway province of Katanga to the central government of the Democratic Republic of Congo, when Moise Tshombe, the secessionist leader, assumed the premiership of the Congo republic.

Ethnoclasses are ethnic groups that resemble classes. They are ethnically and culturally distinct minorities, often descendants of slaves and immigrants whose circumstances led them to specialize in distinctive economic activities, usually of low status. Ethnoclasses in advanced industrial societies, and often disadvantaged, include the Muslim minority in France, people of color in Britain and the United States, and Koreans in Japan. This is also the case of blacks in some nine countries of Latin America.

In developing countries, ethnoclasses at times are economically advantaged, but politically restricted, merchants and professionals, such as the Chinese minorities in much of Southeast Asia, Indians in East Africa, and Lebanese in much of West Africa.

Militant sects are religiously defined politicized minority peoples, and include Islamic minorities in societies dominated by other religious traditions, such as Turks in Germany, Muslim Albanians in the former Yugoslavia, Arabs in Israel, and Malay Muslims in Thailand. They also include the warring Sunni, Shiite, and Druze in Lebanon; the Shiite in Sunni-dominated Iraq and Saudi Arabia; and the Kashmiris and Sikhs in India. Some non-Muslim groups include the Jews of Argentina, the Copts of Egypt, and the Baha'is of Iran.

Whether categorized or characterized as national peoples (ethnonationalists or indigenous peoples), or minority peoples (ethnoclasses, communal contenders, or militant sects), the essence of the phenomenon remains a group's shared perception about something that sets it apart from other groups. The saliency of identification varies over time given the situational and circumstantial nature of ethnicity. Cultural, economic, and political differentials between a group and others tend to reinforce identification.

Historical Context of Conflicts

The identity of citizenship competes with such other identities described above. They involve race, ethnicity, religion, region, class, and so forth, and they pose enduring challenges for the domestic political order. The period since 1945 has seen a weakening of such norms and a growing intolerance of diversity within states. Some scholars have located the answer to this trend in the global process of modernization, characterized by growth of the modern state and the state system, development of the market economy, and the communications revolution.

Historically, ethnic groups, nations, empires, and other forms of large-scale social organizations (Islam, Christendom) have coexisted, but since the seventeenth century, the state has been the dominant form of social organization. This state has been a territorially defined entity (some with colonies beyond their borders) imbued with sovereignty and claiming the full allegiance of all its subjects/citizens.

Prevailing ideologies and political movements within state systems dramatically influenced ethnic conflict. In the 1920s and 1930s, anti-Semitic doctrines in Germany and other European countries promoted ethnic polarization. They competed with communist doctrines in the Soviet Union and elsewhere, which emphasized a common interest of all national (even international) communist peoples and minimized the significance of ethnic and other particularistic identities.

In the 1940s and 1950s, anti-colonial sentiments found expression in nationalist movements in Asia, Africa, and the Caribbean to challenge European colonial domination. Such sentiments, in time, resulted in a marked increase in the number of states claiming exclusive loyalties of diverse peoples. For a while, then, nationalists succeeded in uniting ethnic groups not only to end colonial rule, but to consolidate their newly won independence. The emergence of the cold war in the late 1940s contributed to the consolidation process as the new states sought support from the cold war competitors in their quest at reining in would-be recalcitrant groups for the preservation of "national unity" and in the interest of "economic development."

By the late 1960s and early 1970s, the process of decolonization was all but completed, though politicized ethnic consciousness soon re-emerged in a number of states such as the Democratic Republic of Congo, Nigeria, and Sudan. More recently, a new kind of resistance to the monopolistic state system has left unaffected few world regions and has led to an accelerating wave of autonomy movements.

In emulating the historic states of the industrialized North, new states developed interests in political consolidation and expansion. This implied the subordination of the interests and relative autonomy of large numbers of ethnic groups to state elites' conceptions of the requirements for the pursuit of national interests. State-building came to mean policies of assimilating national and minority peoples, curbing their historical autonomy and extracting their material and human resources for the state. The building of communist states in Eastern Europe after 1945 followed a similar pattern. There were

exceptions as with overseas Chinese in Southeast Asia who were able to share power and prosperity at the center of the new state. Elsewhere, as in Africa, the reach of state power was limited in some areas, and this enabled some groups to retain de facto local autonomy.

The state-building process has been accompanied by development of the market economy and a revolution in communications technology. In the former case, colonial imperialism, itself a by-product of the industrial revolution, grafted large populations of colonized peoples onto the global capitalist economic system primarily assigning to them the role of providing raw material and being absorbers of finished products. In the latter case, the communications revolution reduced distance, removed isolation, and disseminated information on such a scale that human relations were irrevocably changed. These developments could not leave unaffected the old-fashioned state system premised on the narrow notions of state sovereignty and the subordination of national and minority peoples.

Two competing trends presently discernible in the treatment of national and minority peoples include the re-emergence of xenophobia in Germany, France, and Britain (as well as movements that demand ethnic purity in formerly heterogeneous federations, such as Serbian nationalism in the former Yugoslavia), and the fact that there are oppressive leaders who defend existing borders at all costs, despite historically justified claims for internal autonomy or independence by national peoples, such as Kurds and Southern Sudanese. Until recently, it was ironic that the new elites of former Asian and African colonies were willing to fight to maintain existing boundaries of states despite arbitrarily drawn borders that accommodated European interests but ignored demographic and cultural realities.

Post–cold war developments now suggest a new global propensity to revisit the old norms of sovereignty and territorial integrity, norms that have been the bases of national claims over groups' rights. Now there seems to be developing a greater disposition to seek to balance national rights with peoples' or human rights. Support for this can be seen in such regional arrangements as the Conference on Security and Cooperation in Europe, and the 1995-enacted Mechanism for Conflict Resolution and Management of the Organization of African Unity.

Regional Manifestations of Conflicts

Employing the term "ethnoreligious" to encompass all categories of conflicts of national and minority peoples, how have the various regional manifestations informed our understanding of the phenomenon? It is here necessary to bear in mind the fact that the modernization process, inclusive of economic development and the communications revolution, provided the broader context for these conflicts since 1945.

Sub-Saharan Africa is the region most associated in the media with the phenomenon of ethnoreligious conflict, especially its negative and intractable features. Often used in the primodialist sense in which it is equated with race, ethnicity as an essentialist and apolitical concept has been challenged by anthropologists who have argued that the concept is relative, its meaning linked to socially defined and publicly expressed ideas about culture and political identities that are flexible and, in contemporary terms, conditioned by the modernization process.

As to the question about whether there is a distinctive nature to ethnicity in Africa, the debate has often been between the primordialists (ethnicity as an immutable set of emotionally charged biological, cultural, linguistic, and religious givens that are the primary source of identity) and the situationalists (ethnicity as an almost totally flexible set of identities, which vary depending on rational calculation of material, political, and other types of advantages, and which are often stimulated by political mobilization led by actors whose primary identities and motives are non-ethnic). There is a middle interpretation that maintains that ethnicity is a shared cultural identity that may be energized in response to political, class, and economic interests or circumstances, or alternatively weakened depending on the same set of circumstances.

Since 1945, all types of ethnoreligious conflicts have occurred in Africa, but communal contenders have been the most common instigators. This prevailing form of conflict stems from competition over political and economic power in the context of unstable, multi-ethnic coalitions, either to be found within single governing parties or among officers in a military regime.

All types of politicized communal groups exist in Africa. Examples of the more intense and violent ethnoreligious conflicts involve ethnonationalist groups, ethnoclasses, and militant sects. Some have been long term (in Burundi, Rwanda, Chad, Ethiopia, Sudan, apartheid South Africa), and others have been relatively short term (civil wars in Angola, Liberia, Nigeria, Uganda, Congo/ Zaire).

In terms of their impact on international relations, communal contentions in the following countries stand out in Africa: Sudan,

Ethiopia, Mozambique, Angola, Liberia, Somalia, Western Sahara, and the great Lakes region, among others. All tend to sustain the situationist position that politicized communal contention over political power-sharing and economic distribution issues is the prevalent form of politically relevant ethnicity in Africa, not the primordialist intractability of the Western media.

Eastern Europe and Russia constitute the third largest concentration of politicized communal groups after Africa and Asia. This region has perhaps received more world attention than others, a fact that once prompted former U.N. Secretary General Boutros Boutros Ghali to lament the "rich man's war" in Bosnia as opposed to the "poor man's war" in Somalia.

Where most countries of Western Europe are nearly culturally homogeneous, single nation-states, those in Eastern Europe and Russia are culturally and ethnically heterogeneous multinational states. Before the breakup of the Soviet Union and Yugoslavia, the two together accounted for thirty-two ethnic groups, or 35 percent of the region's population. The ideology of Marxist–Leninism managed to contain the cultural and ethnic tensions implicit in aggrieved situations of such diversity. With its demise or challenge, a dramatic change occurred in ethnic relations and the status of minorities in this region.

Three of the federated, multinational states of the region—the Soviet Union, Yugoslavia, and Czechoslovakia—have disintegrated because their constituent republics exercised their constitutional rights of secession from the political union. As if that was not enough, at least two of the successor sets of states—the Soviet Union and Yugoslavia—are now themselves at risk of massive disruption in social relations and have each in

fact experienced civil wars. Yugoslavia has been dismembered into five sovereign states—Croatia, Slovenia, Macedonia, Bosnia-Herzegovina, and Montenegro and Serbia (the last two making up the rump state of Yugoslavia today). But ethnopolitical cleavages within each of the new units, particularly Bosnia and Croatia, have occasioned wars accompanied by "ethnic cleansing," or genocide, on such a scale that the world community, though reluctantly and belatedly, was drawn into the conflicts if not to attempt resolution, at least to contain them. The efforts continue with new outbursts of violence, such as in the Serbian province of Kosovo where ethnic Albanians assert their identity in response to overbearing Serbian nationalism. Then, too, the Russian Federation has been challenged with rebellion in Chechnya, a rebellion apparently not-yet-fully contained. Resolution remains outstanding as well in the conflict between the two former Soviet republics of Azerbaijan and Armenia over the region of Nagorno-Karabakh.

In Eastern Europe and Russia, an elite-led social revolution has brought freedom to subject nations and national ethnic groups. This had provided an opportunity for the peoples concerned to redefine themselves and their relations with one another on an equal footing, hopefully in a peaceful setting. Thus, minorities that are disadvantaged and aggrieved have in less than a decade become governing majorities. Soon those new governing majorities began to face their own minorities, whose new-found assertiveness has put them at even greater risk of communal or inter-ethnic conflict.

North Africa and the Middle East together have thirty-one politicized minorities comprising 28.8 percent of the total population. Kurds and Palestinians are the most numerous among those who lost out in the twentieth-century process of modernization through state formation. There are also the Saharawis (who continue to resist incorporation by Morocco), the Berbers of North Africa, and the Azerbaijanis of Iran (who have recently been or are currently in conflict with their states).

Since World War II, North Africa and the Middle East have seen the greatest magnitude of communal protest and rebellion in comparison to groups in any other world region. While there is less inequality and greater accommodation in North Africa, the problem tends to be severe in the core of the Arab world with the denial of national aspirations of the Palestinians and the Kurds.

The Palestinians in Israeli-occupied territories represent a dispersed group seeking greater autonomy and independence. They are in fact a national people dispersed throughout the world, with politically active segments in Jordan, Israel, Lebanon, the West Bank and Gaza, and Jerusalem. The bilaterally negotiated Oslo Accords of September 1993 have led to the creation of a Palestinian Authority in the West Bank and Gaza, though a number of intractable issues remain outstanding between the Palestinians and the government of Israel.

The Kurds are also a dispersed national people, but their situation differs from the Palestinians in that they are a non-Arab, mostly Sunni Muslim people, 21 million in number, and living in Turkey, Iran, Iraq, and Syria. They number 10 million in Turkey alone where their existence has only recently been recognized by the authorities, and where a Kurdish Workers' Party has used guerrilla and terrorist tactics to pursue independence. This is the case both because of a lack of good faith in accommodating their grievances by the government of Turkey, but also because of fears of potential irredentist claims on Iraq, Iran, Syria, and Turkey, should an independent Kurdish state be established in the region.

Relations among communal groups in North Africa and the Middle East are shaped in a fundamental way by Islamic doctrine and practice. Where shari'ah, or Islamic law, reigns supreme, there is no separation of state and religion. The perennial tension between secular forces and pious Muslims is a result of the inability of modernizers to reduce a religious culture to a personalized path to salvation. With the democratic gains of the Islamic Salvation Front in Algeria, which began in 1992 and have yet to fade away in the midst of pervasive conflict in that country, Muslim modernizers face increasing challenges. On this account, the ethnoreligious conflicts in this region have no easy answers. If revivalists achieve electoral victories eventually in Algeria, Jordan, and Egypt, can they build modern states based on Islamic principles? Or is modernity incompatible with Islamic principles? How compatible is the ever-increasing separation among ethnic or national groups with the doctrinally prescribed unity of the religious community?

Minorities in Western democracies and Japan, from a global perspective, are distinct from those in other world regions because they usually express their grievances through protest as opposed to rebellion, and the responses of their governments tend generally to accommodate their interests, not to enforce their subordination or incorporation. But seemingly intractable problems remain in Northern Ireland and Canada's Quebec.

These regions have the smallest number of minority populations (twenty-four groups or 84 million people), including ethnoclasses of African, Islamic, and Asian origins in Western Europe and the United States. In these countries, one also finds the indigenous rights movements. In France, Spain, Italy, Britain, and Canada, ethnonational demands have generally been resolved or managed by resource and autonomy concessions.

Northern Ireland has not been amenable to this approach because the region is not homogeneous. Accommodation of Catholic interest antagonizes Protestants, and vice versa. Nevertheless, there seems to be a silver lining in the so-called Good Friday accords of 1998 and the endorsement of the agreement in Northern Ireland and the Irish Republic. A middle course for genuine power-sharing between the Catholic and Protestant contenders seems to have been worked out, though challenges remain.

Quebec nationalism within the Canadian federal system is another remaining challenge. A near vote in 1995 on secession seriously threatened national unity and has resulted in a political impasse. While there is little potential for violence here, unlike the situation in Northern Ireland, a resolution to the impasse could produce negotiated sovereignty for Quebec, and thus lend further credence to the principle of the rights of peoples to exit sovereign states.

In world regions as varied as Eastern Europe and Russia, sub-Saharan Africa, North Africa, the Middle East, and the Western democracies, ethnoreligious conflicts have played themselves out over the past half-century with devastating effects for an increasingly large number of national and minority peoples.

Though widely portrayed in the media as ethnic in the primordial sense, ethnoreligious conflicts in Africa have been predominantly situational and circumstantial with only a tinge of the primordial. This tinge derives from the fact that because ethnicity is shared

cultural identity, it may be accelerated or de-accelerated depending on the political, class, economic, and other interests at hand. Understanding these factors, analyses of causes and issues—not some pre-conceived or pre-ordained tribal Hobbesian chaos—remain the challenge to getting a handle on the disparate conflicts on the African continent.

Belatedly recognized because dormant in the womb of a Marxist social order, and effectively kept in check by the politics of the cold war, the cultural heterogeneity one finds in Eastern Europe and Russia is essentially little different from that found in Africa though forces acting upon them may differ. When ethnic Albanians rise in rebellion against their Serbian overlords the principles that animate their action and the identity that energizes them is little different from Eritreans confronting their Ethiopian overlords until the early 1990s. The configuration of regional forces may differ, as well as the available resources and the pace of change in response to demands, but challenges to the state system and to fundamental humanitarian principles show little difference.

In North Africa and the Middle East, the magnitude of ethnoreligious conflict has since 1945 been the greatest, especially in the core of the Arab world. Kurds and Palestinians have suffered disproportionately the effects of modernization through state-building. Thus, their ethnoreligious identity has been energized by the unwillingness of the authorities under which they are forced to live to genuinely recognize them and consider granting them access or negotiating exit.

Challenge of International Response

As indicated at the outset, a major characteristic of the past half-century has been a growing realization of the co-existence with the state of ethnoreligious and other groups. Where once states claimed exclusive rights over their citizens, increasingly competing identities challenge such rights. The nature of the challenge is itself a subject of controversy since the international order recognizes the sovereign state and its exclusive prerogatives. Challenge to the state is tantamount to challenge to the international order, and the ethnoreligious challengers are deemed to have no independent status in the international system.

Yet these culturally bounded groups are quite capable, given the often fierce loyalties of their members, of presenting the international community with major humanitarian disasters—including genocide, "ethnic cleansing," huge internal and external displacements of civilian populations, and deaths of millions of the most vulnerable in societies around the world.

Often intractable and enduring, there is no world region that has been free of such conflicts, and a new wave has been unleashed in the aftermath of the end of the cold war. Some of these conflicts have been joined with geopolitical rivalries and border disputes, further complicating their resolutions.

It bears repeating that a primary factor in the political saliency of ethnoreligious identity is unequal treatment by the larger society or national government. Nevertheless, such an ethnic grievance must be mobilized, and the mobilization process may involve movement from ethnic disadvantage to grievance, to protest, or to rebellion. There are often many factors involved, including the "demonstration effect," or groups emulating others; "cessation of suppression," or sudden liberation, as occurred in Eastern Europe and Russia; and the availability of "ethnic entrepreneurs" who provide leadership. But the most crucial of the factors is the response of the state to these manifestations of mobilization. Does it cultivate loyalty by granting access, does it coerce loyalty, or does it negotiate exit?

Once mobilized, ethnoreligious grievances raise a number of questions for the state and the international order, the principal one being how to address two contradictory principles that co-exist in international law—the principle of sovereignty, territorial integrity, and non-interference, and the right to intervene in domestic jurisdiction in cases of serious violations of human rights and humanitarian principles.

One strategy requires a difficult and delicate balancing that redirects conflict into established channels that preserve minority rights—and accommodate the basic interest of the state. The U.N. Agenda for Peace, formulated by Secretary General Boutros Boutros Ghali on June 17, 1992, outlines four types of responses to ethnoreligious conflicts: preventive diplomacy (creative measures to pre-empt conflict); peacemaking (international action for peaceful settlement); peacekeeping (use of military personnel in non-combatant roles, such as monitoring cease-fires); and post-conflict peacebuilding (international action to address root causes of conflict such as economic despair, social injustice, and political oppression).

Another strategy for conflict resolution involves the special case of secession as a solution. Traditionalists seem to be concerned about the impact on the international system of largely heterogeneous states should ethnoreligious groups be given legal status and corresponding rights. Put simply, the question is how to balance the rights of states, already established, with the rights of groups, currently in contention. Though simple, the question is daunting. On the one hand, the state-centric system is not likely to become obsolete in the near future. On the other hand, there is increasing sentiment supportive of autonomy as a viable option in some cases.

The way forward for all types of ethnoreligious conflicts is not to attempt a reconstruction of the state system so that territorial boundaries are more closely aligned to ethnic borders. That would simply raise more complex issues such as those that the successor states to the Soviet Union and Yugoslavia are currently grappling with. Rather, the way forward is to acknowledge and strengthen ethnoreligious groups within the existing state system by the devolution of authority, among other measures. Scholar Elise Boulding contends that devolution would significantly enhance the structural problems of the modern state and thus cast ethnoreligious conflicts as "part of the process of solving" problems rather than the problems themselves.

For the international community, the challenge is to develop and strengthen norms for the protection of collective rights within the emerging international system. Such protected rights should include the "rights to individual and collective existence and to cultural self-expression without fear of political repression" or other forms of reprisal. Such rights should be accompanied by state or regime obligation to refrain from the imposition of ethnoreligious standards or agendas on other peoples.

Unless the international community upholds such obligations, and otherwise develops human rights and humanitarian law, as well as equips itself with some measure of political will to address ethnoreligious conflicts, the global community and its member states will join national and minority peoples in being the losers as these conflicts threaten peace and security within and beyond the borders of states everywhere.

D. Elwood Dunn

Bibliography

Allen, T., and J. Eade. "Anthropological Approaches to Ethnicity and Conflict in Europe and Beyond." *International Journal on Minority and Group Rights* 4 (1997): 217-246.

Boulding, Elise. "Ethnicity and New Constitutive Orders: An Approach to Peace in the Twenty-First Century." Paper prepared for a Festschrift (Memorial Conference) for Kinhide Mushakoji, 1990. See Gurr, "Communal Conflicts."

Crocker, Chester A., and Fen Osler Hampson, with Pamela Aall, eds. *Managing Global Chaos: Sources of and Responses to International Conflicts.* Washington, D.C.: U.S. Institute of Peace Press, 1996.

Gurr, Ted Robert. *Minorities at Risk: A Global View of Ethnopolitical Conflicts.* Washington, D.C.: U.S. Institute of Peace Press, 1993.

———. "Communal Conflicts and Global Security." *Current History* 94, no. 592 (May 1995): 212-217.

Gurr, Ted Robert, and Barbara Harff. *Ethnic Conflict in World Politics.* Boulder, CO: Westview Press, 1994.

Huntington, Samuel P. *The Clash of Civilizations and the Remaking of World Order.* New York: Simon and Schuster, 1996.

Kegley, Charles W., Jr., and Eugene Wittkopf. *World Politics: Trends and Transformations,* 6th ed. New York: St. Martin's Press, 1997.

Moynihan, Daniel Patrick. *Pandaemonium: Ethnicity in International Politics.* New York: Oxford University Press, 1993.

Smith, Anne-Marie. "Advances in Understanding International Peacemaking." USIP Publication, n.d.

United Nations. *An Agenda for Peace: Preventive Diplomacy, Peacemaking and Peace-keeping.* Report of the Secretary General (Boutros Boutros Ghali) pursuant to the statement adopted by the Summit Meeting of the Security Council on January 31, 1992. New York, 1992.

Terrorism and International Incidents

Although terrorists frequently think of themselves as being at war, terrorism is not always "war by other means." Criminals seeking only personal gain engage in it, as do other people whose goals are not political. Their perceived enemies can be domestic, foreign, the powers and classes dominating the entire international order, or some combination thereof. Moreover, terrorism has sometimes grown directly out of wars. These were wars that ended, officially, but then at least one side sought to go on fighting by using terrorist techniques. Not surprisingly, such exercises in terrorism can easily contribute to the outbreak of new large-scale wars. Two examples of this process are worth examining closely: the Israel-Palestine struggle and the India-Pakistan struggle over Kashmir. These cases are important because of the impact they still have upon the rest of the world.

What is terrorism? There is no one generally accepted definition, but we can define it, for the purposes of the present limited discussion, in the following tentative fashion: Terrorism is violent activity that aims to go beyond the immediate victim or victims to create a climate of fear within a wider group, and thereby coerce that larger group to give into certain demands and behave in a way that the terrorists desire. Terrorism is also violence designed to bring publicity to a grievance or cause and thus to gain recognition and even legitimacy for that cause. Typical terrorist methods include car bombings in crowded streets, time bombs exploding on aircraft, and shootings in public places such as airports. Other terrorist tactics include assassination, massacre, hostage-taking, and airplane hijacking. One feature of terrorist operations is that they often wound, maim, and even kill innocent people, including civilians who know nothing of the terrorists' aims.

States (i.e., established governments) do practice terrorism, very often against their own people, even to the point of committing mass murder. In many instances between the 1940s and the 1990s, international and internal terrorism has been carried out by individuals or small groups of persons, although formal governments or informal revolutionary "alternative" governments may stand behind them.

The Israel-Palestine Case

The war that created the State of Israel is often called the 1948 War, but it really lasted from 1947 to 1949. It began as a fight between Jewish regular and guerrilla forces (including some Jewish terrorist groups) against Arab irregulars. Regular Arab military formations from neighboring Arab countries soon intervened, however. Arabs both inside and outside Palestine rejected the idea of dividing what had been a single British-controlled region into an Arab mini-state and a Jewish mini-state, while Jews in Palestine were determined to create their own viable nation-state. This was not a war in which either side's higher levels of command could realize political and military aims in consistent and orderly ways, although the Jews always had a better command and control structure than did their adversaries. On both sides, the perceptions, emotions, and decisions of local commanders (and local people), facing realities on the ground, usually proved to be far more important than plans formulated elsewhere.

Two national narratives, containing elements of both truth and myth, came out of the messiness and fog of the 1948 Israeli Independence War. These stories or histories have played vital roles in fostering continuous feelings of victimization among Israelis and Palestinians. The Palestinian narrative is centered upon loss of land and expulsion of people (via physical removal and terrorism) who they believed belonged on that land. Consistent and centralized Jewish (Zionist) planning allegedly forced most Palestinians to flee to other Arab countries as refugees, while their land became subject to foreign expropriation and occupation. There is little, if any, recognition in this narrative of the confused and localized wartime situations in which many Arab civilians did leave Palestine for reasons that are not all attributable to Israeli planning. Nor does the Palestinian narrative really grapple with the idea that the Jews of Palestine had reason to believe that most of them surely would have been expelled (or worse) had the 1948 War turned out favorably for the Arab cause.

The Arab narrative portrays the new "Israel" as an illegitimate creation of both Zionist (Jewish fanatical exclusivist and even racist) aggression and Western imperialism. The Western world had placed Palestine under British rule after World War I. After World War II, the West wanted to use it to compensate Jews for crimes that the Western world had committed and to maintain a foothold in the Middle East. But such ambitions were being pursued at the expense of Palestinians and other Arabs. The Arabs were a third-world people, just emerging from colonialist domination. Naturally, they did not (in the 1940s or later decades) possess the political or military resources needed to resist the huge amount of foreign power being employed against them.

One implication of the Palestinian narrative was that recognition of the so-called State of Israel by Arab states and movements, and meaningful political negotiation with it, would either be ruled out or conducted in a clandestine fashion only. After all, Zionist occupation of Palestinian and Arab territory was an affront to the entire Arab world. The Israelis were not to be viewed as a genuine nationality, but only as Jews (members of a religious group) who were currently holding Arab land.

For the Jewish side, a key point has been the attempt in the 1940s by the British, and by Palestinian and other Arab forces, to deny the Jewish people a refuge and homeland in its historical place of origin. The main aim of both Arab irregular forces and regular armies was to drive out or even kill most of those Jews who were already in "Eretz Israel" and to prevent more from coming. These were Jews who were part of, or were being assisted by, the Zionist movement, which was a genuine, and ultimately successful, national liberation movement. Under Zionist leadership, Jews were returning to their ancestral land after centuries of persecution and genocide abroad. Jewish victory in Palestine meant creation of the first independent Jewish country since ancient times. This would be a country that could absorb returning Jews from all over the world, including survivors of the Nazi extermination effort in Europe, and acquire the military might to defend itself.

Central to the Israeli national narrative is the idea that Palestinians generally fled on their own volition from what would be Israeli territory and were not expelled. Another idea is that most of what happened to the Palestinians was justified, given the conditions of a war for Israeli survival. Still another argument is that a "population exchange" actually occurred, in that large numbers of Jewish refugees from Arab countries had to be absorbed by Israel after the war. These points were important in sustaining a long-held Israeli view that recognition and legitimacy need not be granted to any Palestinian cause. Instead, the solution to what was simply an Arab refugee problem lay in Arab states agreeing to absorb all homeless Palestinians into their own societies. If they refused to do so (and most did), it was for the political purpose of keeping the Israel-Arab conflict alive. It is only in the 1980s and 1990s that a regular debate has existed within Israeli public discourse over the independently established fact that a great many Palestinians were expelled during the 1948 War.

Despite modifications that may have been made in these conflicting narratives over time, they have helped to foster not just terrorism but the entire post-1949 Arab-Israel conflict. The terrorist dimension of that conflict had an identifiable first phase, which lasted from 1949 to 1956. A key feature of that phase was the linkage between state-sponsored Arab terrorism, Israeli reprisal, and the start of the full-scale Middle East war in 1956. Palestinians had been infiltrating Israel ever since the 1948 War. Some did so for private purposes, but as time passed, they usually came as part of organizationally

sponsored or government-sponsored terrorist efforts. By 1955, Israel's leaders were concluding that their counter-terrorist policy of occasionally sending regular Israeli army troops into neighboring Egypt and Jordan to stage military reprisal raids was not having the desired deterrent results. It was also likely to become too costly for Israel, militarily. These conclusions should be counted among the multiple causes of the 1956 War.

During the next phase, between the 1956 and 1967 Middle East wars, an important objective of the Palestinian organization Al-Fatah, at least for a time, was to involve Arab countries in a general liberation war against Israel rather than allow the status quo to become a permanent reality. The Al-Fatah sought to raise tension along Israel's borders. The Syrian-supported raids it staged were an immediate cause of the crisis that ultimately led to the 1967 Six-Day War. Other vital factors, however, such as the ambitions and maneuvers of particular Arab states and leaders (chiefly Egypt's Gamal Abdel Nasser), were more important in producing the 1967 explosion.

With Israel's defeat of the armed forces of Egypt, Syria, and Jordan in June 1967, and its capture of territory (the West Bank and Gaza Strip) containing large numbers of Palestinian inhabitants, the relationship between Palestinian activists and Arab governments changed drastically. The classic phase of the Israel-Palestine terrorist struggle began when Palestinian organizations came to the forefront of international attention as autonomous actors waging their own campaigns, with their own objectives in mind. Palestinian guerrillas, terrorists, "freedom fighters," and commandos, as they were variously called by observers of differing political persuasions, may still have needed financial, diplomatic, and other kinds of backing from Arab states, but the Palestinians had seized the initiative. Paradoxically, they were not important contributors to the outbreak of the next major Middle East war, variously called the Yom Kippur War or the Ramadan War of 1973. But they helped to spark inter-Arab wars—namely, the Jordanian-Palestinian-Syrian conflict of 1970–1971 and the Lebanese civil wars of the 1970s and 1980s. Finally, they themselves became embroiled in a major war with Israel in 1982, when the Israelis attacked the extensive military infrastructure that the Palestine Liberation Organization (PLO) had built in Lebanon by that time. The Israelis also went after the PLO in Beirut, and became deeply entangled in Lebanese affairs for some time.

The PLO has been the most prominent of the Palestinian groups and for many years has served as the chief diplomatic representative of almost the entire Palestinian nationalist movement. Arab states officially granted it this status in 1974. The PLO has also provided Palestinians, whether they live within Israeli-occupied territory or abroad, with a loosely structured framework of quasi-governmental institutions. Founded in 1964, the PLO has eluded the control of any regular Arab government, at least since the Al-Fatah and Yasir Arafat became dominant within the PLO in 1969.

The PLO's component terrorist factions have retained their own individual identities, while the PLO has also included conventionally organized troops, as well as civilians from various kinds of social and educational organizations. The factions have differed ideologically but could cooperate under the PLO umbrella, at least intermittently, so long as they could sustain some form of consensus on political aims and methods. As Arafat and the PLO gradually moved toward political-diplomatic-governmental role-playing

in the 1970s, 1980s, and 1990s, various important terrorist groups have loosened their links with the PLO. Some have ceased to work meaningfully inside it, at least temporarily.

Major terrorist operations were associated with the Al-Fatah in the 1970s. After the PLO was defeated by regular Jordanian military forces in 1970–1971 and ultimately driven from the strong foothold it had established on Jordanian soil, the group known as ''Black September'' was formed to serve as the Al-Fatah's unofficial terrorist arm. Most of its early actions were taken against Jordanian targets, but Black September's outstandingly famous (or notorious) act was the kidnapping and killing of Israeli athletes who had been sent to the international Olympic games, held in Munich, Germany, in 1972. Reportedly, Black September was disbanded in 1973, but terrorist incidents attributable to the Al-Fatah continued to take place.

Among the other PLO-affiliated groups that captured enormous international attention by the early 1970s was the Popular Front for the Liberation of Palestine (PFLP), led by George Habash. Terrorism by the PFLP included bombings, shootings, and aircraft hijackings staged inside and outside the Middle East in the 1960s and 1970s. One example of its international reach was its mid-air bombing of a Swiss airliner en route to Israel in 1970, killing all fifty-five persons aboard. The PFLP's September 1970 multiple hijackings of airliners were one of the major factors precipitating the 1970–1971 Jordanian Civil War. In this incident, commercial aircraft were hijacked in Europe, landed in the Jordanian desert, and then destroyed after their passengers deplaned, all to the embarrassment of Jordan's King Hussein. Another major action was the massacre of travelers at

Israel's Lod Airport in 1972, an operation actually carried out by a PFLP ally, the Japanese Red Army. The PFLP also initiated the famous Entebbe incident of 1976, when terrorists hijacked an Air France jet to Uganda and held its Jewish passengers hostage at Entebbe Airport until most were rescued by attacking Israeli commandos. The PFLP has also been active through most of the 1990s.

The Al-Fatah and the PFLP were among the five or so major terrorist components of the PLO during its early years. Another actor worthy of mention is the Abu Nidal organization, which in 1974 broke away from the PLO. Under the leadership of Abu Nidal, it has killed and injured hundreds of people in attacks carried out in many countries, and at such places as the airports of Vienna and Rome. It has targeted not only the United States, Great Britain, France, and Israel, but the PLO as well. Its targets have included PLO representatives, usually tied to the Al-Fatah, who in the 1970s and 1980s may have been involved in fostering talks with Israelis. It is suspected of assassinating one of the most famous veteran PLO leaders, Abu Iyad, in 1990.

As of 1998, the historic coalition of PLO terrorist groups is not functioning. Only Yasir Arafat's Al-Fatah stands behind the PLO, although other factions have not abandoned it fully and the Al-Fatah no longer functions in the terrorist mode. More important now than the PLO is the Palestinian National Authority (PNA). This is a limited governmental entity that Arafat and his current followers and allies have established on the soil of the West Bank and Gaza Strip, in keeping with agreements reached as part of (what might be called) the Madrid-Oslo peace process of the 1990s.

The PLO's evolution from a body that had been generally classified as terrorist in Israel and the West to an institution that Israel could officially accept as a negotiating partner involved a number of major steps. One was a 1973 commitment by Arafat to the idea of building a Palestinian mini-state on any occupied territory that Israel might relinquish. At this point, the PLO goal of recapturing all of Palestine had not been abandoned, nor had Israel's right to exist been recognized. Nevertheless, what would eventually be a phase-by-phase softening of Arafat's and the PLO's public positions on Israel (yet not necessarily the private ones) had begun.

Another major move toward respectability was the recognition granted by the 1974 Rabat conference of Arab states of the PLO as the only entity entitled to speak for the Palestinians internationally. It was followed by the speech Arafat made to the United Nations General Assembly later in 1974, and the passage of pro-Palestinian U.N. resolutions that same year. These events reflected and affirmed the already widespread international perception of the Palestinians as a nationality with rights. Terrorism and the publicity generated by it, along with the efforts of Arab governments, had helped to put both the Palestinian cause and the PLO on the world map. So had the political leanings of other third-world governments and the Communist bloc.

The PLO and the Palestinians also gained some international sympathy from their 1980s misadventures in Lebanon, where the PLO had been eliminated as a political and military force and Palestinians experienced military destruction and massacre at the hands of Lebanese Christians, Israelis, and Syrians. The Palestinian cause made significant political gains (in terms of international publicity and sympathy) with their "Intifada"—a popular revolt against Israeli rule in the occupied territories, begun in 1987, the main features of which were Palestinian demonstrations, non-violent civil resistance, and violent (if usually non-lethal) actions such as throwing rocks and Molotov cocktails.

Another crucial step, although it may have looked like yet another Palestinian disaster to all who were watching closely at the time, was the PLO's support of Saddam Hussein during the 1990–1991 Kuwait crisis and the Gulf War. The PLO became isolated diplomatically and financially, when it alienated much of its traditional support base among the governments of Arab states.

In the early 1990s, Israel and the PLO leadership under Yasir Arafat negotiated a new relationship. As part of the Madrid-Oslo peace process, each side officially recognized the other, and granted each other a certain limited degree of legitimacy. The financial isolation of the PLO just after the Gulf War pressured Arafat and his immediate followers to follow the Madrid-Oslo road. So did the relative marginalization of the Tunis-based leaders of the PLO, while the Intifada was being directed locally. Other influences included political competition that the PLO was experiencing from Islamic fundamentalists operating amid the Palestinian population in Israeli-occupied territory. The disappearance of the Soviet Union, the superpower that had backed the Palestinian cause in various political, military, and material ways, was important, too.

Israel's top leaders at the time, Foreign Minister Shimon Peres and Prime Minister Yitzak Rabin, eventually perceived an opportunity to alter the entire Israel-Palestine discourse and took it. Among the Rabin-Peres government's reasons for Israel's radical change in direction were the rising threat of Islamic fundamentalism and the decline in Israel's value to the United States as a stra-

tegic asset and "unsinkable aircraft carrier," now that the cold war had ended. Prompting from the United States was involved, although it was not nearly as decisive as the major decisions (such as agreeing to hold secret meetings in Norway) that the negotiating parties took upon themselves. In addition, by the early 1980s, the Rabin-Peres camp in Israeli politics had been coming to the conclusion that Palestinians had been constructing their own sense of nationality for some time, in response to Zionism.

But in 1995, Rabin was assassinated by one of his countrymen (who fits the terrorist profile). Rabin's ally and successor as prime minister, Shimon Peres, was defeated in a parliamentary election fought within a deeply divided Israel in 1996. These events did much to slow the peace process, if not kill it. In 1998, deadlocked positions between the highly nationalist, religious, and territorial-minded Netanyahu cabinet in Israel and the leadership of the Palestinian National Authority have set back Israel-Palestine relations considerably, perhaps fatally.

Palestinian religious terrorism was a significant factor in the process that brought the right-wing cabinet of Prime Minister Binyamin Netanyahu into office in 1996. It is true that the Islamist groups responsible for this round of terrorism were not only expressing their opposition to the peace process but were also responding to certain Israeli actions, including the assassination of a major terrorist personage. Continued Palestinian terrorism has demonstrated to many Israelis that the "peace process" is not bringing them security.

The best known of these Islamist terrorist groups is the Hamas (Islamic Resistance Movement). It became active during the Intifada and is an offshoot of the Islamic Brotherhood, a loose multinational fraternity of

Islamic fundamentalist organizations with a long history in the Middle East. Hamas methods, used devastatingly both before and after the 1996 Israeli parliamentary election, have included grisly suicide bombings of city buses in Israel. Although Palestinian Islamists have staged no major campaigns in 1998, their potential for violence, and the apparent existence of a modus vivendi between them and the Arafat camp, has been a source of great security concern and suspicion for the Israeli government.

Even if the PNA has been effectively preventing and combating terrorism, a claim that has been given credence by Washington, it has received little credit for doing so from Israel's government, and perhaps properly so. One tactic utilized by Yasir Arafat, as he dealt with the highly fractious Palestinian and Arab political scene in which he operates, is to say different things to different audiences. It is a habit that surely helps him as he functions as an aging charismatic personality, a former terrorist turned international statesman, an authoritarian leader, and an accomplished master of political maneuver and survival. He has hinted about ultimate Palestinian nationalist ambitions, which can only sustain a profound distrust of him, a distrust that many Israelis have never abandoned. Similarly, Israel's Netanyahu is not merely distrusted by the entire Palestinian camp but has been vilified for acting on the basis of his hard-line nationalist instincts and his need to maintain a cabinet coalition that contains some rigid ideologues.

The Case of Kashmir

Between 1947 and 1949, India and Pakistan fought a war over Kashmir. These two nations had both been part of British India until 1947, and Kashmir remained disputed territory after the partition of India. The Kashmir dispute is complex and subject to many conflicting interpretations. For the purposes of this discussion all that need be said is that the first India–Pakistan war ended with India holding the lion's share of the disputed territory. A cease-fire line, rather than a settled border, thereafter divided what became one of the states in the Indian federal union (the state of Jammu and Kashmir) from what Pakistanis call "Azad" (free) Kashmir. India has continued to claim all of Kashmir since 1949, while Pakistani sentiment has been strongly irredentist.

The two countries fought again over Kashmir during their 1965 war, and Pakistan again could not accept the outcome. The 1965 war was partly the result of a Pakistani attempt to infiltrate trained operatives into Kashmir, which might have started a revolt, involving terrorism, if the local population had been willing to support it. But popular support did not materialize at that time.

The third India-Pakistan war (1971) was not directly triggered by events in Kashmir, even though fighting did take place there. This war also left Pakistan dissatisfied over the Kashmir question, especially since territory was lost that had once clearly been part of Pakistan—namely, East Bengal (which became the independent nation called Bangladesh). Therefore, it should not be surprising that Pakistan in 1989 seized the opportunity to support a genuine Kashmiri Muslim insurgency against Indian rule. Pakistan has supplied personnel, training, weapons, sanctuary, and diplomatic support to insurgent groups that have faced the hundreds of thousands of Indian security personnel sent to suppress them.

While religion may seem to be the prime motivating factor in the Kashmir situation, especially since Islamic fundamentalism and

Hindu nationalism are involved, various forms of nationalism and ethnicity are the more important causative forces at work here, as in the Israel-Palestine contest. Pakistani nationalism is based upon something called the "two-nation theory." Its central argument has been that Muslims and Hindus in South Asia each constitute nations and not just religions. An extension of that argument is that Pakistan was created to provide independent nationhood for the South Asian Muslim community, and therefore Kashmir, with its Muslim majority, should be an integral part of Pakistan. For a Pakistani to respect the idea that Kashmiri Muslims might legitimately belong to either a Hindu nation called India or the "secular" nation that India has officially proclaimed itself to be is to derogate Pakistan's own raison d'être.

Indian nationalism has had "the secular state" as one of its underlying principles, even though the definition of that principle has been the subject of debate in recent years. The original definition, in vogue when India and Pakistan first fought over Kashmir, was the so-called Nehruvian definition (generally associated with India's first prime minister, Jawaharlal Nehru). It held that, while religion and the state would not be kept separate, no religion would receive favored treatment from the Indian governmental structure. Instead, all religions would be respected by it, and the adherents of all religions would be treated as equal Indian citizens within an Indian (not Hindu) "nation in the making." Independent India therefore could and should contain Muslims, and the fact that a region of India might have a Muslim majority within it could not properly justify separatism, or any Pakistani territorial claims.

The Nehruvian version of secularism became compromised in the decades since his death, by the granting of special rights for Muslims among other things, but it still has resonance so far as Kashmir is concerned. Even the Bharatiya Janata Party (BJP), the Hindu nationalist party that leads the 1998 coalition cabinet in New Delhi, claims to be genuinely secularist while decrying the "pseudo-secularism" that supposedly privileged Indian Muslims for too long. The BJP evidently wants Muslims to be part of Indian life, even if they are a subordinate part. This is so despite the suspicion, negative stereotyping, and occasional hostility that members and backers of the BJP have exhibited in various (and often very violent) ways.

A third variety of nationalism is part of the Kashmir conundrum, although a term like "subnationalism" may describe it more accurately. "Kashmiriyat" (Kashmiri-ness) was an ill-defined, "syncretistic," or "composite," ethnic identity that both Muslim and Hindu Kashmiris historically shared, an identity or sense of uniqueness derived from cultural assimilation and blending, as well as evolution of a common language. The breakdown or unraveling of the old Kashmiriyat in the last several decades turned Muslim activists against Hindus, but apparently there is still an ethnic flavor to Kashmiri Muslim identity and militancy. Persons believing in Kashmiriyat reportedly hold a variety of views, ranging from believing that Kashmir should become independent to believing in autonomy, but they do not want to see Kashmir simply merge with Pakistan.

Competing historical narratives play an important role in the Kashmir conflict, as they do in the Israel-Palestine struggle. Important to the Kashmiri nationalist narrative is the idea that Kashmir has been a distinctive cultural entity since ancient times. Diverse streams of thought, including Buddhism and forms of Hinduism, combined together with Islam (after the fourteenth century) to make Kashmir a great arts and learning center. Moreover, Kashmir's has been a tolerant, humanist, Sufi-influenced version of Islam that differs from the Wahabi-Sunni tradition found in Pakistan and large portions of India. Kashmir's composite culture includes customs and habits that Hindus and Muslims borrowed from each other.

The Kashmiriyat narrative claims that the powers surrounding Kashmir have oppressed and even enslaved it for several centuries. A struggle for self-determination and democracy, begun in Kashmir in the first half of the twentieth century, has continued through various phases up to the time of this writing. Kashmir's 1947 accession to India was only provisional, according to this view. It could only have been continued if the Indian government's commitment to secularism, democracy, and the kind of federalism that provided for Kashmir's autonomous management of its own internal affairs, had remained unimpaired. But the Indian government betrayed its ideals and promises, so far as Kashmir was concerned.

In the pro-Pakistani narrative, the key to Kashmir's historical identity is that it has been Muslim, and therefore should have gone to South Asia's new Islamic nation-state, Pakistan, in 1947. Its accession to India was one of many wrongs involved in the process of partitioning the British-Indian empire. Pakistan should now support as much as it can Kashmir's authentic struggle to free itself from Indian rule.

The pro-Indian narrative stresses the point that Kashmir's humane version of Islam resulted not only from Sufism, but also from those elements of Hindu culture that permeated it. Whatever legal or historical quibbles may be raised against the process by which Kashmir joined India, close historical examination by fair-minded people will show that process to have been entirely proper. Moreover, the best way to preserve Kashmir's unique culture and religion is to keep it within a democratic and secular India.

Another part of the Indian narrative is that the present crisis in Kashmir should be viewed simply as Pakistani-sponsored terrorism. Pakistan allegedly made a concerted effort to infuse Islamic fundamentalism into Indian-held Kashmir from the 1970s onward, by financially supporting an expansion in the number of Islamic schools and using them for indoctrination purposes. In addition, Pakistan's Inter-Service Intelligence (ISI) agency recruited guerrillas and terrorists by luring young men from Indian-controlled Kashmir into Pakistan, and then training, arming, and sending them back over the border. Such Pakistani efforts were made easier by the Soviet Union's war in Afghanistan and the increase in Asian Islamic fundamentalist sentiment that the war and the Soviet Union's eventual collapse helped to foster. Kashmiri fighters could be motivated by visions of Muslim brotherhood extending across Kashmir, Pakistan, Afghanistan, and into Central Asia.

India's claims about external causes of the Kashmir crisis do have considerable merit. One other such cause that should be emphasized (as has been done in India) is the Islamic fundamentalist wave in Middle Eastern and Asian affairs that was produced by the Iranian revolution of 1979. By the end of the 1980s, the timing was right for the spread of Islamism into the Kashmir affair.

So was participation in the Kashmir struggle by Afghan war veterans, and by Pakistan's ISI, which had learned lessons about guerrilla warfare from its major role vis-à-vis Afghanistan.

Internal Kashmiri causes of rebellion should not be ignored. These causes include the Kashmir population's rising political consciousness, produced by economic development, increased literacy, and media exposure. This change in political awareness was ultimately frustrated and alienated by the Indian government's mishandling of Kashmir's internal political, administrative, and security affairs.

Of the numerous Kashmiri rebel groups, the most important are the Jammu and Kashmir Liberation Front (JKLF) and the Hizb-ul Mujahideen (HMJK). The JKLF reportedly served as the rebellion's vanguard between 1989 and 1991 and may still be the most popular political movement. Its ideology is ostensibly secular-nationalist, although that ideology most likely overlaps significantly with those of the religious groups. The JKLF favors Kashmir's independence.

The HMJK is one of the groups favoring accession to Pakistan. Until 1997, the HMJK was reported to be the best-armed and the single largest underground group, probably because it had better Pakistani material support than its rivals did. Its outlook is generally described as being not only pro-Pakistani but highly religious, and it has apparently done much to cause Hindus to depart from Kashmir's famous central valley. A substantial number of the HMJK cadres are reputed to be foreigners, chiefly Afghans. In general, Pakistan has increasingly had to rely on non-Kashmiris (Pakistani nationals and some Muslims from the Middle East and Central Asia) to sustain the insurgent military campaign.

The two main Kashmiri rebel organizations, which have visited occasional violence on each other, never took part in a shadow-government like the PLO; however, many (if not all) of the insurgent groups, including the JKFL and HMJK, have formed an above-ground organization called the All-Parties Hurriyat [Freedom] Conference (APHC). The APHC serves as a weak linking institution for the whole movement, and its chairman sometimes acts as a spokesperson for the whole insurgent cause, or so recent newspaper articles would suggest. The APHC has sponsored non-violent activities, such as strikes, demonstrations, and boycotts, and has even appeared moderate enough to be called upon by the Indian side, on at least one occasion, to play a mediator's role.

Nevertheless, the tactics of the Kashmiri insurgents have, in the main, been shockingly violent. Their activities have included robbery, extortion, and rape, as well as killing Hindu non-combatants for ethnic-cleansing purposes. Non-military people in Kashmir have been abducted and/or killed, including foreign tourists. One rebel group, the Islamic fundamentalist (and pro-Pakistani) Harkat-ul-Ansar (HUA), has been linked to a particularly newsworthy episode of hostage-taking, in which five innocent tourists from Western countries became an international cause célèbre and have apparently died.

If many Kashmiri rebel actions fall within the bounds of non-terrorist guerrilla warfare, others conform to the limited definition of terrorism with which this discussion began. Certain Indian activities, however, such as the abduction, torture, and execution of rebel suspects, the indiscriminate firing on civilians, and permitting "renegade" Muslim squads to attack civilians, make India another state that (like Israel) has in some ways crossed the fuzzy boundary between practicing counter-terrorism and practicing terrorism itself.

Comparisons and Conclusions

Many widely accepted ideas about terrorism are contravened or only weakly supported by the Israel-Palestine and Kashmir cases, including the ideas that one man's terrorist is another man's freedom fighter; terrorism is a predictable and natural response to historical injustice, persecution, and hopelessness; terrorism is the weapon of the weak; and terrorism does not lead to major political achievements.

"One man's terrorist is another man's freedom fighter" is mainly a slogan and not some higher form of truth, if viewed in the context of the Kashmir and the Arab-Israeli struggles. "Freedom fighters" are often in a position to choose between terrorist tactics and others that may be equally effective. Muslim militants may kill non-combatant Hindus in Kashmir, but there is no absolute necessity to do so. As Palestinians themselves found during the Intifada, non-violent actions can be just as effective politically, both within the Israeli-occupied territories and abroad. Therefore, whether a "freedom fighter" is also a terrorist is largely a matter of human will and choice. Both Palestinians and Kashmiris seem to find non-violent political action unsuitable, probably for historical and cultural reasons.

Is terrorism "a predictable and natural response to historical injustice, persecution, and hopelessness"? The possibility of human choice, the vagaries of human perception, and the influences wielded by such cultural factors as ethnicity, religion, mythology, and historical experience, all serve to make this proposition problematic. Non-violent pro-

tests, and violent revolutions, guerrilla wars, civil wars, and even international wars, may naturally follow from the above-mentioned causes (except perhaps for hopelessness which is more likely to lead to passivity). But terrorism is another matter. There is little about terrorism that is predictable and natural. Many historical injustices have not been followed by terrorism, while terrorism can occur in relatively just and liberal societies. Quite possibly, the increasing availability of both high-tech and deadly low-tech weaponry, as well as the ever-greater expansion of communications and travel opportunities since World War II, make terrorism a more attractive choice for individuals, groups, and governments than was true in the past. But opportunity still does not dictate choice.

What may influence the decision-making of potential terrorists is the fact that, far from being the "weapon of the weak," terrorists can operate from positions of considerable strength. The Palestinian terrorist groups and those found in Kashmir might be weaker, in the conventional military sense, than their opponents, but theirs' are not conventional military battles. Nor are their resources inconsiderable, given the financial backing (hundreds of millions of dollars for the PLO and its components) and the massive amounts of weapons and other supplies that they receive over time. Strength is also derived from the sanctuary, training, diplomatic protection, and publicity that they receive from private and governmental backers. Furthermore, terrorists can and do draw strength from international terrorist networks, such as that which has been forged by the Islamist financier and organizer Usama Bin-Laden.

Kashmiri insurgents are in a rather unusual position of strength, as of 1998, even if they are on the defensive because of relentless Indian pressure. Standing behind them is a Pakistan that possesses the nuclear technology and conventional weaponry to deter India from eliminating insurgent bases found in the Pakistan-held part of Kashmir, or even hotly pursuing squads of militants into Pakistani territory. Air attacks on those bases, like the ones Israel frequently inflicts on Palestinian camps and installations, are also unlikely to happen. Even if Pakistani support for particular Kashmiri groups may wax and wane for various reasons, Pakistan's military parity with India leaves Islamabad free to engage in "proxy warfare" in Kashmir and elsewhere, while avoiding another full-scale India–Pakistan war, one that might well "go nuclear."

Can terrorism chalk up major political achievements? Certainly Palestinian terrorists have done so, although their success has to be placed in its proper context. By itself, terrorism would have accomplished little for the Palestinian nationalist cause without huge amounts of financial and other kinds of backing from entire blocs of established states. Nor could much Palestinian success have come without having a leadership cadre that could keep some semblance of dialogue and cooperation going on within the movement and could provide it with both a sense of (Arafat-style) strategic direction and

adroit diplomatic representation. The Kashmiri insurgency seems to lack these essentials, and may well be fated to go on using terrorist tactics indefinitely, with little chance of winning major victories.

Steven Hoffman

Bibliography

Chomsky, Noam. *Pirates and Emperors: International Terrorism in the Real World.* New York: Black Rose Books, 1991.

Crenshaw, Martha, and Pimlott, John, eds. *Encyclopedia of World Terrorism.* Armonk, NY: Sharpe Reference, 1997.

Horowitz, Irving Louis. *Taking Lives: Genocide and State Power.* New Brunswick, NJ: Transaction Publishers, 1997.

Howard, Lawrence, ed. *Terrorism: Roots, Impact, Responses.* New York: Praeger, 1992.

Oliverio, Annamarie. *The State of Terror.* Albany: State University of New York Press, 1998.

Poland, James M. *Understanding Terrorism: Groups, Strategies, and Responses.* Englewood Cliffs, NJ: Prentice Hall, 1988.

Sederberg, Peter C. *Terrorist Myths: Illusion, Rhetoric, and Reality.* Englewood Cliffs, NJ: Prentice Hall, 1989.

Tanter, Raymond. *Rogue Regimes: Terrorism and Proliferation.* New York: St. Martin's Press, 1998.

Tucker, David. *Skirmishes at the Edge of Empire: The United States and International Terrorism.* Westport, CT: Praeger, 1997.

Wieviorka, Michel. *The Making of Terrorism.* Chicago: University of Chicago Press, 1993.

International Arms Trade

The massive international arms trade has been as much a hallmark of the post–World War II period as the wars it has spawned and aggravated, though the commerce in weapons has origins in the pre-war era. In the 1930s, for example, a congressional investigation cited the "merchants of war"—that is, U.S. weapons suppliers—as the significant culprits in drawing the United States into World War I. By supplying arms to belligerents, Congress argued, the United States inevitably joined their ranks, forced to defend the trade by going to war.

The result was the so-called cash and carry legislation that required the pre–U.S. intervention World War II belligerents to pay for their supplies—including arms—in advance and pick them up in their own ships from U.S. ports. The "cash and carry" law was not the last time that this connection between the arms trade and U.S. involvement in overseas war would be made. Like later efforts to curb U.S. arms sales abroad, however, the legislation of the 1930s ultimately proved futile.

Still, the arms trade of the first half of the century—even during the maelstrom of World War I—has paled in comparison to that of the post–World War II era, and particularly in the last thirty years. Unfortunately, the United States is not the only country involved. Today, arms sales have become a significant component in the export profiles of most industrialized countries, and a host of industrializing ones. Moreover, the market for arms has spread to all corners of the globe.

The Quantity of Arms Sales

Though overall statistics are tricky to assess, due to varying kinds of measurements and a lack of verification in many instances, the quantities of arms sales and arms transfers—that is, under military aid packages—is enormous. According to the Congressional Research Service, it was estimated that some $33 billion in international arms orders were made in 1996, the last year available for overall statistics, though this was a substantial decline from the peak year of 1992, when the total reached $42 billion, a result of Persian Gulf countries replacing their armaments destroyed in the Gulf War.

Between 1945 and 1960, international arms sales were relatively minimal. The United States, for example, sold just $500 million worth of weapons annually during these years. This relatively low figure was due to several causes. First, large parts of the third world were still colonized, and thus not a market for arms. And those countries in Asia and Latin America that were independent were generally too impoverished to purchase much in the way of weapons overseas.

Thus, much of the market for weapons was in the first and second (former Communist) worlds, and many of the countries there had arms industries of their own. Indeed, in the cold war atmosphere of those years, the United States—and, to a lesser extent, the Soviet Union—actively rebuilt the arms industries of the former Axis powers, despite wartime agreements not to do so.

The dynamics of the early cold war also

worked to limit arms sales. Neither the United States nor the Soviet Union saw the third world as the significant battleground of their ideological struggle until the early 1960s, thus limiting the need to arm combatants.

By the late 1960s, however, the post–World War II revival of first- and second-world economies was contributing to the rise in arms sales to those countries. It was the events of the 1970s that produced the great secular rise in international arms sales. Again, several factors contributed to this trend. First, in the wake of the Vietnam debacle, the United States embarked on what was called the Nixon Doctrine, whereby Washington would help set up regional powers to act as surrogates for the United States. This obviously involved beefing up the armories of these various third-world countries.

On the demand side, the quadrupling of oil prices made it possible for a number of states rich in hydrocarbon resources to pay for vast weapons increases. Thus, between 1971 and 1975, U.S. arms sales alone climbed from about $1.4 billion annually to nearly $16 billion, with concomitant rises in the arms sales of other industrialized countries, both in the first and second worlds, though dominated by the former.

Indeed, by the mid-1970s, the issue of international arms sales was becoming a politicized one in the United States, Britain, and several other Western democracies. In the United States, candidate Jimmy Carter made the reduction of arms sales a key plank in his foreign policy platform. Nevertheless, while President Carter offered the first significant American effort to limit arms sales, the policy was so riddled with loopholes and exceptions that it did little more than contain the upward trend in sales. In 1980, foreign military orders still amounted to some $16 billion.

The Reagan years witnessed a quantum increase in U.S. arms sales, matched by those in other industrialized countries. Indeed, not only did the Reagan administration remove the limitations on weapons sales and transfers enacted during the Carter presidency, but policy-makers actively moved to streamline the process, by offering new financial arrangements and subverting congressional oversight in both legal and, in the case of Iran and the contras of Nicaragua, illegal ways. By 1982, U.S. arms sales totaled more than $22 billion.

This substantial increase was matched by the Soviet Union, also seeking to bolster its allies' military capacities—and its own balance of payments—in the face of increased U.S. arms sales. In 1973, the Soviet Union delivered some $5.3 billion in weapons overseas; by 1982, the total was nearly $11 billion. While European arms exporters—though motivated less by strategic than economic factors—also increased their sales from roughly $5 billion in 1974 to $13 billion. In addition, the 1980s also saw the arrival on the international arms market of several major industrializing country suppliers, including, most notably, Brazil, China, and Israel.

Under presidents George Bush and Bill Clinton, yet another factor has played into increasing U.S. arms sales, a factor that has been imitated by other major weapons suppliers. In the wake of the cold war, both Bush and especially Clinton have made trade promotion—including that of arms sales—a major component of their foreign policy, with U.S. arms sales peaking in the early 1990s.

This policy has required competing arms suppliers to do the same. Moreover, the collapse of the Soviet Union and the end of the cold war has left a vast arms manufacturing capacity in both the West and the former Communist bloc. Russia, in particular, has been desperately using arms sales to bring in much-needed foreign exchange in the 1990s. Still, a lowering of tensions in the weapons-buying Middle East and economic downturns in many third-world countries has led to a slackening demand in the arms business and concomitant decline in arms orders and deliveries in recent years.

The Quality of Arms Sales

Just as there has been a general upward trend in the quantity of weapons offered in the international arms market, so too has the variety and sophistication of available weapons increased in recent decades. Essentially, there are two kinds of arms transfers: those involving weapons and weapons systems, and those including the technology to manufacture weapons. The latter can include licensing agreements, co-production deals, or more rarely, the supply of turn-key factories.

Throughout the 1960s, most arms exports consisted of weaponry of a rather unsophisticated nature or of obsolete vintage. For example, most of the military aircraft that was sold abroad by the United States in this period consisted of hand-me-downs from its own military services. By the early 1970s, increased quantity was being matched by increased complexity, as wealthier and more sophisticated buyers in both the first and the third worlds demanded newer equipment of more recent vintage. Thus, by the late 1970s and early 1980s—even despite the Carter administration's half-hearted effort to deny weapons systems that would upset regional balances of power—the United States was selling arms that were but a generation or two less advanced than those used by its own military services. These included such

near top-of-the-line items as F-15 and F-16 fighters, M-60 tanks, and Sidewinder air-to-air missiles. The restraint of the Carter years disappeared with Reagan, whose administration shifted from a policy constrained by fears of a local arms race to a view that appropriate weapons for export by the United States meant anything that, in the words of expert Michael Klare, produced a "net contribution to enhanced deterrence and defense."

This, naturally, created a spiral in the sophistication of weapons sold by other suppliers, since the United States not only led the world in its volume of arms sales but in the quality of the weapons it sold as well. For reasons of geopolitical competition, the Soviet Union was forced to respond by upscaling the weapons it exported, if the balance of power between its surrogates and those of the United States was to be maintained. This was especially the case when the more complicated systems tended to be bested by American exports, as was the case in the 1967 Arab-Israeli War. For the big four European arms suppliers, it was more a question of economic competition. To win a share of the most lucrative markets—particularly in the Middle East—the French, English, Italian, and German arms industries were required to improve the weapons they sold as well. Between 1975 and 1982, for example, the Soviet Union sold over 3,000 supersonic aircraft to the third world, along with over 18,000 surface-to-air (SAM) missiles. The former included such items as late-model MiG 23s and 25s. The big four European arms suppliers also sold about 500 such aircraft and nearly 3,000 missiles.

This tendency toward high-end items has only increased since the end of the cold war. With oversized arms industries in much of the industrialized world—as well as in the

Soviet Union—the pressure to stay afloat economically has forced manufacturers to aggressively market their cutting-edge technology. Moreover, national governments in the first world and the former Communist bloc have become actively engaged in promoting the most sophisticated wares of their arms industries, largely for economic and domestic political reasons—that is, to maintain employment.

Of course, these are the big-ticket items. The vast bulk of arms shipments abroad—and those that get little media or bureaucratic scrutiny—involve small arms, useful for both military and policing purposes. These include handguns, rifles, grenades, and landmines; counter-insurgency gear, including jeeps, trucks, helicopters, and light attack planes; and riot control equipment, including tear gas, handcuffs, armored cars, and truncheons. In the late 1970s, the United States exported over 50,000 rifles, 600,000 tear-gas grenades, and 55 million rounds of small-arms ammunition to third-world police forces. While between 1975 and 1982, the Soviet Union and Europe provided over 1,200 light aircraft, some 2,800 helicopters, and nearly 17,000 armored cars to third world military and police forces.

In addition, sales of goods classified in the so-called gray areas have also increased. These include items that can be used for both civilian and military/police purposes, such as jeeps, trucks, transport planes, communications gear, and computers. Such items are often sold to countries under arms embargoes, since they can be classified as material for civilian use. During the 1970s and 1980s, for instance, a number of American and European companies sold such equipment to the embargoed apartheid regime in South Africa.

Just as in weapons, the United States has led the world in weapons-making technology during the post–World War II era. Until the early 1970s, however, most of the licensing and co-production deals arranged by the United States involved NATO powers, plus Australia and Japan. While the Soviet Union generally shared its arms-making expertise with its Warsaw Pact allies and mainland China. By the late 1970s, however, the same forces pushing arms manufacturers to offer more complex weapons systems—that is, competition, the increasing sophistication and wealth of arms buyers, as well as the growing desire of third-world countries to develop their own arms industries—were leading to more technology transfers.

Still, most such U.S. transfers involved a handful of special cases—countries with historical ties to the United States or of great strategic significance. Thus, in 1978, the United States had just eight technology transfer programs with four countries: Taiwan, South Korea, the Philippines, and Turkey. While several other countries had licensing agreements with U.S. arms suppliers, including Argentina, Brazil, and Israel. Under the Reagan administration, licensing changed dramatically and, by 1982, included Egypt, Pakistan, Saudi Arabia, Singapore, and Thailand.

Moreover, the kinds of technologies produced increased in sophistication to a degree that South Korea was co-producing F-15s. In general, European arms manufacturers have been more circumspect in their technology transfers, largely for economic reasons. They do not want to give up their technology edge. As for the Soviet Union, most of its third-world buyers did not possess the capacity to utilize technology transfers, while more advanced industrializing countries tended to prefer the higher-quality weaponry of the United States and Europe.

Finally, many of these technology deals involved the temporary assignment of technicians from the supplying nations, usually private and civilian in the case of the West and military personnel in the case of the Soviet Union. At the same time, both Western and Soviet firms and countries have welcomed students and technicians from third-world nations, as part of their commercial and strategic relationships. Working for firms in the arms-supplying states, they then take that know-how back to their native country and use it to develop arms production facilities there.

Of course, not all of the technology transfers can be blamed on the first and second worlds. A number of third-world countries made it a point to develop their own arms manufacturing capacity, especially when embargoed by the first and second worlds because of war, political isolation, or egregious human rights violations. Thus, Israel, Taiwan, and South Africa developed their own arms industries in the 1970s, while sharing technology among themselves. At the same time, both India and Pakistan, locked in strategic struggle and embargoes during their several wars, made it national policy to develop arms-making capacities of their own.

Nor is the problem of technology transfers strictly confined to sophisticated weapons systems. In recent years, there has been a growing international awareness of the destructive capacity of landmines and small arms, both decidedly low-tech items. It is estimated that no less than fifty countries have the capacity to produce small arms, while another two dozen or so can make landmines.

Who's Selling and Why

As noted above, the six most important arms-supplying countries for most of the post–World War II era have been the United States, the Soviet Union, and the big four European countries—France, Britain, Germany, and Italy. These main suppliers have been supplemented by those in Japan, Sweden, Czechoslovakia, and several other European countries. In more recent years, a number of industrializing countries have joined the ranks of major arms suppliers. The most important of these include Brazil, China, and Israel. In the past few years, with the stigma of apartheid lifted, it appears that South Africa is joining the ranks of arms suppliers.

Still, the United States has remained the number-one arms exporter through the entire period in both the quality and cost of weapons, though there have been individual years when it was outstripped by the Soviet Union and even France. Between 1974 and 1982, for example, the United States signed arms agreements with third-world countries that amounted to more than $82 billion, while the big four European sellers contracted for roughly $65 billion among them, and the Soviet Union made deals for about $70 billion. The total world market for arms export orders in those years was roughly $260 billion. Thus, the United States controlled about one-third of the business, while the big four and the Soviet Union accounted for roughly another 25 percent each. These numbers have not changed much in recent years. In 1996, the United States received about 35 percent of all arms orders, in a $35 billion trade, while Russia's had fallen to about 15 percent, or roughly $5 billion.

For the United States, there have been a variety of motives for selling arms abroad, though these have changed over time and vary from country to country. During the cold war, political and strategic imperatives tended to predominate. These included the need to support U.S. allies, military burden-sharing—particularly in the wake of the Vietnam War—political influence and leverage, superpower competition, access to bases, access to political and military elites, and in the case of anti-riot and counter-insurgency equipment, the desire to bolster friendly regimes against internal unrest. A final factor that tended to make political and strategic factors paramount over economic ones—especially during the first thirty or so years of the cold war—was that the business of arms sales was rather small, accounting for a tiny proportion—about 1 percent in the 1950s and 1960s—of all U.S. exports.

For the Soviet Union, the motivations were roughly similar to those of the United States, though Moscow had a few idiosyncratic reasons of its own to promote the sale of arms. These included a desire to establish secure borders. Thus, the Soviet Union made a major point of selling arms to friendly countries on its periphery, first in the Warsaw Pact countries and then in Asia. The latter included long-term sales arrangements with India and Iraq. In addition, Moscow has used arms sales and transfers in its competition with mainland China to win the allegiance of leftist regimes in the third world.

For the big four European powers, strategic considerations were also important, though they remained secondary to economic ones, even at the height of the cold war. To bolster their influence in regions they considered to be in their traditional sphere of influence, France and Britain in particular sold weapons to former colonies in Africa and the Middle East. Finally, there have been the so-called pariah states, such as Israel, South Africa, and Taiwan. In each of these countries—and particularly in Israel—arms sales represented a way to shore up support in a hostile world.

In the post–cold war era, economic consid-erations have tended to outweigh other factors in the promotion of arms sales abroad. This is not to say, of course, that strategic matters are no longer considered or that economic concerns were never factored into the arms sales equation during the cold war. Indeed, it is difficult at times to separate economic from strategic considerations, since the bolstering of friendly regimes can have a direct economic impact on the arms-selling country.

In addition, the arms industry itself—though largely a creation of the cold war in the United States and the Soviet Union—has taken on an economic imperative of its own. Thus, both the United States and the Soviet Union defrayed the cost of their own arms purchases and costs by sharing the burden with allies. Since manufacturing costs tend to go down with increased output, selling abroad was a way to lower the costs of new weapons or subsidize the cost of new weapons by selling the old. In the case of technology transfers, this could also provide a way to share the cost of research and development as well.

Of course, strictly economic factors were important during the cold war as well. Indeed, one of the explanations for the explosive growth in U.S. arms sales in the 1970s was an outgrowth of the Vietnam War, when the demand for weapons by the domestic military services shrunk, forcing manufacturers to look abroad to keep their factories running and their profits up. Moreover, the declining domestic demand for armaments was exacerbated by the fact that it came at a recessionary moment. Thus, for domestic reasons—specifically, maintaining employment in the arms manufacturing sector—politicians gave the green light to companies interested in selling their arms abroad.

For the United States—as well as the Europeans and even the Soviet Union—there were foreign economic considerations in the promotion of arms exports in the 1970s and 1980s. Specifically, all their economies faced increasing balance-of-payments crises, due in part to the spiraling cost of oil in the case of the West and the increasing stagnation of the agricultural sector in the case of the Soviet Union. Thus, the governments in all of these countries utilized arms sales to win back some of the money they were paying to OPEC or grain-exporting countries. In the case of the United States, this was direct, since it was the Persian Gulf countries that became the biggest arms buyers during this period, being awash, as they were, in petro-dollars.

Since the end of the cold war, other economic factors have come into play. Both for the United States and, even more critically, for the Soviet Union, the end of the cold war has signaled a crisis in the arms business, with declining domestic demand. Not surprisingly, both Moscow and Washington have moved from permitting and indirectly encouraging arms sales to actively working with arms manufacturers, as part of the normal governmental policy of promoting the exports of its own manufacturers. Indeed, the administrations of George Bush and Bill Clinton—both especially assiduous in developing cooperative relations with exporters or potential exporters—have had few qualms about extending this new relationship to encompass arms manufacturers.

Indeed, it can be argued that political and strategic factors have at times been harnessed to economic considerations. Some experts, for example, have argued that the Gulf War represented, at least in part, a way to show-off new weapons systems to potential buyers around the world. More recently, with the Clinton administration's approval of more sophisticated arms sales to Latin American governments, there is evidence that the needs of the domestic arms industry were taken into account to an important degree. In addition, the Clinton administration has been heavily criticized for its sales of certain technologies—with military capabilities—to China. While the publicly stated position of the administration was that it was ignorant of these deals or that the deals did not involve critical technologies, some observers note that the hidden message was: If America does not offer the technology, someone else will, thus winning the economic and political benefits of doing so in the process.

Who's Buying and Why

During the first thirty or so years of the post–World War II era, as noted above, most arms purchases were made by the industrialized countries of Europe, as well as Japan. Beginning in the 1970s, however, a variety of factors came into play that encouraged various parts of the third world to increase their arms purchases. First and most importantly were the countries of the Middle East, especially those rich in petroleum resources and, with the hike in oil prices of those years, awash in petro-dollars. These included Iraq (buying largely from the Soviet Union and Europe), the Persian Gulf Arab countries (making purchases mostly from the United States and Britain), and, above all, the Shah's Iran (buying almost exclusively from the United States).

Between 1976 and 1980, Saudi Arabia purchased roughly $5 billion in weapons on the international market: 40 percent from the United States, 20 percent from Britain, and another 20 percent from France and West Germany combined. At the same time, Iraq bought nearly $8 billion in weapons, 60 percent of which came from the Soviet Union. Iran, however, outbid them all, with weapons purchases well in excess of $8 billion, 75 percent of which were made in the United States.

Moreover, the so-called frontline states—that is, those facing the enormous power and arsenal of the Israeli Defense Forces—purchased large quantities of arms in the late 1970s, when tensions with Israel remained high. Between 1976 and 1980, Syria, for example, bought some $6.6 billion in arms, roughly 80 percent of which was from the Soviet Union and much of which was intended to replace equipment destroyed in the 1973 Arab-Israel War and its incursions into Lebanon in the late 1970s.

Notably, the downturn in the price of oil has done little to shrink the purchasing appetites of countries in the region. The volatile political climate, regional rivalries, and near-constant state of war in the region ensure a steady demand, which arms-supplying countries—eager to balance their oil payments—have been actively filling. This steady trend can be observed over the course of the 1990s. While arms sales to the region peaked in the wake of the Gulf War—as nations in the region were forced to replenish their depleted arsenals—they have not been reduced too substantially in the period since. In 1990, before the war, the Persian Gulf countries purchased $37.2 billion in arms; in the wake of the Gulf War in 1992, they bought $42.2 billion in arms. In 1996, Saudi Arabia alone purchased $5.2 billion, making it the largest arms importer in the world.

In the 1980s, the market for weapons in the Middle East was enhanced by increasing purchases on the other side of Asia. During these years, the industrializing countries of East Asia—the so-called tiger economies—found themselves increasingly able to pur-

chase weapons and pay for them through exports. At the same time, they sought to bolster their own defense capacities, largely to counter the overwhelming power of mainland China. Thus, Taiwan, South Korea (which, of course, also faced a well-armed foe in North Korea), Singapore, and later Malaysia, Thailand, and especially Indonesia hiked their defense purchases dramatically in the 1980s. The latter purchased some $1.5 billion in arms between 1984 and 1993, over one-third of which was from the United States.

Finally, there are a variety of reasons why governments—particularly those in the third world—choose to buy weapons on the international arms market, aside from the fact they cannot or choose not to manufacture them domestically. While these factors obviously vary from country to country, they can be summarized into the following general categories. First, and most importantly, are legitimate defense concerns, either against an external foe or, in the case of unpopular regimes, against domestic opposition. Other external factors include a desire to project an image of strength abroad for reasons of national pride or to gain concessions in territorial disputes, off-shore resources, and so forth. Internally, military leaders may use weapons purchases to gain the upper hand in their struggle with other national elites.

Economic factors come into play as well. A country may want to purchase weapons or, more usefully, weapons technology to enhance its own research and development capacities. In this instance, it is noteworthy that more and more countries—especially in East Asia—have been demanding technology transfers as a precondition for arms sales, a stipulation that supplier governments—eager to bolster their own defense industries—have been increasingly willing to meet.

The Impact of the Arms Trade

Arms-supplying nations have consistently argued that their sales of weapons do not contribute to armed conflict. Rather, they say, the sales help promote regional and global security by providing effective deterrence, regional balances of power, and the means for governments to stabilize disruptive and subversive domestic elements. While the facts speak otherwise and will be addressed shortly, it is also important to note that many countries admit that arms sales—albeit by rival suppliers—contribute to instability. Thus, throughout the cold war, the United States and the Soviet Union exchanged charges that the other was undoing carefully nurtured balances of power in various regions of the world.

In addition, Washington accused the Soviet Union of fomenting unrest and subversion by providing arms either to left-wing insurgents or to belligerent leftist countries. At the same time, Moscow said that the United States was supporting regressive and unpopular regimes by providing them with the military and police supplies they needed to remain in power. In the 1980s, Moscow added the charge that the United States itself was fomenting subversion by supplying weapons to anti-Communist insurgents in such places as Afghanistan, Angola, and Nicaragua.

More recently, there has been a shift in rhetoric among arms-supplying countries. No longer do they accuse each other of fomenting conflict by selling weapons abroad—a charge that is too difficult to make given the universality of the business and the eagerness with which various industrialized governments pursue it. Now, the criticisms involve the sophistication of arms involved, particularly those involving so-called weapons of mass destruction (namely, of the chemical, biological, and nuclear types) and vehicles (particularly missiles) by which to deliver them. In recent years, various members of the U.S. government have charged China, France, Russia, and even Israel of selling inappropriate military technology to countries the United States considers dangerous, such as Iran. Meanwhile, other countries contend that the United States sets a double standard for itself and the rest of the world, selling arms to countries like Turkey and Indonesia—which used them to invade Cyprus and East Timor, respectively, in 1974—while condemning sales to Iran in the 1980s.

Aside from the charges hurled at each other by the arms-supplying nations, there remain the simple numbers of wars and human rights violations involving governments that have made substantial purchases of arms in the international marketplace. The United States—as the largest supplier of arms—finds itself with the dubious distinction of having its weapons involved in more wars than any other arms-exporting nation. It is estimated that among the fifty or so ongoing conflicts in the third world and former socialist bloc states in the early 1990s, U.S. weapons were involved in some forty-five, or 90 percent, of them. In more than half the wars, the United States continued to provide arms after the wars had begun. Moreover, in many countries with ongoing insurgencies—such as Israel, Egypt, Somalia, Indonesia, and Mexico—the United States remained the largest supplier of counter-insurgency or riot control weaponry and equipment.

Finally, it should be noted that in exceptional situations, egregiously large arms purchases can have a destabilizing effect not just within a given region but within the political system of a single country. Many observers argue that the Shah's enormous military outlays were one of the causes of the 1979 Islamic revolution in Iran.

Nor is the damage done by the arms trade merely confined to periods of war. Though the international community has recently acted to ban their sale, there remain some 50 to 70 million unmapped anti-personnel landmines scattered across current and former war zones around the globe. In places like Angola and Cambodia, it is estimated that these mines produce a new death or crippling injury every day. Small arms, too, can continue to haunt countries long after the war is over. It is estimated that there are currently some 75 million assault rifles in circulation around the world. This abundance means they can be had readily and cheaply, for as little as $6 in places like Mozambique. Just as the end of a war means an abundance of weapons, it also means an abundance of demobilized soldiers and guerrillas, a recipe for banditry in many parts of the third world, and particularly in Africa.

Finally, it is important to note the consequences for the arms-supplying countries themselves of their weapons sales abroad. These consequences can be divided into three types. First, there is the boomerang effect, in which the weapons sold have been used against the soldiers of the countries that have supplied them. In the case of the United States, four of the last five times it has sent troops into a combat or peace keeping situation—Panama, Iraq, Somalia, and Haiti—it has faced an enemy armed with U.S. weapons. (The exception to this trend has been Bosnia.) A related consequence is referred to by the term used in the intelligence establishment—"blowback." This involves a policy pursued by the United States that comes back to haunt it. The best example of this involves the training and arming of Islamist

militants to fight the Soviet Union in Afghanistan. Both the 1988 attacks on U.S. embassies in Kenya and Tanzania and the World Trade Center bombing in 1993 involved terrorists trained and formerly armed by the Central Intelligence Agency in Afghanistan.

At the same time, there are costs—both direct and indirect—to the taxpayers in arms-supplying countries. First, there are the enormous subsidies paid to the arms manufacturers by the government. In most countries, these come in the form of military aid to friendly countries—allowing them to purchase the weapons manufactured by that country's arms companies with taxpayer money—low-interest loans and credits offered by the arms-selling country to customers, and promotional activities on behalf of arms manufacturers. In the United States, for instance, it is estimated that together these subsidies amounted to some $7.6 billion in 1995 alone, nearly one-half the total value of the weapons exported. Indirect costs can be even higher. As weapons suppliers offer more sophisticated systems to other countries, a vicious cycle is perpetuated. Because first-world arsenals, especially that of the United States, are expected to be at least one generation more advanced than arsenals elsewhere, selling more sophisticated weapons creates the imperative for developing newer ones for the domestic military.

Efforts at Control

With most arms sales in the period from 1945 to 1977 confined to first world and Warsaw Pact countries—where the cold war rarely turned hot—there was little concern or need for controlling the international trade in weaponry. The proliferation of sales to the countries of the Middle East—and especially

Iran—in the mid-1970s, however, brought the issue to the fore, at least within the American political context. As noted above, presidential candidate Jimmy Carter voiced serious concerns about U.S. involvement in the international arms trade during his campaign. After coming to power in 1977, Carter enunciated a new policy in which the United States would "henceforth view arms transfers as an exceptional foreign implement, to be used only in instances where it can be clearly demonstrated that the transfer contributes to our national security interests."

To that end, the Carter administration imposed specific controls on arms sales. These included a total ceiling based on 1977 levels, the banning of modification of advanced systems for export purposes, the prohibition on co-production deals, an end to governmental promotion of arm sales, a linkage between human rights and arms sales, and efforts at multilateral negotiations among the major arms-supplying countries both in the West and the Communist bloc.

Carter's efforts, however, were hamstrung from the beginning in several ways. First, they contained many exemptions, exceptions, and waiver possibilities. NATO and ANZUS (Australia and New Zealand) countries, as well as Japan and Israel, were never included. Second, the rules allowed the president to waive these limitations in "exceptional circumstances." Thus, under a variety of domestic and foreign pressures, Carter was increasingly wont to utilize waivers to allow for arms sales. These pressures included a rising political right at home, which criticized the administration's arms sales limitations as being detrimental to the projection of U.S. power and interests abroad.

Paradoxically, Carter's own efforts at peace—in the Camp David Accords between Egypt and Israel in 1979—required him to provide more military aid to these two countries. Ultimately, however, there remained the fact that as long as other countries were willing to sell arms to undesirable customers, a unilateral set of limitations by the United States remained unfeasible. Thus, arms orders approved by Washington increased from $8.8 billion in 1977 to $11.7 billion in 1978, and included such controversial deals as the selling of 200 modern jet aircraft to three Middle Eastern countries.

As noted above, the Reagan years witnessed a near-total disregard for limitations of any kind. Indeed, the new administration actively promoted arms sales, as a means of shoring up U.S. power abroad and fighting Communism. With the United States taking the lead, international arms sales soared in the 1980s and early 1990s, once again provoking efforts to establish some kind of controls on the sale of weapons abroad. These initiatives, however, have largely been aimed at the two extremes of the trade. First have been the attempts to create treaties limiting the transfer of technologies required to construct weapons of mass destruction—including chemical, biological, and nuclear weapons—and their delivery systems. The effectiveness of these treaties has been limited. For example, it is understood that Iraq acquired much of the technology it needed to build chemical and biological weapons from Germany and the United States. More recently, while India seems to have developed its nuclear weapons manufacturing capacity on its own, most observers believe Pakistan received help from China, which included the technology to construct missiles capable of carrying nuclear weapons as well.

At the same time, there has been a concerted effort to limit the international trade in small arms. In 1997, most of the international community signed a treaty banning the production, sale, and use of anti-personnel landmines. (The United States, citing its needs to defend South Korea, refused to sign as of this writing.) The push in recent years to set international limits on the trade in small arms, especially assault rifles, has been stymied by several factors. First, domestic lobbying groups in the United States—most significantly, the National Rifle Association—have pressured politicians and negotiators not to sign any treaties that limit the domestic sales of small arms.

Secondly, there are the logistical problems involved in limiting the international trade in small arms. Unlike such big-ticket items as aircraft, tanks, and missiles, it is virtually impossible to police the trade in small arms by conventional methods, such as inspections and satellite reconnaissance. This has led to talk of designing small arms with built-in obsolescence devices or designing ammunition that scars weapons, thus demobilizing them after a certain period of use. Still, the fact that small arms—as well as landmines—can be manufactured cheaply and easily with low-tech equipment means that limitations on international sales may be difficult if not impossible to sustain. Critics counter that any limitation is worth the

effort, since it is bound to dry up some of the lethal supply.

James Ciment

Bibliography

Boutwell, Jeffrey, Michael Klare, and Laura Reed. *Lethal Commerce: The Global Trade in Small Arms and Light Weapons.* Cambridge, MA: American Academy of Arts and Sciences, 1995.

Grimmett, Richard. *Conventional Arms Transfers to the Third World, 1986-1993.* Washington, D.C.: Congressional Research Service, 1994.

Hartung, William. *And Weapons for All.* New York: HarperCollins, 1995.

———. *US Weapons at War.* New York: World Policy Institute, 1995.

Klare, Michael. *American Arms Supermarket.* Austin: University of Texas Press, 1984.

Klare, Michael, and Peter Kornbluh. *Low Intensity Warfare: Counterinsurgency, Proinsurgency, and Antiterrorism in the 1980s.* New York: Hill and Wang, 1988.

Rana, Swadesh. *Small Arms and Intrastate Conflicts.* New York: United Nations Centre for Disarmament Affairs, 1995.

Sampson, Anthony. *The Arms Bazaar.* New York: Viking Press, 1977.

Sennott, Charles. "Armed for Profit: The Selling of U.S. Weapons—A Special Report." *Boston Globe,* February 11, 1996, supplement.

United States Arms Control and Disarmament Agency. *World Military Expenditures and Arms Transfers, 1990.* Washington, D.C.: U.S. General Printing Office, 1990.

REGIONAL MAPS

REGIONAL MAPS

North America

RUSSIA

ARCTIC
OCEAN

GREENLAND

ICELAND

U.S.

Great Bear
Lake

Great Slave
Lake

Athabasca
Lake

Reindeer
Lake

Hudson
Bay

CANADA

PACIFIC

OCEAN

Lake
Winnepeg

Lake of
the Woods

Lake
Nipigon

Lake
Superior

Lake
Huron

Lake
Michigan

Lake
Ontario

Lake
Erie

Great Salt
Lake

UNITED   STATES

ATLANTIC

OCEAN

MEXICO

GULF OF
MEXICO

0	250	500 Miles
0	250	500 Kilometers

Mexico and Central America

Caribbean Islands

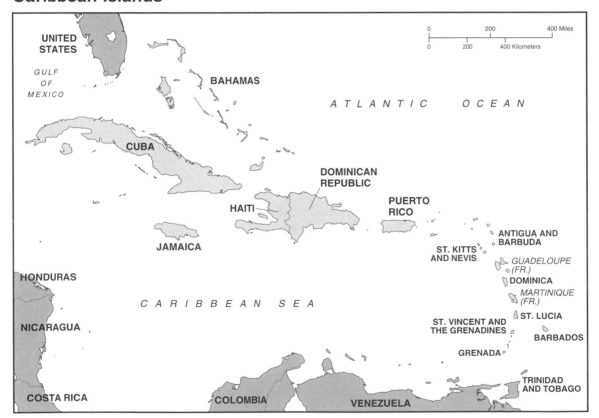

South America

Europe

Middle East

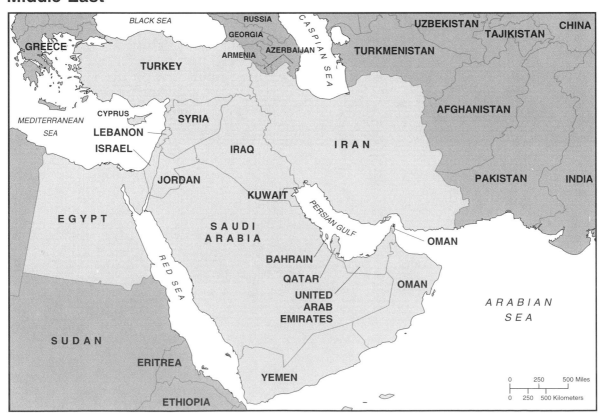

Africa

Indian Subcontinent

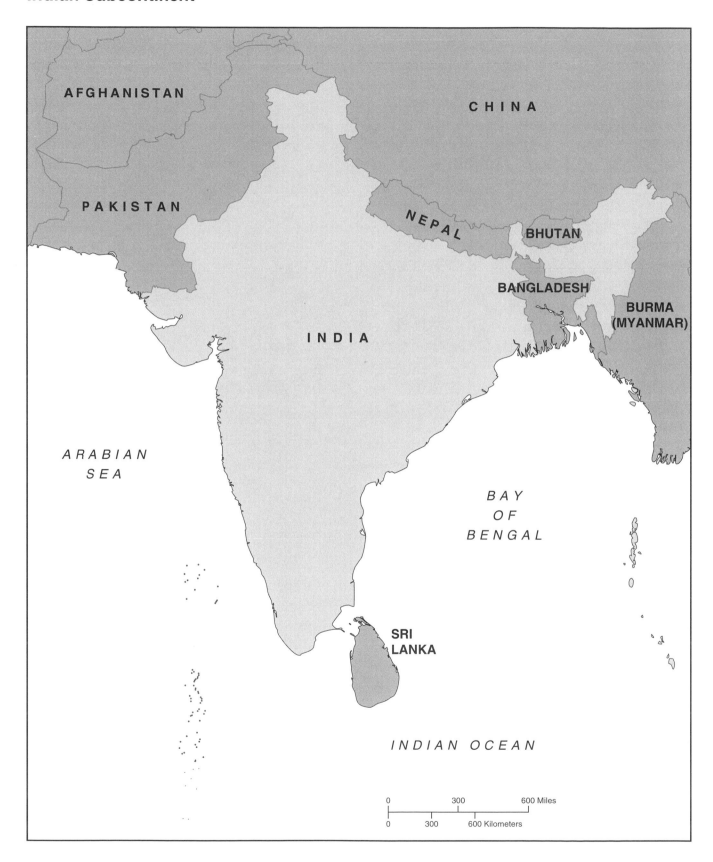

Former Soviet Union

China and Surrounding Areas

Southeast Asia

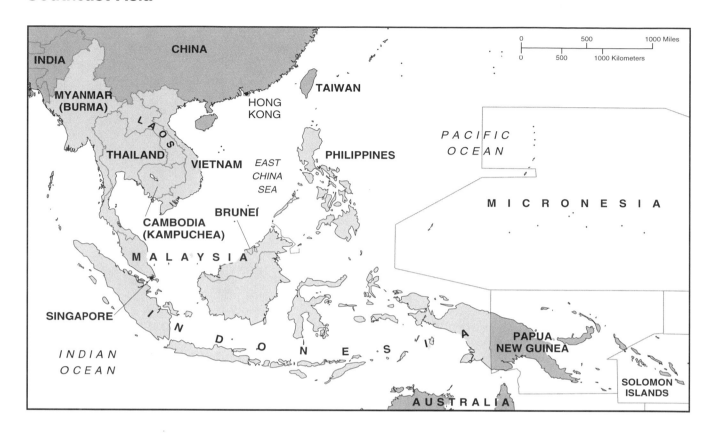

ALLIANCES

AND

TREATIES

ANZUS Pact

The ANZUS pact was a cold war alliance between Australia, New Zealand, and the United States—hence the acronym "ANZUS"—dedicated to preserving peace and security in the Pacific Ocean region. The treaty, officially called the Pacific Security Treaty, was signed on September 1, 1951, in San Francisco, and took effect in April 1952.

Pact interaction was coordinated by annual meetings of the pact council, made up of the Foreign Ministers of the three involved countries; decisions by the pact council had to be unanimous. The pact also made provision for military representatives to meet separately and arranged for military maneuvers among the three members.

Reasons for ANZUS

The ANZUS pact was to be the foundation of security in the Asian-Pacific region. The threats to regional security that the pact was designed to counter were not specified, but there were two clear security motives behind its creation.

First, the United States intended the pact to reassure a nervous Australia, which was concerned about the recent decision to allow Japanese rearmament. Japan had been disarmed at the end of World War II, but cold war pressures had convinced Japanese and American leaders that Japan would have to recreate some kind of armed forces for its own protection. Japan's new military was designed to be non-threatening; its ground, air, and naval branches were called the Self-Defense Forces, and even as late as 1998, they were forbidden to send combat troops abroad. Nevertheless, Australia and New Zealand, with memories of World War II still vivid, were distrustful. The ANZUS pact served to allay their fears by assuring them that the United States would guarantee their security.

Second, the pact was a direct response to the cold war confrontation between the United States and the Soviet Union. Although the cold war began in Europe, it had soon spread to Asia. In 1949, China's long civil war had ended in the victory of Mao Zedong and the Chinese Communist Party, and 1950 saw the beginning of the Korean War (1950–1953). These defeats and near-defeats had created concern in the United States regarding the dangers of communism in the Asia-Pacific region.

ANZUS was created to fit in with the U.S. policy known as "containment." Containment was designed to keep the Soviet Union from spreading its influence to any other nations. By creating regional alliances such as ANZUS—as well as the Southeast Asia Treaty Organization (SEATO) and the North Atlantic Treaty Organization (NATO)—the United States hoped to hem in any further attempts at Soviet expansion.

Functioning

When the ANZUS pact was signed, it was clear that the United States was the senior partner in the alliance. In 1952, Australia and New Zealand had a combined population of about 11 million; compared to the U.S. population of 150 million. With relatively tiny armed forces, the main contribution of Australia and New Zealand was their navy and air bases. The two smaller ANZUS countries became ports of call for the U.S. navy, making it logistically easier for the United States to exert its influence on the Asian heartland. Australia also allowed the United States to base satellite tracking stations on its territory.

The ANZUS pact made it clear that the United States had become the superpower to which the rest of the West turned. This caused ruffled feelings in Great Britain, which, before World War II, had been the primary protector of Australia and New Zealand. Britain objected to the fact that the pact had been negotiated without any British consultation, but American diplomat John Foster Dulles argued that the inclusion of Britain would have been seen by Asian countries as harking back to the colonial era. Australia and New Zealand remained part of the British Commonwealth, but ANZUS demonstrated that America was now their most important ally.

Even before the ANZUS pact took effect, the military alliance among the three signatories was being consummated by the commitment of small contingents of Australian and New Zealand troops to the Korean War. Although the troops were sent under United Nations auspices, it was clear that Australia and New Zealand were confirming their support of their strategic alliance with the United States.

The ANZUS pact was made somewhat obsolete by the 1955 creation of SEATO—which included the ANZUS signatories and added Great Britain, France, Pakistan, and the Philippines—but relations between the ANZUS allies remained good. During the Vietnam War, Australia and New Zealand again sent soldiers to fight alongside their American ally.

With the ending of SEATO in 1977, the ANZUS pact took on greater importance. Although vital regional issues were fewer after the fall of Vietnam, the annual pact meetings provided a forum for the three powers to discuss issues of mutual interest, including the Soviet invasion of Afghanistan and the invasion of Cambodia by Vietnam.

ANZUS began to break apart in 1984 with the victory in New Zealand of David Lange and his Labour party. Lange, fulfilling a campaign promise that had been inspired by the anti-nuclear movement, banned nuclear-powered or nuclear-armed warships from entering New Zealand's harbors. Since many American vessels were either nuclear powered or carried nuclear weapons, this made it difficult for U.S. warships to participate in joint ANZUS exercises. The United States responded in August 1986 by suspending its treaty obligations to New Zealand. The treaty was not officially dissolved, and Australia continued to abide by its provisions, but as a three-power pact it was effectively inoperative.

ANZUS Today

After the effective withdrawal of New Zealand from the ANZUS pact, the formal military alliance had, for most practical purposes, ended. The United States and Australia continued to maintain close military links under the auspices of the pact, but their relationship had been transformed into a two-power alliance.

The collapse of the Soviet Union (1991) and the decline of communism as an international threat had also made the ANZUS pact much less relevant. Australia and New Zealand, on good terms with most of their Asian neighbors, did not have the same need of a superpower protector.

There were some attempts to revive the pact in the late 1980s and 1990s, but without success. It seemed likely that the pact would become part of cold war history.

Carl Skutsch

See also: Cold War Confrontations; Southeast Asia Treaty Organization (SEATO).

Bibliography

Baker, Richard W., ed. *The ANZUS States and Their Region: Regional Policies of Australia, New Zealand, and the United States.* Westport, CT: Praeger, 1994.

Donnini, Frank. *ANZUS in Revision: Changing Defense Features of Australia and New Zealand in the Mid-1980s.* Maxwell Air Force Base, AL: Air University Press, 1991.

Arab League

The Arab League (its official name is the League of Arab States) was founded in Cairo on March 22, 1945. The founding states were Egypt, Iraq, Lebanon, Saudi Arabia, Syria, Transjordan (Jordan), and Yemen. (Egypt was expelled in 1979 after signing the 1978 Camp David Accords with Israel, but was subsequently readmitted into the League.) The Arab League currently has as member states more than twenty Arab nations in the Middle East and North Africa, including Libya, Sudan, Algeria, Kuwait, and Palestine (represented by the PLO). Each member state receives one vote in the League Council, which coordinates all League activity. Its headquarters is located in Cairo.

Historical Background

The Arab League was born at the end of the colonial era. Arabs had lacked any independent nation of their own since the beginning of the Ottoman Turkish Empire. The defeat of the Turks in World War I did not, however, gain the Arabs their freedom. France and Great Britain declared that the Arab territories that had been under Turkish control would now become protectorates and would be guided toward independence at a pace chosen by the Europeans. Britain occupied Iraq, Palestine, and Saudi Arabia, while France took Lebanon and Syria. Arab leaders, many of whom had fought alongside the British in their war against the Turks, chafed under this enforced tutelage. Arab intellectuals and leaders discussed the possibility of creating a unified Arab state, free from the divisions enforced by European occupation.

Prominent among the leaders pushing for Arab unity was Nuri al-Sa'id, an Iraqi Arab who had fought with the British in World War I and supported them during World War II. With British help Nuri was made prime minister of Iraq and used his position to attempt to organize a unified Arab state under the Hashimite kings of Iraq. In 1942, Nuri put forward a plan calling for a single nation to be created out of the territories of Palestine, Syria, Jordan, and Lebanon; this Greater Syrian state would be linked together with Iraq in an Arab League, which would be open to other Arab nations as they gained their independence. Nuri hoped that this confederation of Arab states would eventually become a single, united Arab nation.

Nuri's idea was supported by Mustafa al-Nahhas Pasha, the prime minister of Egypt (also under British domination), who called for an Arab conference to be held at Alexandria in September 1944. This Arab conference was attended by delegates from Egypt, Iraq, Syria, Transjordan, and Lebanon, and by observers from Saudi Arabia, Yemen, Morocco, Libya, and Palestine. Despite Nuri's desire for a more centralized organization, the participating states were unwilling to surrender the independence that they were on the verge of gaining to a Pan-Arab state. The league they created, therefore, was a loose confederation of Arab states; its goals were to coordinate, not control, the Arab states' activities. The focus of the 1944 discussions was on economic rather than political cooperation. The vision of the league that was born out of these discussions was of a mutual aid society for the Arab world. The

Pact of the League of Arab States was signed by its founding members in March 1945.

Activities of the League

The Arab League was not created as an overtly political organization, and its most successful activities have always been in the realm of economics. An Economic Council, having as its members the Ministers of Economic Affairs for the member states, was founded in 1953 and was given the responsibility of helping to coordinate Arab economic activity.

In 1957, the League established the Council of Arab Economic Unity, whose mandate was to create economic integration among Arab states. The council was responsible for creating the Arab Common Market, an attempt to mirror the economic cooperation existing within the European Common Market. Similarly, the Arab Monetary Fund, established in 1976, was designed to be the Arab equivalent of the International Monetary Fund, providing loans for those members who were in need of assistance in developing their economies. In 1973, the League founded the Arab Bank for Economic Development in Africa, which was dedicated to assisting African states with debt repayment and capital investment.

The founding of the Israeli state in 1948 politicized the League, as all of its members were opposed to the creation of a Jewish state in Palestine. As early as 1945, the Council of Arab Unity passed a resolution calling on its members to boycott Zionist (Jewish) firms in Palestine. In April 1950, the League drafted a Joint Defense and Economic Cooperation Treaty, which went into effect in August 1952. The Joint Defense Treaty led to the creation of a Joint Defense Council, run by foreign and defense ministers, and a Permanent Military Commission, containing the military leaders of the member states. Under the Joint Defense Treaty, the Arab League led an economic boycott of Israel coordinated by the League's Special Bureau for Boycotting Israel. (One of the side effects of the League's boycott was the banning of Elizabeth Taylor movies in Arab countries, because the actress was known to be a financial supporter of Israel.)

The Arab League was also responsible for creating the Palestinian Liberation Organization (PLO). In 1948, the Council of Arab Unity had formed an All-Palestine Government to represent the needs of the Palestinian refugees who had fled the newly forming state of Israel, but this body had failed to attract widespread support among Palestinians. In 1964, therefore, the League authorized the creation of a more autonomous organization, the PLO, headed by Ahmad Shuqayri, a Palestinian activist. By creating the PLO, the League hoped to be able to maintain control over the growing forces of Palestinian nationalism; however, in 1969, Palestinians, unwilling to continue to serve as pawns of the League, transferred the leadership of the PLO to Yasir Arafat, the head of an aggressive activist group called Al-Fatah. After 1969, the PLO ceased to be a tool of the Arab League, and Arafat and the Palestinians attempted to plot their own course toward a Palestinian state.

For the most part, the Arab League did little more than play a coordinating role for the Arab world's opposition to Israel. The many wars fought between Israelis and Arabs have been supported by Arab League members but have not been controlled by the League itself; such a role was beyond the scope of its decentralized organization. The League did declare (in 1974) its support for the PLO as the "sole, legitimate representative of the

Palestinian people," a move which undercut Jordan's King Hussein, who had previously claimed a role as the spokesman for Palestinian affairs. The League's opposition to Israel led it to expel Egypt in March 1979 as already stated; Egypt was then subjected to the same economic boycott as Israel (although Sudan and Oman, Egyptian allies, did not join in the boycott).

The Arab League has also attempted to intervene in other regional conflicts. In 1961, the Arab League sent a multinational force of Saudi, Egyptian, Jordanian, and Sudanese troops to guard Kuwait's borders against threats from Iraq. In 1976, the Arab League created an Arab Deterrent Force to supervise (unsuccessfully) attempts to end the fighting in Lebanon.

The 1990 occupation of Kuwait by Iraq helped to damage the Arab League's sense of cooperation. Most Arab states (although not always their populations) supported the U.S. efforts to expel Iraq from Kuwait; the significant exception was Jordan, whose close economic ties to Iraq forced it to attempt to maintain a neutral stance during the war. At an August 1990 League meeting, twelve of the twenty attending nations condemned the Iraqi invasion, demanded a withdrawal of Iraqi troops from Kuwait, and voted to support the creation of an Arab army to defend Saudi Arabia against Iraqi aggression. Subsequently, some Arab League members, including Saudi Arabia and Egypt, joined in the counter-invasion of occupied Kuwait. Other members, including Libya, Sudan, and the PLO, were sympathetic to Iraq, engaged in what they perceived to be a war against Western imperialism.

It was in this context of division within the Arab world that the capital of the Arab League was relocated back to Cairo (after 1979, the League headquarters had been moved to Tunis). In 1991, the League elected an Egyptian, Ahmad Esmat Abd, as its secretary general, returning Egypt to its previous position of preeminence within the League.

Significance

The Arab League has failed to achieve unity in the Arab world but it has served as a focus for Arab cooperation on issues of shared interest. If some of its greatest successes are in the area of cultural achievements (such as the Arab League Educational, Scientific, and Cultural Organization and the Academy of Arab Music), this is simply because the political and economic problems of the region are beyond the scope of such a loosely structured organization. And despite its divisions, which were exacerbated by the 1990–1991 Persian Gulf Conflict, the League has remained united in its support for the Palestinian goal of creating an independent nation-state.

Carl Skutsch

See also: Iraq: Gulf War, 1990–1991; Israel: War of Independence, 1948–1949; Israel: Palestinian Struggle Since 1948; Lebanon: Civil War, 1975–1990; Palestine: Intifada, 1987–1992.

Bibliography

Hasou, Tawfig Y. *The Struggle for the Arab World: Egypt's Nasser and the Arab League.* Paris: KPI, 1985.

Hassouna, Hussein A. *The League of Arab States and Regional Disputes: A Study of Middle East Conflicts.* Dobbs Ferry, NY: Oceana Publications, 1975.

Khalil, Muhammad. *The Arab States and the Arab League: A Documentary Record.* Beirut: Khayats, 1962.

MacDonald, Robert W. *The League of Arab States: A Study in the Dynamics of Regional Organization.* Princeton: Princeton University Press, 1965.

Central Treaty Organization (Baghdad Pact)

Originally known as the Baghdad Pact—after the city in which it was signed in 1955—the Central Treaty Organization (CENTO) was an organization designed to promote mutual security and economic cooperation among its member states. These originally included Iran, Iraq, Pakistan, Turkey, and Great Britain. Promoted by the United States, which joined the organization as an ancillary member in 1956, the Baghdad Pact was one in a series of regional security alliances stretching from the North Atlantic to the South Pacific, designed to counter armed outside aggression or internal subversion fostered by Communist Moscow and Beijing. The pact was renewable every five years.

Under the original treaty, the organization was governed by a council, which met once a year, and a secretariat that met on a more regular basis. The secretariat included four divisions: political and administration, economic, public relations, and security. While the military staff planned joint exercises and military coordination, the economic committee focused on projects in agriculture, scientific research and education, mining, health, and communications and public works. For the most part, the development projects concerned transport and communications, including the development of highways, railroads, and micro-wave transmission that had both military and civilian uses.

In fact, the Baghdad Pact was little more than a paper organization. Following the 1958 nationalist revolution of Abd al-Karim Qasim in Iraq, which overthrew the pro-Western monarchy established by the British in 1930, Baghdad pulled out of the organization, forcing the name change to CENTO and the removal of the organization's head offices to Ankara.

During most of the 1960s and 1970s, the group largely focused on the above-mentioned economic projects, the largest of which was a railroad linking Turkey and Iran. The absence of unrest in the region—with the exception of Pakistan's wars with India—meant the organization had few security issues to deal with. Indeed, U.S. policy-makers, who saw the real threat to the security of CENTO members coming from Moscow, viewed Pakistan's struggle with India as a diversion.

By the mid-1970s, with the collapse of Vietnam and the Southeast Asia Treaty Organization and the general retreat of U.S. power from the Asian mainland, CENTO was even less a factor in the military power relationships of southwestern Asia than it had been in the 1950s and 1960s. Unable to cope with the rise of Islamic revolutionaries in Iran—who pulled that country out of the organization following their rise to power in

February 1979—CENTO was dissolved within a year.

James Ciment

See also: Cold War Confrontations; Iran: Islamic Revolution, 1979; Iraq: Revolution and Coups, 1958–1968; North Atlantic Treaty Organization (NATO); Southeast Asia Treaty Organization (SEATO).

Bibliography

Bethke, Gerald. *Should the United States Continue to Support CENTO? An Individual Research Report.* Carlisle Barracks, PA: US Army War College, 1973.

Kechichian, Joseph. *Security Efforts in the Arab World: A Brief Examination of Four Regional Organizations.* Santa Monica: Rand Institute, 1994.

Non-Aligned Movement— The Bandung Conference

The non-aligned movement, begun at the Bandung Conference of 1955, was the deliberate attempt by a group of countries to move away from allying themselves with either the United States and its allies, or the Soviet Union and other Communist states. The cold war was at its height; the Soviet Union and the United States were insisting that the world's nations must choose sides; and the non-aligned movement chose an alternative route. In a world divided between the rich Western "first world" and the communist "second world," Bandung created the possibility of a "third world," which would have its own interests, not connected to East-West conflicts. Although its actual achievements are difficult to pin down, it helped to define an era and gave a number of countries a means by which they could attempt to avoid joining either Communist or Western camps, while expressing an alternative ideology of third-world cooperation.

The Bandung Conference

From April 18 to 24, 1955, representatives from twenty-nine nations met at Bandung, Indonesia, for an Asian–African conference. The delegates came from all the independent nations of Asia and Africa—except Korea and Israel. Organized by five newly independent nations—Indonesia, Burma (Myanmar), Ceylon (Sri Lanka), India, and Pakistan— and hosted by Indonesia's Sukarno, Bandung was supposed to be an assertion of national pride in the face of dying colonialism. The sponsors wished to create a forum in which the national voices of countries outside Europe and America would be heard, and in which some kind of joint policies might be arrived at. Among their prime concerns was the continued existence of colonialism, as exemplified by the still-thriving French Empire.

The leaders at Bandung included men who would go on to lead the non-aligned movement—Indonesia's President Sukarno, India's Prime Minister Jawaharlal Nehru, Egypt's President Gamal Addel Nasser—but Bandung did not have any clearly articulated ideology. In fact, Bandung included countries who were openly allied to the West (Turkey and South Vietnam), as well as Communist allies of the Soviet Union (China and North Vietnam).

These varied participants at Bandung were only able to adopt a few vague proclamations, which included a statement condemning "colonialism in all of its manifestations" as well as a ten-point collection of principles that called for "the promotion of world peace and cooperation."

Nevertheless, the roots of the non-aligned movement were at Bandung. For the first time nations of the South, the under-industrialized world, had met together without consulting the rich nations of the North. Bandung was their declaration of independence.

The Non-Aligned Movement

The idea of non-alignment was suggested by Bandung, but it was not clearly articulated as an ideology until the first Non-Aligned Conference, held in Belgrade in 1961. This conference was the result of an increasingly cooperative relationship between three leaders: Josip Broz Tito of Yugoslavia, Nasser of Egypt, and Nehru of India. All three believed that their countries had a shared interest in withstanding the threat of domination by both the capitalist West and the communist East.

A key year in forming the non-aligned consciousness was probably 1956. The Suez Canal Crisis, in which British, French, and Israeli troops invaded Egypt, demonstrated to Nasser and others that colonialism was still alive in the West. Similarly, the Soviet Union's simultaneous brutal suppression of the Hungarian revolt made it clear that the East could be equally threatening.

The three founders of non-alignment—Tito, Nasser, and Nehru—had all survived confrontations with the rich powers of the world. Tito had stood up to Stalin and saved Yugoslavia from becoming another East European puppet of the Soviet Union; Nasser had nationalized the Suez Canal, facing down British and French attempts to retake it; and Nehru had successfully led the fight against British control of India. This commonality of experiences and interests led the Yugoslav, Egyptian, and Indian leaders to work more closely together during the late 1950s.

The idea of a meeting of non-aligned states crystallized during 1960. That year, sixteen African nations had achieved independence, bringing United Nations membership up to 100, of which more than two-thirds were from either Asia, Africa, or Latin America. Many of these nations felt isolated by the East-West conflicts, and wished instead to focus on problems that they considered more immediately relevant to their situation, such as economic development and ethnic strife. They wanted a forum to discuss issues that were outside the Soviet-American struggle for influence.

Many of them also considered the cold war a danger to the entire globe. In 1960, cold war tensions heated up, with the downing of an American U-2 spy plane over the Soviet Union, and the collapse of a planned summit between the Soviet Union and the United States. Since both superpowers had atomic weapons, any confrontation had the potential of destroying the world.

The time seemed to be ripe for creating a third force in international politics, one which would help to defuse East-West animosities. In 1961, Tito, Nasser, and Nehru organized a September summit at Belgrade.

Twenty-five nations attended the first Non-Aligned Conference at Belgrade. The conference's agenda was directed toward defusing cold war tensions. The participants called upon the United States and the Soviet Union to suspend their "war preparations" and to initiate communications in order to avoid future conflict. The conference also criticized colonialism, called for an end to nuclear testing, and asked all nations to work toward general disarmament.

Non-aligned conferences were held at regular intervals thereafter, such as in Cairo in 1964, Lusaka in 1970, Algiers in 1973, Colombo in 1976, and Havana in 1979, but they found it difficult to achieve more than general calls for an end to cold war polarization. There were too many differences in policy among the many non-aligned nations. The Arab states were often focused on the issue of Israel, while Africa was usually reluctant to condemn the West and thereby risk the aid payments upon which their countries depended. Cuba, which hardly qualified as non-aligned, tried to push the movement in an anti-American direction but was opposed by Yugoslavia and others. The result was no result. The non-aligned movement lacked sufficient unity and coherence to have a substantial effect on international politics.

The departure of the non-aligned old guard also lessened the impact of the movement. With the death of Nehru in 1964, and Nasser in 1970, the non-aligned movement lost two of its greatest leaders. Tito survived until 1980, but was eclipsed by younger leaders, like Fidel Castro, who continued to push the non-aligned movement in anti-Western directions. While Castro had some rhetorical successes, he and the other new-generation leaders lacked the moral stature and vision of their predecessors. The non-aligned movement gradually lost its focus and sense of purpose.

Nevertheless, non-alignment was not a complete failure. If nothing specific was achieved, the non-aligned movement was still able to articulate a vague but real alternative to the cold war ideologies of the United States and the Soviet Union. It argued for a world in which nations could cooperate and coexist without being drawn into ideological wars. If many non-aligned nations failed to live up to this goal, it did not diminish their success in charting a new course from that being put forward by the rich northern states.

The non-aligned movement survived the end of the cold war; a twelfth conference was held in New Delhi in 1997. More than 100 nations attended.

American Attitudes

America and its allies tended to see the non-aligned movement as a pro-Soviet political movement. In the American view, to be neutral in the struggle against the Soviet Union was to be supporting Soviet expansionism. That Fidel Castro, Cuba's Communist dictator, was a leader in the non-aligned movement also helped to convince American leaders of the movement's leftist leanings. Furthermore, the nations of the non-aligned movement attacked Western imperialism more often than they criticized Communist abuses. Although this was because most non-aligned nations had once been colonies of one or another Western power, and remained suspicious of the intentions their former conquerors might still harbor, the United States, whose historical memory was quite short, often discounted the legitimacy of their fears.

The U.S. view of the non-aligned movement had some basis in fact. Many of its leaders were Communists (Castro and Tito) or Communist sympathizers (Nasser, Ghana's Kwame Nkrumah, and Nehru). But being a Communist was not the same as being an ally of the Soviet Union; America's failure to realize this subtle difference would handicap its foreign policy throughout the cold war. Not all nations that criticized Western imperialism were dupes of the Soviets.

Communist Responses

The Communist states, particularly China, were, at first, somewhat better at appealing to the non-aligned movement. China had sent Zhou Enlai to the Bandung conference and, by waving the banner of its own anti-colonialist history, managed to convince some of the participants that China could be a useful friend to the third world. China and the Soviet Union were aided in their overtures to the non-aligned world by the leftist tradition in which many of the non-aligned had spent their political adolescence. For leaders such as Nkrumah, who had strong socialist leanings, the Communist world could be appealing.

Openness toward the Communist bloc was damaged by the 1962 border war between India and China, as well as by the Soviet Union's initial refusal to halt nuclear testing, as called for by the first Non-Aligned Conference. It soon became clear to all but the most devoted admirers of the Soviets—as Cuba's Castro was obliged to be—that the Soviet Union was only interested in the non-aligned movement if it would help in advancing its own superpower agenda.

Although Castro managed to achieve some success in leading the non-aligned movement in an anti-Western direction, particularly after the 1979 meeting in Havana, the general trend of the non-aligned states was to move away from a harsh anti-Western position. The fall of the Soviet Union only accelerated this tendency.

Analysis

The non-aligned movement's goals were many: to protest against the polarization of the world, to lessen the tensions that the cold war had created, and to improve the economic status of the less-developed world. Its failure was due as much to the difficulty of the problems which it hoped to address as it was to the inherent conflicts and cross-currents within the movement. And as the cold war faded, the non-aligned movement became increasingly irrelevant. In the 1960s and 1970s the Soviet Union and the United States had felt obliged to seek the support of the countries of the non-aligned bloc, but with the cold war gone, the industrialized world no longer had to be concerned about third-world issues.

Still, the non-aligned movement had helped to create the image of the third world, in the minds of the other two worlds, as well as in its own. With the United Nations as its forum, the non-aligned movement became an alternate voice to that of the two competing alliance systems.

The non-aligned movement was also the parent of a host of other Asian, African, and Latin American regional and international organizations; OPEC, the OAU, and the G-15 all owe their birth, in part, to the same currents that created the non-aligned movement.

Carl Skutsch

See also: Organization of African Unity (OAU); United Nations.

Bibliography

David, Steven. *Choosing Sides: Alignment and Realignment in the Third World.* Baltimore: Johns Hopkins University Press, 1991.

Jackson, Richard L. *The Non-Aligned, the UN, and the Superpowers.* New York: Praeger, 1983.

Willetts, Peter. *The Non-Aligned Movement.* East Brunswick, NJ: Nichols, 1978.

China: U.S. Recognition

Historical Background

The defeat of Chiang Kai-shek's Nationalist forces on mainland China by the Chinese Communists in 1949 presented the United States with a difficult foreign policy problem. Rather than surrender, Chiang and his followers reassembled on Taiwan (Formosa), the Pescadores, and a number of islands off the coast of China. Despite his defeat, he continued to claim that his government was the legitimate government for all of China, and he promised to return to the mainland sometime in the future. At that time, there existed two governments claiming legitimacy. Ordinarily this situation would not create much of a problem, but Chiang's defeat occurred just as the cold war was heating up and the Korean War was about to begin. After the official establishment of the People's Republic of China (PRC) on October 1, 1949, some governments extended diplomatic recognition to the new government in Beijing, others simply withheld recognition, and some, including the United States, continued to recognize the government of Chiang Kai-shek. By the end of 1950, only twenty-seven nations extended diplomatic recognition to the Beijing regime.

President Truman's Dilemma

President Harry Truman also had to contend with the fact that some critics of his administration thought his policies helped bring about the communist victory in China. The bitter partisan criticism directed at President Truman made him aware that he would pay a heavy political price for extending diplomatic relations to the Beijing regime. Truman was aware that the Nationalist government controlled a powerful lobby in Washington that was able to influence the Congress.

In addition to the internal political problems President Truman had to cope with, Mao's victory created a Sino-Soviet bloc that helped make communism a more potent force in world politics. Mao's victory gave the Communists a territorial base in China that could be used to help spread communism throughout Asia. Several months after his victory, Mao traveled to Moscow, and on February 14, 1950, the two countries signed a thirty-year treaty of friendship, alliance, and mutual assistance.

The question of the United States extending diplomatic recognition to the Beijing regime was resolved with the outbreak of the Korean War in June 1950. On June 27, President Truman ordered the Seventh Fleet to patrol the Taiwan Strait to prevent clashes between Taiwan and the mainland. His actions in effect neutralized Taiwan and involved the United States in China's civil war. The consequences of that action remained significant long after the United States and China normalized their relations in January 1979. When China's troops crossed the Yalu River in October 1950 to help defend North Korea, the question of extending diplomatic recognition became moot. China's entry into the Korean War meant that its military forces were engaged in combat against the forces fighting under the authority of the United Nations.

Other actions by the Truman administration contributed to the deterioration of Sino-American relations. In April 1951, the United States resumed military aid to the Nationalist government on Taiwan. In September, a conference convened in San Francisco for the signing of a peace treaty with Japan. China was not invited to attend. After completing the peace treaty, the United States and Japan signed a mutual defense treaty designed to help contain the People's Republic of China. The United States also negotiated the ANZUS treaty with Australia and New Zealand in 1951.

The Korean War was a major issue in the 1952 presidential campaign. Republicans charged the Truman administration with being responsible for the outbreak of the conflict and of being unable to end it. On October 24, 1952, General Dwight Eisenhower pledged that if he won the election he would travel to Korea to explore the best way to bring an end to the conflict. His pledge helped him win the election. He made the trip in December.

President Eisenhower

In his first State of the Union message President Eisenhower rescinded President Truman's order issued in June 1950 preventing the Nationalist forces on Taiwan from attacking the mainland. The media referred to this policy as the "unleashing of Chiang Kai-shek." The policy gave the impression that the United States would support Chiang Kai-shek's attacks on the mainland. The Chinese Communist forces launched an offensive in Korea in May 1953, after a preliminary agreement to end the war. President Eisenhower let the leaders in Beijing know that if the offensive continued he would use nuclear weapons to end the war.

A Korean armistice was signed in July 1953, but Sino-American relations did not improve. Beijing provided substantial military assistance to the Vietminh communist forces attempting to oust the French in Vietnam. When the first Indochina War ended in July 1954 by partitioning Vietnam along the seventeenth parallel, the mainland government then turned its attention to Formosa and the offshore islands. This resulted in another Sino-American crisis.

In 1954, the Eisenhower administration decided to help Chiang Kai-shek's government defend Quemoy and Matsu, two islands close to the mainland. The American commitment to aid Chiang Kai-shek was made more credible because of the strengthening of the American military presence in the region. In December 1954, the United States and the Republic of China signed a mutual defense treaty. In January 1955, Congress approved the Formosa Resolution. It authorized the president to take whatever steps he thought necessary to protect Formosa and, if need be, the offshore islands as well.

In 1958, China again tried to win control of the offshore islands and this created another crisis. The Eisenhower administration considered using nuclear weapons if a war did break out. At a news conference in November 1958, President Eisenhower denounced China for its refusal to provide the United States with information about Americans unaccounted for during the Korean War. China did nothing to help resolve this sensitive issue.

China's officials opposed a number of policies initiated by the Eisenhower administration. In addition to the defense treaty signed with the People's Republic of China in 1954, the United States also signed a defense treaty with South Korea in August 1953 and negotiated the Southeast Asia Treaty Organization (SEATO) in 1954. The United States continued to take the lead in keeping the Beijing regime out of the United Nations.

Throughout his administration, President Eisenhower and Secretary of State John Foster Dulles repeatedly voiced their opposition to recognizing the Beijing regime. In August 1958, the Department of State issued a memorandum explaining the reasons for their opposition. Neither Eisenhower nor Dulles thought that recognition would benefit the United States. Indeed, they believed that recognition would be detrimental to America's national interests because it might give communism greater legitimacy and thereby help it spread throughout Asia. Secretary of State Dulles often expressed the opinion that the Beijing government was illegitimate, unrepresentative of the Chinese people, and did not respect international law. Taiwan was an important ally in helping to contain communism in Asia and any policy that weakened Taiwan could have a detrimental impact on the containment effort.

Presidents Kennedy and Johnson

In their 1960 presidential debates, Richard Nixon and John F. Kennedy expressed some differences regarding the offshore islands of Quemoy and Matsu. Kennedy did not think the United States should risk war with China because of the two islands. Nixon, however, said they were important not because of their intrinsic value but because of their relationship to Taiwan. Neither candidate proposed recognizing the Beijing regime. After Kennedy's inauguration, he had to deal with a number of complex issues, including the Berlin crisis. The question of recognizing China was not an immediate concern nor was he optimistic that Sino-American relations would soon improve.

In June 1961, at a news conference in Paris, he expressed doubt that Sino-American differences would be resolved. Interestingly, President Kennedy and Soviet Premier Nikita Khrushchev had similar views regarding China. In July, Khrushchev sent a letter to Communist party leaders around the world accusing China of pursuing aggressive policies particularly in relation to Taiwan. A few weeks later, the U.S. Senate adopted a resolution recommending that the United States not recognize the Beijing government or allow it to enter the United Nations. In August 1961, the House of Representatives approved the same resolution.

Secretary of State Dean Rusk opposed any change in U.S. policy. He favored containing and isolating China. Rusk was Assistant Secretary of State for Far Eastern Asian Affairs during the Truman administration, and he played a major role in shaping America's policies toward Korea and the People's Republic of China. He consistently opposed extending diplomatic recognition to the Beijing regime. His views regarding China were very similar to those of former Secretary of State Dulles.

As the Sino-Soviet ideological conflict escalated, Moscow often accused China of pursuing aggressive policies that threatened nuclear war. The one thing the United States and the Soviet Union had in common was opposition to Beijing. Both the United States and the Soviet Union held China responsible for the October 1962 Sino-Indian War. In July 1963, the United States and the Soviet Union signed the nuclear test ban treaty; China called it a "big fraud" and refused to sign it. In October 1964, China tested its first nuclear device. In May 1965, a second nuclear device was tested, and in June 1967, China detonated its first hydrogen bomb.

After President Kennedy's death, the United States massively intervened in Vietnam and the hostility between the United States and the People's Republic of China continued. In a speech in February 1964, Secretary of State Rusk said he did not think that Sino-American relations would soon improve. He accused China of supporting subversive movements throughout the world and taking a more militant line in promoting communism than did the Soviet Union. He criticized China's refusal to renounce the use of force in the Taiwan Strait. He said China was responsible for violating the 1954 Geneva Indochina agreements and the 1962 Geneva accords on Laos. In April 1965, President Lyndon Johnson, in a speech at Johns Hopkins University, accused China of promoting violence throughout the world. He did not think recognizing the Beijing regime would help in resolving international disputes.

In March 1966, Rusk pointed out that the United States had many contacts with the People's Republic of China. Between 1955 and 1966, there were 129 meetings between American and Chinese diplomats in Warsaw and Geneva, but the talks failed to yield positive results. To the extent that the United States became more deeply involved in the Indochina conflict, and because of Beijing's support for Hanoi's policies, there were few opportunities and little desire to improve Sino-American relations.

President Nixon

About a year before the 1968 presidential election, Richard Nixon, in an article for *Foreign Affairs,* suggested that improved Sino-American relations could come about in the future. After his election, he hoped that China, and perhaps the Soviet Union, could contribute to peace and stability by helping to end the Vietnam War. Nixon's approach to changing America's policies was gradual, nuanced, and initially did not require any overt response on the part of the People's Republic of China.

Nixon's most important problem when he became president was ending the Vietnam War or, at a minimum, withdrawing American military forces as quickly as possible without endangering America's prestige. During his presidential campaign, he told the American people, "New leadership will end the war and win the peace in the Pacific." Unlike his predecessor, Nixon wanted to engage Moscow and Beijing in the peace process.

Nixon knew the Soviet Union would not welcome improved Sino-American relations, and he was aware of domestic political opposition to any change in American policies. Non-recognition of mainland China had been in place since 1949.

Nixon had to deal with a number of problems in attempting to improve Sino-American relations. One was the fact that the

United States continued to recognize the government in Taipei as the official government for all of China. As a logical corollary of this policy, the United States took the lead in keeping the Beijing government out of the United Nations.

Despite the obstacles, President Nixon wanted a change in policy and there were a number of reasons for this. In addition to its territorial size, China was developing a formidable nuclear arsenal and contained one-third of the world's population. Nixon wanted the United States to more effectively exploit Sino-Soviet conflict; however, to accomplish this, the United States needed to improve relations with China. In the triangular relationship involving China, the Soviet Union, and the United States, Washington would benefit the most if it had better relations with the two communist nations than they had with each other. That is the essence of triangular diplomacy.

The idea of bringing about a fundamental change in the Sino-American relationship met with a good deal of opposition from various groups. Bureaucrats will often resist change because they are more comfortable with consistency rather than innovation. When a policy has been in place for more than twenty years, it develops a constituency with a stake in the status quo.

Opposition also came from individuals who thought that China was a greater threat to the United States than was the Soviet Union. In 1965, China's defense minister, Lin Biao, wrote an article titled "Long Live the Victory of the People's War." In it, he presented ideas developed by Mao Zedong for the eventual victory of the communist nations over the West. Lin said the ideas of Mao were applicable to Vietnam and would eventually lead to America's defeat there. In retrospect, most of his ideas seem rather na-

ive; however, at the time, some American officials, such as then Secretary of Defense Robert McNamara, compared the article to *Mein Kampf* and Mao Zedong to Adolf Hitler. There was also the fact that Beijing provided the government in Hanoi with various types of assistance during the Vietnam War. At the time, American officials did not have much information on the growing rift between Hanoi and Beijing.

Finally, in 1966, Mao Zedong began the Cultural Revolution that kept China in turmoil for several years. During this time, China had few diplomatic contacts with other nations and was hostile to both superpowers. The Cultural Revolution seemed to confirm that China was not a responsible member of the international community.

Ironically, some opposition to the recognition of the Beijing regime came from those who thought the Soviet Union was the major threat to the United States and, therefore, nothing should be done that would destabilize the Soviet-American relationship. They opposed recognizing China because of its potential detrimental impact on arms control agreements between the superpowers. Later, Cyrus Vance, secretary of state under President Jimmy Carter, wanted to defer extending diplomatic recognition to the Beijing regime until negotiations for the SALT II treaty were completed. He opposed those policies that he thought would derail the SALT process.

Opposition also came from supporters of the Taiwan government. A pillar of China's foreign policy was the refusal to allow governments to extend diplomatic recognition to both Taipei and Beijing. Mao Zedong insisted that countries sever their ties to Taipei if they wanted to extend diplomatic recognition to the PRC. If Taiwan was an ally and China an adversary, switching allegiance made no sense. To improve Sino-American relations at the expense of the government in Taipei was seen as a betrayal of a loyal ally.

Finally, there were those who did not think the benefits of extending recognition to the Beijing regime outweighed the costs. Many nations had followed the American lead in refusing to recognize the Beijing government and had voted with the United States to keep the Beijing government out of the United Nations. The United States could not extend diplomatic recognition to Beijing and also keep it out of the United Nations.

Nixon decided that efforts to improve relations with China should be undertaken with little fanfare. He did not want the opponents of change to coalesce and sabotage his efforts. A degree of secrecy, he thought, was essential for success.

President Nixon's approach to changing America's policy vis-à-vis China was gradual and subtle. Small changes were made over a period of time. Nixon did not know how China would react to his initiatives. There was not much evidence that the leaders in Beijing were interested in better relations. His overtures could be rebuffed with possibly dire political consequences both at home and abroad.

The process of deciding how to normalize relations with China began in 1969 when President Nixon ordered a review of Sino-American relations to determine if a more constructive relationship was possible. He then initiated a number of policies as a signal to Beijing that America was interested in better relations. In November 1969, he ordered the Seventh Fleet to cease patrolling the Taiwan Strait. President Truman had ordered the patrols after the outbreak of the Korean War in 1950 to prevent the mainland government from attacking Taiwan. In April 1971,

Nixon, meeting with the American Society of Newspaper Editors, said he would like to visit China someday. He knew China's officials would monitor and evaluate his comments. He told a number of foreign leaders, including President Charles de Gaulle of France and Pakistan's president Yahya Khan, that the United States was interested in better relations with China. In June 1971, the United States ended its twenty-one-year embargo on trade with China. Beijing's receptiveness to these initiatives was also influenced by policy changes made by Nixon that were not directed at China yet had a significant impact on Sino-American relations.

One major change occurred in June 1969. President Nixon announced that 25,000 American troops would leave Vietnam. He promised that further withdrawals would occur. He was committed to the policy of "Vietnamization." Even if the war did not end, American military personnel would eventually be completely withdrawn. This was a dramatic departure from previous policies. In the 1960s, President Kennedy and, to a much greater extent, President Johnson justified America's intervention in Vietnam in part as a means to contain China. One day before Nixon's announcement of the troop withdrawal, Soviet party leader Leonid Brezhnev, at a meeting of Communist parties from around the world, called for the creation of an Asian Collective Security Pact. Its purpose was to contain China. The contrast between the policies of Nixon and Brezhnev was not lost on the leaders of China. The American military presence in Asia was declining; the Soviet military presence was increasing.

In July 1969, President Nixon briefed reporters on the Island of Guam. He articulated what came to be known as the Nixon

Doctrine. The importance of the doctrine for Sino-American relations was that the United States would no longer provide the manpower to fight wars in Asia. For the United States, there would be no more Vietnams.

When Nixon took office, a steady stream of editorials in China's publications depicted him as a reactionary committed to pursuing aggressive foreign policies. There were, however, factors that helped make China more receptive to Nixon's initiatives, such as the growing military might of the Soviet Union and the large Soviet military presence on the Sino-Soviet border. In 1969, there were several hundred military incidents along the border, some potentially very serious. In a clash along the Ussuri River in March, both sides suffered casualties. This was followed by anti-Soviet demonstrations in Beijing and anti-Chinese demonstrations in Moscow. Throughout the 1960s, the polemics in the Sino-Soviet conflict became more acerbic and more personal. China accused Brezhnev of pursuing policies similar to those of Adolf Hitler. The Russians said the same thing about Mao Zedong. In 1969, statements by both the Chinese and Soviet governments suggested the possibility of large-scale conflict between the two. American officials did not discount the possibility of a Sino-Soviet war.

Other factors contributing to the Sino-Soviet dispute included the Soviet invasion of Czechoslovakia in 1968 and the formulation of the Brezhnev Doctrine. A broad reading of the doctrine, also known as the doctrine of limited sovereignty, would imply that the Soviet Union had the right to intervene militarily in China if it was deviating from Marxist-Leninist thought and practices. In response, China accused the Soviet Union of invading Czechoslovakia to maintain a co-

lonial empire supported by hegemonic policies. The word "hegemony" became a key word in the Sino-Soviet polemical clashes. China used it as code word for Soviet imperialism. Whenever China signed an agreement with another government, the leaders in Beijing tried to get an anti-hegemony clause in the agreement.

The leaders in Beijing were also apprehensive because of Soviet efforts to isolate and encircle China. In March 1966, the Soviets distributed a letter to Communist parties in Eastern Europe accusing China of attempting to start a war between the United States and the Soviet Union to weaken both nations. The Soviets accused China of splitting the world communist movement and revising Marxist-Leninist doctrines. In the communist world, the charge of revisionism was a very serious one. In January 1966, the Soviet Union signed a treaty with the People's Republic of Mongolia that permitted the stationing of Soviet military forces in Mongolia. The Sino-Mongolian border was about 2,500 miles long. In 1966, some experts, including China's foreign minister, Chen Yi, believed there were more Soviet troops along China's border than in Eastern Europe. Finally, in August 1971, India and the Soviet Union signed a treaty of peace, friendship, and cooperation. At the time, both countries were involved in conflicts with China.

The government in Beijing also took steps to improve Sino-American relations, steps that did not require any American response. In 1969 and 1970, China released several Americans who had been in jail in China. In April 1971, Beijing invited an American table tennis team to tour China; American newsmen were allowed to cover the team's activities. On July 9, 1971, one of the most dramatic events in the cold war era occurred.

Henry Kissinger, the Assistant for National Security Affairs, made a secret trip to China. He accepted, on behalf of President Nixon, an invitation to visit China. Nixon made the journey in February 1972.

Nixon Goes to China

A significant aspect of the 1972 Beijing summit was that President Nixon decided to go to China before going to meet the Soviet leaders in Moscow. The choice was dictated by Soviet procrastination in deciding a date for a Brezhnev–Nixon meeting. The president had hoped to meet with Brezhnev sometime in 1970. The Soviets refused to set a date. They thought they could extract concessions from Nixon regarding the Western presence in Berlin, the proposed SALT I treaty, and the convening of a European security conference. The Soviets were unaware of the steps taken to arrange a Nixon–Mao meeting. When the trip to Beijing was announced, the Soviets proposed that Nixon visit the Soviet Union first. He declined the offer.

President Nixon arrived in China on February 21, 1972. Shortly after his arrival, he was summoned to meet with Mao Zedong. They talked for more than an hour discussing Sino-American issues. The meeting was cordial and the cordiality made it evident that improved relations between the two countries was taking place. Unlike some other summits, the important aspect about the meeting in Beijing was that specific issues were not as consequential as the opportunity for American and Chinese leaders to deal with each other directly for the first time. During the summit, it became evident that China viewed the Soviet Union as an aggressive imperial power. The very fact that

Nixon was in Beijing underscored China's fear.

To ensure the success of the summit, the leaders in Beijing minimized the importance of Taiwan but made no concessions regarding the future of the island. It did, however, prove to be a contentious issue in putting together the final communiqué. The two sides had approximately twenty hours of talks trying to construct an acceptable communiqué. They succeeded on February 27.

The Shanghai communiqué was an unusually important document for a number of reasons. First, the president's visit was a great historic event. Governments around the world would carefully study the communiqué. Second, the communiqué was intended to give the foreign policy bureaucracies in Beijing and Washington a new sense of direction. Although there had been diplomatic contacts between the two countries, most of them were *pro forma* and failed to yield positive results. Finally, the communiqué was a difficult document to assemble because the United States still recognized the government on Taiwan as the "official" government of China and this was a major source of friction between Washington and Beijing.

The two sides departed from conventional diplomatic procedure in that they decided to delineate their disagreements in the document, particularly in relation to Japan, Korea, Indochina, and, the most contentious issue of all, Taiwan. Premier Zhou Enlai insisted upon listing the differences. He did not want to issue a banal document full of generalizations. The American part of the communiqué emphasized the need to end the Vietnam War on the basis of self-determination. President Nixon also reaffirmed American support for South Korea and Japan.

China's part of the communiqué expressed

support for North Vietnam and the communist insurgencies in Laos and Cambodia. China supported North Korean proposals for unifying the country and opposed the rearmament of Japan. Both sides agreed that Taiwan was a major obstacle to overcome if they were to establish diplomatic relations. They also agreed that neither power should seek "hegemony" in the Asia-Pacific region and both would oppose any nation seeking to do so.

The United States repeated what was acceptable to both Chinese governments—namely, that there was only one China, and Taiwan was a part of it. President Nixon indicated his desire to reduce the American military presence on Taiwan, but the reduction, he said, would depend on the degree of tension in the area. At the time, the American Mutual Defense Treaty with Taiwan was still in force. The net effect of the Shanghai communiqué was that despite major Sino-American differences vis-à-vis Taiwan, both sides demonstrated their determination to improve relations.

Henry Kissinger attributed the success of the summit to the fact that China and the United States were finally dealing with each other based on balance-of-power politics and geopolitical realities rather than ideological rivalry.

The Taipei government was discouraged and concerned about the new direction of American policy, but the United States continued to formally recognize the government in Taipei, not Beijing. Nevertheless, Taiwan suffered a major setback. In October 1971, the United Nations General Assembly voted to recognize the Beijing regime as the official government of China; Taiwan was expelled. The United States voted to seat the Beijing government but voted against the expulsion of Taiwan.

The Russians complained that the United States began to improve relations with China only when Sino-Soviet differences had become acute. This led the Soviets to question the motives behind America's policy of rapprochement, but they were careful not to do anything that would cause Nixon to cancel his proposed trip to Moscow in May 1972.

After Nixon's re-election in 1972, he had to deal with the Watergate crisis. This occupied him until his resignation in August 1974. When President Gerald Ford succeeded Nixon, normalizing relations with the People's Republic of China was not high on his agenda. Ford did not want to antagonize the conservatives in the Republican party, many of whom opposed Nixon's policies vis-à-vis China.

President Carter

In the 1976 presidential campaign, Jimmy Carter supported normalizing relations with the People's Republic of China, but he also wanted to improve relations with the Soviet Union. He decided to make human rights the centerpiece of American foreign policy, and this decision complicated Soviet-American relations. The combination of emphasizing human rights and seeking to normalize relations with the People's Republic of China seemed, from the point of view of Moscow, to be deliberately provocative.

A major dispute erupted within the Carter administration between Secretary of State Vance and National Security Advisor Brzezinski. Vance favored a policy of "evenhandedness," in which the two communist nations would be treated in the same way. Zbigniew Brzezinski favored a policy of "balance," which meant giving the Beijing government preferential treatment. President

Carter vacillated between the two until the Soviet Union invaded Afghanistan in 1979. He then sided with Brzezinski. In April 1980, Vance resigned.

Although the Soviet Union feared the Sino-American rapprochement, Moscow gave no indication it was willing to moderate its policies to improve relations with the United States. The Soviets intervened in Angola in 1975. They also intervened in Ethiopia and Yemen. The 1970s was a decade of Soviet expansionism. Soviet leaders believed that the correlation of forces had shifted in their favor at a time when the United States was still suffering from the Vietnam trauma.

To exacerbate matters, the Soviets were often in violation of the human rights provisions of the 1975 Helsinki Final Act. Some dissidents were arrested because they were monitoring Soviet compliance with the Final Act. When it became apparent that President Carter would continue to speak out about human rights abuses, dissidents arrested in the Soviet Union were given longer jail terms than they would have received in the past. In 1977, the Soviet Union refused to allow American Ambassador Malcolm Toon to deliver a July 4 address to the Soviet people. The Soviets canceled his talk because of references to human rights. That same year, the Soviet Union began deploying SS-20 missiles in Europe. The SS-20 was an intermediate-range mobile missile capable of launching three nuclear warheads. The deployment threatened the existing balance of power in Europe and contributed to a deterioration in the Soviet-American relationship. Given the threatening nature of Soviet policies, President Carter decided to move forward in normalizing relations with China.

A number of issues needed to be resolved but none were more difficult than the question of Taiwan. What kind of contacts could the United States continue to have with the Taipei government after extending diplomatic ties to Beijing? What was to be done with the 1954 mutual security treaty? Could the United States continue to provide military arms and equipment to Taiwan?

An Agreement Is Reached

To normalize relations, President Carter had to meet China's demands without appearing to abandon Taiwan. He did not want to alienate members of Congress who supported the Taiwan government.

On May 20, 1978, Brzezinski arrived in Beijing to further the normalization process. He was authorized to agree to three demands made by China. The United States would terminate diplomatic relations with Taiwan, would withdraw all troops from the island, and would abrogate the 1954 mutual security treaty. The United States also had demands. It wanted to maintain unofficial relations with and continue selling military equipment to Taiwan, and it did not want the Beijing government to contradict statements made by the American government regarding the peaceful resolution of the Taiwan issue.

The American mutual security treaty with Taiwan proved to be a contentious issue. The United States was willing to abrogate the treaty but wanted to do so in a legitimate way. Article X of the treaty permitted each signatory to abrogate the treaty after giving a one-year notice. In 1950, the Soviet Union and China signed a thirty-year treaty that contained a similar clause. In 1979, the Beijing government announced that the treaty would lapse in 1980. The United States seized upon this, and said that Washington wanted to end the treaty with Taiwan in the same way. The American position prevailed. The one issue that was deferred but not resolved was that of supplying Taiwan with military equipment once the mutual security treaty was terminated. China wanted the sales ended, but President Carter knew that if he agreed he would have difficult problems with Congress. The issue remained contentious in the Sino-American relationship long after the treaty with Taiwan was abrogated.

On December 5, 1978, President Carter announced that the United States and the People's Republic of China would establish diplomatic relations on January 1, 1979. The two governments also agreed that China's vice premier Deng Xiaoping would visit the United States. Thus ended a thirty-year period during which time Washington recognized the Nationalist government as the only legitimate government of China.

Kenneth L. Hill

See also: China: Chinese Civil War, 1927–1949; China in the United Nations—Beijing or Taipei?

Bibliography

Broadwater, Jeff. *Eisenhower and the Anti-Communist Crusade.* Chapel Hill: University of North Carolina Press, 1992.

Brzezinski, Zbigniew. *Power and Principle: Memoirs of the National Security Advisor.* New York: Farrar, Straus, Giroux, 1983.

Carter, Jimmy. *Keeping Faith: Memoirs of a President.* New York: Bantam Books, 1982.

Dulles, Foster R. *American Policy Towards Communist China, 1949-1969.* New York: Crowell, 1972.

Geyelin, Philip. *Lyndon B. Johnson and the World.* New York: Praeger, 1966.

Hungdah, Chiu, ed. *China and the Taiwan Issue.* New York: Praeger, 1979.

Kissinger, Henry. *White House Years.* Boston: Little Brown, 1979.

Melanson, Richard. *Reevaluating Eisenhower. American Foreign Policy in the 1950s.* Urbana: University of Illinois Press, 1987.

Nixon, Richard. *RN: The Memoirs of Richard Nixon.* New York: Grosset and Dunlap, 1978.

Oksenberg, Michel. *China and America: Past and Future.* New York: Foreign Policy Association, 1977.

Whiting, Allen. *China and the United States: What Next?* New York: Foreign Policy Association, 1976.

China in the United Nations— Beijing or Taipei?

United Nations Membership

Although the architects of the United Nations Charter favored universal membership, the ideal was not easy to achieve. One major problem was that after 1949 two governments claimed to be the legitimate government for all of China.

On October 1, 1949, the People's Republic of China (PRC) was formally inaugurated after the Communists succeeded in defeating the Nationalist forces led by Chiang Kai-shek. Rather than surrender, Chiang and his troops fled to Taiwan, the Pescadores, and a number of offshore islands. Chiang vowed to continue the struggle to defeat the communists and return to the mainland. Regrouping on Taiwan enabled Chiang and his forces to claim that his government remained the legal government for all of China. Chiang's government continued to represent China at the United Nations. Although the literature on

this subject often referred to the question of whether China should be "admitted" to the United Nations, the question was one of representation, not membership. Delegates of the Nationalist government attended the June 1945 San Francisco conference that approved the United Nations Charter. China, or more precisely, the Republic of China, along with France, Great Britain, the Soviet Union, and the United States were charter members of the United Nations and permanent members of the Security Council, each with the right of veto.

The United States and the Republic of China cooperated to defeat Japan in World War II but differences developed when China's civil war resumed in 1945. President Harry Truman sent General George C. Marshall to China in December 1945 to mediate the conflict between the Nationalists and the Communists but his mission failed. The Chinese Communist victory in 1949 and the establishment of the People's Republic of China dramatically changed the Sino-American relationship. The defeat of Chiang Kai-shek's Nationalist forces, combined with growing Soviet-American differences, had a significant impact on politics in America.

Sino-American Differences

The problem of deciding which government should represent China in the United Nations was complicated because of Beijing's policies after 1949, American domestic politics, the Korean War, the Vietnam War, and cold war disagreements between the super-powers.

The United States and China did a number of things after 1949 that soured Sino-American relations. There was, however, one problem that predated 1949. The United States and the Republic of China were allies during World War II. Both were working to defeat Japan. To aid that effort, the United States provided Chiang Kai-shek with substantial military aid. The Communists, under the leadership of Mao Zedong, opposed anything that strengthened the Nationalists. When there is a civil war, intervention can never be neutral—one side or the other benefits.

In January 1950, China seized U.S. consular offices in Beijing. In response, the United States accused China of violating the 1901 and 1903 consular treaties. On January 14, 1950, all American consular personnel in China were withdrawn. In December 1950, the Beijing government ordered the seizure of all U.S. property and froze all U.S. bank deposits. China was retaliating for the economic sanctions imposed on it after the outbreak of the Korean War in June 1950. China's entry in the war in October 1950 foreclosed any possibility that the United States would extend diplomatic recognition to the Beijing regime or permit it to represent China in the United Nations.

The Korean War brought about a much closer relationship between the United States and the Taiwan government. They negotiated a mutual defense treaty in 1954 that made the United States a major player in the Chinese civil war. Consequently, the United States could not support expelling the Taiwan government from the United Nations. After 1949, the leaders in Beijing made it evident that they considered the United States to be their major adversary, and at least for a time, the Soviet Union was an ally. Their Marxist ideology and the support Chiang Kai-shek received from the United States shaped the perception of China's leaders.

Politics in America

America's domestic politics influenced Washington's determination to keep the Beijing government out of the United Nations. In particular, two events troubled many Americans. One was the Communist victory in China in 1949. China was an American ally during World War II, and President Franklin D. Roosevelt insisted that China should become a permanent member of the United Nations Security Council with the right of veto. The United States provided the forces of Chiang Kai-shek with considerable military aid during the war, and Americans volunteered to fight with China to help defeat Japan. When the Chinese Communists were victorious in 1949, despite massive American military assistance to the Nationalists, many Americans were shocked. They wanted an explanation of why their ally lost. The second event that troubled Americans was the successful test of an atomic bomb by the Soviet Union in 1959. This occurred several years sooner than expected. Some politicians thought both Mao's victory in China and the Soviet testing of an atomic weapon came about because of espionage activities sponsored by the Soviet Union. Accusations were made that individuals working in the State Department and other government agencies were either communists or sympathetic to communist causes.

In a Senate debate in January 1950, Robert Taft, a leading Republican, accused the Truman administration of pursuing policies intended to defeat Chiang Kai-shek. Republican Senator Kenneth Wherry made a similar accusation. Senator Taft subsequently accused the State Department of advocating "pro-communist" policies. In a speech in February 1950, Senator Joseph McCarthy claimed to have a list of 205 individuals that were members of the Communist party and continued to work for the State Department. He charged that the secretary of state knew about these individuals and their Communist party membership. Until he was censured by the Senate in December 1954, Senator McCarthy was one of the most powerful and most feared politicians in America. For a number of years after 1949, the Democrats were saddled with the charge that they "lost" China. The bitter partisan controversy between the Republicans and the Democrats made it difficult for the United States to extend diplomatic recognition to the government in Beijing. This nonrecognition was linked to the question of China's representation at the United Nations. For many Americans the two issues were linked.

Although politicians made many unsubstantiated allegations regarding espionage, there were, nevertheless, instances that gave the allegations some credibility. In January 1950, Alger Hiss, who worked for the State Department for fourteen years, was found guilty of perjury. He was accused of passing secrets to the Soviet Union but because the statute of limitations expired, he was not tried for espionage. In February 1950, Klaus Fuchs, a British scientist who worked on the development of the atomic bomb at Los Alamos, admitted he passed atomic secrets to the Soviet Union. In March 1951, Julius and Ethel Rosenberg were found guilty of passing atomic secrets to the Soviet Union. Both were executed. These events fueled the partisan controversy and helped win the Taiwan government a degree of support in the United

States. The controversy made normalizing relations with mainland China impossible.

The Korean War

The Korean War began in June 1950. In response to the North Korean attack, President Truman dispatched American military forces to help repel the aggression under the authority of the United Nations. The Security Council, because of the absence of the Soviet delegate, was able to approve collective security measures for the defense of South Korea. The conflict took on a new dimension when the United Nations forces crossed the thirty-eighth parallel in October 1950. The United States wanted to unify Korea. If the U.N. forces succeeded, American troops could be stationed along the Chinese border, a situation intolerable to the Beijing government.

In response to the U.N. decision to cross the thirty-eight parallel, China entered the conflict. It did so for basically the same reasons that influenced the American decision to intervene. The United States wanted to protect the independence of South Korea; China wanted to protect the independence of North Korea. A unified Korea under the leadership of Syngman Rhee, a fervent anti-communist, could be used as a base of support for attacks against China.

China's intervention in the Korean conflict meant that its forces were waging a war against the United Nations. Under these circumstances, many members of the world organization would not vote to accept the credentials of the Beijing delegation.

In January 1951, both houses of the U.S. Congress passed resolutions expressing opposition to seating the Beijing government in the United Nations. Further complicating matters was the decision of the United

Nations General Assembly in February 1951, largely as a result of American influence, to brand China an aggressor because of its entry into the Korean War.

At a news conference in November 1958, President Dwight Eisenhower denounced the Chinese for their refusal to provide the United States with information about Americans unaccounted for during the Korean War. China did nothing to help resolve this sensitive issue.

American officials in both the Kennedy and Johnson administrations were aware that China was supporting the efforts of North Vietnam to win control of South Vietnam. As the United States became more deeply involved in the conflict, Sino-American relations became more hostile. China, not the Soviet Union, was considered the major threat to the security interests of the United States.

Between the end of World War II and the outbreak of the Korean War, Soviet-American relations became increasingly hostile. The two nations differed over a great many issues, including the implementation of the Yalta and Potsdam agreements, the civil war in Greece, Soviet demands on Turkey, the unification of Germany, access to Berlin, Germany's war reparations, a Soviet role in the occupation of Japan and Italy, control of atomic weapons, Soviet territorial demands on Iran, the unification of Korea, the Marshall Plan, the Cominform, the 1948 Czech coup, and the return of German and Japanese prisoners of war. Although most of these conflicts had little if anything to do with the government in Beijing, they nevertheless influenced American policy vis-à-vis the PRC. American policy-makers assumed that as a member of the communist bloc, China supported whatever policies Moscow

advocated. Americans seemed to pay less attention to Soviet policies and more attention to the rhetoric of China's leaders, who consistently labeled the United States a paper tiger and minimized the significance of nuclear weapons.

Debate in the United Nations

In January 1950, the Soviet Union introduced a resolution to the United Nations Security Council to expel the Republic of China. The resolution was defeated by a six-to-three vote. India, the Soviet Union, and Yugoslavia supported the resolution; China, Cuba, Ecuador, Egypt, France, and the United States opposed it. In response to that action, Jacob Malik, the Soviet representative to the Security Council, announced that he would attend no more meetings until the representatives of the Republic of China were expelled.

In March 1950, Secretary General Trygve Lie tried to formulate a compromise proposal regarding China's representation that would end the Soviet boycott. He said a distinction should be made between diplomatic recognition between two countries and representation in the United Nations. He saw no reason why nations could not cooperate with each other in the United Nations despite the fact that they had no formal relations outside the U.N. Israel was admitted to the world body but failed to secure diplomatic recognition by the Arab nations. Lie's efforts ended with the outbreak of the Korean War.

Supporters of the Beijing regime made a number of arguments to back their position. One was that the United Nations could not be considered a universal organization if a country with a population of 700 million, a quarter of the world's population at the time, was not represented. Some delegations believed that the Beijing government was discriminated against because of its political system and friendship with the Soviet Union. For some proponents, a more compelling argument for having the Beijing regime in the United Nations was that China was acquiring a nuclear arsenal. In October 1964, China successfully tested its first atomic device. In May 1965, a second device was tested. In 1967, China tested a hydrogen bomb. At about the same time that China was developing its nuclear arsenal there was a growing international recognition that the control of nuclear weapons required the cooperation of all the nuclear powers, including the PRC. In November 1965, the United Nations General Assembly approved a resolution calling for a conference on disarmament. The Beijing government said it would not cooperate with the United Nations as long as the Taiwan government continued to represent China.

In 1966, an article in the *People's Daily* stated that China would not sign a nuclear non-proliferation treaty. The article accused the United States and the Soviet Union of using the United Nations to prevent countries other than the superpowers from acquiring nuclear weapons. China's refusal to cooperate with the United Nations strengthened the conviction of those nations that believed Beijing's presence in the world organization was essential if international problems were to be successfully addressed.

From 1950 to 1961, the United States succeeded in keeping the issue of China's representation off the agenda of the General Assembly. This "moratorium" ended in December 1961, and the issue was again debated. Despite this setback, the United States scored another victory. The General Assembly rejected a Soviet proposal for seating the Beijing regime. The Assembly then approved an American-supported resolution stating that China's representation was an important question requiring a two-thirds vote for approval rather than just a simple majority.

Support for the seating of the Beijing regime gathered strength as the membership of the United Nations increased beginning in December 1955. Most of the new members identified with the non-aligned movement rather than with either of the cold war blocs. When the question of China's representation first arose in the 1950s, the United States had an overwhelming influence on U.N. policies. That influence diminished as more Afro-Asian nations became members.

American officials continued their efforts to keep the Beijing regime out of the United Nations. Members of the Kennedy administration held China responsible for the 1962 Sino-Indian War. China was accused of violating the principles of the United Nations Charter by seeking to resolve its differences with India by resorting to military means. The conflict troubled Americans because India often championed causes favored by the Beijing regime.

Opponents of the Beijing regime cited China's activities in Tibet as another example of China's disregard for human rights. The question was not whether Tibet was independent or a part of China but rather the issue was freedom of religion. The anti-religious campaigns in Tibet seemed to be additional evidence that the Beijing regime was unwilling to abide by the principles in the United Nations Charter.

During the Eisenhower administration, Secretary of State John Foster Dulles often expressed the opinion that the Beijing government was illegitimate, unrepresentative of the Chinese people, and did not respect international law. The Eisenhower administration developed a close relationship with the government on Taiwan. That relationship made certain the mainland would not succeed in winning control of those areas ruled by Chiang Kai-shek. The United States could not protect Taiwan and recognize the Nationalist government as the legitimate government for all of China, and then vote to recognize the Beijing regime in the United Nations.

The Situation Starts to Change

After his election victory in 1968, President Richard Nixon was determined to fundamentally change American policies vis-à-vis China. As Sino-American relations improved, the arguments for keeping the Beijing regime out of the United Nations diminished. The United States could not very well begin the process of normalizing relations with Beijing and at the same time continue to oppose Beijing taking its seat in the United Nations.

In November 1970, Algeria introduced a resolution to expel the delegates representing the Republic of China and to recognize the delegates representing the People's Republic of China. The General Assembly approved the resolution by a vote of 51:49:25. This was the first time a majority voted in favor of seating the Beijing regime. Unfortunately, a two-thirds vote was needed for approval, not a simple majority. The vote made it evident that it was only a question of time before the Beijing regime was recognized by the United Nations General Assembly as the legitimate government for all of China.

At a news conference on June 1, 1971, Nixon said a "significant change" was developing in the United Nations regarding the representation of China. He knew that more and more nations favored recognizing the Beijing regime. At the time, President Nixon was working to improve Sino-American relations.

In April 1971, Beijing invited an American table tennis team to tour China; American newsmen were allowed to cover the team's activities. On July 9, one of the most dramatic events in the cold war era occurred. Henry Kissinger, the Assistant for National Security Affairs, made a secret trip to China and while there, he accepted on behalf of President Nixon, an invitation to visit China.

In 1971, the General Assembly again took up the question of China's representation. On August 2, Secretary of State William Rogers announced that the United States would vote in favor of seating the Beijing regime but would vote against expelling the Taiwan government (Republic of China). The decision to vote against expelling Taiwan was a political decision dictated by American domestic politics. President Nixon knew that Beijing would not accept a two-China policy. Beijing would not accept a United Nations seat unless Taiwan was expelled. On October 25, 1971, by a vote of seventy six to thirty-five, the General Assembly accepted the credentials of the Beijing regime and voted to expel Taiwan. The General Assembly Resolution stated "that the representatives of the Government of the People's Republic of China are the only lawful representatives of China to the United Nations."

Public opinion in America reacted sharply and unfavorably. The Gallup poll reported that support for the United Nations dropped to an all-time low. Many congressmen wanted to reduce America's financial contribution to the United Nations. Senator Barry Goldwater suggested that the United States cut off all funds for the world organization. Third-world countries, however, greeted the seating of the Beijing regime with much enthusiasm. Some welcomed the American defeat, but others simply welcomed the fact that an independent, third-world country now had a seat on the United Nations Security Council.

Kenneth L. Hill

See also: China: Chinese Civil War, 1927–1949; China: U.S. Recognition.

Bibliography

Blum, Robert. *U.S. Policy Towards Communist China: The Alternatives.* New York: Foreign Policy Association, 1966.

Chen, Lung-chu. *Formosa, China, and the United Nations.* New York: St. Martin's Press, 1967.

Dallin, Alexander. *The Soviet Union at the United Nations: An Inquiry into Soviet Motives and Objectives.* New York: Praeger, 1962.

Dulles, Foster R. *American Policy Towards Communist China, 1949 1969.* New York: Crowell, 1972.

Hilsman, Roger. *Foreign Policy in the Sixties: The Issues and the Instruments.* Baltimore: Johns Hopkins University Press, 1965.

Kim, Samuel. *China, the United Nations, and World Order.* Princeton: Princeton University Press, 1979.

Luard, Even. *A History of the United Nations.* New York: St. Martin's Press, 1982.

Melanson, Richard. *Reevaluating Eisenhower: American Foreign Policy in the 1950s.* Urbana: University of Illinois Press, 1987.

Nixon, Richard. *RN: The Memoirs of Richard Nixon.* New York: Grosset and Dunlap, 1978.

Oksenberg, Michel. *China and America: Past and Future.* New York: Foreign Policy Association, 1977.

Creating West Germany, 1945–1955

1945 Occupation Zones

Historical Background

In July 1945, U.S. President Franklin D. Roosevelt, British Prime Minister Winston Churchill, and Soviet Premier Josef Stalin met in Potsdam, a suburb of Berlin, to coordinate plans for the occupation of Germany. The Allies agreed to eliminate all traces of nazism, to demand reparation payments, to introduce democratic reforms, and to implement a policy of demilitarization. The primary purpose of the victorious powers was to put into place policies that would guarantee that Germany would never again endanger the peace in Europe.

Germany was divided into zones of occupation; each of the Big Four—France, Great Britain, the Soviet Union, and the United States—occupied one zone. Berlin was divided in the same way. Berlin became a major problem for the western Big Three—France, Great Britain, and the United States—because it was located inside East Germany. The Soviet Union controlled the access routes into the city. The victors decided to govern Germany through an Allied Control Council (ACC) composed of military commanders from each of the four zones. Decisions required unanimous agreement. The victors agreed to govern Berlin through an Inter-Allied Governing Council, also known as the Kommandatura.

Council of Foreign Ministers

At the 1945 Yalta conference, the three heads of government—Churchill, Roosevelt, and Stalin—agreed that their foreign ministers should meet regularly to foster cooperation and coordinate policies. At Potsdam, the three leaders decided to create a Council of Foreign Ministers (CFM), including France and China. The ministers were to meet whenever their governments thought it necessary for them to do so. In addition to promoting cooperation and coordinating policies, the CFM was responsible for preparing peace treaties for the defeated nations.

Germany surrendered in May 1945. The first CFM meeting convened in London three months later, and it quickly became evident that promoting cooperation among the victorious powers would be no easy task. The Big Five ministers, representing China, France, Great Britain, the Soviet Union, and the United States, had some preliminary discussions regarding German reparations, control of the Ruhr and the Rhineland, and demilitarization. They also discussed peace treaties for some of the defeated nations. On October 2, 1945, Soviet Foreign Minister V.M. Molotov, without any warning, interrupted the negotiating process by insisting that only those nations that signed the terms of surrender for the defeated nations could participate in the negotiations. At the 1945 Potsdam conference, Great Britain and the United States accepted the Soviet position limiting the number of nations eligible to sign the peace treaties. They assumed, however, there would be no limit on the right to participate in the negotiations. When the London conference opened, Molotov appeared to accept this process permitting each of the Big Five to participate. On October 2, Molotov announced that any previous agreements regarding the peace treaties were not valid because of the Soviet interpretation of the Potsdam agreement. Given the abbreviated nature of the meeting, German issues did not receive much attention.

The failure at London was significant because the ministers were simply exchanging ideas to determine the policy preferences of each of the five governments. Molotov's objection pertained to procedure, not substance. Although each of the Big Five had the right of veto in the United Nations Security Council, they could not veto procedural issues. If the participants at London could not agree on procedure, the probability of reaching a substantive agreement on Germany's political future was not encouraging.

Meetings in Moscow and Paris

Fearing the consequences of the failure at London, U.S. Secretary of State James Byrnes took the initiative and succeeded in arranging a meeting in Moscow with the foreign ministers of Great Britain and the Soviet Union. Byrnes did not invite France and China because the Moscow meeting was based on the Yalta agreement, not Potsdam.

The agenda for the Moscow meeting was a rather long one dealing mostly with non-German issues. The ministers remained in session from December 16 to December 27. The results were somewhat encouraging. The ministers appeared to resolve a number of problems relating to Japan, Korea, China, Bulgaria, Romania, and atomic energy. The issues, in most cases, were not actually resolved but commissions were created to deal with them. This apparent progress generated hope that future CFM meetings might successfully formulate policies dealing with Germany.

The second CFM meeting convened in Paris in April 1946. Secretary of State Byrnes submitted the draft of a twenty-five-year treaty for the disarmament and demilitarization of Germany. The purpose of the treaty was to make certain that Germany could not again threaten the peace in Europe. He hoped that once a treaty demilitarizing Germany was completed the Allied nations could then turn their attention to framing a peace treaty. This was a necessary requisite to bring closure to World War II and to permit a return to normalcy. The European nations could not get on with the job of economic and political reconstruction until they reached an agreement on the type of postwar world the victors wanted. Unfortunately, they had clashing visions and different priorities. These were reflected in the division of Germany and the various proposals for unifying Germany.

Byrnes presented the treaty on demilitarization to the foreign ministers to enable them to discuss it and to recommend changes to make it more effective. France and Great Britain welcomed the treaty. Molotov did not reject it, but he pointed out some of its alleged weaknesses without offering any remedies to improve upon it. He wanted a government established before completing a peace treaty. There was, however, no sign this would soon happen. The Soviets preferred retaining control over East Germany rather than promoting German unification on terms not completely acceptable to Moscow. The Soviets were insulating their zone of occupation in Germany and Berlin to prevent any interaction with the three Western powers.

Although Germany was divided into zones of occupation, the Potsdam agreement called for treating it as a single economic unit. This did not happen. Consequently, Germany was an economic burden on the three Western occupying powers. In July 1946, in an effort to kick-start Germany's economic recovery, Secretary of State Byrnes offered to merge the economy of the American zone of occupation with that of any other zone. He recognized the imperative of economic unity if there was to be economic recovery.

At the Paris meeting of the Council of Foreign Ministers, on July 10, 1946, Foreign Minister Molotov presented the Soviet plan for the future of Germany. He opposed separating the Ruhr from Germany, deindustrialization, and the dismemberment of Germany. He wanted Germany to have a central administration that could be transformed into a government, but only after a long period of occupation. The Soviets wanted $10 billion in reparations and wanted the occupation to remain in place until the reparations were paid. Western experts estimated that if the Soviet plan was accepted, Germany would be paying for more than fifty years.

Byrnes in Stuttgart

In September 1946, Secretary of State Byrnes, in an address in Stuttgart, West Germany, discussed American goals for Germany given the lack of cooperation among the occupying powers. He was in part responding to Molotov's July 10 address. Byrnes called for the establishment of a provisional German government, the elimination of economic barriers between the zones of occupation, and an increase in Germany's level of production. He agreed that the Ruhr and Rhineland, important industrial areas, should remain a part of Germany. He wanted to reduce the size of the occupation force but he pledged there would be an American military presence in Germany for a long period.

Byrnes's speech was an important turning point in the cold war. By promising to remain in Germany, he was trying to reassure the French who were apprehensive about a German recovery. He was also telling the Russians that the United States was not going away. The decision to remain in Germany as long as necessary meant in effect that the United States was there to prevent a Soviet advance. He wanted to reassure the people of West Germany who were fearful of the Soviet Union.

The proposals put forward by Byrnes and Molotov about the future of Germany clearly revealed a wide gap between the two. Although neither individual spoke about the European balance of power, that was the essential issue. The European nations could not be certain how a unified Germany would influence the European distribution of power. The French feared that a unified Germany could again become a threat. Other European nations shared the French fear, as did the Soviet Union. Germany, because of its past behavior, was not trusted.

In December 1946, the United States and Great Britain agreed to an economic union between their two zones to become effective on January 1, 1947. Although not intended at the time, this proved to be the first step in creating a West German state. The French refused to join the merger. The French government continued to think that Germany, not the Soviet Union, remained the greatest threat to peace. The Communist party in France enjoyed much popular support, followed the Soviet line in foreign policy, and was a part of the coalition governing France.

The Moscow CFM Meeting

In January 1947, George Marshall replaced James Byrnes as secretary of state. He traveled to Moscow in March for another CFM meeting. By this time, the cold war was heating up; the gulf between the United States and the Soviet Union was widening; and there was no agreement on unifying Germany. On March 12, two days after the CFM meeting convened, President Truman appeared before a joint session of Congress to articulate the Truman Doctrine. Given the many differences that developed between the Soviet Union and the Western Big Three

since the end of World War II, reaching an agreement to unify Germany was not a realistic probability. Secretary of State Marshall did not expect to make much progress in completing a peace treaty for Germany.

At the Moscow CFM meeting, the differences between the two sides regarding Germany became more evident. They differed over the structure and powers of a central government, the economic system, reparations, territorial boundaries, and the question of how nations that fought against Germany should participate in the formulation of a peace treaty. The Western powers wanted a federal form of government with very limited powers given to the center. The Soviets wanted a more centralized government. Marshall feared that a German government with centralized powers would make it easier to carry out a communist coup d'etat. The United States wanted to eliminate the economic barriers separating the four zones, but the Soviets rejected the proposal. They would not approve any policy that threatened to diminish their control. The fact that the Big Four could not reach an agreement on economic unity made it unlikely they could agree on Germany's reunification. Great Britain and the United States differed with the Soviet Union but they also had major disagreements with France.

Marshall did not think the German problem could be resolved because of conditions in Europe. If conditions continued to deteriorate, the Soviets might be able to extend their power beyond the areas already under their control. By 1947, the contours of a postwar world were not yet clear. Economic conditions in Europe were horrendous, and American policy was in the process of transition. The time was not ripe for an agreement on Germany and would not be for a long time.

An important difference between the 1947 Moscow CFM meeting and those held in the past was the pessimism that much could be accomplished. The Western nations, particularly Great Britain and the United States, were beginning to recognize the necessity of cooperating among themselves. By 1947, Secretary of State Marshall and British Foreign Secretary Ernest Bevin realized that rebuilding Germany was necessary for the economic recovery of Europe. This goal was also essential to reduce the costs of the occupation. The economies of France and Great Britain had not recovered from the effects of World War II nor did it seem that recovery would soon occur. The American Congress was determined to reduce spending and to facilitate the transition to a peacetime economy. The Allied victory was proving to be very costly.

On July 15, 1947, the Joint Chiefs of Staff issued a new directive for governing Germany. The directive replaced the one issued in May 1945, based on the Morgenthau Plan. It called for the deindustrialization of Germany. The July 1947 directive recognized the need to develop the West German economy by connecting it to the European Recovery Program (ERP), also known as the Marshall Plan. West Germany would serve as the engine to bring about the economic recovery of Western Europe. The need for progress was imperative. In 1947, people were rioting in the Western occupation zones because of an inadequate supply of food and poor economic conditions.

In August 1947, Great Britain and the United States agreed to raise production levels in their zones of occupation. France refused to do the same. By the end of 1947, France, Great Britain, and the United States realized they had to do more to improve living conditions in Germany and Europe. The Marshall Plan, announced in June 1947, was

beginning to take shape, but it would take time to see results. Reviving the German economy was essential.

The London Six-Power Meeting

In February 1948, ministers representing Belgium, France, Great Britain, the Netherlands, Luxembourg, and the United States met in London. By this time, the United States and Great Britain accepted the fact that the Council of Foreign Ministers was not an effective instrument for resolving problems. They also recognized that the economic provisions of the Potsdam agreement were not working. Germany was not treated as a single economic unit. The purpose of the London meeting was to review policies vis-à-vis Germany and to propose new policies. Topics on the agenda included creating a West German government, control of the Ruhr, the German economy, and security measures.

The ministers remained in session until March 6 discussing various proposals dealing with the agenda items. In February 1948, the communists seized power in Czechoslovakia despite the fact that they already controlled the important ministries. The Czech coup had a significant impact on the Western Allies. It indicated that Stalin would be satisfied with nothing less than the complete domination of the East European nations. He was not likely to relinquish control over East Germany.

In notes to France, Great Britain, and the United States, the Soviet Union claimed that any decisions agreed to by the ministers meeting in London would violate the Potsdam agreement. The Soviets insisted that decisions regarding Germany needed the approval of the four occupying powers. The Western Big Three rejected this line of argument.

Marshal Sokolovsky, the Soviet representative on the Allied Control Commission, insisted that the Big Four discuss the tripartite declaration issued by representatives of Czechoslovakia, Poland, and Yugoslavia on February 18. The declaration criticized the economic merger of the Anglo-American zones, charged that the Western powers were not doing enough to demilitarize or to denazify West Germany, and complained about inadequate reparations. The declaration issued by Czechoslovakia, Poland, and Yugoslavia was a response to the London six-power meeting. On March 20, 1948, the Soviet Union withdrew from the Allied Control Council because of the London meeting and the refusal of the Western powers to keep the Soviet Union informed about decisions made there. In April, Soviet authorities began to restrict Allied rail and road traffic to West Berlin.

The London conference resumed on April 28. The ministers continued to discuss control of the Ruhr, security issues, and the relationship between West Germany and the European Recovery Program. During the negotiations, the French demonstrated a reluctance to proceed with the establishment of a provisional government for West Germany. The United States and Great Britain were prepared to act despite French reservations. The British and American ministers feared that any lack of progress in establishing a provisional government would be exploited by the Soviet Union and resented by the people of West Germany. The London meeting ended on June 2. The ministers issued a communiqué several days later.

The ministers at the six-power conference created an international authority for the Ruhr, gave West Germany permission to establish a constituent assembly to draft a constitution, and they promised to keep their troops in Germany until a secure peace was established. There was agreement on the need for close cooperation among the three Western zones in Germany and the ERP. The ministers began to lay the groundwork for a West German state.

On June 24, 1948, the foreign ministers of Albania, Bulgaria, Czechoslovakia, Hungary, Poland, Romania, the Soviet Union, and Yugoslavia issued a statement at the close of a meeting in Warsaw. They accused the Western nations of violating the Potsdam agreement, attempting to bypass the Council of Foreign Ministers, ending four-power control of Germany, and rebuilding its industrial and military potential. The Soviets were determined to do all they could to prevent the establishment of a West German state.

The decisions made in London threatened the existing balance of power both in Germany and in Europe. The result was a dramatic increase in international tensions. In June 1948, the Soviets began to block traffic into West Berlin. Eventually all traffic was brought to a halt. The United States then instituted the Berlin airlift to feed the population of West Berlin and to provide for its basic needs. The Berlin airlift was successful; West Berlin would not be abandoned. In July, the Soviets withdrew from the Berlin Kommandatura because of the decisions made at the London six-power meeting. The Berlin blockade ended any hope there would be a four-power agreement on German reunification.

Soviet Actions

In January 1949, the Soviet Union launched a peace campaign. The change in policy came about in response to Western policies. The Western Allies were gaining strength. In April 1948, the communists suffered a major defeat in elections in Italy; the communists were no longer in the French government; the London six-power meeting laid the foundation for a West German state; the Marshall Plan was producing results; and there was progress in establishing NATO. As part of the peace campaign, the Soviets called for the convening of another CFM meeting. The Western powers assumed that the Soviets wanted a meeting to divide the Allies among themselves and from West Germany.

In January 1949, Dean Acheson replaced George Marshall as secretary of state. In April, he met with the British and French foreign ministers who were in Washington for the signing of the NATO treaty. Acheson wanted an agreement among the three regarding policies toward West Germany and West Berlin. Stalin expressed an interest in ending the Berlin blockade, but in return he wanted to convene another CFM meeting. The Soviet proposal was accepted. Secretary of State Acheson was determined to prevent the Soviet Union from disrupting Western plans for Germany. Policies had to be in place before the CFM meeting, in Paris, convened.

On May 8, 1949, West Germany adopted a constitution, referred to as the Basic Law. A Council of Foreign Ministers meeting convened on May 23. By this time, the Soviets knew they could not prevent the creation of a West German state. The Soviets lifted the blockade of Berlin before the meeting convened. The blockade had not hampered efforts to unify West Germany nor did it impact on the European economic recovery then in progress. In 1949, West Germany became a full partner in the European Recovery Program. The balance of power, according to Secretary of State Acheson, was shifting in favor of the West.

During the Paris CFM meeting, the Soviets made it clear they wanted to go back to the Potsdam agreement. This would enable them to continue to control East Germany and would give them a renewed voice in West German affairs. They also wanted to reactivate the Allied Control Council and the Kommandatura. The Western nations rejected the Soviet proposals. The CFM meeting ended on June 20; little was accomplished.

Building a West German State

On September 15, 1949, the Bundestag elected Konrad Adenauer as chancellor by a margin of one vote. On September 21, the Federal Republic of Germany (FRG) formally came into being. The Occupation Statute, intended to take the place of a peace treaty, became operative. It defined the new relationship between the Bonn government and the three Western Allies. West Germany was not yet sovereign, but the Bonn government now had more control over its own affairs. The military government was abolished, but the military occupation remained. In October, the Soviets established the German Democratic Republic (GDR), but Moscow remained in total control. Secretary of State Acheson denounced the Soviet action as an illegal act because the people of East Germany were not consulted.

On November 9, 1949, Acheson met in Paris for two days of talks with the foreign ministers of Belgium, France, Great Britain, Luxembourg, and the Netherlands. The purpose of the meeting was to determine the future relationship between West Germany and the six Western powers. The basic problem confronting the ministers was to reconcile the need for Germany's economic and political recovery with the security interests of the European nations and the costs of that security. The problem was complicated because there was strong anti-German sentiment in many European nations. The memories of World War II were still vivid. The ministers decided to give their High Commissioners in Germany responsibility for negotiating with the German government measures granting it more control over its affairs.

On November 22, 1949, Chancellor Adenauer and the three High Commissioners signed an agreement, the Petersberg agreement, giving the West German government broad powers and primary responsibility over its own affairs. West Germany received permission to begin consular relations with other powers. In return, Bonn pledged to continue its denazification program. Chancellor Adenauer made it clear that he would seek a revision of the Occupation Statute when the time was right. The Western Allies were committed to reviewing the statute after twelve months to determine if revisions were necessary.

The Petersberg agreement represented a new approach to the Bonn government. West Germany was treated as an equal partner, and its prestige became a major priority of the Western Big Three. The foundation was laid for ending the occupation and for integrating West Germany into various European institutions. The Soviets opposed all these policies but were unable to change them or prevent their implementation.

Attitudes regarding the re-arming of West Germany changed dramatically because of North Korea's attack on South Korea in June 1950. Comments by East German officials suggested that what happened in Korea could also happen in Germany. If the communists were willing to resort to military actions in Asia would they not be willing to do the same thing in Europe? The North Korean

attack resulted in the militarization of the cold war. Plans were made to strengthen NATO, increase military spending, build up military forces, and re-arm West Germany.

Re-arming Germany

In September 1950, the Western Big Three foreign ministers agreed to take steps to terminate the state of war with Germany. They also reached a consensus on the need to re-arm West Germany. If a war occurred in Europe, Germany would have to be defended. The Western nations did not want to assume this burden without a West German contribution. Secretary of State Acheson and Foreign Secretary Bevin agreed that when German military forces were established they should be under the command of NATO; however, France was not quite ready to accept a re-armed West Germany. The ministers agreed that an attack on West Germany or West Berlin would result in a Western response even if Western troops were not the victims. Prior to this, the Western nations would respond only if their occupation forces were attacked. The Western Big Three created a commission to determine how to modify the Occupation Statute to permit West Germany greater freedom.

In October 1950, the Soviet Union and the satellite nations met in Prague and issued a communiqué denouncing the decisions of the Western powers to re-arm West Germany. They were again accused of violating the Potsdam agreement and of wanting to exploit West Germany for their own economic benefits. The communist nations wanted an affirmation that West Germany would not re-arm.

The Soviets suddenly became interested in negotiating a peace treaty for a unified Germany. They wanted a four-power peace treaty completed immediately, and they wanted to convene an all-German constitutional convention to prepare for a provisional government. East and West Germany were to have equal representation at such a convention. At the time, the East German population was about 18 million, the West German population about 47 million. On October 25, Secretary of State Acheson issued a statement refuting the allegations made in the Prague communiqué and rejecting all the proposals.

In November 1950, the Soviet Union called for a meeting of the Council of Foreign Ministers to discuss the Prague proposals made the previous month. The Soviets wanted a CFM meeting devoted exclusively to Germany. The three Western Allies rejected the Soviet approach but expressed a willingness to convene a meeting with a broader agenda.

In December, the North Atlantic Council, the major decision-making body of NATO, issued a statement calling on France, Great Britain, and the United States to explore the best way for West Germany to participate in the defense of Europe. The Western powers informed Chancellor Adenauer that they would replace the Occupation Statute only after West Germany agreed to contribute to the defense of Western Europe. Re-arming West Germany was a delicate issue for Chancellor Adenauer. Many West Germans opposed re-arming because it could result in the permanent division of Germany. There was also the possibility that re-arming could provoke a Soviet military response.

The three High Commissioners in West Germany received instructions to explore with the Bonn government means to create a new relationship with the three Western powers on a contractual basis. A contractual agreement would end the occupation. The Soviet Union was aware of this changing re-lationship. On December 30, 1950, the Western powers were again accused of wanting to re-arm West Germany and rebuild its military capabilities. The Soviets expressed a willingness to attend a preliminary conference to discuss an agenda for a Big Four foreign ministers' meeting.

In January 1951, the United States responded to the December 30 note from the Soviet Union. The United States opposed having a meeting of the Big Four to discuss German issues only. The United States said there were other factors that contributed to Soviet-American tensions; they too had to be addressed. The Soviets insisted that the most important problem was the re-arming of West Germany but they agreed to discuss other issues. At this stage, the Soviets just wanted to convene a meeting to halt or modify Western policies toward Germany.

The Western Big Three did not think negotiations with the Soviet Union would be fruitful but they could not ignore Soviet demands for a CFM meeting. There were a number of Germans, including the leader of the Social Democratic Party Kurt Schumacher, who feared that re-arming West Germany would perpetuate the division of Germany. Promoting German national unity was the Soviet trump card. If Soviet policies were successful, the people of West Germany would appear to have an option. They could choose remilitarization and alliance with the West or national unity based on Soviet proposals. The Western Big Three did not underestimate the appeal of national unity to the German people.

On March 5, 1951, deputies of the Big Four met in Paris to lay the groundwork for a CFM meeting. These preliminary talks lasted four months and ended in failure. The goals of the two sides vis-à-vis Germany were incompatible. No agreement was possible. The two sides, for example, could not agree on the ground rules for conducting an election.

In December 1951, the United Nations General Assembly approved a Western-sponsored resolution appointing a commission to determine if conditions in Germany were suitable for holding national elections. The Western Big Three wanted national elections to elect a central government. They wanted to be sure the elections were conducted in a climate of freedom that included the right to cast a secret ballot. The Soviet Union refused to allow the commission to enter East Germany.

In February 1952, the foreign ministers of France, Great Britain, and the United States met in London with Chancellor Adenauer to determine how West Germany would participate in a European army. In 1950, French Premier René Pleven submitted to his cabinet the Pleven Plan to create a European Defense Community (EDC). The EDC would permit West Germany to participate in the defense of Europe. The EDC was to be a European army composed of six nations including the Benelux nations, France, Italy, and Germany. The French cabinet did not approve the Pleven Plan until May 1952.

A Soviet Proposal

On March 10, 1952, the Soviet Union, in a note to the Western powers, proposed completing a peace treaty for Germany with permission for it to have its own armed forces. All foreign troops would have to leave Germany, and it would be prohibited from joining any military alliance directed against any of the nations that were allied in the effort to defeat Nazi Germany. The Soviets wanted to disrupt the negotiations regarding the proposed contractual agreement and the creation of the EDC. The Soviets were well aware

that the French remained apprehensive about Germany rebuilding its military might.

The Western powers opposed re-arming Germany without sufficient constraints to make certain it would not again become a threat to peace in Europe. They also rejected, as did Chancellor Adenauer, a policy of neutrality because of its potential dangers. A neutral Germany could be tempted to enhance its power by exploiting Soviet-American differences. The Western powers also rejected the Soviet demand that a united Germany should be prohibited from joining a military alliance if it wished.

The Contractual Agreements

In May 1952, the Soviets sent a threatening note to the Bonn government alleging that the contractual agreements were intended to keep West Germany under the military control of the three Western Allies. The threatening tone of the Soviet note backfired and strengthened support for the contractual agreements. On May 26, 1952, they were signed in Bonn. Some controls remained because Germany and Berlin remained divided.

Two days later, a number of agreements were signed in Paris, including the European Defense Community. Belgium, France, Italy, the Federal Republic of Germany, Luxembourg, and the Netherlands signed the EDC treaty. None of the treaties could be implemented until all were ratified. The contractual agreement and the EDC were part of a single package.

In December 1953, the Western Big Three accepted a Soviet invitation to convene a CFM meeting in Berlin. The ministers met in January. Although Soviet Foreign Minister Molotov opposed the re-arming of West Germany, the Soviet Union was unwilling to modify its policies to reach an agreement on German reunification. The conference ended without any agreement on Germany.

France Rejects the EDC

On May 19, 1954, the West German Bundestag ratified the contractual agreements and the EDC treaty. On August 30, France rejected the EDC and thereby nullified years of difficult and complicated negotiations. The French rejection required negotiating a new agreement to restore sovereignty to Germany. Great Britain and the United States decided to repair the situation as quickly as possible. In September 1954, the foreign ministers of Belgium, Canada, France, West Germany, Italy, Luxembourg, the Netherlands, the United Kingdom, and the United States met in London to explore alternative ways to restore sovereignty to West Germany and connect it to NATO. The ministers reached a number of agreements, but they needed more time for negotiations. They met again in Paris in October.

A West German State

At the Paris meeting, the ministers completed agreements regarding the re-arming of West Germany, the restoration of its sovereignty, and an end to the occupation. West Germany, as a gesture to France, voluntarily agreed not to build atomic, biological, or chemical weapons, nor build jet bombers, jet fighters, or guided missiles. The nine Western ministers agreed to expand the Brussels treaty and to invite West Germany and Italy to become members. West Germany was also invited to join NATO. Great Britain made a major concession by pledging to keep four army divisions and a tactical airforce in Europe indefinitely. This was to reassure the French.

On November 13, 1954, the Soviet Union issued invitations to all the nations of Europe with which it had diplomatic relations and to the United States to attend a European security conference. The United States and its European allies rejected the invitation. American officials assumed the Soviets were trying to prevent the ratification of the Paris agreements.

On May 5, 1955, the Federal Republic of Germany officially regained its sovereignty. The occupation ended, and West Germany joined NATO. Chancellor Adenauer succeeded in winning independence for West Germany. It was now a part of the European security structure. The grant of sovereignty, however, deepened the division of Europe.

The divisions of Berlin, Germany, and Europe would continue until the end of the cold war.

Kenneth L. Hill

Bibliography

Acheson, Dean. *Present at the Creation.* New York: Norton, 1969.

Byrnes, James F. *Speaking Frankly.* New York: Harper and Brothers, 1947.

Clay, Lucius. *Decision in Germany.* Garden City: Doubleday, 1950.

Deighton, Anne. *The Impossible Peace: Britain, the Division of Germany and the Origins of the Cold War.* Oxford: Clarendon Press, 1990.

Djilas, Milovan. *Conversations with Stalin.* New York: Harcourt, Brace and World, 1962.

Goldman, Eric. *The Crucial Decade and After: America, 1945-1960.* New York: Knopf, 1960.

Mastny, Vojtech. *The Cold War and Soviet Insecurity.* New York: Oxford University Press, 1996.

Messer, Robert L. *The End of an Alliance: James F. Byrnes, Roosevelt, Truman, and the Origins of the Cold War.* Chapel Hill: University of North Carolina Press, 1982.

Naimark, Norman. *The Russians in Germany: The History of the Soviet Zone of Occupation, 1945-1949.* Cambridge: Cambridge University Press, 1995.

Truman, Harry. *Memoirs: Years of Trial and Hope.* Garden City: Doubleday, 1956.

Economic Community of West African States (ECOWAS)

The Economic Community of West African States (ECOWAS) was established by treaty in 1975 and ratified the following year. The original signatory countries were: Benin, Burkina Faso, Côte d'Ivoire (Ivory Coast), Gambia, Ghana, Guinea, Guinea-Bissau, Liberia, Mali, Mauritania, Niger, Nigeria, Senegal, Sierra Leone, and Togo. Cape Verde joined the organization in 1977.

Originally intended as an economic organization—ECOWAS was designed to coordinate tariff, agriculture, labor, and monetary policies of the various member states—the organization has come to play an important peacekeeping role in West Africa in the 1990s, particularly through its involvement in the civil wars in Liberia and Sierra Leone. In 1981, the member states signed protocols—reaffirmed in 1991—calling for non-aggression toward other member states, as well as for the provision of mutual defense assistance. A revised treaty, signed in 1993, committed the members to work toward regional peace, stability, and security.

Peacekeeping in Liberia

The first trial of the ECOWAS security protocols came in Liberia. In August 1990, the ECOWAS Cease-fire Monitoring Group (ECOMOG)—consisting of 4,000 troops from Gambia, Ghana, Guinea, Nigeria, and Sierra Leone—were sent into Liberia to enforce a cease-fire between the warring factions there, as well as to re-establish public order and establish an interim government in preparation for elections. (The Liberian conflict had begun in December 1989, when Charles Taylor and his National Patriotic Front of Liberia [NPFL] invaded the country from the Ivory Coast, in an effort to topple the dictatorship of Samuel Doe.)

The intervention was only partially successful. An interim government was established, under President Amos Sawyer, but it had virtually no authority outside the capital of Monrovia and its immediate environs. Elections were scheduled for May 1992, before which time ECOMOG forces were supposed to occupy Liberian harbors and airports, as well as establish a buffer zone along the Sierra Leone border. Because of the resistance to ECOMOG by the NPFL, this was not possible.

Indeed, the ECOMOG mission had strong political overtones from the beginning. Since its inception, the West African peacekeeping force has been seen, and indeed has been, a largely Nigerian effort. Its command structure and most of its troops largely came from Nigeria, a country that by sheer population and economic might has dominated West Africa since at least the 1970s. Moreover, ECOMOG politics have been fractured by divisions between Nigeria and the other member states, particularly the larger Francophone ones like Senegal and the Ivory Coast.

Because Taylor was heavily sponsored by the latter's former president, Felix Houphouet-Boigny, Nigeria's rulers have been highly suspicious of him and, during the first several years of the ECOMOG mission, did everything they could to prevent his coming to power. When Doe surrendered to ECOMOG in August 1990, the Nigerian commander made sure he was not turned over to Taylor. Instead, they handed him over to Prince Johnson, a former Taylor lieutenant who had parted ways with the NPFL leader. Johnson ultimately tortured Doe to death. More importantly, ECOMOG thwarted two of Taylor's offensives to capture the capital in 1990 and 1992. Then in October of 1992 ECOMOG went on an offensive against Taylor, after the NPFL had failed to demobilize and prepare for elections as required under the ECOWAS-sponsored Yamoussoukro accord of 1991, which Taylor was a signatory to. The offensive, however, which included heavy bombardment of the Taylor-held country around Liberia's second city of Buchanan, failed.

Part of the animosity between ECOMOG and Taylor concerned access to Liberia's wealth of rubber, timber, iron ore, gold, and diamond resources. Indeed, a map of the fighting between ECOMOG and Taylor matched the locations of Liberia's major extractive industries or the ports where the resources could be shipped from. All parties to the conflict were interested in controlling these areas. This included not just ECOMOG—some of whose officers were engaging in smuggling activities—but Taylor's rivals as well, including two factions representing the Krahn ethnic group that had

ruled under the Doe dictatorship: the United Liberation Movement (ULIMO) and the Liberian Peace Council (LPC).

In April 1993, ECOMOG announced that ULIMO had been disarmed and demobilized. But all was not as it seemed in the confusion of the civil war. Many Liberian and international observers believed that ULIMO was being supported by ECOMOG and that its forces, rather than being demobilized, were, in fact, being integrated into ECOMOG. According to the NPFL, ECOMOG was no longer a neutral force.

Yet another ECOWAS-sponsored accord was signed by the faction leaders in July 1993, anticipating full disarmament and elections by February 1994. At the same time, ECOMOG was expanded to include more troops from more countries, including a contingent from non-member Tanzania, brought in to assuage the NPFL's concerns about the neutrality of ECOMOG. A new interim government, with the pro-Taylor Wilton Sankuwulo as president, was installed in Monrovia the following year. This, of course, angered the other factions and sank both the 1993 agreement and a 1995 agreement signed in Ghana.

Throughout 1995 and 1996, intensive multi-sided fighting continued between and among the NPFL, ECOMOG, ULIMO, the LPC, a breakaway ULIMO faction, and the remaining elements of the Armed Forces of Liberia (AFL). Clashes between the ULIMO breakaway faction—known as ULIMO-J, because of its leader Roosevelt Johnson—and ECOMOG in the west of the country in December 1995 and January 1996 left 16 peacekeepers dead and saw the capture of 130 more, all of whom were Nigerians. The fighting between ULIMO-J and ECOMOG was rumored to be the effect of an agreement reached between Nigerian strongman Sani

Abacha and Taylor made during a secret trip the latter took to the Nigerian capital of Abuja in mid-1995. By this time, ECOMOG forces had been augmented to some 12,000, versus an estimated 60,000 rebel fighters in the various factions. While the latter—and especially the NPFL—controlled most of the interior of the country, ECOMOG was largely isolated around the capital and in the various ports.

Peacemaking in Liberia

In April 1996, in an attempt to end the war, Taylor attacked Monrovia itself. In extensive fighting between the NPFL and remnants of the AFL, the city was heavily damaged and tens of thousands of people—already internally displaced—fled to nearby countries. The April fighting shocked both ECOMOG and the international community into renewing their efforts to uphold the Abuja accords, signed in early 1995. In addition, a new ECOMOG commander, Victor Malu, was sent in to remake the force. Malu, considered one of the finest officers in the Nigerian army, took command in July.

Malu immediately began making plans to station ECOMOG throughout the country, in preparation for a general disarmament process that would end on February 1, 1997. Whether from war weariness or ECOMOG's new assertiveness, the faction leaders complied, and by early February, most of them had demobilized, though rumors persisted that caches of weapons remained hidden in more remote areas of the country. Adding to the stories of hidden weapons were revised counts of combatants. The figure of 60,000 was reduced to 35,000—based on the disputed fact that many fighters came and went from one faction to another—of which some 30,000 had been demobilized.

Under the Abuja accords, all factions were required to formally disband and form themselves into political parties by the end of February. In addition, all potential candidates for political office in the elections scheduled for May 1997—including most of the faction leaders—were required to resign from their positions in the interim government. All persons and parties complied, though for logistical reasons the elections were postponed until July.

In those elections, for which an augmented ECOMOG force of 16,000 supplied the logistics and security, Taylor was overwhelmingly elected. Because of his past history of hostility toward ECOMOG, it was expected that the new president would immediately move to have ECOMOG leave the country. But Taylor has not moved precipitately, and though ECOMOG's numbers have declined, they remain in many parts of Liberia as of this writing.

Sierra Leone

While members of the Sierra Leone army were serving with ECOMOG forces in Liberia, political conflict and rebel fighting continued in their home country. In 1992, fighting broke out between Taylor's NPFL forces—which were being aided by and were aiding rebel forces in Sierra Leone—and the Sierra Leonean army after the NPFL invaded the country. Taylor claimed he was merely pursuing elements of ULIMO that were using the country as a base for attacks on his faction. In January 1992, ECOWAS-led discussions in Monrovia led to a cease-fire between the NPFL and the Sierra Leone government, though this was often violated by NPFL-ULIMO fighting in the border area.

In May 1995, as fighting continued between government forces and the Revolutionary United Front (RUF) rebel forces, Sierra Leone president Valentine Strasser—who came to power in a military coup—requested that ECOWAS mediate. Strasser, however, was forced out of office by yet another military coup in January 1996 and elections were held the following month. With 36 percent of the vote, Ahmed Tejan Kabbah and his United National People's Party were elected to power. The new president's efforts to oust recalcitrant members of the military from power led to a coup by Major Johnny Paul Koroma in May 1997.

Condemned by ECOWAS and much of the international community, Koroma's government was isolated, facing international economic sanctions and an invading ECOMOG force, headed by the Nigerians. In June, the fighting began when Nigerian gunships shelled the capital of Freetown. Throughout the summer and fall, heavy fighting occurred around the capital and numerous Nigerian-ECOMOG soldiers were killed or captured. In February 1998, however, ECOMOG had defeated the Sierra Leone coup leaders and forced them into exile, leading to the reinstatement of President Kabbah.

James Ciment

See also: Liberia: Civil War, 1989–1997; Sierra Leone: Civil Conflict, 1990–1998.

Bibliography

Adeleke, Ademola. "The Politics and Diplomacy of Peacekeeping in West Africa: The ECOWAS Operation in Liberia." *The Journal of Modern African Studies* 33, no. 4 (1995): 569-593.

Kpundeh, Sahr John. *Politics and Corruption in Africa: A Case Study of Sierra Leone.* Lanham, MD: University Press of America, 1995.

European Defense Community (EDC), 1952–1954

Historical Background

The North Atlantic Treaty Organization (NATO) was established in April 1949. The alliance members then had to determine the role West Germany would play in defending Europe. British and American officials realized that defending Europe without a West German contribution would be enormously difficult. By 1952, West Germany, because of its location, size, and potential power, was a major player in European politics. If a war broke out in Europe, Germany would undoubtedly be involved. That is where Soviet and Western troops directly confronted each other.

The French recognized the necessity for a West German military contribution, but they also feared a re-armed Germany. The memories of World War I and II remained vivid. The French were particularly determined to keep West Germany out of NATO. As a NATO member, Germany could build its own army and a general staff. There was a need to re-arm Germany, but France wanted to limit and control the process by placing limits on personnel and armaments.

West Germany's chancellor Konrad Adenauer reluctantly agreed to re-arm West Germany, but he insisted that it be treated as an equal. Equality was a political necessity to help guarantee parliamentary approval for re-arming. There was much opposition to re-arming. The Social Democrats, the major opposition party in the German parliament, adamantly opposed re-arming. They believed that a re-armed West Germany would end any possibility that the Soviet Union would agree to German unification. Adenauer could insist that West Germany be treated as an equal because the United States and Great Britain recognized that they needed West Germany to help deter a Soviet military attack.

Origins of the EDC

In July 1950, French Premier René Pleven proposed what came to be known as the European Defense Community (EDC). His proposal called for establishing a European army, including West German military units, controlled by supranational institutions. Under the terms of the EDC treaty, the EDC would have a European commander, would be subordinate to NATO, and would remain in force for fifty years. The EDC members included France, West Germany, the Netherlands, Italy, Belgium, and Luxembourg. The purpose of the EDC, from a French point of view, was to prevent the establishment of a German army under the control of a German government.

Representatives of the six participating

nations signed the EDC treaty on May 27, 1952. Although the treaty was signed, many nations, including the six signatories, had reservations. Britain's prime minister Winston Churchill thought the treaty unworkable. He envisioned a commanding officer unable to communicate with his troops because they all spoke a different language. There was also the question of sovereignty. The smaller countries, Belgium, the Netherlands, and Luxembourg would have most if not all of their military forces under a supranational authority. Governments would have no control over their troops assigned to the European army.

Although France proposed the EDC, the French had more reservations about the treaty than anyone else did. Many members of the French National Assembly were determined to prevent the creation of a European army. The treaty was opposed by the Communists, the Gaullists, and members of the Socialist party. Although there were many reasons for the opposition, the most important reason was that France did not want to see Germany re-armed whatever the safeguards. It continued to think of Germany as its primary enemy, not the Soviet Union.

Exacerbating French fears was the fact that a large number of their troops were in Indochina and the North African colonies. In 1952, there was no indication that the Indochina War would soon end. As a result of these troop deployments, it was conceivable that there would be more German than French troops in the EDC. Initially, France was to provide fourteen divisions, West Germany and Italy twelve each, and the Benelux nations five. If France had to send more troops to Indochina, the number of its troops in the European army would be reduced.

Belgium was concerned because Great Britain was not a part of the EDC. Belgium, along with the Netherlands and Luxembourg, was fearful of being dominated by either Germany or France. The Italian government preferred membership in NATO as an alternative to the EDC.

Chancellor Adenauer wanted Germany to regain its sovereignty and independence. This was his primary goal. To accomplish this, West Germany had to contribute to the defense of Europe. Adenauer had the support of Great Britain and the United States. Both governments recognized the need to end the occupation but they also wanted measures in place to make certain Germany would not again threaten Europe. They wanted Germany integrated into European institutions as the best means for preventing a future German threat.

The Soviet Union opposed any scheme that included the re-arming of West Germany. The one trump card held by the Soviets was the desire of the German people for unification. In March 1952, in identical notes to France, Great Britain, and the United States, the Soviet Union called for a four-power meeting to discuss German unification and national elections. The Soviets proposed the withdrawal of all troops from Germany, which would be prohibited from joining any military alliance directed at any nation that had waged war against Nazi Germany during World War II. The purpose of the Soviet proposal was to derail the EDC negotiations. Great Britain and the United States recognized the Soviet proposal for what it was, a delaying tactic. The French, however, wanted to try again to reach an agreement with the Soviet Union. During the debate on the EDC from 1952 to 1954, the Soviet Union put forth a number of proposals regarding German unification. The United States and Great Britain rejected them all. France, because of its fear of a re-armed

Germany, was more willing to explore the Soviet proposals.

The EDC countries signed the treaty in May 1952. The expectation was that it would be ratified within a reasonable period of time, but the ratification process took longer than anyone expected. The Netherlands ratified the treaty in January 1954, Belgium and West Germany in March, and Luxembourg in April. Italy was expected to ratify the treaty shortly thereafter.

In April 1954, Great Britain signed an agreement with each EDC member pledging to keep its military forces in Europe indefinitely. President Eisenhower made a similar pledge regarding American forces. The British and American pledges were intended to win support in the French National Assembly for ratification of the EDC treaty. The pledges were also designed to reassure the French who worried about the possibility that West Germany, once it re-armed, would withdraw from the EDC and again threaten Europe.

France Rejects the EDC

On August 30, 1954, the French National Assembly killed the EDC treaty. A number of factors caused the defeat. Undoubtedly, the most important was the fear of a re-armed Germany. Nothing that British or American officials said or did could eliminate that fear. French political leaders knew that re-arming West Germany was inevitable. Their approach to the issue was based on emotion, not reason.

Other factors contributed to the defeat of the EDC treaty. The Soviet Union launched a ''peace campaign'' after the death of Soviet

Premier Joseph Stalin in March 1953. The Soviets abandoned their territorial claims on Turkey made by Stalin in 1945. The Korean War ended four months after the death of Stalin. The first Indochina War ended in July 1954. To the French, the Soviet Union looked a lot less threatening in 1954 than it had in the past. If the Western powers and the Soviet Union could agree on German unification, the re-arming of Germany could be postponed. The French wanted ''peace at any price.''

The rejection of the EDC by the French National Assembly negated the ''contractual agreements'' restoring sovereignty to West Germany. The EDC and the ''contractual agreements'' were part of a single package. New agreements were needed to restore sovereignty to West Germany and to enable it to contribute to the defense of Europe. Great Britain and the United States did not want to waste any more time. They were determined to re-arm West Germany with or without the cooperation of the French.

In October 1954, the United States and the representatives of eight allied nations agreed that West Germany should join NATO. The occupation of West Germany ended the following year. It was now a fully sovereign nation.

Kenneth L. Hill

See also: Creating West Germany, 1945–1955; North Atlantic Treaty Organization (NATO).

Bibliography

La Querrelle de la CED. *France Defeats EDC.* New York: Praeger, 1957.
McGeehan, Robert. *The German Rearmament Question: American Diplomacy and European Defense after World War II.* Urbana: University of Illinois Press, 1971.

Japan: World War II Peace Treaty, 1951

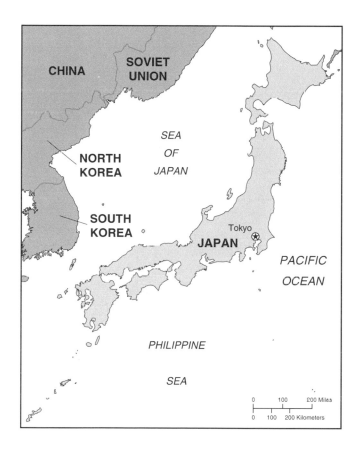

Historical Background

After World War II, American officials and those of other victorious nations had the task of writing peace treaties for the defeated nations including Germany and Japan. Officials in Washington realized that a prolonged occupation of either country would eventually prove counter-productive. Completing peace treaties for the two defeated enemies presented dissimilar problems. One crucial difference was the role of the Soviet Union.

The Soviet Union was a major player in European politics and was a significant factor in defeating Germany in World War II. American power was decisive in defeating Japan; the Soviet role was marginal. On August 6, 1945, the United States dropped an atomic bomb on Hiroshima. Two days later the Soviet Union declared war on Japan. On August 9, the United States dropped an atomic bomb on Nagasaki. On August 15, Emperor Hirohito accepted the American surrender terms. Soviet troops never entered Japan.

The first Council of Foreign Ministers (CFM) meeting convened in London in September 1945. Great Britain, the Soviet Union, and the United States established the council at the 1945 Potsdam conference. Although neither China nor France attended the Potsdam meeting, they became members of the CFM. The primary function of the council was to write draft treaties for the nations defeated in World War II. The CFM could also deal with any issues given to it by the governments of the Big Five—China, France, Great Britain, the Soviet Union, and the United States. At the London conference, the Soviet Union disagreed with the other participants on procedural issues. Consequently, the conference ended in failure. They reached no agreements regarding the occupation of Japan or the writing of a peace treaty. The failure of the first CFM meeting was not a good omen.

Soviet-American Differences

Secretary of State James Byrnes feared that the failure at London would rupture the wartime alliance that defeated Germany and Japan. In Moscow in December 1945, he took the initiative in convening a meeting of the foreign ministers of the Big Three—Great Britain, the Soviet Union, and the United States. He did not invite the ministers of France and China. Byrnes thought it might be easier to reach agreements with the Soviet Union if only three negotiating partners were at the table rather than five.

The agenda for the Moscow meeting was a long one and included questions regarding the occupation of Japan. The United States and the Soviet Union agreed to establish a Control Council in Tokyo composed of representatives of the United States, China, the Soviet Union, and one individual who represented Great Britain, India, Australia, and New Zealand. The council was to carry out directives of the Far Eastern Commission (FEC), located in Washington. The FEC was organized in February 1946 to give those nations that fought Japan a voice in the occupation. The commission consisted of eleven nations including China, Great Britain, the Soviet Union, and the United States, each with the right of veto. The other members were Australia, Canada, France, India, New Zealand, the Netherlands, and the Philippines. Despite the creation of the Allied Control Council and the FEC, Soviet influence on America's occupation policies was kept to a minimum. This in part reflected the

growing tension in Soviet-American relations after 1945.

Although the occupation of Japan was less challenging than that of Germany, American officials were nevertheless confronted with a daunting task. Japan had a larger population than Germany; it had been a great power for a long period; and many American occupation officials were unfamiliar with Japan's culture and value systems. In 1945, President Harry Truman named General Douglas MacArthur Supreme Commander for the Allied Powers (SCAP) in Japan. His duties were largely determined by Washington and his own policy preferences. With no troops in Japan, the Soviets lacked leverage to influence American policy.

General MacArthur had to disband the 4 million military personnel in Japan plus those returning from overseas. He took steps to introduce democracy, bring war criminals to trial, write a new constitution, abolish Shintoism as a state religion, conduct national elections, break up the monopolies, and make certain the Japanese people had enough to eat.

The United States and the Soviet Union differed on the procedure for completing a peace treaty for Japan. In July 1947, the United States proposed to the members of the FEC that negotiations begin to draft a treaty. The American plan was to have preliminary talks, complete a draft treaty based on the recommendations of those consulted, and then convene a conference to vote on the treaty. Approval would require a two-thirds vote, and no nation would have the right of veto.

The Soviets rejected the American proposal. They based their rejection on the Potsdam agreement, which created the CFM and gave it authority to draft peace treaties for the defeated nations. American officials did not think the Potsdam agreement was relevant to Japan. When the Potsdam conference convened in 1945, the Soviet Union was not at war with Japan. In fact, the Soviet Union and Japan had signed a neutrality agreement in April 1941, and it was operative when the Potsdam conference convened.

By 1947, Soviet-American relations were becoming more hostile, and this was evident whenever a CFM meeting convened. There were two meetings in 1947, and both exacerbated Soviet-American differences. The Soviet Union used its veto power to prevent peace treaties for Germany and Austria from being completed. The Soviets would not have an opportunity to block a treaty with Japan. The United States wanted to complete a peace treaty for Japan with or without the cooperation of the Soviet Union. The occupation of Japan could not continue indefinitely.

In September 1950, President Truman decided that negotiations should begin on a Japanese peace treaty. His decision was in part a response to the outbreak of the Korean War. Officials in Japan feared that the Korean War might be a prelude to an attack on Japan. American officials believed that a peace treaty with Japan combined with a defense treaty would reassure Japan. A defense treaty would protect Japan and would help calm the fears of those subjected to Japanese aggression during World War II.

In October 1950, the Soviet Union received a memorandum from the United States suggesting provisions to be included in a peace treaty for Japan. One proposal dealt with the future of Formosa (Taiwan), the Pescadores, Southern Sakhalin, and the Kurile Islands. The United States suggested that if, after one year, the Big Four—France, Great Britain, the Soviet Union, and the United States—could not agree on the future of these territories the issue would go to the United Nations General Assembly.

The Soviet Union responded to the October memo and raised a number of questions and objections. It insisted that the 1943 Cairo Declaration and the 1945 Potsdam agreement settled the status of Formosa and the Pescadores. The Yalta agreement, according to the Soviets, settled the status of the Kurile Islands and Southern Sakhalin. From Moscow's point of view, these issues were settled and there was no need for further negotiations.

Negotiating a Treaty

In January 1951, President Truman appointed John Foster Dulles to conduct negotiations for a peace treaty. Dulles was a leading Republican and could help win Senate ratification of a treaty when completed. His job was to consult with officials in those countries that had fought Japan in World War II. Shortly after his appointment, he departed for Japan to confer with General MacArthur and Japanese officials. As an illustration of how much things had changed since the occupation began, Dulles intended to treat the Japanese as equals. He would not, however, permit them to bargain with him regarding restrictions imposed on Japan by the terms of surrender. He also insisted that if the Japanese entered a military treaty with the United States they must do so voluntarily. The occupation would end whether Japan agreed to a military alliance or not.

Besides consulting with General MacArthur and Japanese leaders, Dulles also met with the leaders of Australia, New Zealand, and the Philippines. He spent several weeks traveling throughout Asia, and on his return to the United States, he met with President Truman. Dulles reported that a broad consensus existed on how to proceed with the treaty-making process. He was confident a treaty could be completed in a relatively short time, perhaps within six months.

On March 1, 1951, Dulles addressed the American people. He reviewed the treaty-making process and the problems to be resolved. Japan's sovereignty was to be restored. There would be no restriction on Japan's ability to develop its economy or its military capability. The United States wanted Japan to be militarily secure and to develop closer ties with the West.

American officials were concerned that the withdrawal of occupation troops from Japan would create a power vacuum the communists would exploit. This concern had to be balanced with the fact that those nations that suffered because of Japanese aggression did not want to confront that danger again. Japan's military infrastructure was destroyed by the war; America's Asian allies did not want it rebuilt.

The outbreak of the Korean War in June 1950 had a profound impact on the United States and its allies in both Europe and Asia. Historically, Korea was an important player in the Asian balance of power. A communist-dominated Korea in alignment with the People's Republic of China and the Soviet Union could threaten Japan's security. American and Japanese leaders agreed that the United States should maintain military bases in Japan after signing a peace treaty. Without an American military presence, Japan could not defend itself if attacked.

The problem of balancing the need to protect Japan with the need to protect its neighbors was resolved by constructing a number of military treaties. In April 1951, President Truman announced that the United States was in the process of negotiating a tripartite defense treaty with Australia and New Zealand. The United States was also negotiating a treaty with the Philippines.

At about this time, the United States was looking at ways that would enable West Germany to contribute to the defense of Europe. Events in Germany and Japan were moving along parallel trails. The two former enemies were regaining their influence as a result of the cold war and the Korean War.

In April 1951, President Truman fired General MacArthur because of insubordination and differences regarding Asian policies. MacArthur wanted to enlarge the Korean War by bombing military targets in China. He also supported using troops from Nationalist China (Taiwan) to help fight the war. Accepting MacArthur's recommendation would have made the treaty-writing process much more difficult, if not impossible. Great Britain and some members of the Commonwealth of Nations had extended diplomatic recognition to the Beijing regime, and some thought the mainland government should be invited to the peace conference.

Dulles returned to Japan to reassure Japanese leaders that the dismissal of the general would not delay completing a peace treaty. He also traveled to France and Great Britain to consult with and learn the views of those governments. There were a number of Anglo-American differences but none were serious. The United States accepted Great Britain as a co-sponsor of the treaty. It would be the result of a joint effort. When Dulles returned to Washington, he was confident America's allies would cooperate in the treaty-making process.

The United States relied primarily on bilateral diplomacy to complete the treaty. The idea of convening a peace treaty conference was rejected because that would enable the Soviet Union to block progress. Secretary of State Dean Acheson also favored the bilateral process, because he wanted to keep the peace treaty as simple as possible. There would be no reparation demands and no punitive provisions, nor would the treaty limit Japan's ability to re-arm. Japan was free to negotiate peace treaties with any nation dissatisfied with the Anglo-American draft.

Soviet Objections

From the end of 1950 until the convening of the peace conference in San Francisco in September 1951, the United States and the Soviet Union exchanged a series of notes regarding their respective positions on the future of Japan. The Soviets did not think the American proposals offered sufficient guarantees to prevent renewed Japanese militarism. They wanted limits placed on Japan's ability to re-arm, and they wanted the limitations to remain in place after the occupation ended. Beijing shared these views. The United States insisted that Japan had the right to protect itself and to negotiate defense treaties with other nations.

The Soviets wanted all foreign troops out of Japan within one year of the signing of a peace treaty. They wanted to prohibit Japan from joining any military alliance. The United States pointed out that the American troops would not remain in Japan as an occupation force. The troops would be there because of a bilateral Japanese-American agreement freely entered into by the Japanese government. The United Nations Charter sanctioned military alliances. Japan had the right to do what the charter permitted.

The Soviets also objected to the failure of the proposed peace treaty to recognize Beijing's control over Formosa (Taiwan) and the Pescadores. In the proposed treaty, Japan renounced all claims to the islands, but their status remained ambiguous. From the American point of view, there were two governments claiming to represent the Chinese people. Both governments could claim jurisdiction over Formosa, the Pescadores, and the offshore islands. In addition, President Truman knew the Senate would reject any treaty that extended the territorial control of the Beijing government.

The Soviet Union also objected to the United States taking possession of the Ryukyu and Bonin Islands. The Soviets wanted them returned to Japan. The United States pointed out that it was only claiming the administering authority for the islands under a U.N. trusteeship. Residual sovereignty remained with Japan. Finally, the Soviets objected to the treaty-making process. They did not think an exchange of notes constituted meaningful negotiations. The Soviets accused the United States of unilaterally drawing up a treaty that other nations could, at best, only hope to modify. The Soviets did not think this process constituted a genuine exchange of ideas.

International Reaction

In July 1951, the United States issued invitations to fifty-five nations to attend a conference in San Francisco for the signing of a peace treaty. Along with the invitations, a revised draft treaty was distributed to enable the invited nations to examine it and to recommend changes before the conference convened. Once the recommendations were studied, a final text would be circulated and would be approved or disapproved at the conference, without amendment.

Prime Minister Jawaharlal Nehru decided that India would reject the invitation because of alleged treaty defects. India wanted the Ryukyu and Bonin Islands returned to Japan because, according to Nehru, these islands were not acquired by Japan as a result of an act of aggression. India also objected to the procedure used in creating the Japanese-American military alliance. India did not think that Japan should enter a military alliance until after it had regained its sovereignty. To do so beforehand would give the appearance that without the one there would not be the other. Finally, India objected to the proposed treaty's failure to return Taiwan and the Pescadores to mainland China and that China was not invited to attend the conference. Nehru's unusual position supported the return of Taiwan and the Pescadores to China while at the same time he objected that the proposed peace treaty did not grant the Soviet Union sovereignty over the Kurile Islands and Southern Sakhalin. Burma and Yugoslavia also rejected invitations.

In August 1951, the United States and Great Britain distributed the final text of a Japanese peace treaty. The August draft differed only slightly from that of July. The clause on reparations was strengthened. It recognized Japan's limited ability to pay reparations, but it was expected to do so in the future. This final draft was what the delegates attending the conference could either accept or reject.

Many nations objected to various parts of the treaty but they recognized that the occupation could not continue indefinitely. When Dulles traveled to the Philippines in 1951, he was aware of the deep bitterness felt by the people toward the Japanese. Japan's occupation of the Philippines had been cruel and destructive. The Philippine government wanted $8 billion in reparations, but the Japanese economy had not sufficiently recovered to permit reparations to be included in the peace treaty. Other nations also wanted reparations. Dulles was sympathetic to these claims, but he wanted them to be dealt with on a bilateral basis in the future. The United States was not seeking reparations.

The San Francisco Conference

Much to the surprise of some American officials, the Soviet Union, Poland, and Czechoslovakia agreed to attend the conference, which opened in San Francisco on September 4, 1951. President Truman addressed the opening session and emphasized the theme of reconciliation. Each delegation had a one-hour period for speeches. Soviet Foreign Minister Andrei Gromyko made a number of motions; all were defeated. During his presentation, he offered a number of amendments, none were considered. He tried to drive a wedge between the Asian delegates and those representing the Western nations, but his effort failed. Two of the Asian delegates accused the Soviet Union of demanding freedoms for the Japanese people that were denied to the Soviet people. At a news conference, Gromyko warned that approving the peace treaty could lead to a new war in the Far East.

On September 8, 1951, forty-nine nations signed the treaty. The Soviet Union, Czechoslovakia, and Poland did not. The treaty contained several major provisions. Japan's sovereignty was restored but was confined to the four islands of Hokkaido, Honshu, Shikoko, and Kyushu. The treaty recognized the need for Japan to pay reparations, but nothing was said about the amount to be paid. Reparation claims were estimated at $100 billion. By signing the treaty, Japan renounced claims to Taiwan and the Pescadores.

After the signing ceremony, the United States and Japan signed a military alliance permitting the stationing of American forces in Japan for an indefinite period. By the terms of the treaty, Japan could not permit any other nation to station military personnel in Japan or to have military bases there without America's approval. If asked by the Japanese government, American troops could help quell an internal rebellion. At the time, the governments in Washington and Tokyo feared a communist uprising. The defense treaty was one component of a security system to protect the free nations of Asia.

A new phase of the cold war began. No one in September 1945 could have foreseen how rapidly the World War II alignments would be replaced by a very different power configuration. America's two wartime allies, China and the Soviet Union, were now adversaries. Two enemies, Germany and Japan, were now allies.

The Occupation Ends

When the occupation ended, Japan and the United States forged a close cooperative relationship. Democracy took root in Japan, and both countries opposed the spread of communism. Japan's anti-Soviet sentiments were due in part to the fact that many thousands of Japanese prisoners of war were still in the Soviet Union. Some estimated the number of POWs at more than 200,000. The Japanese also objected to the loss of the Kurile and the Southern Sakhalin islands. Japan's hostility toward the Soviet Union was also the result of the fact that the Soviet declaration of war against Japan violated the 1941 neutrality agreement. The Soviets violated the 1941 treaty, fought in the war about one week, and won control over Japanese territory.

In March 1952, the United States Senate gave its approval to the peace and defense treaties signed with Japan, the American-Philippine defense treaty, and the tripartite agreement with Australia and New Zealand.

The United States and Japan were at peace.

Kenneth L. Hill

See also: ANZUS Pact.

Bibliography

Acheson, Dean. *Present at the Creation.* New York: Norton, 1969.

Brines, Russell. *MacArthur's Japan.* Philadelphia: J.B. Lippincott, 1948.

Johnson, Sheila. *American Attitudes Towards Japan, 1941–1975.* Washington, DC: American Enterprise Institution, 1975.

Mastny, Vojtech. *The Cold War and Soviet Insecurity.* New York: Oxford University Press, 1996.

Montgomery, John. *Forced to Be Free: The Artificial Revolution in Germany and Japan.* Chicago: University of Chicago Press, 1957.

Reischauer, Edwin. *The United States and Japan.* Cambridge: Harvard University Press, 1965.

Sebald, William. *With MacArthur in Japan.* London: Cresset Press, 1967.

Shiels, Frederick. *America, Okinawa, and Japan.* Washington, DC: University Press of America, 1980.

Truman, Harry. *Memoirs: Years of Trial and Hope.* Garden City: Doubleday, 1956.

Wilcox, Wayne. *Asia and the International System.* Cambridge: Winthrop Press, 1972.

Middle East Negotiations

The history of Middle East negotiations has been a long and extremely convoluted one. While a few of the negotiations have led to lasting peace treaties, or to temporary armistices and cease-fires, many have failed completely. This fitful history of regional diplomacy has basically involved three kinds of negotiations over the fifty or so years since the end of World War II. These are: (1) talks between Israel and the Arab world, (2) talks between the Israelis and the Palestinians, and (3) talks among the Arab parties (these have also included issues not pertaining to Israel).

With the exception of the multilateral talks that began in 1991—known as the Madrid round, after the city where they were first held—all the negotiations have been conducted on a bilateral level. At least one set of talks—the Camp David Accords—was mediated by the United States, while the Madrid negotiations involved both superpowers. The rest have been conducted largely without outside mediation.

Aside from the many substantive issues dividing the various parties in the Middle East, the history of negotiations in the region has been plagued by two general obstacles. First has been the problem of recognition. Perhaps more than anywhere else in the world, here it has been difficult to get the parties even to recognize one another. Until Camp David, no Arab country was willing to officially recognize the legitimate existence of the state of Israel. And not before the Oslo Accords was any Israeli government willing to accept the Palestine Liberation Organization (PLO) as a legitimate representative of the Palestinian people, de-spite the fact that the PLO was clearly the accepted voice and representative of the vast majority of the Palestinian people. Indeed, it was against Israeli law for any government official to even meet with PLO representatives until 1993.

Even more obstructive were Israeli attitudes about Palestinians. For many years, most Israeli officials, in both the Labor and Likud parties (roughly, the moderate left and right on the country's political spectrum), did not even recognize the existence of a distinctive Palestinian people, preferring instead to see them as a subset of the Arab world and viewing Jordan as partly their state. This view allowed Israeli governments to avoid the very uncomfortable issues of Palestinian nationalism and statehood.

A second obstacle to Middle East negotiations for many years concerned forums and context. That is to say, until Camp David, every Arab government made Israeli recognition of the PLO a prerequisite for direct Arab-Israeli talks. These governments also insisted that there would be no talks until Israel lived up to various U.N. resolutions—passed after the 1948, 1967, and 1973 wars—requiring the Jewish state to settle the issue of Palestinian refugees and, in the case of the latter two, to withdraw from the lands occupied in 1967. Israel consistently tried to separate these matters, hoping to achieve peace with its neighbors without conceding recognition of the PLO or discussing the possibility of a Palestinian state.

In addition, the Arab states have always pushed for an international forum for talks, preferably under U.N. aegis and with the inclusion of the Soviet Union. Israel, which largely views the United Nations as a hostile body, consistently pushed for bilateral talks with Arab states, fearing that Israel would be outnumbered and outpressured in a multilateral forum. The United States, Israel's superpower patron, has largely gone along with this insistence for reasons of its own; Washington did not want the kind of Soviet participation that an international forum implied, fearing that it would lead to increased Soviet influence in a region deemed crucial to U.S. national security. This demand only eased with the collapsing power of the USSR in the early 1990s, when the United States accepted Soviet participation in the Madrid talks.

While the many wars between the Arab states and Israel have all been followed by meetings to discuss cease-fires and other immediate issues pertaining to the specific conflict of the time, there have been four key sets of negotiations in the region since World War II: the talks leading to the Camp David Accords between Egypt and Israel in 1978, the multilateral Madrid negotiations from 1991 to 1993, the Oslo Accords and the subsequent negotiations between the Palestinians and Israelis on their implementation that began in 1993, and the negotiations that achieved the Israeli-Jordanian peace treaty of 1994.

Modern History of the Middle East Through Camp David

Following World War I, the former Ottoman Empire lands in the Middle East were divided into League of Nations mandates, administered by the French and the British. France was given control of Syria (which then included Lebanon), and Britain was put in charge of Iraq, Transjordan, and Palestine.

By 1946, all these states, except Palestine, had been given their formal independence. Palestine, however, presented special problems, owing to the presence of an increasing population of Jews who had been migrating to the region since the late nineteenth century in the hopes of creating a Jewish state.

Beginning in 1917, Britain promised the Jews a homeland, while at the same time reassuring the Arabs in Palestine that their rights would be protected. The mutual exclusiveness of these promises produced a series of multi-sided conflicts between the Jews, the Arabs, and the British, as well as a series of British position papers that tried to glide over the problem. Exhausted by World War II and facing independence movements throughout its far-flung empire, Britain in 1947 admitted it had failed to find a workable solution for Palestine, informing the United Nations that it would turn over administration of the region to the United Nations on May 15, 1948.

The United Nations set up a commission that issued a report calling for the division of Palestine into separate Arab and Jewish states, with Jerusalem administered as an international city. This solution pleased the Zionists, but rancored the Arabs, who did not like the fact the United Nations would give 55 percent of the territory to a group representing just over 10 percent of the population of Palestine. Arab governments around the region and representatives in Palestine rejected the compromise. On May 14, 1948, however, the Jews acted unilaterally, declaring an independent state in the zone ascribed to them by the United Nations, but arming themselves and preparing to conquer more territory.

The following day, the Arab states of Egypt, Transjordan (now Jordan), Syria, and Iraq retaliated, moving in to defend the zones ascribed to the Arabs. After a year of fierce fighting, with numerous atrocities on both sides, the Israelis achieved not only independence, but also control over more than 70 percent of Palestine. In the process, several hundred thousand Palestinians fled or were forced to leave—Israelis say the former; Arabs insist on the latter—creating a problem that would stymie Arab-Israeli relations through the present day. During the summer of 1949, armistices—though not formal peace treaties—were signed between all the belligerent states. Israel's official borders were left to be determined.

A state of belligerency between the Arab states and Israel continued to exist through the 1970s, exacerbated by Israeli participation in the British- and French-inspired Sinai War of 1956 and, more importantly, by Israel's capture of Egyptian, Jordanian, and Syrian territory in the Six-Day War of 1967. This result triggered yet another wave of Palestinian refugees, a U.N. resolution calling for Israel to pull out of the newly Occupied Territories, and official—albeit internationally unrecognized—Israeli incorporation of East Jerusalem. The war also prompted the infamous three "no's" of the Khartoum Summit of 1967, whereby the Arab League refused to make peace, negotiate, or even recognize the Jewish state.

Earlier, in 1964, Egyptian President Gamal Abdel Nasser organized the PLO. At first, the organization and its military wing were meant to be subordinate to Egypt. But in 1968, Yasir Arafat's Al-Fatah militants defeated the Israeli army at the Battle of Karameh. Following the Arab defeat of 1967, the victory was cheered by Arabs, propelling Arafat, Al-Fatah, and the Palestinian cause to the front stage of the Middle East conflict. No more was it said that the Palestinians themselves should wait upon Arab armies. In 1969, Arafat and Al-Fatah took control of the PLO. Still, the defeat of 1967 stuck in the throats of Arab leaders, who sought the chance to reverse their losses. Nasser tried—and failed—with his War of Attrition. But his successor, Anwar Sadat, though only achieving a stalemate with Israel in the 1973 war, seemed to have succeeded in rescuing Arab pride and demonstrating to Israel that the status quo could not stand.

Meanwhile, inter-Arab relations were undergoing a change too. Since 1948, Jordan's King Hussein had maintained that he spoke for the Palestinian people, since half his country's population consisted of Palestinians. But at the Arab summit of 1974, the governments of the region officially recognized the PLO as the representative of the Palestinian people. This contradicted the dominant line of the ruling Labor party in Israel, which had been pushing for a Palestinian-Jordanian confederation that would include the West Bank. This position would lose its relevance with the victory of the hard-line Likud coalition in 1977 Israeli elections. Under Likud, Israel would vastly expand its settlement program in the Occupied Territories, seemingly in preparation for incorporating them into the Jewish state for good.

Israeli inflexibility, however, was matched by a new willingness of the Egyptians to negotiate. Sadat, the more pro-Western, less bellicose successor to Nasser, was now satisfied that he had upset the unacceptable post-1967 status quo in the Sinai with the stalemate of 1973, a result made even more palatable by the fact that his oil-rich Arab allies had demonstrated the power of their resources over the West with their oil boycott of 1973–1974. In one of the boldest moves in modern Middle East history, Sadat flew to

Jerusalem in late 1977 and spoke to the Israeli Knesset, or parliament. The stage had been set for the first significant negotiations between Israel and an Arab state: the Camp David talks.

Camp David

Sadat's speech to the Knesset—expressing sympathy for Jewish security fears and invoking the memory of the Holocaust—touched the Israeli people. But it was intended as much for Washington as for Jerusalem. Having expelled thousands of Soviet advisors from Egypt in 1972, Sadat was eager to establish warmer relations with the United States, knowing that it was better situated than was the USSR to offer the kinds of technical and economic assistance the Egyptian government needed to improve the quality of life of its people.

The speech had its intended effect. U.S. President Jimmy Carter—with his longtime interest in the Middle East and a penchant for mediation—invited both Sadat and the newly elected Likud Prime Minister Menachem Begin to the presidential retreat at Camp David for a marathon summit. After thirteen days of intensive talks in September 1978, the three leaders—who would collectively win a Nobel Peace Prize for their efforts—announced they had reached not one but two sets of accords.

The first Camp David Accord concerned the Palestinians. It called for a transitional period of five years in which the Occupied Territories would gradually be given an autonomous status and the right to elect its own government. Ultimately, this would lead to a set of final status talks in the early 1980s, with Jordanians and Egyptians—including Palestinians from the territories—negotiating on behalf of Palestinians generally.

Most observers expected the talks to lead to a Jordanian-Palestinian confederation.

The second Camp David Accord was more straightforward. It called for the signing of a peace treaty within three months, wherein Egypt would recognize Israel and guarantee its security in exchange for Israeli withdrawal from the Sinai. As far as Sadat was concerned, the two accords were a package, but subsequent events proved otherwise.

The Arab states all condemned Sadat and cut off relations with Egypt. Shortly after the talks, Israel invaded southern Lebanon, ostensibly to clear out PLO enclaves that had been using the region for attacks on northern Israel. Many Arabs—including many Egyptians—said that Israel had used the Camp David Accords to secure its western flank before attacking on its north. Sadat, they said, had been played for a fool. Moreover, the Likud government continued to accelerate the pace of Jewish settlement-building in the Occupied Territories.

Beleaguered and ostracized, Sadat too began to wonder whether Begin had negotiated in good faith at all, since the outcome of Camp David served Israeli needs so precisely. That is to say, Israel had achieved an immediate bilateral peace with its most formidable Arab neighbor in exchange for vague promises of Palestinian autonomy in the future. Moreover, Sadat was disappointed at America's inaction. While the United States was delivering a massive aid package to Cairo as promised, it was doing little to pressure the Israelis to live by the agreements mediated by its own president. In the end, Sadat would pay the ultimate price for his dealings with Israel, when he was gunned down by Islamist militants in his own army who objected to the agreement.

For their part, Israeli hard-liners—especially those on the far right of the Likud coalition—had their own suspicions. They had given up the vast Sinai territory—with its oilfields, Israeli investments, and strategic defensive depth—for nothing more than an Egyptian promise to abstain from hostilities. There was talk that the Arabs were merely trying a new tactic in their decades-long quest to destroy the Jewish state.

Madrid

During the 1980s, both the Reagan administration and the more conservative Arab leaders proposed a series of plans to solve the Palestinian crisis and, they hoped, the overall Middle East situation. Both the so-called Reagan Plan of 1982 and the plan proposed by U.S. Secretary of State George Shultz were based on the Jordanian option, that is, the Jordanian-Palestinian Federation on the West Bank. King Fahd of Saudi Arabia added another element to the mixture, when he offered to use his influence to pressure Arab states to recognize Israel once the latter had agreed to the formula laid out in the Reagan Plan. But the Likud government was in no mood to negotiate, rejecting all three plans and continuing its policy of settlement building in the Occupied Territories. Unbowed by Israel's fiasco in Lebanon, both Begin and his Likud successor Yitzhak Shamir hewed to a hard line, refusing any concessions to the Palestinians.

The despair of the Palestinians in the territories was becoming more palpable with each passing year. Subject to economic exploitation, political oppression, and daily humiliations, they had little to hope for. The PLO, ejected from its bases in Lebanon by the Israelis and Syrians, was now ensconced

1,500 miles away in Tunisia, where comfortable officials, paid by donations from the oil-rich Arab states, seemed to grow more and more complacent. The ultimate insult, however, came at the Arab summit in Jordan in November 1987, when Hussein snubbed Arafat, and the delegates placed the Palestinian issue second on their agenda, after the Iran-Iraq War—the first time this had ever occurred.

But as they had done once before after the 1967 war, the Palestinians decided to take things into their own hands. Just a month after the Jordan summit, a spontaneous popular uprising broke out across the territories. Known as the *intifada*, Arabic for "shaking off," as in "shaking off Israeli rule," the protests changed every equation in the region, though it took some time for the full effect of the intifada to be felt. In 1988, King Hussein renounced his claims on the West Bank and suspended his administration there, thus killing the so-called Jordanian option. (Under post-1967 agreement, Israel permitted Jordan to continue administering basic social services in the West Bank.)

But the real impact of the intifada was felt in Tunis. There, Arafat found the balance of power within the PLO forever changed. Whereas previously, the Palestinians in refugee camps and the diaspora—that is, Palestinians who had once lived in Israel proper and insisted on the destruction of the Zionist state—had dominated the organization, now the Palestinians in the territories were in command. Having seen Israeli power close up and wanting relief from Jewish oppression, they were willing to compromise with a two-state solution. This permitted Arafat to abrogate those parts of the Palestinian covenant calling for the destruction of Israel, a prerequisite for talks with the United States.

(These talks ended soon after, when Arafat refused to condemn a Palestinian attack on a Tel Aviv beach a year later.)

With the Persian Gulf War, the situation in the region changed once again. Victorious over Iraq and no longer threatened by a collapsing Soviet Union, the United States pushed for multilateral talks between Arabs and Israelis, partly to reward the Arabs for their support of the coalition against Saddam Hussein. (Bush rewarded Israel for its non-involvement in the war by unfreezing loan guarantees destined for new settlements in the Occupied Territories.)

The Madrid negotiations included Israel, the main Arab states, the United States, the Soviet Union, and the ghost of a Palestinian presence, incorporated into the Jordanian delegation. The Madrid process included a two-track approach: a negotiation of the Palestinian problem along with talks to resolve the unsettled state of Jordanian and Syrian relations with Israel. Inevitably, the talks failed. Israel was unwilling to budge on Palestine, which prompted the Arab states to refuse to negotiate the second track.

Still, Madrid would come to have an important effect on subsequent relations between the Palestinians and the Israelis, and, by implication, on relations between Jordan and Israel as well. First, Arafat—excluded from the summit—feared that other Palestinian representatives might sign a separate deal with Israel, undercutting his position and perhaps jeopardizing the possibility of a Palestinian state. Second, the failure of Madrid—combined with the ongoing intifada and a financial crisis produced, in part, by the costly building of settlements and the security infrastructure needed to support them—led Israeli voters to oust the Likud government and replace it with a Labor majority in the 1992 elections. All these factors, then, prompted both Arafat and the new Israeli prime minister, Yitzhak Rabin, to seek a new and secret forum to settle their differences.

Oslo

Almost immediately after the 1992 elections, Rabin and Foreign Minister Shimon Peres began looking for ways to meet with the PLO. When the Norwegian prime minister offered his country as a venue, both the Palestinians and the Israelis accepted. Meeting in and around Oslo, the secret talks got off to a tentative start, especially on the part of the Israelis who refused to send representatives from the foreign ministry until pressed to do so by PLO representatives. Eventually, Deputy Foreign Minister Yossi Beilen joined the team.

The first order of business was establishing the scope of the discussions and how binding the agreement, whatever it included, should be. The PLO wanted a comprehensive agreement, with an ironclad linkage between an interim accord and the final status talks. Israel refused to concede either. Indeed, the Israeli position dominated the talks, forcing the PLO to accept little more than a set of rules for further negotiations. In return, it received official Israeli recognition as the sole representative of the Palestinian people. Ultimately, both sides agreed that the final status talks would take place three years after the signing of the Oslo agreement, leaving the PLO and the Palestinians in limbo between subjection and sovereignty.

Still, the Declaration of Principles, as the Oslo Accords were officially known, and the internationally televised handshake between Rabin and Arafat on the White House lawn after its signing in September 1993 inaugurated a new era in Israeli-Palestinian relations. There was widespread celebration in both Israel and the Occupied Territories, though this could not disguise the fact that important elements in both societies were utterly opposed to both the agreement and the very idea of Israeli-PLO talks. Right-wing Israelis feared that Rabin was selling out legitimate security concerns by placing them in the hands of a Palestinian authority headed by someone they considered to be an unrepentant terrorist. Worse, he was admitting that Israel might not have a legitimate right to govern all the territories to which they maintained it was entitled—territories which, the religious among them believed, God had given them in perpetuity.

Ironically, Arafat's opponents in the Palestinian community agreed, though from the opposite perspective. For the Islamists of Hamas, any agreement that accepted the existence of a Jewish state on holy Muslim lands was anathema. Similarly, the presence of a Zionist state—in the heart of the Arab Middle East—was deemed unacceptable by Arafat's secular, left-wing opposition both inside and outside the PLO. Though the Oslo Accords, thin and lacking substance, offered little beyond Israeli recognition of the PLO, these opposition forces recognized what Rabin and Arafat also knew. Once started, the peace process would propel further negotiation and an ultimate settlement by virtue of its own momentum. That appraisal, as it turned out, would prove far too optimistic.

Post–Oslo Accords

As noted earlier, the Oslo Accords offered little in the way of substance. Beyond Israeli recognition of the PLO, they simply offered protocols and schedules for future talks, an agreement that the new Palestinian Authority would include Gaza and Jericho, and a deadline for the final status negotiations. Still, both the PLO National Council and the Israeli Knesset endorsed them. Now came the hard part, working out the details of Israeli withdrawal, Palestinian security arrangements, and substantive issues concerning Jewish settlements, water supplies, Jerusalem, and the ultimate status of a Palestinian entity.

While negotiators for the PLO and the Israeli government sat down at the Egyptian resort town of Taba, terror struck in the form of a militant religious Jew firing upon Muslim worshipers in Hebron, killing twenty-nine before being beaten to death by survivors. Hamas soon responded with a series of suicide bus bombings that left more than a dozen Israeli soldiers and civilians dead. Despite the violence, both sides pledged themselves to continue the talks, though the Israelis began hedging on the deadlines for future negotiations.

On May 4, negotiators, now meeting in Cairo, announced they had reached an agreement. In contrast to the dozen or so pages of the Oslo Accords, the Cairo document—outlining the specifics of the so-called Gaza-Jericho first plan—was hundreds of pages long, with dozens of annexes and hundreds of reservations, qualifications, and exceptions. For Arafat's opponents, it offered little indeed: limited Palestinian Authority jurisdiction over Gaza and the West Bank town of Jericho. Israel would continue to occupy almost all the West Bank, though its troops could not go into these Palestinian-occupied areas.

Indeed, Palestinian society was torn apart by the agreement. While Arafat supporters celebrated—cheering the arrival of the first Palestinian forces in Jericho and Gaza—Hamas militants protested. As the demonstrations escalated in the fall of 1994, Arafat's police opened fire, killing thirteen and wounding dozens more. It was the worst violence in the Occupied Territories since the signing of the Oslo Accords, and, more ominously, it represented the first great clash between Palestinians themselves. Though the two sides reached an agreement, Hamas launched yet another bombing campaign against Israel, prompting border closures and demands that Arafat crack down on the militants.

This placed the PLO leader in an awkward position. To keep Israel negotiating, he had to deal with his own radicals harshly. This, in turn, jeopardized his own legitimacy among the Palestinian people. Meanwhile, the Rabin government was having its own problems, as the Hamas bombing campaign began to have a corrosive effect on Israeli public opinion, decreasing the level of support for the Labor government and the Oslo process. At the same time, both the PLO and the Rabin government had staked their political reputations and futures on the agreement, and were thus committed to further talks.

After a series of deadlines had passed, the two sides signed a second set of implementing accords in September 1995. Under these, Israel agreed to pull out of some 450 Palestinian villages and towns before the January 1996 Palestinian elections. While this withdrawal placed over 70 percent of the people in the territories (minus the Jewish settlers) under Palestinian authority, it still left the bulk of the rural areas in Israeli hands. In effect, said Palestinian critics of the plan, it was turning their lands into a Middle Eastern version of South African homelands, isolated and crowded enclaves surrounded by Israeli forces and settlers. Moreover, the

agreement ignored the two most contentious cities in the territories, Hebron and Jerusalem. In the former, a small group of ultra-Orthodox Jewish settlers maintained a provocative presence in the overwhelmingly Muslim city. As for Jerusalem, both sides claimed it as their capital—or, in the Palestinians' case, their future capital—though Israel insisted on keeping all of it. Settlement of this issue, both sides agreed, would have to await final status talks.

On November 4, 1995, the volatile situation in Israel and Palestine was once again inflamed, this time by the assassination of Rabin by a right-wing Jewish university student. At first, the event propelled the peace process. Rabin's memory as a martyr for peace was now invoked by Peres, his successor, to build support for the peace process. Public opinion polls showed an upswing in support, a trend mirrored on the Palestinian side by the overwhelming victory of Arafat and his Al-Fatah party in the January 1996 elections.

Still, the Palestinian issue is nothing if not unpredictable. Determined to destroy what was considered to be a sellout of Palestinian aspirations, Hamas launched a series of devastating suicide bombings in Israeli cities in the spring of 1996. This, as well as a disastrous offensive against Islamic militants in Lebanon, undermined support for Peres's candidacy as the May 1996 Israeli general elections drew close. Those elections, of course, ended in the victory of Likud standard bearer Binyamin Netanyahu, who had made no secret of his serious reservations about the peace process during the campaign.

Though warned by the Americans, the PLO, and Arab leaders not to renege on agreements signed by his predecessor, Netanyahu both refused to meet with his Palestinian counterpart and initiated provocative moves, such as the opening of a tunnel beneath the holy Muslim sites on the Temple Mount. A symbolically charged issue, the tunnel opening sparked a series of Palestinian demonstrations that culminated in exchanges of gunfire between Palestinian and Israeli security forces.

With the peace process seeming to unravel, President Clinton sent special envoy Dennis Ross to arrange a settlement over the outstanding issue of Hebron. Months of negotiating resulted in a January 1997 agreement dividing the city into Israeli- and Palestinian-controlled zones, though many Hebronites criticized the fact that 450 Jewish settlers were treated the same as some 100,000 Muslim residents of the city.

Contentious and unpopular, Hebron proved to be the last major agreement reached between the Palestinian Authority and the Israeli government. Netanyahu's insistence on continuing settlement expansion—as well as building entirely new ones in Arab East Jerusalem—has been largely responsible for the near-frozen relations and lack of progress in Palestinian-Israeli negotiations through most of 1998.

James Ciment

See also: Egypt: War of Attrition, 1967–1970; Israel: War of Independence, 1948–1949; Egypt: Sinai War, 1956; Israel: Six-Day War, 1967; Israel: Yom Kippur War, 1973; Palestine: Intifada, 1987–1992.

Bibliography

Aruri, Naseer. *The Obstruction of Peace: The US, Israel and the Palestinians.* Monroe, ME: Common Courage Press, 1995.

Corbin, Jane. *The Norway Channel: The Secret Talks That Led to the Middle East Peace Accord.* New York: Atlantic Monthly Press, 1994.

Kaufman, Edy, Shurki Abed, and Robert Rothstein, eds. *Democracy, Peace and the Israeli-Palestinian Conflict.* Boulder, CO: Lynne Rienner, 1993.

Lesch, Ann Mosely, and Mark Tessler. *Israel, Egypt and the Palestinians: From Camp David to Intifada.* Bloomington: Indiana University Press, 1994.

Makovsky, David. *Making Peace with the PLO: The Rabin Government's Road to the Oslo Accords.* Boulder, CO: Westview Press, 1996.

Quandt, William. *Peace Process: American Diplomacy and the Arab-Israeli Conflict Since 1967.* Washington, DC: Brookings Institution, 1993.

Quigley, John. *Palestine and Israel: A Challenge to Justice.* Durham, NC: Duke University Press, 1990.

Said, Edward. *Peace and Its Discontents: Essays on Palestine in the Middle East Peace Process.* New York: Random House, 1996.

North Atlantic Treaty Organization (NATO)

The North Atlantic Treaty Organization (NATO) was established under the North Atlantic Treaty signed in 1949 by a number of non-Communist European nations, along with the United States and Canada. Officially, the treaty was a mutual military and defense pact, calling for the common defense of all members against outside attack. In reality, the treaty was largely designed to create a U.S. security umbrella over those non-Communist European nations perceived to be threatened by Soviet expansionism during the early years of the cold war.

The North Atlantic Treaty was initially signed by twelve signatories in 1949. These initial countries included Belgium, Canada, Denmark, France, Iceland, Italy, Luxembourg, Netherlands, Norway, Portugal, Great Britain, and the United States. In 1952, Greece and Turkey acceded to the treaty, with West Germany following in 1955. While Spain joined in 1982, it did not fully participate in the military organs of NATO until 1996. France, while remaining a member of NATO, withdrew from NATO's integrated military structure in 1966. It resumed participation in some of NATO's military activities and organizations in 1996.

The Atlantic Alliance is ruled by the North Atlantic Council, consisting of permanent representatives from each country, or heads of state or foreign ministers. Meetings of the council are held at least twice a year, with the secretary general of NATO serving as the council's chair. Decisions are made by common consent rather than majority vote.

Founding of NATO

At the end of World War II, much of Western Europe lay in ruins—its economy shattered by the war, its citizens without morale, and its political institutions weak. Although itself heavily damaged by the war, the victorious Soviet Union appeared to be in a dominant position, with its vast military machine in occupation of much of the European continent east of the Elbe River in Germany. Between 1946 and 1948, Moscow imposed pro-Soviet, Communist regimes in every country east of the Elbe, except Greece, which had been defended first by Britain and then by the United States—the latter under the aegis of the Truman Doctrine, which promised aid to forces fighting against indigenous Communist rebels. (Yugoslavia remained Communist, but outside Soviet conrol.)

Despite this aid to Greece, there was a fear among internationalists in the United States that the American people would demand a return to isolationism in the wake of World War II, as there had been after World War I. Unlike in the 1920s, however, there was no Western country capable of maintaining international leadership in the post–World War II era except the United States. Both Britain and France were barely capable of fighting rear-guard actions against their disintegrating empires. Only the United States, internationalists in Washington believed, could halt the tide of Communist expansion.

In 1948, the United States launched its second great post-war initiative to build a strong, non-Communist Western Europe (the first was the Truman Doctrine). Known as the Marshall Plan, it extended billions of dollars in aid money to West European countries, in the hope that this might spur economic revitalization and undermine the appeal of Communist politicians who were arguing that capitalism had produced the prewar depression that had caused World War II. The plan was an overwhelming success for the United States and the cause of anti-Communism. In revitalizing economies and staving off total economic collapse, it stabilized the democratic, non-Communist political order across Western Europe.

At the same time, a number of West European governments were also concerned about the revitalization of their militaries, fearing both the reality of the Soviet threat and the potential of a revitalized German military threat. In March 1948, Britain, France, and the Benelux countries signed a collective defense treaty known as the Brussels Treaty. Still, the signatories knew that they were in no position to defend themselves against the Soviet Union without the assistance of the United States, the world's only other superpower.

Within a month of signing the Brussels Treaty, the European signatories were in negotiations with the governments of the United States and Canada to draw these two North American nations into the agreement. A year later, in 1949, the collective defense treaty that established NATO was signed by the initial twelve signatories during a meeting in Washington. For the United States,

membership in NATO was a unique diplomatic endeavor. This would be the first time since its 1778 treaty with France that the United States had formed a permanent alliance with another country.

At the core of the treaty was Article 5, which stated that "an armed attack against one or more of [the member states] in Europe or North America shall be considered an attack against them all; and consequently they agree that, if such an armed attack occurs, each of them, in exercise of the right of individual or collective self-defense recognized by Article 51 of the Charter of the United Nations, will assist the Party or Parties so attacked by taking forthwith, individually and in concert with the other Parties, such action as it deems necessary, including the use of armed force, to restore and maintain the security of the North Atlantic area." Other key stipulations of the treaty called for centralized military command (Article 9) and military assistance from the United States to other members (Article 3, eventually totaling $25 billion over twenty years in direct military aid.)

Early Stresses

Among the most important issues in the early years of the alliance was what to do about West Germany. For most West European countries, the memory of Nazi occupation was still very fresh in the early 1950s. The idea of allowing West Germany to rearm was frightening. Yet, at the same time, it was recognized that Bonn was the key to the alliance's success. The large German population, the growing German economy, and the country's geographic position astride the invasion routes from the East made its membership in the alliance critical. Additionally, it was also feared that keeping West Germany out of the alliance would force Bonn to seek closer ties with both East Germany and its Soviet patron, as a means of self-defense.

Thus, the members of NATO—and particularly France—wanted to find a "safe" way to integrate West Germany into a Western military alliance. The direct control offered by the centralized military command of NATO seemed to offer the key, and in 1955, West Germany joined the alliance. While considered one of the great successes of post–World War II European recovery, it could, and was, argued that the alliance integrated West Germany into the Western bloc of nations. It also helped to foster the growing animosity between the Western and Eastern blocs. Within a short time after Bonn joined NATO, the Soviet Union organized a similar military alliance, known as the Warsaw Pact, among its East European neighbors, thus hardening the military lines of the cold war.

Ironically, it was one of the original signatories of the Brussels Treaty—France—that proved to be the most recalcitrant member of the alliance in its first two decades. Under the nationalist leadership of President Charles de Gaulle, who came to power in 1958, France began to make its dissatisfaction with the U.S. dominance of NATO known. At the same time, and zealous of its own sovereignty, Paris resented the presence of "foreign" military officials and bases—that is, NATO member military officials and bases—on its soil. De Gaulle also feared that membership in NATO would draw France "automatically" into wars that it might prefer not to become involved in. With these considerations in mind, Paris opted to withdraw from the centralized command structure of NATO in July 1966, though it remained a member of the alliance.

Nuclear Defense

From the very beginning, NATO faced a critical defense problem. Its combined conventional force was no match for the overwhelming manpower and weaponry of the Soviet bloc, even with the participation of the United States and the placement of over 300,000 U.S. soldiers on bases on West European soil. Thus, early on, NATO's strategy involved a back-up plan for nuclear defense, mainly a U.S. nuclear defense. During the 1950s, the United States offered its nuclear umbrella to Europe and extended its policy of Mutually Assured Destruction (MAD) to include its NATO allies. Still, many West Europeans did not believe that the United States would risk a nuclear attack on its own territory to defend Europe against an invasion. It was this thinking that ultimately led Britain, and especially the more vulnerable France, to develop independent nuclear retaliatory forces of their own.

To alleviate European fears, the United States began to deploy U.S. nuclear weapons on West European bases in 1957. Thus, the various NATO members made sure that the Soviet superiority in conventional weapons and men was countered by both nuclear weapons and technologically superior conventional weapons. The decision to place these missiles near the Soviet Union, and especially in neighboring Turkey, is seen by many as one of the reasons Moscow chose to begin deploying missiles in Communist Cuba in 1962. Kennedy and Soviet Premier Nikita Khrushchev would eventually work out a secret agreement whereby the missiles were removed from Turkey in exchange for a halt in Soviet missile deployment to Cuba.

With détente and the easing of tensions between Western and Eastern Europe in the 1970s, however, the political thinking in many West European countries began to change. Rather than fearing U.S. abandonment in the face of a Soviet invasion, many—especially among the young and on the left—feared that Europe would become a proxy battleground for a U.S.-Soviet confrontation. Thus, when the Reagan administration decided to deploy medium-range Pershing missiles in Western Europe in the early 1980s—the so-called euro-missiles—the decision was met with vast protests, particularly in West Germany and Britain, America's two most important allies in Europe. Still, the deployments went ahead.

The Collapse of the Soviet Union

Until the 1960s, the Soviet Union seemed capable of meeting what it considered to be the NATO military threat, while at the same time achieving substantial economic growth at home. But by the 1970s, it was becoming clear to many Soviet watchers in the West that this balancing act was becoming increasingly difficult for Moscow to maintain. Its cumbersome centralized economy began to come undone under the dual requirements of meeting NATO military advances while, at the same time, fulfilling the growing consumer demands of the Soviet public.

Under Premier Leonid Brezhnev—who ousted Khrushchev in 1964—and others of his generation who had faced and met the Nazi threat, the Soviet bureaucracy increasingly placed a greater emphasis on maintaining military parity with the West. The economy deteriorated, especially as the sti-

fling political atmosphere limited the development of the information economy so essential to post–industrial era growth. In 1985, the ruling politburo, recognizing the dilemma the country had fallen into, chose a young reformer named Mikhail Gorbachev to be premier.

Gorbachev had recognized that the Soviet economy was incapable of achieving both military parity with the West and providing the Soviet people the modern consumer lifestyle for which they yearned. On the latter front, he instituted perestroika, or economic restructuring. As for the military side of the equation, he immediately moved to ease tensions with the West and begin the process of demilitarization of the Soviet economy. Unfortunately, his political reforms proved the undoing of his own administration, as well as of the Soviet Union and Communist Eastern Europe.

Beginning in the early 1980s, workers in Poland had begun to organize resistance to the Communist government in that country, but had been harshly suppressed under a military regime backed by Moscow. The Solidarity labor movement in Poland came to renewed life after the rise of Gorbachev, who made it clear to the leaders in Warsaw, and other East European capitals, that Soviet arms would no longer be used to defend unpopular regimes. By the end of 1989, the Communist governments in every East European nation had either been overthrown or forced to share power with non-Communist parties.

At the same time, allowing more free speech, Gorbachev opened up a Pandora's box of criticism in his own country that ultimately led to the breakup of the Soviet Union, as the various nationalities—beginning in the Baltic states—began to demand their independence. A failed coup in August

1991 led to Gorbachev's ouster and the end of the Soviet Union. NATO, initially erected to counter the Soviet military threat following World War II, now lacked an enemy and, its critics said, a reason for being.

Peacekeeping and Expansion

This lack of mission and sense of direction for NATO seemed to be epitomized by the organization's hesitant response to the Yugoslav crisis and the war in Croatia and Bosnia. With the collapse of communism in Eastern Europe in 1989 the centrifugal nationalist forces in Yugoslavia—heretofore held in check by the repressive Communist regime of Josip Broz Tito—came to the fore, causing several of the component republics of the former Yugoslavia to break away from Belgrade.

Because of the large Serbian minorities in two of those breakaway republics, the Serbian-dominated Yugoslav government decided to support irredentist Serbian elements in Croatia and Bosnia. The war in Croatia—though bloody and destructive—was relatively short lived and was largely resolved before NATO could respond. The war in Bosnia, however, was not.

NATO was presented with several questions that went to the heart of the organization's existence in the post–cold war world. Without the threat of the Soviet Union, what did mutual self-defense mean? Did it include preventing or stopping a war in a non-member state? How could this be perceived as a self-defense issue? Eventually, under U.S. prodding, NATO's leadership ultimately found the answers to these questions. First, the war in the Balkans threatened to inundate West European countries with tens and even hundreds of thousands of un-

wanted refugees. More importantly, the war threatened to draw in NATO members such as Turkey and Greece, perhaps on opposite sides of the conflict. And finally, it was feared that the Russian Federation—heir to the Soviet Union—might side with its fellow Slavic and Orthodox Christian allies, the Serbs.

Thus, in July 1992, NATO's leaders announced that they were willing to support the peacekeeping activities of the U.N. force in Bosnia and Croatia, known as the U.N. Protection Force in Yugoslavia (UNPROFOR). In April 1993, NATO warplanes began to patrol the skies over Bosnia to enforce restrictions on military aerial activity mostly conducted by the Serbian government in support of Serbian militias inside the country. By August, NATO agreed on air attacks, largely against Serb positions, which it began to carry out after Serb artillery attacks on the Bosnian capital of Sarajevo and other cities in August 1994.

In 1995, the United States began to take a more central role in resolving the Bosnian conflict, largely because it felt that the Europeans could not agree on what to do. By November, NATO and the various parties to the Bosnian conflict signed the Dayton Peace Accords, named after the Ohio city where they were drawn up. Among other things, the Dayton accords called for the establishment of a NATO-led peacekeeping ground force in Bosnia, known as the Implementation Force (IFOR). Ultimately, some thirty-one NATO and non-NATO countries supplied peacekeepers for IFOR, and some Russian participation was included in the decision making. As of this writing, the Dayton accords and IFOR have proved to be a solid success, though tensions remain high in the region as new fighting in the Albanian-dominated Serbian province of Kosovo threatens to degenerate into a Bosnian-style civil war in 1998.

The relative success of the Yugoslav peace-keeping mission has revitalized NATO and given it a new sense of mission. This renewed vitality is evidenced in the 1998 decision to expand the alliance to include the Czech Republic, Hungary, and Poland, with other former East European states slated for membership in the future.

James Ciment

See also: Bosnia: Civil War, 1992–1995; Croatia: War with Serbia, 1991–1995; Warsaw Pact; Yugoslavia: Disintegration, 1990s.

Bibliography

Drew, S. Nelson. *The Future of NATO: Facing an Unreliable Enemy in an Uncertain Environment.* New York: Praeger, 1991.

Gottfried, Kurt, and Paul Bracken, eds. *Reforging European Security: From Confrontation to Cooperation.* Boulder, CO: Westview Press, 1990.

Kelleher, Catherine McArdle. *The Future of European Security: An Interim Assessment.* Washington, DC: Brookings Institution, 1995.

Shea, Jami. *NATO 2000: A Political Agenda for a Political Alliance.* Washington, DC: Brassey's, 1990.

Sherwood, Elizabeth D. *Allies in Crisis: Meeting Global Challenges to Western Security.* New Haven, CT: Yale University Press, 1990.

Organization of African Unity (OAU)

The Organization of African Unity (OAU) was founded on May 25, 1963. Its charter stated that its aims were to protect the interests of all African states, to eradicate colonialism, to improve economic conditions, and to promote unity and solidarity among African states. The OAU was created in a climate in which some African statesmen dreamed of creating a truly united Africa; the OAU was, for these men, a compromise or a stepping stone, depending on their degree of optimism. As it turned out, the OAU accomplished substantially less than had been originally hoped—Africa's many internal divisions made any real unity impossible—but it still served the useful purpose of giving African nations a forum to debate their shared problems. As of 1998, the OAU represented fifty-three member nations.

The OAU had its intellectual roots in the Pan-African movement of the early twentieth century. This movement, originating in America and the West Indies, was led by the descendants of slaves who wished to reforge a link with Africa as part of an effort to raise the self-esteem and pride of blacks who lived in the Americas.

The first Pan-African congress was organized by Sylvester Williams, a Trinidad lawyer, and was held in 1900. After Williams's death, W.E.B. Du Bois, an American, took over leadership of the Pan-African movement and organized four Pan-African congresses between 1919 and 1927. Du Bois and the Pan-Africans argued that all people of African descent should work together to achieve freedom, both in the New World and in colonial Africa. Delegates to the congresses came both from the Americas and from African colonies.

Du Bois's work was echoed in the "back-to-Africa" movement (1914-1925) of Marcus Garvey, a Jamaican journalist. Garvey wanted American and West Indian blacks to return to Africa to create a great nation, free from white control.

By the time a fifth Pan-African congress was organized, in 1945 in Manchester England, the driving force behind Pan-Africanism had moved from the Americas to Africa. Du Bois presided over the congress, but the initiative behind its creation came from African leaders, including Kwame Nkrumah of Ghana and Jomo Kenyatta from Kenya. This congress, more radical than its predecessors, demanded immediate freedom for Africa and argued that unity of African peoples was the only way to achieve freedom from the colonial powers.

Alongside these Pan-African movements, other African leaders were also working together to form regional alliances. These generally were linked along linguistic lines, with the colonies controlled by Great Britain forming groups separate from those controlled by France. These linguistic barriers would continue past independence, making it more difficult for the newly independent states of Africa to cooperate.

In the 1950s and 1960s, Pan-Africanism's strongest proponent was Kwame Nkrumah, one of the delegates to the 1945 Pan-African congress. Nkrumah led Ghana to independence in 1957 and immediately began to push for integration with other African states. In 1958, Nkrumah and Sekou Touré, leader of Guinea, announced a merger of their two nations into the Ghana-Guinea Union. Nkrumah and Touré then called for a "Union of Independent States of Africa."

In December 1960, Mali joined with Ghana and Guinea to create the Union of African States, which was designed to be the nucleus of a United States of Africa. The leaders of the three countries invited others to join them. Although some African leaders expressed some interest, including William Tubman of Liberia, most were reluctant to join any such union. (And the Union itself never became more than a symbolic one, quickly forgotten. The three nations continued to be ruled independently, and soon even the pretense of unity was dropped.)

It became clear that many leaders, while interested in the idea of cooperation, were reluctant to give up their hard-won national sovereignty. Particularly when it was unclear how any Pan-African state might be ruled—Nkrumah and Touré both were developing into autocratic leaders who allowed little opposition to their policies within their own countries. Instead, other leaders offered an alternative to Nkrumah's vision of a tight federation of African states, suggesting that Africa might be better off gathered under the umbrella of a loose association.

The Formation of the OAU

The various regional organizations that had been forming in post-independence Africa—the All-African Peoples' Conference (AAPC),

the Pan-African Movement of East and Central and Southern Africa (PAFMECSA), and the Organisation commune africaine et mauricienne (OCAM)—held a series of congresses and conferences between 1959 and 1962, all of which attempted to find some common ground for cooperation among African states. These gatherings were still either regional (East, West, or South African) or linguistic (English or French African) in focus.

Two of these conferences, the Brazzaville Conference of December 1960 and the Casablanca Conference of January 1961, demonstrated some of the fault lines preventing African unity. The Brazzaville group, representing twelve former French colonies, advocated cooperation based on "culture and community of interests"—meaning language—and was generally moderate in its criticism of colonialism. The Casablanca group, which included Ghana, Guinea, Egypt, and Libya, took a more radical position, committing itself to giving economic support to anti-colonial movements in Africa.

In 1961, Liberia and Ethiopia, neither of which had attended the Brazzaville or Casablanca meetings, organized a conference at Monrovia that invited members from both groups. This Monrovia group met again in 1962 at Lagos. The twenty states meeting at Lagos agreed to create an Organization of Inter-African and Malagasy States. The Casablanca group, however, boycotted both conferences.

Finally, in May 1963, the Ethiopian emperor Haile Selassie organized a meeting at Addis Ababa that included all the independent African states, with the exception of Morocco. (One of the issues that had divided the Brazzaville and Casablanca groups—Algeria's war of independence against France—became moot when France agreed to give up control of Algeria in late 1962; this resolution made it possible for the two groups to meet.)

At the Addis Ababa Conference, those leaders, particularly Ghana's Nkrumah, who wanted a federal union of African states, were outvoted by their colleagues who preferred the idea of a looser union. It was a victory of the moderate Brazzaville and Monrovia groups over the more radical Casablanca group. So, instead of creating an Organization of African States, the thirty leaders at Addis Ababa signed a charter (May 25, 1963), which brought into existence the Organization of African Unity.

In honor of Haile Selassie's efforts, the permanent headquarters of the OAU was located at Addis Ababa.

The OAU in Operation

The OAU's aims were large and vague. Its charter called for the promotion of African solidarity, cooperation in improving living standards, defense of sovereignty and territorial integrity, and the elimination of colonialism. The emphasis in the OAU charter was the protection of national sovereignty. Unlike Nkrumah's Casablanca group, the leaders of the OAU did not want the organization to interfere in any way in the internal affairs of their countries. Article 3 of the charter emphasized that member states should adhere to the principle of non-interference in internal affairs of other member states and that disputes should be settled peacefully, through negotiations. The OAU was to be a coordinating body, not an enforcement body. Nkrumah's vision of a Pan-African Union would not be realized.

Although the OAU, as a matter of policy, deliberately refused to intervene in the affairs of its members, it did leave open to itself two areas of international activity. First,

the OAU, as part of its charter, was committed to mediating disputes between African member states—and there would be many of these. Second, the OAU dedicated itself to ending colonialism in Africa.

Anti-Colonialism

By the mid-1960s, there were three major colonial powers left in Africa: the Portuguese with their colonies in Angola, Mozambique, and Guinea-Bissau; the ex-British colony of Rhodesia; and the Republic of South Africa.

To deal with these colonial remnants, the OAU called for sanctions by its members as well as by the international community. These calls had minimal effect at first. The world, while it might condemn the racist practices of the colonial holdouts, was unwilling to suffer economically to punish them. Even some African states ignored the OAU's call: Zambia and Botswana had little choice but to trade with the white regimes that surrounded them. These efforts by the OAU failed because of the weakness of its membership. Divided they could do little.

Some member nations of the OAU did offer refuge for freedom fighters from Angola, South Africa, and Rhodesia, but this was something they might have done even without an OAU. A more subtle victory of the OAU was to keep the issue of colonialism alive in United Nations debates. In order not to appear to be supporting racist regimes, the United Nations passed resolutions that called for self-determination for the peoples of Africa. This raised the consciousness of the Western world regarding the situation in Africa and thereby increased the pressure upon the white regimes. This pressure was partially responsible for the 1975 withdrawal of Portugal from its African possessions.

Similarly, United Nations sanctions, recommended by the OAU, helped to force Rhodesia to agree to allow a black government to take control of that country in 1980. South Africa was the longest colonial holdout. It was not until the late 1980s that F.W. de Klerk, also under international pressure, began to dismantle the apartheid system.

The degree to which the OAU can take credit for the defeat of the colonialist regimes is debatable—only a part of its already small budget was devoted toward supporting black freedom fighters—but certainly its constant pressure on international organizations, especially the United Nations, added to the pressure that eventually caused Portugal to withdraw and whites in Rhodesia and South Africa to surrender power.

Mediation of Disputes

In the mediation of intra-African disputes, as in decolonialization, the OAU had a limited but real effect. Although its decentralized character tended to limit its willingness to interfere in African conflicts, the OAU acted on a number of occasions to attempt to end conflicts that seemed to be escalating out of control. As befit its conservative agenda, it almost always intervened on the side of the established government and ignored demands of recognition by rebel or secessionist forces—the major exception being its recognition of the Polisario rebels in the Western Sahara.

The early successes of OAU negotiators include helping to achieve a cease-fire in the Algerian-Moroccan border dispute of 1963–1965, easing the withdrawal of British troops from Tanzania in 1964, and offering mediation in the Somalian-Ethiopian and Somalian-Kenyan border disputes, which were settled in 1967.

Less successful were the OAU's efforts to bring the Nigerian Civil War (1967–1970) to an end. The membership of the OAU was divided on the Nigerian struggle: The majority supported the territorial integrity of Nigeria (which was in line with the OAU charter), while a minority, including Tanzania and Gambia, supported the secessionist government in Biafra. Only the 1970 surrender of Biafra resolved this OAU disagreement. Neither was the OAU able to stop the civil war in Sudan, which began again in 1983 (although the OAU had helped to mediate the first Sudanese Civil War, which ended in 1972).

The OAU's limited success in resolving intra-African disputes was the result of limited means—the member nations of the OAU provided it with a relatively small operating budget—and its reluctance to commit troops to any conflict. The OAU did authorize member states to send peacekeeping forces to Chad in 1979 and 1981, but the peacekeepers—with virtually no financial support from the OAU—were unable to stop the fighting and were quickly withdrawn. The Chad conflict continued despite OAU calls for a cease-fire.

More successful was the 1990 intervention in Liberia after the collapse of Samuel Doe's government. Although this intervention was carried out by troops under the command of the Economic Community of West African States (ECOWAS), it had the blessing of the OAU. Liberia continued to be troubled by internal strife, but the ECOWAS force did provide a degree of stability which had been lacking.

In 1996, the OAU began discussions regarding the possibility of creating an OAU-sponsored rapid reaction force that would be capable of intervening in African conflicts— the immediate catalyst for the talks was the ongoing ethnic violence in Burundi. It remained unclear whether the OAU would follow any steps that would break with its tradition of mediation rather than intervention.

Analysis

The OAU failed to accomplish great things because, as defined by its charter, it lacked sufficient unity for effective action. An OAU created along the lines that Nkrumah envisioned might have been more effective, but it was almost certain that it would never have been able to function—the nations of Africa had too many barriers dividing them, from ethnicity to language. Nevertheless, the OAU provided a forum for debate, moderated some of Africa's uglier conflicts, and contributed to the end of colonialism in Africa.

Carl Skutsch

See also: Non-Aligned Movement—The Bandung Conference; Economic Community of West African States (ECOWAS).

Bibliography

Amate, C.O.C. *Inside the OAU: Pan-Africanism in Practice.* New York: St. Martin's Press, 1986.
Harris, Gordon. *Organization of African Unity.* New Brunswick, NJ: Transaction, 1994.

Organization of American States (OAS)

The Organization of American States (OAS), whose membership includes every nation-state in the Western Hemisphere except Cuba (which was ousted following its Communist revolution in 1962), was founded in 1948. Largely a consulative body, with little power to initiate military action, representatives of the member states (one per country) meet annually in the various capitals of the member countries. The chair rotates yearly among members. The organization includes several permanent committees and commissions, the most important of which deal with economic development and human rights. There is also a court of human rights within the organization.

The OAS, though officially organized in 1948 as part of a larger U.S. and Western initiative to develop a strong anti-Communist diplomatic system at the beginning of the cold war, has its roots in the late nineteenth century. In 1889–1890, representatives of virtually all of the independent states of the Western Hemisphere met in Washington to form the International Union of American Republics, largely to promote regional trade. Following several name changes and international conferences, the organization was officially founded at the Ninth Conference of the Pan-American Union (the last pre-OAS organization) in Bogota, Colombia, in 1948.

Anti-Communism and Peacekeeping

In 1954, under U.S. initiative, the member states signed the Declaration of Solidarity for the Preservation of the Political Integrity of the American States against the Intervention of International Communism, a move largely made in response to the rise of the leftist president, Jacobo Arbenz of Guatemala, who was overthrown in a U.S.-sponsored coup that same year. In 1962, the strong, anti-Communist tenor of the organization was evinced in its decision to oust Cuba after it was found to be allowing Soviet nuclear missiles to be stationed on its soil. The OAS voted to back U.S. efforts to remove the weapons. The crisis in the Dominican Republic in 1965, in which a leftist coup led to anarchy and a U.S. invasion, led to the formation of the OAS's Inter-American Peace Force.

The first effort at OAS peacekeeping came in 1969 when two member states, Honduras and El Salvador, engaged in a border conflict. Initially sent in to investigate human rights violations, an OAS task force eventually arranged a cease-fire and an exchange of prisoners. The rising level of tension throughout the region led to the decision, made at the annual meeting in Buenos Aires in 1970, to shift decision-making power from an executive council to the more representative General Assembly. High on the latter's agenda was the growing level of anarchy in many South American republics, including extortion and kidnapping by terrorist groups. At the same time, during the 1960s and early 1970s, the OAS moved to establish protocols and institutions, including the founding of the Inter-

American Development Bank to promote economic development.

In the early 1980s, the organization was called upon to resolve two international and two internal conflicts in Latin America: the border war between Ecuador and Peru, the war between Argentina and Britain over the Falkland Islands/Islas Malvinas, the leftist insurgency in El Salvador, and the rightist, U.S.-supported insurgency in Nicaragua. Its failure to play a significant role in any of these conflicts—with the possible exception of the Peru-Ecuador war—led to efforts to try and revitalize the organization. Two reforms adopted at the 1985 meeting included a strengthened executive branch of the organization and a decision to allow member states to mediate conflicts even if all the participants to a conflict had not agreed to set the matter before the OAS.

Independent and local efforts to end the fighting in Central America—which led to the signing of the Esquipulas II agreement in 1987 (signed by Costa Rica, El Salvador, Guatemala, Honduras, and Nicaragua) came to involve the OAS as well. Under Esquipulas, the secretary general of the OAS was invited to become a member of the international commission set up to implement the agreement. Two years later, the OAS sent a team to resolve the crisis in Panama, in which the government refused to abide by election results, but was unable to reach a solution.

Democratization and the End of the Cold War

By the late 1980s, the OAS was becoming more deeply involved in the democratic movement that was sweeping Latin America. Between 1990 and 1993, OAS observer teams were sent to monitor elections in Nic-

aragua, Dominican Republic, Haiti, Paraguay, and Suriname. (Eventually, the requirement of representative democracy for membership was enacted as the Protocol of Washington in 1992.) With the exception of Haiti, all of these countries effectively transferred power from non-elected to elected officials.

The situation in Haiti, in which the military ousted the legally elected government of Jean-Bertrand Aristide, led to an OAS decision to place a full embargo on that island nation. Together with the United Nations, the OAS orchestrated a conference on Governor's Island in New York in 1993, which led to a peace agreement in which the army would step aside and allow Aristide to resume his position as president of the republic.

Continued intransigence by the military and unrest on the island, however, forced the UN-OAS contingent sent to Haiti to implement the Governor's Island accord to leave. In May 1994, most of the OAS—with the exception of Anguilla and Argentina—voiced their opposition to the U.S. decision to intervene militarily in Haiti in order to return Aristide to the presidency. The return of Aristide in October 1994 seemed to end the crisis, though the OAS has expressed doubts about the democratization of the island and continued abuses by military and paramilitary forces in Haiti since then.

With the collapse of the Soviet Union and the end of the cold war in the 1990s, many member states of the OAS were no longer willing to support the U.S. hard line against Communist Cuba. In 1995, the organization's permanent human rights committee voted to condemn the U.S. embargo on food and medicine to Cuba as a violation of international human rights and OAS principles. In

1996, the OAS also decided to consider whether the Helms-Burton Act—U.S. legislation that punished foreign individuals and companies doing business in Cuba—was a violation of OAS rules and principles.

At the same time, the spread of democracy in Latin America and the growth of regional trade has led to more open cooperation between the United States and Latin-American nations, which for a long time resented and feared U.S. power in the hemisphere and interference in their internal affairs. At the OAS-sponsored Summit of the Americas, held in Miami in 1994, the members voted to set up structures to combat regional terror-ism and push for a Free Trade Area of the Americas by the year 2005.

James Ciment

See also: Argentina: Falklands/Malvinas War, 1982; Cuba: Missile Crisis, 1962; Dominican Republic: Coup and U.S. Invasion, 1965; Ecuador: Border Dispute with Peru, 1947; El Salvador: Soccer War with Honduras, 1969; Guatemala: Coup Against Arbenz, 1954; Haiti: Civil Conflict, 1990s; Nicaragua: Contra War, 1980s; Panama: U.S. Invasion, 1989.

Bibliography

Sheinin, David. *The Organization of American States.* New Brunswick, NJ: Transaction Publishers, 1995.

Vaky, Viron P. *The Future of the Organization of American States: Essays.* New York: Twentieth Century Fund Press, 1993.

Organization of the Islamic Conference (OIC)

The Organization of the Islamic Conference (OIC) was founded in 1971 by Muslim states including Saudi Arabia, Egypt, Morocco, Malaysia, and Indonesia. In 1998, membership included more than fifty countries, among them Albania, Chad, Iraq, Pakistan, and Syria. Its headquarters is in Jeddah, Saudi Arabia.

Historical Background

The OIC was born from a desire among Islamic leaders to recreate the Islamic unity that had been lost with the ending of the Ottoman Turkish Caliphate during World War I. The Caliphate had provided a religious center for the Islamic world long after its political power had faded. Its disappearance in 1918 left behind a gap in the Islamic world. Islam, these leaders felt, might also give stability to nations that had just recently achieved their independence (before 1945, most of the Islamic world had been under the control of European powers) but had only a vague sense of nationalism. Organizations such as the Muslim Brotherhood, founded in 1928, were popular because of their emphasis on creating a society based on the teachings of the Koran.

By the 1960s, a few Muslim political leaders were trying to forge an Islamic community of nations. Both King Faisal of Saudi Arabia and the Malaysian prime minister, Abdul Rahman, attempted, unsuccessfully, to create an international Muslim organization. Arab nationalists, however, such as Gamal Abdel Nasser of Egypt, were scornful of creating a political movement based on religion, which they considered backward-looking and reactionary. Nevertheless, the idea of Muslim solidarity gained during the middle 1960s.

The creation of the State of Israel in 1948 gave additional focus to Islamic unity. Many Muslims were hostile to the new state, which they believed had usurped the rights of the Muslim Arabs of Palestine. The success of Jewish nationalism helped to spark a renewed sense of pan-Muslim identity. The Israeli capture of the Old City of Jerusalem in the June 1967 Six-Day War also aroused Muslim antagonism, as Jerusalem is considered by Muslims to be the third holiest place on earth, after Mecca and Medina.

The key event that triggered the creation of the OIC was when an Australian man set a fire at the Al Aqsa Mosque in Jerusalem in August 1969. The act shocked the Islamic world; many Muslims believed that the Israeli authorities, if not behind the attack, had at least been responsible for the climate that made it possible. The Al Aqsa Mosque, located on the Temple Mount by the Dome of the Rock, is believed to be where the Prophet Mohammed ascended into heaven, and is holy for that reason. Some Muslims believed that the fire was part of a plot to push them off the Temple Mount—a belief given some validity by the fact that some extremist Jewish groups have agitated for exactly that result. In response to the Al Aqsa fire, Amin al-Husaini, the former Mufti (Muslim religious leader) of Jerusalem, issued a call to all Muslim heads of state for an immediate Muslim summit. Blaming the Israelis for the fire, al-Husaini warned that "this Jewish crime is a striking example of the malicious Jew's intention to commit similar crimes in other countries." Without echoing the Mufti's virulent anti-Semitism, other Muslim leaders supported the idea of holding an Islamic summit. Impressed by the outrage in the Muslim world—Muslim nations in the United Nations sponsored a resolution condemning Israel for the fire—even nationalist leaders like Nasser supported the idea of a summit.

The Founding of the OIC

The first Islamic summit was held in September 1969 in Morocco. Attended by representatives—most of whom were heads of state—from twenty-four countries, the summit issued a resolution stating that "Muslim governments would consult with a view to promoting among themselves close cooperation and mutual assistance in the economic, scientific, cultural, and spiritual fields, inspired by the immortal teachings of Islam." The following year, a conference of foreign ministers met in Jeddah, Saudi Arabia, to fabricate an institutional foundation for the new Organization of the Islamic Conference. In 1972, the council of foreign ministers agreed upon a charter for the new organization.

The first aim of the OIC, as proclaimed in its charter, was "to promote Islamic solidarity among member states." The third aim was "to endeavor to eliminate racial segregation and discrimination and to eradicate colonialism in all its forms" (this plank would be used as the justification for criticiz-

ing Israel's treatment of Palestinians in the occupied territories). Making this focus on Palestine explicit, the fifth aim of the charter was "to coordinate all efforts for the safeguard of the Holy Places and support of the struggle of the people of Palestine, and help to regain their rights and liberate their land." The first official meeting of the OIC was held in Lahore, Pakistan, in 1974. The most recent meeting was in Tehran, Iran, in 1997.

Activities of the OIC

The OIC has a number of subsidiary organizations that operate year round, including the Islamic Development Bank, the Islamic Solidarity Fund, and the Islamic News Agency. Founded in 1975, the Islamic Development Bank, which is particularly active, is dedicated to providing loans to Muslim member countries in accordance with Islamic law. The IDB also provides funds to Islamic communities in non-member countries. The Islamic Solidarity Fund has helped to establish Islamic universities in Niger, Uganda, Bangladesh, and Malaysia.

In the arena of international politics, the OIC has served mainly as a coordinating body for Muslim nations in areas of mutual interest. Its one consistent international policy has been the promotion of Palestinian independence and the return of Jerusalem to Arab Muslim control. In the 1981 conference, for example, the OIC called for a jihad for the liberation of Jerusalem and the occupied territories. This jihad took the practical form of an economic boycott against Israel. The OIC also expelled Egypt from the organization in 1979 as punishment for signing the 1978 Camp David Accords with Israel. (Egypt was also expelled from the Arab League.) Egypt was accepted back into the organization in 1984 because of its importance. The OIC took a more moderate position regarding Israel after 1991, ending its call for jihad and supporting peace negotiations with Israel.

Beyond the issue of Palestinian rights, the OIC has acted when issues of importance to the Islamic community arose and has attempted to provide leadership and coordination of policy among Muslim nations. Its leaders attempted to strike a middle ground between the more radical non-aligned movement and the more divisive Arab League.

Among the OIC's activities have been condemning the 1980 Soviet invasion of Afghanistan (the OIC demanded an immediate withdrawal of Soviet troops, a demand which Moscow ignored); attempting, in 1987, to resolve the ongoing Iran-Iraq war (unsuccessfully); and condemning the 1990 Iraqi invasion of Kuwait. In March 1989, the OIC denounced Salman Rushdie, author of the novel *The Satanic Verses* (1988), for having blasphemed against Islam in his writing—parts of the book depict a Mohammed-like character as a figure of fun. (Iran's Ayatollah Khomeini was more harsh, calling upon Muslims to "execute" Rushdie and putting a 6 million dollar bounty on his head.)

After an initial period of foot-dragging, the OIC also became very active in supporting the cause of the Bosnian Muslims during Bosnia's internecine civil war. In 1992 and 1993, the OIC asked that the United Nations lift the arms embargo placed on Bosnia and intervene militarily to prevent further attacks by Serbian militias against Bosnian Muslim villages. Many members of the OIC suggested that the reluctance of the United Nations to intervene in Bosnia was based upon anti-Muslim prejudice. The Iranian representative was quoted as saying that "the behavior of the United Nations and the Security Council shows that they themselves want the Muslims to be driven out of Bosnia-Herzegovina, and that they approve of the crimes committed by the Serbs through their silence." In 1995, the OIC declared the weapons embargo illegal and encouraged its members to smuggle arms to support the Bosnian Muslims.

In the OIC's December 1997 meeting, held in Teheran, Iran, member states discussed the possibility of creating a Muslim common market, a Muslim news agency and satellite network, and of improving the position of women in the Muslim world. The OIC also condemned Israel for "state terrorism" and demanded an end to the building of settlements on Arab land. The meeting saw a limited reconciliation between Saudi Arabia and Iran, which represent two extremes of the observant Islamic world. (One of their main points of contention has been support for the United States. Saudi Arabia remained an American ally, while Iran condemned it as the "great Satan.") Finally, the OIC condemned terrorism in the name of Islam, a pointed attack on the actions of Muslim extremists in Algeria, Pakistan, and Egypt.

Carl Skutsch

See also: Afghanistan: Soviet Invasion, 1979–1989; Bosnia: Civil War, 1992–1995; Cold War Confrontations; Iraq: Gulf War, 1990–1991; Israel: War of Independence, 1948–1949; Israel: Palestinian Struggle Since 1948; Israel: Six-Day War, 1967; Palestine: Intifada, 1987–1992.

Bibliography

Ahsan, Abdullah. *The Organization of the Islamic Conference: An Introduction to an Islamic Political Institution.* Herndon, VA: International Institute of Islamic Thought, 1988.

Baba, Noor Ahmad. *Organisation of Islamic Conference: Theory and Practice of Pan-Islamic Cooperation.* New York: Sterling Publications, 1994.

The Southeast Asia Treaty Organization (SEATO)

During World War II, American policy-makers assumed that the Big Five—China, France, Great Britain, the Soviet Union, and the United States—would cooperate with each other to maintain the peace once the war ended. What happened after the war was quite different. France and Great Britain were no longer world powers. Both countries struggled for years to recover from the devastating effects of World War II. Civil war resumed in China and ended with a Communist victory in 1949. The United States and the Soviet Union clashed over many issues including peace treaties for the nations defeated in World War II, the civil war in Greece, and territorial demands by the Soviet Union on Turkey and Iran.

America's primary concern after 1945 was rebuilding and protecting the nations of Western Europe. The Marshall Plan in June 1947 and the creation of NATO in April 1949 were the primary instruments for achieving those goals. From 1945 to 1950, American policy-makers were primarily focused on Europe, but that changed when North Korean troops invaded South Korea in June 1950. President Harry S. Truman decided that American forces, under the authority of the United Nations, should defend South Korea. Suddenly, the United States became the dominant power seeking to contain communism in Asia.

The outbreak of the Korean War convinced President Truman and Secretary of State Dean Acheson that one way to contain communism was to create a series of interlocking military alliances. In August 1951, the United States and the Philippines signed a defense treaty. In September, the United States signed a defense treaty with Australia and New Zealand. That same month the United States signed a defense treaty with Japan.

When the Korean War began, France was engaged in the hopeless task of trying to defeat the Communist forces in Indochina under the leadership of Ho Chi Minh, who was a dedicated Communist but was also a nationalist seeking to end French colonial rule. The United States provided France with substantial military and economic aid but the Communists kept winning. In July 1954, France agreed to partition Vietnam along the seventeenth parallel. The Communists won control of North Vietnam. South Vietnam became independent. The end of the first Indochina war brought about a sharp decline in French influence in Southeast Asia. The United States moved in to fill the vacuum of power.

Establishing SEATO

President Dwight D. Eisenhower decided to continue the alliance-building policy of President Truman. Eisenhower believed that negotiating a defense treaty with other interested nations would be an effective means to contain communism in Southeast Asia. On September 8, 1954, about six weeks after France signed an agreement ending the first Indochina war, Secretary of State John Foster Dulles flew to Manila to sign a treaty creating the Southeast Asia Treaty Organization (SEATO). Members of the treaty included Australia, France, Great Britain, Thailand, Pakistan, the Philippines, New Zealand, and the United States. There was a protocol to the treaty extending its coverage to Cambodia, Laos, and South Vietnam. President Lyndon B. Johnson used the protocol to justify America's intervention in the Indochina conflict.

There were only two Southeast Asian nations in SEATO, the Philippines and Thailand. The Thai government had some legitimate concerns regarding the threat of communism. Communists were active in northeastern Thailand, and there was the possibility that North Vietnam would be willing to extend aid and support to the Thai Communists. Thai leaders were also concerned about Communist activity in Laos. The Communists in Laos, known as the Pathet Lao, were under the control of North Vietnam.

The Philippines joined SEATO in large part because of historical factors. The Philippines had already signed a bilateral defense treaty with the United States that permitted the United States to use military bases in the Philippines. At the time the SEATO treaty was signed, the Philippines confronted no external threat.

Pakistan joined SEATO primarily because of its hostile relations with India. As a member of SEATO, Pakistan could expect to receive American military assistance, which would strengthen Pakistan's military capability vis-à-vis India. Including Pakistan in SEATO antagonized the government in New Delhi, and this became an irritant in Indo-American relations for many years. When negotiations were taking place to organize

SEATO, Prime Minister Jawaharlal Nehru urged his Congress Party to organize demonstrations against the treaty. He labeled American efforts to organize the treaty an "unfriendly act."

France and Great Britain were unlikely to play an active role in the treaty because both countries were in the process of downsizing their colonial empires. France had just lost a war in Indochina. It was, therefore, unlikely that the French government would recommit its troops to fight in Indochina on behalf of American objectives. After France withdrew from Indochina in 1954, it had to cope with challenges to its power in North Africa.

The British government was sensitive to the fact that India, a member of the British Commonwealth, opposed the treaty. India was one of the leaders of the non-aligned bloc of nations, most of whom opposed military alliances. These nations believed that military alliances were a cause of war and therefore should be avoided. They also believed that Western military alliances were a form of neo-colonialism.

In 1954, India was trying to develop better relations with China. The government in Beijing opposed SEATO because its purpose was to contain communism. Finally, India opposed SEATO because the Nehru government thought it would have to use its scarce resources to build its military capabilities to deal with any threat from Pakistan.

The British recognized that their resources were insufficient to enable them to play a dominant role in Asia. The decision to join SEATO was simply a reflection of Great Britain's desire to cooperate with the United States. In 1954, when it became evident that France was going to be defeated in Vietnam, President Eisenhower tried to convince Prime Minister Winston Churchill to support an Anglo-American intervention to save the French, but Churchill refused. Great Britain was not likely to again become involved in a major conflict in Asia for reasons that did not directly impinge on Britain's national interests.

Australia and New Zealand joined SEATO in part because the United States extended its protective umbrella to both those countries through the 1951 ANZUS treaty. After World War II, Australia and New Zealand could no longer rely on Great Britain's military might.

The Structure of SEATO

SEATO was unlike NATO. The latter had a unified command with troops under its control. SEATO had no unified command, nor were troops available for its use. The members of NATO shared common historical experiences and recognized a common threat. The SEATO members had little in common and did not agree on a common threat. Australia and New Zealand, for example, were primarily concerned that Japan would re-arm and again become a menace. Neither China nor North Vietnam threatened Pakistan. No nation was threatening the Philippines.

For Eisenhower and Dulles, the SEATO treaty was largely symbolic. They hoped it would raise the morale of Asian members worried about the ultimate goals of China or North Vietnam. The treaty did not commit the United States to maintain any military forces on the Asian mainland nor did the treaty guarantee an American response to an act of aggression. If aggression did occur, the treaty members were only obligated to consult each other.

Theoretically, SEATO was designed as a guarantee underpinning the 1954 Geneva accords that ended the first Indochina war. In that sense, it was similar to the defense treaty

the United States signed with South Korea. The purpose of that treaty was to deter North Korea from launching another attack across the thirty-eighth parallel. SEATO was a warning to North Vietnam not to cross the seventeenth parallel. American officials were to learn that the differences between Korea and Vietnam were more important than the similarities. The American treaty with Korea was bilateral. If North Korean forces again attacked South Korea, the United States would not have to consult with other countries to determine how to respond. SEATO was a multilateral treaty. The treaty members would have difficulty reaching a consensus because of clashing national interests.

Just before President Eisenhower left office, there was mounting evidence that the Communists were seeking to win control of Laos. The president was willing to increase aid to the Indochina states but was unwilling to commit American forces to fight there. There were a number of ways to interpret the SEATO treaty. At a news conference in February 1954, President Eisenhower, in response to a question, said he could not imagine the United States getting involved in the Vietnam War. Although he made that statement before SEATO was organized, from 1954 on he gave no indication that the United States would intervene in Vietnam despite the renewal of the war in 1956.

The Vietnam War

President Johnson frequently cited the SEATO treaty to justify America's intervention in Vietnam. There was, however, nothing in the treaty that required the United States to militarily intervene the way it did. If SEATO had not existed, President Johnson would have found some other way to justify his policy of intervention. In 1974, President Richard M. Nixon withdrew American military forces from Vietnam. A year later, the Communists won control over all of Indochina. SEATO was ineffective if not counterproductive.

In 1977, SEATO was dissolved. It was ineffective in containing communism in Indochina in part because it was viewed as an instrument of Western colonial control. Ho Chi Minh and his followers were symbols of Vietnamese nationalism.

Kenneth L. Hill

See also: ANZUS Pact; Japan: World War II Peace Treaty, 1951; North Atlantic Treaty Organization (NATO); Korea: Invasion of the South by the North, 1950–1953; Vietnam: First Indochina War, 1946–1954; Vietnam: Second Indochina War, 1964–1973.

Bibliography

Barnett, Doak. *Communist China and Asia.* New York: Harpers, 1960.

Modelski, George. "Indochina and SEATO." *Australian Outlook* (March 1959): 27–54.

———, ed. *SEATO: Six Studies.* Sydney: Halstead Press, 1964.

The United States: The Marshall Plan

Background

When World War II ended in 1945, it was difficult to differentiate between the winners and the losers. The war destroyed much of Europe, and people in both the victorious and the defeated nations needed such basic things as food and shelter. The war had lasted about six years and there was no hope for a rapid recovery. After the war, the United States provided the nations of Europe with billions of dollars in aid. By 1947, it was evident that despite the help, economic conditions were not improving. One of the ironies of the post-war period was that the victorious powers could not regain their economic strength without rebuilding the German economy. The aggressor in World War II had to be revived for the good of Europe.

In March 1947, President Harry Truman appeared before a joint session of Congress and presented what came to be known as the Truman Doctrine. His message was a warning to the Soviet Union that the United States was prepared to do what was necessary to protect free nations from the threat of communism. The Soviet threat, however, was not just military. The greatest danger was that the European nations would collapse because of economic and social conditions.

The Soviet Union and the European Communist parties exploited Europe's post-war economic and social conditions. By 1947, the nations of Eastern Europe, with the exception of Czechoslovakia and Hungary, were firmly encased in the Soviet bloc. Indigenous Communist parties, particularly those in France and Italy, supported Soviet policies and blamed the economic and social conditions on capitalism in general and on the United States in particular. Both the French and the Italian Communist parties enjoyed much popular support, winning more than 30 percent of the popular vote and controlling a proportionate number of seats in their respective legislative bodies.

The 1946–1947 winter added to the suffering. It was a brutally cold winter. In Great Britain, there were times when the electrical power system completely shut down due to shortages of coal. In February 1947, Anthony Eden, a leader of the Conservative party, said Great Britain was facing its greatest industrial crisis in twenty years. Gales, blizzards, and freezing weather aggravated an already disastrous situation. In some places, there was an adequate supply of coal, but inadequate transportation prevented delivery. Trains, trucks, and shipping were often unable to move because of the weather. The result was steep levels of unemployment. The unfavorable weather exacerbated the misery and discomfort of people already suffering from food, fuel, and clothing shortages. When the winter snows began to melt, flooding destroyed agricultural crops. In March 1947, 50,000 to 100,000 Germans demonstrated in the British zone of occupation because of food shortages. This was the first overt anti-British display of violence since the occupation began.

When Germany was defeated in 1945, the nations of Europe wanted to impose restrictions to prevent it from again endangering the peace. It was divided into four zones of occupation and although the 1945 Potsdam agreements called for Germany to be treated as a single economic unit, this did not happen. Germany had four economic systems until Great Britain and the United States brought about an economic merger of their zones in January 1947. British and American officials realized that Europe's economic recovery required a rebuilding of the German economy and a massive infusion of capital to reconstruct the industries destroyed by World War II.

If the people of Europe continued to suffer without any hope for improvement, the Soviet Union could extend its control and influence throughout the continent. There was the possibility that the Communists could do in Europe what Nazi Germany had failed to do. The United States was determined this would not happen.

The people of Europe had to cope with the destruction caused by World War II, the activities of the Communist parties, and the unfavorable weather. The demobilization of military forces and the influx of refugees from Eastern Europe exacerbated these problems. In some countries, those who fought with the partisans wanted revenge against those who collaborated with the Nazi regimes. This was a particularly severe problem in France. The Communists enjoyed a degree of popularity in Europe because they had joined with the partisans in fighting the Nazi occupation forces.

The Marshall Plan

President Truman appointed George Marshall secretary of state in January 1947. In May, he met with several of his aides to analyze proposals that would help bring about the economic recovery of Europe. The European trading system had collapsed; there was nothing to trade. Each nation was attempting to cope with the crisis, but there was no overall plan for economic recovery. A collective effort was needed.

Marshall and his advisors agreed that the European nations had to formulate a plan for economic recovery but the United States must be in charge. In a commencement address at Harvard University on June 5, 1947, Marshall unveiled his ideas to bring about the economic recovery of Europe. He presented no plan nor did he provide specific proposals. He offered the European nations economic assistance provided they would cooperate with each other. Marshall required the European nations to do three things. He called on each nation to (1) draw up a balance sheet of its needs and resources, (2) develop a blueprint for self-help, and (3) indicate how American dollars could best be used. He insisted that the initiative for recovery must come from the European nations and the initiative must include a coordinated plan. Marshall's address had an electrifying impact on Europe. Under-Secretary of State Dean Acheson had alerted British leaders about the importance of Marshall's address. Britain's Foreign Secretary Ernest Bevin was ready to take the initiative in responding to Marshall's challenge.

American policy-makers had to decide

what countries to include in the European Recovery Program (ERP), the official name for the Marshall Plan. Many analysts, both in the United States and in Europe, considered Truman's message to Congress in March 1947 to be the official beginning of the cold war. Should the United States invite the Soviet Union and its satellites to participate in the program? This presented the Truman administration with a difficult problem. If it was not invited, the Soviet Union could blame the United States for increasing international tensions by dividing Europe into blocs. Critics such as Henry Wallace, a vice president under Franklin Roosevelt, thought that Truman's policies were unnecessarily antagonistic toward the Soviet Union. Wallace wanted the United States to establish a $50 billion fund to be administered by the United Nations. The aid would go to all the nations of Europe, including the Soviet Union and the nations of Eastern Europe.

If the Soviet Union decided to participate in the program, the Congress almost certainly would have refused to appropriate any money. The Congress was unlikely to provide America's major adversary with financial assistance that would diminish the assistance available for allies. Opponents of the Soviet Union had no difficulty in justifying their opposition. They could point to violations of the Yalta and Potsdam agreements, Soviet support for the Communist rebels in Greece, Soviet territorial demands on Turkey, and the disruptive role of Communist parties throughout Europe. The American people, given the many disagreements between the United States and the Soviet Union since the end of World War II, would not support congressional efforts to help the Soviet economy.

In 1946, Republicans won control of the

Congress and many of the new members were committed to budget reductions. Some members of Congress, from both political parties, were reluctant to support the Truman Doctrine because of the costs. The Marshall Plan was going to cost much more than aid to Greece and Turkey. If the Soviet Union and the satellite nations were included in the Marshall Plan, the cost would be astronomical.

President Truman decided to invite the Soviet Union, but few American officials thought it would accept. The leaders in Moscow apparently never considered participating in the program to try to sabotage it.

In March 1947, Secretary of State Marshall attended a Council of Foreign Ministers meeting in Moscow. The failure of the conference to resolve any of the major issues, particularly those pertaining to Germany and Austria, reinforced the idea that negotiating with the Soviet Union was unproductive. Marshall believed that as long as conditions in Europe remained as they were, the Soviets would go on trying to expand their power and influence. Since the end of World War II, the balance of power had shifted to favor the Soviet Union. A readjustment of the balance required that the nations of Europe regain their economic vitality.

Officials in Washington responsible for the Marshall Plan believed that, with the exception of Greece, economic assistance was much more important than military assistance. The Soviet Union, given its own economic problems, was not an immediate military threat. The greatest danger facing the nations of Europe was internal collapse, not external aggression.

The Marshall Plan recognized the necessity of looking at the problems of individual nations, relating those problems to other nations, and connecting economic issues with security and political issues. France, for example, would not agree to increase the level of industry in Germany without some guarantee to limit its military potential. The economic recovery of Europe was dependent on Germany. In 1947, German coal production was about 20 percent of prewar levels. That had to be substantially increased.

After Marshall's address at Harvard in June 1947, Foreign Secretary Ernest Bevin went to Paris to meet with his counterpart, Foreign Minister Georges Bidault. Bidault insisted on inviting the Soviet Union to participate in the talks. He feared that failure to invite the Soviets would alienate the French Communist party. It would then blame France and Great Britain for failing to promote cooperation among the wartime allies. An invitation to the Soviet Union was extended and accepted. Tripartite talks began in Paris on June 27, 1947.

Initially, it appeared that the Soviet Union was genuinely interested in Marshall's proposal. Foreign Minister Vyacheslav Molotov arrived in Paris with a large number of advisors. It quickly became apparent that the Soviet approach to Europe's economic recovery differed from what Marshall had in mind. The Soviets wanted to modify his approach. Molotov wanted the United States to be more specific about the amount of aid to be given. Each nation would then draw up its own list of needs. The United States would dispense aid on a national basis without any coordination on the part of the European nations. In contrast, France and Great Britain proposed creating a steering committee composed of representatives from the three countries and some from other countries. The steering committee would study Europe's needs and propose remedies. The Soviets charged that this approach violated national sovereignty. The Soviets opposed the transparency Marshall's proposal required. Nations engaged in an adversarial relationship do not often cooperate for their mutual benefit. The cold war was like a zero-sum game. A benefit for the West was a loss for the Soviet Union.

On July 1, 1947, Secretary of State Marshall accused the Soviet Union of maliciously distorting his proposal for Europe's economic recovery. The Soviets charged that the proposed ERP was an instrument to allow the United States to dominate the nations of Europe. Henry Wallace made the same charge. Marshall pointed out that the United States wanted to alleviate the suffering of the people in Europe. He readily acknowledged that a prosperous Europe would benefit the United States. The Marshall Plan was in keeping with America's national interest, but at the same time, others would also benefit. Marshall attached three conditions to American aid: (1) The assistance had to be effective, (2) it could not serve selfish political or economic interests, and (3) the aid had to be used specifically for economic rebuilding.

The three ministers had five meetings. On July 2, the last day of the tripartite talks, Molotov read a prepared statement rejecting the Anglo-French proposals. He warned France and Great Britain about the consequences of their action if they participated in the ERP.

On July 4, 1947, France and Great Britain invited twenty-two nations to send representatives to Paris to formulate a plan for their economic recovery. Czechoslovakia initially accepted the invitation, but after Premier Klement Gottwald visited with Marshal Joseph Stalin, he rejected the invitation. Stalin would not permit any of the satellite countries to participate in the ERP. On July 12, 1947, representatives of sixteen nations met in Paris to discuss Marshall's proposals.

They established the Committee on European Economic Cooperation (CEEC) to collect facts, determine needs, and develop a coordinated plan to deal with their needs.

In December 1948, President Truman informed Congress that he thought the ERP would cost $17 billion over a four-year period. He requested more than $6 billion for the first fifteen months of the program. The president asked the Congress to act quickly because the people in Europe were desperate. He warned that they could turn to totalitarianism if their situation did not improve. Most members of Congress recognized that the collapse of Europe would have a profound impact on the United States. There was, however, reluctance on the part of some members of Congress to commit to such a huge program requiring the expenditure of billions of dollars. Some congressmen questioned whether the United States could afford such a program. They feared the United States was already overextended in its commitments.

Convincing Congress to appropriate money for the most expensive peacetime program in American history was no easy task. Members of the Truman administration spent a great deal of time responding to questions from members of the House and Senate. Republican Senator Robert Taft opposed the plan, as did former president Herbert Hoover. Henry Wallace traveled throughout the United States and Europe attacking Marshall's proposals. The president and members of his administration emphasized that without the ERP the Communists might win control of one or more governments in Europe. The president prevailed. On April 3, 1948, ten months after Marshall's address to Harvard, he signed the ERP legislation. The Congress appropriated more than $6 billion for a twelve-month period. On April 5, Truman

appointed Paul Hoffman to head the Economic Cooperation Administration (ECA). The ECA was responsible for administering the Marshall Plan. This meant coordinating policies from different branches of the government and then coordinating those policies with the European recipients of the aid.

The Soviet Union

Although the Soviet Union needed economic aid, Stalin would not agree to participate in the ERP. The Soviets worried about an economically revived Germany. The United States remained committed to keeping Germany disarmed, but there was no guarantee the commitment would last. German leaders would undoubtedly make more demands to ease the occupation. The United States and its allies found themselves in the awkward situation of needing German cooperation if Europe was to recover. The Soviets were well aware that including West Germany in the recovery program could lead to a permanent division of the country. West Germany could make a much more significant contribution to the West than East Germany could make to the Communist bloc.

If the Eastern European nations participated in the ERP, the Soviet Union could conceivably lose its ability to control their policies. Stalin had just acquired an empire; he was determined to maintain total control. Keeping Western influence outside his empire was what the iron curtain was all about. The very fact that Poland and Czechoslovakia expressed an interest in participating in the ERP demonstrated that not all the nations of the Soviet bloc had the same interests.

In 1947, the Soviet Union had two major foreign policy goals in Europe. One was to establish a monolithic Communist bloc. Controlling the bloc could prove difficult if a bloc member became dependent on U.S. aid. The second goal was to prevent the formation of a Western bloc aligned with the United States. That is precisely what the Marshall Plan threatened to do. The United States, for example, made it clear to the nations of Western Europe that requests for aid would be more sympathetically received if there were no Communists participating in the government. In 1948, Secretary of State Marshall threatened to cancel aid to Italy if the Communist party won the April election. The United States insisted that the recipients of aid exclude Communists from government positions.

A successful ERP would undoubtedly damage Communist parties throughout Europe. Communism would not appeal to people enjoying economic prosperity. It is rather astounding to realize that the Soviet Union was committed to do whatever was necessary to prevent the ERP from succeeding. The French and Italian Communist parties did all they could to prevent success. Their primary weapons were strikes, propaganda, demonstrations, and confrontations, including the use of violence.

To make certain that the Communist parties in Europe did not deviate from Moscow's policies, the Soviet Union created the Cominform (the Communist Information Bureau) in October 1947. The Cominform was specifically created in response to the Truman Doctrine and the Marshall Plan. In addition to the Communist parties of the satellite nations, the Soviet Union invited the leaders of the Communist parties in France and Italy to attend. The two parties were instructed to do all they could to make certain the Marshall Plan did not succeed. When the French and Italian Communist leaders returned from Poland, a wave of strikes and violence occurred in both countries.

One interesting aspect of the first Cominform meeting was the absence of representatives of the Greek Communist party. This suggests that as early as the autumn of 1947, a Communist victory in Greece was not a major Soviet priority, although it continued to be a major objective of Yugoslav foreign policy.

Conclusion

The Marshall Plan lasted from April 1948 to December 1951 and cost approximately $12.5 billion. The plan had political, economic, and psychological components. As an economic policy, the plan was a success. People enjoyed higher incomes, production increased, and the standard of living improved. During the ERP period 75 percent of trade restrictions in place in 1947 were removed. Intra-European trade just about doubled, as did steel production. The improved economic conditions contributed to great political stability in most of the countries receiving aid. In France and Italy, the Communist parties lost some of their appeal. In neither country did they participate in governing coalitions. Perhaps the most notable contribution of the Marshall Plan was psychological. For the people of Europe there was renewed hope and vitality. John McCloy, the U.S. High Commissioner for Germany, said the improvement of economic and social conditions in Germany during the ERP could almost be called a miracle. Perhaps equally important was the fact that the Bonn government was recognized as a stable loyal ally by other nations in Western Europe and the United States.

The Marshall Plan laid the foundation for European integration. One of the subsidiary benefits of the plan was that it helped promote cooperation between and among the nations of Europe. That contributed to the integration process that lasted well beyond the plan itself. In 1952, the European Coal and Steel Community was established and that eventually led to the creation of the Common Market in 1958. The political and economic success of the plan also contributed to the success of the North Atlantic Treaty Organization (NATO) when it was established in April 1949. The economic recovery enabled the countries of Europe to make bigger contributions to their own defense.

The Marshall Plan produced a number of unfavorable consequences, although some of them could not be avoided. The division of Europe into rival blocs became a defining characteristic of the cold war. The United States did not want Communists participating in the governments receiving American aid. The Soviet Union purged members from Communist parties throughout Eastern Europe. Berlin was divided, Germany was divided, and the Marshall Plan divided Europe. Those divisions remained in place until the end of the cold war.

The Marshall Plan succeeded in rebuilding the nations of Western Europe, but that very success fueled cold war tensions. Nevertheless, the Marshall Plan was one of the great achievements of the Truman administration.

The ERP is an excellent example of enlightened self-interest. The economic recovery of Western Europe diminished the threat of Communism and highlighted the advantages of democratic nations cooperating with each other. The success of the ERP shifted the balance of power in favor of the United States and its allies. The people living on the Western side of the dividing line in Berlin, Germany, and Europe were doing much better than those on the Eastern side.

Kenneth L. Hill

See also: Greece: Civil War, 1944–1949.

Bibliography

Acheson, Dean. *Present at the Creation.* New York: Norton, 1969.

Barker, Elizabeth. *Britain in a Divided Europe, 1945–1970.* London: Weidenfeld and Nicolson, 1971.

Beloff, Max. *The United States and the Unity of Europe.* Washington, DC: Brookings Institution, 1963.

Best, Richard A. *Cooperation with Like-Minded Peoples: British Influence on American Security Policy, 1945–1949.* New York: Greenwood, 1986.

Hoffman, Paul G. *Peace Can Be Won.* New York: Doubleday, 1951.

Hogan, Michael J. *The Marshall Plan: America, Britain, and the Reconstruction of Western Europe, 1947–1952.* Cambridge: Cambridge University Press, 1987.

Kindelberger, Charles P. "The Marshall Plan and the Cold War." *International Journal* 23 (Summer 1968): 369–382.

Leffler, Melvyn P. *A Preponderance of Power: National Security, the Truman Administration, and the Cold War.* Stanford: Stanford University Press, 1992.

———. "The American Conception of National Security and the Beginnings of the Cold War." *American Historical Review* 89 (April 1984): 346–381.

Milward, Alan S. *The Reconstruction of Western Europe 1945–51.* Berkeley: University of California Press, 1984.

The United Nations

Historical Background

Before the twentieth century, international cooperation existed on an alliance-by-alliance basis only. Countries made agreements designed to advance their national interests and kept them so long as those interests continued to be served. European, African, Asian, and American histories were partly the stories of these alliances being made and unmade as circumstances changed.

By the nineteenth century, however, some statesmen and diplomats were beginning to suggest that something more was needed. With the advent of railroads, diesel-powered ships, and the telegraph and telephone, the world was becoming a smaller, more interconnected place. Moreover, the industrial revolution had led to the development of weapons—the modern rifle, the machine gun, and the artillery shell—which made modern conflicts between nations likely to be more bloody than any of the past.

To avoid future wars, the emperor of Russia proposed two peace conferences, both of which took place at The Hague. The emperor hoped that the Hague Peace Conferences—the first held in 1899, the second, in 1907—would help to prevent future wars, or at least ameliorate some of their more gruesome consequences. Little was settled at the Hague conferences—the nations involved did not wish to give up their sovereign rights to wage war as they pleased—but they did result in the creation of an international court

of arbitration, the Hague Tribunal, which was a precursor of the United Nations.

The Hague Tribunal was able to successfully arbitrate a number of international disagreements, but could do nothing to stand in the way of World War I. That cataclysmic war—at least 10 million died—convinced many participants that a stronger organization was needed. The U.S. President Woodrow Wilson championed the idea of a international congress of nations which would work to prevent future wars. The result of their efforts was the League of Nations, established at the Paris Peace Conference of 1919.

The League of Nations was the direct ancestor of the United Nations. It had a council that included the major European powers and an assembly that was supposed to include all the independent nations of the world. The League, however, was handicapped at birth by two great flaws: The United States Senate refused to ratify the treaty that brought the League into existence, which meant that the world's greatest economic power would not be a part of this first international organization, and the League had no clearly delineated method of punishing aggressors. These failures left the League helpless in the face of aggression; it was unable to stop Japan's invasion of Manchuria, Italy's conquest of Ethiopia, or Germany's rearmament and absorption of Austria and Czechoslovakia. Most importantly, the League could do nothing to stop World War II. With the onset of the war in 1939, the

League became largely irrelevant, and it dissolved itself in 1946.

Creation of the United Nations

Just as the League of Nations grew out of World War I, the United Nations was an offshoot of World War II. This second world war was even bloodier than the first—at least 50 million died—and the need for an organization that could prevent future wars seemed vital.

Discussions concerning the creation of the United Nations began well before World War II was over. On August 13, 1941, in the midst of the war, Prime Minister Winston Churchill of Britain and President Franklin Roosevelt of the United States signed the Atlantic Charter, a non-binding declaration calling for a world free of violent conflict and suggesting that to prevent future wars some kind of international organization should be formed. The Atlantic Charter was seconded by the January 1, 1942, Declaration of the United Nations. This declaration was primarily a wartime agreement between the countries fighting Germany, Italy, and Japan, but it also echoed the Atlantic Charter's call for an international organization. October 1943 saw the signing of the Moscow Declaration on General Security, which explicitly called for the creation of an international organization. The Moscow Declaration was signed by the Big Four: the United States, the Soviet Union, Britain, and China.

The first planning conference for the United Nations was carried out by the Big Four at a Dumbarton Oaks estate in Washington, D.C., during August and September 1944. The conference was a success, with all four agreeing to the basic framework upon which an international organization would be built—including the creation of a Security Council, General Assembly, and International Court. Further discussions, elaborating on the Dumbarton Oaks meeting, took place among the Big Three—the United States, the Soviet Union, and Britain—at the Yalta Conference in February 1945. Also at Yalta, the powers agreed to sponsor a United Nations Conference which would be held on April 25, 1945, in San Francisco.

Fifty nations met in San Francisco to draft the United Nations Charter. The document they signed on June 26, 1945, included all the elements that had been worked out by the major powers during 1943 and 1944, but the other participating countries also added modifications that turned the Charter into something other than a dictate from above. The central purpose of the new organization, according to the Charter, was "to save succeeding generations from the scourge of war . . . [and] to reaffirm faith in fundamental human rights." After the San Francisco meeting, the delegates returned to their countries to obtain ratification by their respective legislatures or rulers. A majority of the signatories had ratified the Charter by October 24, 1945, which became the date of the founding of the United Nations. All participating nations had ratified the Charter by December 27, 1945—there were fifty-one signatories, including Poland, which had not participated in the original San Francisco meeting, but was allowed to be considered an original founder of the United Nations. The first meeting of the United Nations General Assembly took place on January 10, 1946.

The United Nations Charter created six central organs: the Security Council, the General Assembly, the Secretariat, the International Court of Justice, the Economic and Social Council, and the Trusteeship Council. The United Nations has since created numerous specialized agencies, including the

United Nations Children's Fund (UNICEF), the United Nations High Commission for Refugees (UNHCR), a variety of conflict-specific peacekeeping organizations (such as the United Nations Peacekeeping Force in Cyprus and the United Nations Military Observer Group in India and Pakistan), and associated but autonomous organizations such as the World Bank and the International Monetary Fund. The budget of the United Nations is funded by its member nations on a sliding scale based on criteria that include national and per capita income.

The Secretariat

The Secretariat is the administrative hub of the United Nations. All the officials and bureaucrats who manage the United Nations are a part of the Secretariat. At the head of the Secretariat is the secretary-general of the United Nations who is elected for a five-year term of office. The secretary-general sets the administrative agendas of the United Nations agencies and serves as the symbolic head of the entire United Nations.

The power of the secretary-general is extremely circumscribed. The secretary-general manages the United Nations' administration bureaucracy, but all significant policy decisions are made by the Security Council and the General Assembly. Nevertheless, the secretary-general's symbolic role and prestige can give him influence in world affairs, and an energetic secretary-general can use his limited power to great effect. The first secretary-general, chosen in 1946, was Trygve Lie of Norway. The secretary-general elected for the five-year term beginning January 1, 1997, was Kofi Annan, the first secretary-general chosen from sub-Saharan Africa. As of this writing, all secretary-generals have been men; recently some women have been considered for the position, including, most notably, Mary Robinson of Ireland.

The Security Council

The Security Council is the center of real power in the United Nations. Of its fifteen members, five—Britain, China, France, the Russian Federation, and the United States—are designated permanent members; these five were the strongest countries in the alliance that successfully defeated the Axis powers during World War II, and they insisted on a preponderance of power in the new world organization. (Until 1971, China's seat was held by the Nationalist government of Taiwan; afterward, it was held by the mainland People's Republic of China.) The ten non-permanent Security Council members are elected to two-year terms by the General Assembly.

While giving five countries special privileges over the other nations of the world is not in keeping with democratic norms, it realistically recognizes the fact that without the cooperation of these powers the United Nations would be as ineffective as its League predecessor.

In day-to-day business, the Security Council needs the votes of nine out of its fifteen members to pass a resolution; however, on substantive issues—those that involve a major United Nations policy decision—the Security Council majority must include all five permanent members. In other words, any of the permanent members have the ability to veto any substantive decision taken by the Security Council.

The Security Council has the responsibility for maintaining world peace and security. If it believes that peace has been threatened by a nation or nations, the Security Council can initiate investigations, issue sanctions, or even organize military action (although this has been quite rare). The cold war handicapped the Security Council, and therefore the United Nations. Both the United States and the Soviet Union were willing to use their veto powers to overturn any decision that went against themselves or their allies. During the cold war, therefore, it was extremely difficult to find any common ground upon which all five permanent members could agree. The decline of communism in the Soviet Union and the subsequent ending of the cold war has made unanimous Security Council decisions more feasible, which has, in turn, strengthened the reputation and influence of the United Nations. The 1990 sanctions against Iraq, followed by the 1991 U.N.-sanctioned invasion, marked the beginning of a new era of United Nations effectiveness.

The General Assembly

The General Assembly is the most democratic part of the United Nations. Each of the United Nations member states (185 as of 1998) sends a group of representatives to the General Assembly, with each delegation getting one vote, no matter what the size of the country it represents. In theory, this gives the United States the same weight in General Assembly debates as Luxembourg.

The General Assembly, unlike the Security Council, lacks any substantive power. It can debate, make recommendations, and censure countries, but its resolutions are nonbinding. Member states are obliged to follow Security Council decrees; they are not required to obey General Assembly resolutions. Unlike the League of Nations, which required unanimity for all decisions, the United Nations General Assembly only re-

quires a simple majority to pass its resolutions.

Nevertheless, the General Assembly's decisions have a moral weight. The General Assembly gives the world an arena within which to debate actions by member nations, including the great powers, and condemn them if they see fit. Its resolutions may be ignored by their targets but have the potential of shifting world opinion in one direction or another; for example, the United Nations' consistent condemnation of South Africa's apartheid system had no binding effect on that country's white government, but it may have helped encourage individuals in member nations to boycott South Africa's economy, and thereby help accelerate the end of the system.

The General Assembly can also pass conventions or treaties. These have no legal validity until ratified by a sufficient number of states, but the mere existence of such documents can often lead enough nations to adopt them so as to give them legal meaning. Finally, the General Assembly, together with the Security Council, is responsible for admitting new nations to the United Nations and for electing certain United Nations officials, including the secretary-general.

Preventing Aggression

Although the United Nations operates in many areas, its primary purpose was and is to maintain peace in the world. Prevention and settlement of disputes is the topic of Chapters Six and Seven of the United Nations Charter.

In its attempts to prevent war and internal turmoil, the United Nations has operated most often under the provisions of Chapter Six, "Pacific Settlement of Disputes." It states that any parties to a dispute "likely to endanger the maintenance of international peace and security, shall, first of all, seek a solution by negotiation, inquiry, mediation, conciliation, arbitration, judicial settlement, resort to regional agencies or arrangements, or other peaceful means of their own choice." The emphasis is on voluntary cooperation. The General Assembly or the Security Council may recommend solutions to a dispute, but Chapter Six does not give them the power to enforce those solutions. Chapter Six, however, does allow the Security Council to investigate any dispute in an attempt to determine which country or countries might be at fault, as well as how the dispute might be resolved.

If the only way to resolve a conflict was to rely on the voluntary methods outlined in Chapter Six of the Charter, the United Nations would be little different than its predecessor, the League of Nations. The United Nations, however, made a break from League precedent by adding provisions for peace enforcement.

Chapter Seven, "Action with Respect to Threats to the Peace, Breaches of the Peace, and Acts of Aggression," gives the Security Council the right to determine whether a threat to peace is occurring and to determine what measures might be taken to forestall that threat. These measures go far beyond the sanctions available to the League of Nations. Within the chapter, Article 41 provides for the possibility of economic and communications embargoes. And if those methods do not work, Article 42 allows the Security Council to use "operations by air, sea, or land forces" to suppress a threat to world peace—in other words, military force. The United Nations has no army of its own, and, therefore, the Charter states (Article 43) that all members "undertake to make available to the Security Council . . . armed forces, assistance, and facilities . . . necessary for the purpose of maintaining international peace and security." These armed forces are made available on a purely voluntary basis; no nation is obliged to contribute troops.

In theory, therefore, the United Nations has the power to take a wide range of actions in defense of world peace. Assuming that nine out of fifteen Security Council members agree, the United Nations can even use military force to punish aggressors. In practice, cold war hostilities made it almost impossible to gain the support of both the United States and the Soviet Union, and without unanimity among the five permanent members, any Security Council resolution would be vetoed. What one superpower viewed as aggression, another might consider a defense of its vital interests. Until the end of the cold war, therefore, the United Nations did less than it might have in fulfilling its promise to prevent aggression.

The Korean War

The one time during the cold war when the United Nations acted vigorously under Article 43 was in Korea, and it was under very unusual circumstances. When North Korean troops came across the border into South Korea late at night on June 24, 1950, the Soviet delegate to the United Nations was absent from the Security Council. The Soviets were boycotting the United Nations to protest the United Nations' refusal to replace the Nationalist Chinese delegate to the United Nations with a Communist delegate from mainland China. Without fear of a Soviet veto, the Security Council was able to pass a

June 25 resolution calling upon member nations to support South Korea in its attempt to defend itself against North Korea.

On July 7, with American troops rushing to assist South Korea, the Security Council created a unified command structure to coordinate the defense of that country. The United States was given the responsibility of leading this U.N. army. Again, as the Soviets were still boycotting the Security Council, the resolution passed.

The U.N. army, operating under the auspices of Article 43, was led by American General Douglas MacArthur. The United Nations label was deceptive, however. The bulk of the troops sent to fight were Americans; the commanders were Americans; and when peace was negotiated, it was negotiated by Americans. Excluding South Korea, which contributed a large number of troops to its own defense, only Britain and Turkey committed as much as an infantry brigade; the rest of the allies sent battalion-size units or smaller. (Luxembourg sent one infantry company.)

The Soviets returned to the Security Council in October 1950, but their vetoes were ignored. The United States convinced the General Assembly to pass a Uniting for Peace resolution in November 1950, which stated that when the Security Council was deadlocked by one permanent member's veto, the General Assembly had the right to take the initiative in recommending military action. While the Uniting for Peace resolution was of questionable legality, it provided the United States with the ability to claim that they were continuing to act under United Nations authority.

The Korean War dragged on for three years, until a July 1953 armistice ended the fighting and left the borders approximately where they had started. In that sense, the United Nations had been a success; it had prevented an aggressor, North Korea, from profiting from its aggression. But it was only able to do so because of the unusual absence of the Soviet delegate.

Peacekeeping

While the United Nations was usually unable to gain support for active military intervention—aside from the exceptional case of the Korean War—it found another role as an observer and peacekeeper. United Nations Secretary-General Dag Hammarskjold (1953-1961) first initiated the use of peacekeepers during the 1956 Suez Crisis—a brief war pitting Israel, Britain, and France against Egypt. Although vetoes by the French and the British representatives prevented Security Council action, the General Assembly voted for a resolution calling for a cease-fire and asked Hammarskjold to supervise the creation of an international force to watch over the (voluntary) withdrawal of the three attackers from Egyptian territory. The United Nations Emergency Force (UNEF) sent 6,000 troops from ten countries to the war zone. Largely because of American pressure on its three allies, the operation was a success. UNEF supervised the withdrawal and then stayed posted along the border between Israel and Egypt until 1967, when it was asked to leave by Gamal Abdel Nasser (just prior to the 1967 war).

UNEF established the ground rules for peacekeeping operations. "Blue helmets"—as the peacekeepers were called because of their distinctive headgear—were sent to a region where all parties were willing to accept their presence as a means of reducing tension, either by observing a border in an attempt to prevent incursions or, on a larger scale, by acting as a buffer force between two countries or forces. Peacekeepers are usually armed, but they may only fight in self-defense and have no mandate to interfere in any armed conflict. The invention of peacekeepers by Hammarskjold was a response to paralysis in the Security Council. But despite Hammarskjold's clever rule-bending, the ability of the peacekeepers to operate remains limited. Only the Security Council has the right to order aggressive action against a country; if any participant in the peacekeeping process wishes the peacekeepers to leave, they must oblige.

Peacekeepers had already served on a smaller scale before 1956. A United Nations Truce Supervision Organization (UNTSO) was stationed in and around Israel after 1948 to monitor the border between Israel and the neighboring Arab states. Another border watch was kept in the area of Kashmir contested by Pakistan and India; these observers, the United Nations Military Observer Group in India and Pakistan (UNMOGIP), began their watch in 1949. Neither border-watching group succeeded in stopping the violence—wars continued to break out in both areas—but their presence may have reduced it for at least a time.

Since the UNEF operation, United Nations peacekeeping forces have been active all over the world, usually only as observers, but sometimes acting as buffer armies. One of the most important buffer roles taken by the United Nations was in Cyprus, where in 1964 United Nations troops were called in to separate the warring communities of ethnic Turks and Greeks. They have remained ever since—2,500 soldiers maintaining a line between Turkish and Greek Cyprus.

The United Nations in the Congo

The most extensive use of United Nations peacekeepers until the post–cold war era was in the Congo (called Zaire from 1966 to 1997). In June 1960, the Congo achieved its independence from Belgium and immediately began to dissolve into a chaotic civil war. After Belgian civilians were attacked during the fighting, Belgium sent troops into the country to protect its citizens and its interests. The Belgians also supported the independence bid of the mineral-rich province of Katanga. On July 12, in response to what seemed a threat to Congo's sovereignty, Congo's new prime minister called for United Nations assistance. The Security Council, prodded by Hammarskjold, agreed to send troops to keep the peace.

The United Nations sent an army of 20,000 men from twenty-nine countries to the Congo. The U.N. army's first job, to supervise the withdrawal of the Belgians from the country, was completed in September 1960. At that point the force lost direction as the Security Council argued over what its mission should be. The Soviet Union wished the United Nations peacekeepers to support the government of Prime Minister Patrice Lumumba and to suppress the rebels in Katanga; the United States was suspicious of Lumumba's left-wing politics and preferred a more neutral stance. After Lumumba was murdered in January 1961, the United Nations force was ordered by the General Assembly to suppress the revolt in Katanga. In September, fighting broke out between Blue Helmets and Katangese rebels. While attempting to negotiate a cease-fire, Hammarskjold, on his way to meet with Katanga's leader, Moíse Tshombé, died in a plane crash.

U Thant, Hammarskjold's replacement as secretary-general, was more aggressive in his leadership of the U.N. army in the Congo. United Nations forces fought the Katangese rebels in December 1961 and again in December 1962, forcibly disarming their soldiers and seizing control of Katangese towns. In January 1963, Tshombé conceded defeat and Katanga was brought back under the Congo government's control. The last United Nations troops left in June 1964 (although fighting continued in the Congo until 1965).

The Post–Cold War United Nations

With the end of the cold war, the United Nations finally has been able to act in the manner that its founders had envisioned. In 1990, it had the first opportunity to demonstrate that in a post–cold war world it could be an effective force in defeating aggression.

Desert Storm

When Iraq invaded Kuwait on August 2, 1990, the United Nations Security Council reacted immediately by passing, by a fourteen-to-nothing vote, a resolution condemning the invasion and demanding a return to negotiations by both parties. When Saddam Hussein refused to comply, the Security Council passed a thirteen-to-nothing resolution calling for economic sanctions against Iraq. United Nations members, led by the United States, also began to send troops to Saudi Arabia to both defend that country and to prepare for a possible counter-attack against Iraq.

The Security Council worked to avoid a war, even sending Secretary-General Javier Perez de Cuellar to Baghdad to negotiate with Hussein. On November 29, 1990, with no results from either negotiations or sanctions, the Security Council passed Resolution 678, which set a January 15, 1991, deadline for Iraqi withdrawal from Kuwait. If Hussein did not meet the deadline, the resolution authorized the use of "all necessary means" to force Iraq to end its occupation. The resolution passed with a twelve-to-two vote; Yemen and Cuba voted against it, while China abstained. On January 17, 1991, the allied armies in Saudi Arabia opened an attack on Iraq, which defeated Hussein's army in a few weeks, forcing its withdrawal from Kuwait.

Although on the surface the Iraqi conflict seemed to represent the fulfillment of the United Nations' goal of achieving collective security, the pace of negotiations and military action was pushed along by the United States and its allies. From the beginning of the crisis, President George Bush made it clear that the United States would not allow Iraq to occupy Kuwait. His attempt to gain United Nations support was guided by a belief that it would be useful, not necessary. And in Security Council debates, it was the United States, seconded by Britain and France, which pushed for increasingly bellicose resolutions. China and Russia were less enthusiastic, and Cuba was actively hostile. Moreover, during the actual campaign, it was American troops that dominated the battlefield and American generals who issued the commands. Twenty-eight nations contributed troops to the war, but only Britain and France contributed more than a division.

In many respects, therefore, the Iraqi conflict was an American operation conducted under the cloak of a Security Council resolution. Subsequent negotiations with Iraq have been affected by this dynamic. The United States has continually pressed for harsher treatment for Iraq, while many members of the United Nations have argued for more temperate behavior.

Cambodia

The United Nations has undertaken several other major military commitments during the 1990s, including Cambodia, Yugoslavia, and Somalia. All achieved a mixed degree of success.

Cambodia had suffered from more than twenty years of civil war and invasion, including a 1979 invasion that ousted the Khmer Rouge regime. In 1991, the Cambodian government was still being supported by Vietnam, while anti-government guerrillas (including both non-Communists and Khmer Rouge) received support from the United States, China, and Thailand. In an October 1991 peace conference, the United Nations agreed to create an administrative structure, the United Nations Transitional Authority in Cambodia (UNTAC), that would supervise Cambodia's transition to peace and democracy. The operation, which cost $2 billion dollars, was a semi-failure. More than 20,000 United Nations representatives, soldiers, police, and civilians were sent into Cambodia and successfully supervised elections in 1993, but they could not force the parties to abide by their results. Fighting between Prince Norodom Ranariddh and Prime Minister Hun Sen's factions continued into 1998.

Nevertheless, despite its limited success, the Cambodian intervention by the United Nations had given China an excuse to stop its support of the Khmer Rouge guerrillas, with the result that by 1998, the Khmer Rouge had disappeared as an effective force in Cambodia's political scene. And in general, the level of violence in Cambodia is far lower than it was before the United Nations mission.

Somalia

The United Nations intervention in Somalia began as a humanitarian effort but developed into a military action.

When the Siad Barre regime fell in 1991,

the entire country descended into a confused civil war between rival factions. The constant fighting combined with one of the worst droughts in modern Somalian history left the country without sufficient food for its people. Attempts by relief agencies to bring food to Somalia were short-circuited by local warlords who confiscated the food and supplies for the use of their own factions.

At first, the United Nations ignored the problem in Somalia. Secretary-General Boutros Boutros-Ghali accused the five permanent members of being racists, suggesting that they were more concerned with white Bosnia than black Somalia. The Security Council responded in April 1992 by sending 500 peacekeepers to Mogadishu. These were too few to face down the warlords, however, and the starvation in Somalia continued.

It was the television images of starving Somali children beamed into American homes that convinced President George Bush to support a Security Council resolution that authorized a military intervention into the country. In December 1992, an American-led United Nations expeditionary force moved into Somalia to create a climate where food could be properly distributed. The 38,000-man multinational force, 25,000 of whom were Americans, overawed the warlords and was able to provide a safe environment for relief efforts.

However, when the United Nations force attempted to impose greater order on the country, the Somali factions reacted with defiance and then open skirmishing. When a firefight in June 1993 resulted in the deaths of twenty-five Pakistanis, the United Nations Security Council, again pushed by the United States, passed a resolution calling for the arrest of those responsible. However, in the fighting that followed, American soldiers were killed and America soon soured on the

Somalia rescue mission. They had sent troops to Somalia to save starving children and did not understand why their troops were being shot at and killed. President Bill Clinton ordered all American troops withdrawn by March 1994.

Without the Americans, the mission floundered, and in November 1994 the Security Council agreed to its termination. On March 3, 1995, the last United Nations troops left the country.

The Somalia operation was perceived as a failure by many, particularly in the United States. Although it had probably saved tens of thousands of lives, it had failed to eliminate the power of the warlords or to restore stability in Somalia. The sight of dead Americans made the United States less inclined to send its troops abroad in future peacekeeping efforts.

Yugoslavia

In Yugoslavia, the United Nations was extremely slow in dealing with a growing catastrophe. The fighting began in June 1991. The Security Council, however, only issued an arms embargo against the entire former Yugoslavia in September, and this did little to slow the fighting between Serbs, Croatians, and Bosnian Muslims. In March 1992, United Nations troops were sent to Croatia to supervise a cease-fire between Croatians and Serbs, but this did nothing to halt the growing violence in Bosnia. A May 1992 economic embargo against Serbia was designed to do just that, but was ignored by the Bosnian Serbs, who continued carrying out an ethnic cleansing campaign against Bosnian Muslims and Croats.

In June 1992, the warring factions did agree to allow United Nations peacekeepers to be stationed in Sarajevo in order to facili-

tate the movement of food into Bosnia, which was near starvation. Eventually the United Nations Protection Force (UNPRO-FOR) reached a strength of 30,000 men, but because it was serving in a Blue Helmet peacekeeping role, it could do little more than protect a few enclaves, including Sarajevo (which continued to be shelled, despite the presence of UNPROFOR units). Thousands of Bosnians, mostly Muslims, continued to be killed every month.

The inactivity of the United Nations was based on a combination of politics and apathy. Politically, the Russians felt bound to Serbia by ties of ethnicity and religion, and therefore dragged its feet in Security Council meetings. Furthermore, there was a strong desire among all the major powers to avoid getting bogged down by committing combat troops to Yugoslavia. The United States and Europe pressured the combatants to make peace, but were unwilling to force them to do so. This attitude slowly changed as television images of the slaughter and suffering were broadcast around the world; international public opinion began to demand that something be done to stop Yugoslavia's suffering.

In July 1995, the Serb destruction of a United Nations "protected" enclave at Srebrenica finally led to a change of policy by the international community. The United Nations, pushed along by the leading NATO powers, agreed to authorize NATO air strikes against Serb positions; this, combined with Muslim-Croat counter-offensives, forced the Bosnian Serbs to sign the November 1995 Dayton Peace Accords. To support the peace, the United Nations authorized 60,000 combat troops to be sent to Bosnia; most of them, however, were NATO regulars, with the largest contingents coming from the United States, Britain, and France.

The United Nations had served a useful purpose in providing humanitarian aid to the starving Bosnian Muslims, but until the United States pressed for air strikes and military intervention, the United Nations lacked the will or the ability to stop the fighting in Bosnia.

Arms Control

In addition to the tasks of peacekeeping and military intervention, the United Nations, under the authority of Article 11 of the United Nations Charter, has worked to reduce the danger of violence in the world by recommending arms control limitations. These efforts have had only moderate success. During the cold war, neither superpower, nor any of their allies, wished to disarm because of their fear of one another; the cold war arms race has resulted in a world filled with thousands of nuclear weapons.

One modest success of the United Nations was the 1968 Treaty on the Non-Proliferation of Nuclear Weapons, which enjoined all signatories to promise to neither give nor accept nuclear technology (although it did not take away weapons from those nations that already possessed them). The treaty was signed by most nations; however, two nuclear powers, France and China, refused to sign it until the early 1990s. In addition, a number of non-nuclear powers refused to sign the treaty, including Israel and South Africa (the latter signed the treaty in 1991). And India and Pakistan's 1998 nuclear tests demonstrate that while nuclear proliferation may have been slowed by the General Assembly's treaty, it has not been stopped.

The General Assembly has also written treaties prohibiting the use of other weapons of mass destruction—meaning biological and chemical weapons—but has had difficulty in getting many nations, including the United States and Russia, to sign them.

The Effectiveness of the United Nations

Despite its reputation for inaction and inefficiency, the United Nations has been at the center of a number of crises and has even managed to resolve a respectable number. During the cold war, its ability to resolve differences between the two alliances headed by the United States and the Soviet Union was next to nil, but not all crises were cold war crises. In the Congo, Israel, Cyprus, and other points of conflict, the United Nations was able to provide a forum for debate, and sometimes even a solution to the conflict. In Korea, the United Nations provided an umbrella under which the United States could act to defend South Korea.

In the post–cold war world the United Nations has been able to ameliorate the damage caused by violence in Bosnia, Yugoslavia, and Somalia, as well as turning back Iraq's invasion of Kuwait. And in numerous smaller hot-spots throughout the world, from El Salvador to Angola, the United Nations' Blue Helmets have helped to lessen tensions and reduce the chance of future violence.

The United Nations is most effective when both sides in a conflict wish to achieve peace and jointly request a United Nations peacekeeping presence as an aid to preventing future violence. The United Nations has greater difficulty dealing with a crisis in which one or both sides wishes to continue to use violence to achieve its ends. In these cases, the United Nations is only able to intervene when such a policy is advanced by some of the five permanent Security Council representatives, and is accepted by the rest. Saddam Hussein's invasion of Kuwait was defeated because the United States was willing to commit its troops to the effort; the intervention in Somalia was a political failure in part because the United States was unwilling to see its soldiers die for a confused conflict in which there were no clear goals or enemies.

The United Nations has had more failures than successes in its attempts to end world violence. During the cold war, of course, conflicts were driven by the competition between the communist and capitalist worlds. But even in the post–cold war world, the United Nations has failed to end the ethnic slaughter in Rwanda, to stop the bloody civil wars in Liberia, or to prevent the nuclear tests of India and Pakistan.

The future of the United Nations probably depends on the behavior of the permanent members of the Security Council. Their veto power allows them to dominate debate within the Security Council and the General Assembly, and this is appropriate, as it is only with the active support of these five powers that the United Nations has the capacity to intervene in the world's most violent and dangerous trouble spots. If the five remain committed and cooperative, the United Nations will be effective; if they do not, its prospects are poor.

Carl Skutsch

See also: Bosnia: Civil War, 1992–1995; Cambodia: Civil Wars, 1968–1998; Cold War Confrontations; Congo (Zaire), Democratic Republic of: Post-Independence Wars, 1960–1965; Korea: Invasion of the South by the North, 1950–1953; Somalia: Civil War Since 1991; Yugoslavia: Disintegration, 1990s.

Bibliography

Baehr, P.R., and Leon Gordenker. *The United Nations in the 1990s.* New York: St. Martin's Press, 1992.

Claude, Inis L. *Swords into Plowshares: The Problems and Progress of International Organization.* New York: Random House, 1971.

Meisler, Stanley. *United Nations: The First Fifty Years.* New York: Atlantic Monthly Press, 1995.

Riggs, Robert E., and Jack Plano. *The United Nations.* Chicago: Dorsey Press, 1988.

Yoder, Amos. *The Evolution of the United Nations System.* Bristol, PA: Taylor & Francis, 1993.

Warsaw Pact

The Warsaw Treaty of Friendship, Cooperation, and Mutual Assistance—popularly known as the Warsaw Pact—was signed in the Polish capital in May 1955. The original signatories to the treaty were the Soviet Union and the Communist states of Eastern Europe: Albania, Bulgaria, Czechoslovakia, East Germany, Hungary, Poland, and Romania. Yugoslavia, under the independent socialist leader Marshal Tito, never joined. The hard-line Albanian government of Enver Hoxha broke with the Soviet Union during the more liberal administration of Nikita Khrushchev and pulled out of the Warsaw Pact in 1961.

The Warsaw Pact was largely a mutual security arrangement, pledging each member to come to the defense of any other member in the face of attack from an outside force. While no such outside force was specifically mentioned, it was clear that the Pact was originally established to defend Eastern Europe against attack by the North Atlantic Treaty Organization (NATO) in Western Europe, which was backed by the United States.

The Warsaw Pact and NATO became the two biggest military blocs of the cold war era, though ironically the two sides never engaged in any serious military actions against each other. They divided Europe between them during an era when war was largely banished from the continent. Cold war critics said the military build-up by both sides was a waste of resources; supporters said the two opposing alliances helped keep the peace, by making the cost of war—particularly nuclear war—too high for any leader on either side to contemplate.

The Warsaw Pact was also created—though this was never mentioned in official documents—to keep various East European states under the military control of the Soviet Union. The original treaty called for the establishment of joint command for all of the member countries' armed forces. While the treaty said that command would be shared among the members, in fact, the Soviet Union was the dominant player in the pact and usually determined what kind of actions the joint force would take. The timing of the Warsaw Pact's signing is revealing—in the wake of the first great rebellion against Communist rule in Eastern Europe, the great East German uprising of 1953.

Headquartered in Moscow, the original Warsaw Pact included a Joint Secretariat, Political Consultative Committee, and, most importantly, a Joint Command of the Armed Forces. This latter command was always headed by a Soviet general. A major expansion of the pact's governing system was undertaken in 1969 with the establishment of the Committee of Defense Ministers, the Technical Committee of the Joint Armed Forces, and the Military Council.

NATO's 1955 decision to re-arm West Germany and incorporate its military into the NATO command was seen as a provocative move by the Soviet Union and its East European allies, all of whom had been invaded by Nazi forces in World War II. In response, the Warsaw Pact moved to incorporate a revived East German military into its organization in 1956.

Crises and Challenges

The first great test of the treaty, however, came in Hungary and had nothing to do with NATO. In 1956, a new liberal and anti-Communist regime under Premier Imre Nagy came to power. Fearing a break in the alliance, the Soviets helped establish a rival regime under Janos Kadar, which then requested that Warsaw Pact troops enter the country. The troops backed Kadar's efforts to force the Nagy government out. Fearing a major confrontation with a nuclear-armed Warsaw Pact force, NATO and the West refused to intervene, convincing many East Europeans that they could not expect liberation with the help of Western powers.

Five years later, Warsaw Pact and NATO troops did face each other, though it was a bloodless confrontation. As the number of East Germans fleeing to West Berlin rose during the late 1950s and early 1960s, East Berlin and Moscow moved to stem the tide. This effort violated post–World War II treaties calling for joint control of the former Nazi capital and the free movement of people. As NATO and Warsaw Pact forces faced off along the line dividing the city, the East Germans and Soviets began building the Berlin Wall. As in Hungary, NATO commanders feared provoking a potential nuclear showdown and backed off. The Berlin Crisis of 1961 represented the first—and last—real showdown of Warsaw Pact and NATO forces in Europe.

Another trying time for the Warsaw Pact came in the spring of 1968, when a liberal Communist government under Alexander Dubcek began removing restrictions on political speech and activities in Czechoslovakia, thus triggering a burst of activism that challenged Communist rule and Czechoslovak membership in the Warsaw Pact. Known

as the Prague Spring, the events set off concerns in Moscow and other East European capitals. In August, Warsaw Pact forces from every country except Romania—which refused to support the invasion—rolled into Prague to remove the Dubcek government and end the experiment in "socialism with a human face."

By the early 1970s, the Warsaw Pact was growing in power, even as the United States was reeling from its withdrawal from Vietnam and the Western alliance was entering a period of sustained recession, set off in part by the sudden rise in petroleum prices following the Organization of Petroleum Exporting Countries boycott of the West in 1973 and 1974. Whereas NATO had maintained a commanding quantitative and qualitative advantage in military hardware throughout the 1960s—largely to counter the Warsaw Pact's greater manpower—that lead had withered by the early 1970s. Moreover, the Soviet Union was beginning to expand its presence throughout the developing world, especially in Africa and Southeast Asia.

Though the United States still maintained a nuclear advantage in the 1970s, there was a growing feeling in both America and parts of Western Europe that the military advantage had shifted to the Warsaw Pact. That and the declining economic fortunes of Western democracies led to the victory of conservative, pro-military build-up candidates across Western Europe and the United States in the late 1970s and early 1980s, including Margaret Thatcher in Britain, Ronald Reagan in the United States, and Helmut Kohl in West Germany.

These leaders moved to vastly expand military expenditures, while deploying a new generation of intermediate-range nuclear missiles—the so-called Pershings—in Western Europe.

While these militaristic moves set off massive protests in both Western Europe and North America, they overwhelmed the leadership of the Soviet Union and its East European allies. Crippled by unresponsive command economies, these countries were unable to both match the West's military build-up and provide the consumer goods that were increasingly being demanded by their own citizens. This realization led to the rise of a new generation of leaders in Moscow who sought a way to reform the top-heavy economy in the Soviet Union, while lessening tensions with the West.

Under the leadership of Mikhail Gorbachev, attempts were made in this direction. Moscow both lifted the lid on political dissent at home and sent a message to East European Communist governments that they could not expect Soviet military backing to put down revolts at home. Gorbachev also began to remove Soviet troops stationed in Eastern Europe.

By the late 1980s, there was a growing realization among the peoples of the Warsaw Pact countries that the Communist governments who ruled over them were little more than paper tigers, unable to fend off popular demands that they reform. By 1989, the protests in East European capitals had reached a crescendo. By the end of the year, every single Communist government in Eastern Europe had fallen and, with the exception of Romania, with almost no bloodshed.

Still, under Gorbachev, the Communists remained in power in the Soviet Union, but not for long. With the economy in a tailspin and political discord on the rise, a fear grew among the more conservative members of the bureaucracy and military that the country was heading for chaos. In August 1991, a military coup was attempted, but when it was faced with massive popular opposition

and dissent in the military's own ranks, it collapsed. In December, Boris Yeltsin, the leader of the Russian Federation (the largest component republic of the Soviet Union), demanded the dissolution of the Soviet Union and its replacement by a Commonwealth of Independent States, which came into effect on December 21.

The Collapse of the Pact

Meanwhile, in Eastern Europe, the new democratically elected, post-Communist governments were beginning to question the continued existence of the Warsaw Pact. The Political Consultative Council of the pact agreed to undertake a major review of the character and functions of the organization so as to transform it into "a pact of sovereign and equal states, based on democratic principals." At its June 1990 meeting, the Warsaw Pact leaders agreed to work with NATO and neutral European countries to form a new European security structure.

The effort failed. In that same month, Hungary became the first state to announce its withdrawal from the Warsaw Pact's joint command, effective at the end of 1991. In September, East Germany united with West Germany and became part of NATO. In November, the members of the pact met and voted for its dissolution. The Warsaw Pact had come to an end after thirty-six years.

In the wake of the Warsaw Pact's dissolution, a new security structure has indeed arisen in Europe, though not the one envisioned by the Warsaw Pact council of June 1990. Hungary, the Czech Republic, and Poland have now joined NATO, and there is talk of spreading the alliance to all the members of the former Soviet bloc. To assuage Russian fears of a new NATO encirclement, Moscow has been included as an associate member of NATO with a voice in its consultations.

James Ciment

See also: Cold War Confrontations; Creating West Germany, 1945–1955; North Atlantic Treaty Organization (NATO); Czechoslovakia: Soviet Invasion, 1968; Germany: The Berlin Crises, 1948–1949 and 1958–1962; Germany: East German Uprising, 1953; Hungary: Soviet Invasion, 1956.

Bibliography

Korbonski, Andrzej. *The Warsaw Pact*. New York: Carnegie Endowment for International Peace, 1969.

Moreton, N. Edwina. *East Germany and the Warsaw Alliance: The Politics of Détente*. Boulder, CO: Westview Press, 1978.

Remington, Robin Alison. *The Warsaw Pact: Case Studies in Communist Conflict Resolution*. Cambridge, MA: MIT Press, 1971.

War and Weapons Conventions

Historical Background

War conventions are relatively modern innovations. Throughout most of human history, the limits of warfare have been determined primarily by custom and the available weapons rather than by written agreements. Tradition put limits on violent confrontations (ancient Greek heroes engaged in hand-to-hand combat, which limited the slaughter to only a few individuals); conferences did not.

It is wrong, however, to blindly accept as a law of nature the trite proverb that "all's fair in love and war" (which, after all, was only coined in 1850). This mind-set has been used as an excuse to avoid thinking about the limitations that exist on war's practice, and on the limitations that might be imposed upon war's future. It is also ahistorical. War has always been governed by limitations determined by tradition, religion, or practicality: The ancient Carthaginian soldier could reasonably expect that if he dropped his spear and threw his hands in the air he would not be killed by his Roman counterpart—if only because the Roman would rather capture a slave than kill an opponent. The Iraqi soldier fleeing his burning tank on the road from Kuwait could also expect mercy from American helicopters, but because the Persian Gulf War was waged in the twentieth century, his safety was assured not merely by tradition but by the force of international law. While it is true that international laws and the treaties governing nations' conduct of war have often been broken, the same is also true for laws governing criminal conduct within nations. Individuals commit murders, and countries break international agreements. Nevertheless, just as laws against murder serve a purpose, so to do international agreements regulating the conduct of war.

The legal and moral justifications for regulating wars rest on two concepts dating from the Middle Ages: *jus ad bellum* (justice of war) and *jus in bello* (justice in war). The justice of any particular war, jus ad bellum, is difficult to determine, usually impossible for the parties to agree upon (for obvious reasons), and is usually best adjudged by outside observers or organizations (this remains a central role of the United Nations, whose charter allows it to determine if an "act of aggression" has taken place—that is, an unjust war—and to intervene if this is the case). Conduct within a war, jus in bello, however, has been successfully restricted by participants through the means of weapons treaties and war conventions.

In the Western tradition, one of the first conscious efforts to limit the conduct of war came with the Truce of God, developed in the eleventh century C.E. The Truce of God, created by Catholic synods, called for a halt to warfare from Wednesday evening to Monday morning and also ordained that no battles should occur during holy seasons, such as Lent and Advent. Similarly, the Peace of

God forbade, on pain of excommunication, attacks on Church buildings, clergymen, women, and peasants. Although both the eleventh-century Truce and the Peace of God, limiting when and against whom wars could be fought, were fairly ineffective (the Middle Ages remained plagued by endemic warfare), they were clearly a response to a general belief that war, as it was being waged, was both immoral and damaging to society, and that it needed to have limitations imposed upon its conduct.

The modern intellectual roots of war conventions begins with Hugo Grotius (1583–1645), whose *De Jure Belli ac Pacis* (On the Law of War and Peace) defended the idea of a war justly waged, emphasizing that innocent bystanders deserved to be exempted from the side-effects of military conflict. In the eighteenth-century Enlightenment, writers such as Emmerich de Vattel tried to develop laws of war that would limit its violence, a particular focus was preventing harm to civilians. These moral theorists laid the groundwork for nineteenth-century agreements, particularly the Geneva Conventions. In a more practical vein, Europe's nations worked to develop a series of protocols governing everything from the rights of neutrals at sea to the exchange of prisoners of war. Some treaties, such as the Rush-Bagot Treaty (1817) between the United States and Britain, might also demilitarize particular regions (Rush-Bagot limited the number of warships allowed in the Great Lakes). These practical conventions were the ancestors of the twentieth-century nuclear arms limitation agreements.

International codes that attempted to limit the conduct of wars, rather than simply smooth their operations, were not developed until the nineteenth century with the establishment of the Geneva Conventions.

Geneva Conventions

The Geneva Convention for Amelioration of Wounded in Time of War (1864) grew out of the efforts of a Swiss citizen, Henri Dunant, who witnessed the slaughter at the Battle of Solferino (1859) and was horrified at the obstacles confronted by those trying to save the lives of wounded soldiers. Dunant's efforts led to the creation of an International Standing Committee for Aid to Wounded Soldiers (1863) based in Geneva. The committee, which in 1880 changed its name to the International Committee of the Red Cross, became the center of a movement dedicated to the improvement of the treatment of wounded soldiers and prisoners of war. The following year, seizing on the momentum created by Dunant, the Swiss government called for an international conference to discuss the medical care of soldiers in the field. The first Geneva Convention, signed in 1864, was ratified by most of the world's major military powers within three years. The convention declared that all establishments and personnel dedicated to the treatment of wounded and sick soldiers—from field hospitals to stretcher-bearers—were to be immune from capture or attack, that wounded of both sides should be provided with medical treatment, and that a red cross would be the symbol used to protect medical buildings and personnel from military attack. A second Geneva Convention (1906) expanded upon these provisions. The third Geneva Convention (1929) added agreements concerning the disposition of prisoners of war, calling for humane treatment and visits by neutral representatives to check on conditions (this often meant representatives from the International Red Cross, which had taken upon itself the duty of supervising the implementation of Geneva Conventions).

The first three Geneva Conventions greatly improved the lot of both wounded and prisoners. During both World War I and World War II, medical care for combatants improved, while prisoners were usually housed in reasonably healthy conditions and sometimes received mail and packages from their families. Adherence to the Geneva Conventions, however, was uneven. During World War II, the Japanese military ignored the conventions and treated their prisoners with murderous severity; the Nazi German government largely followed the conventions in its treatment of American and British prisoners, but ignored it when dealing with captured Soviet soldiers.

To extend and clarify the scope of the Geneva Conventions, which seemed particularly important after the horrors of World War II, a fourth conference was held in Stockholm in 1948. This conference agreed on four conventions, all ratified on August 12, 1949, to govern the conduct of war. The first covered the treatment of wounded soldiers; the second covered the treatment of wounded sailors; the third addressed the rights of prisoners; and the fourth called for humane treatment of civilians by an occupying army. The first three conventions were simply expansions on the original conventions of 1864, 1906, and 1929. The fourth made illegal those anti-civilian practices that had been carried out by both the German and Japanese governments during the war, including deportation of civilians, the taking of hostages, torture, and collective punishment and reprisals.

In 1977, two protocols were added to the 1949 Geneva Conventions, extending protection to guerrilla soldiers and fighters in civil wars. These last protocols seemed necessary to many because of the changing nature of warfare in the twentieth century, but have been the least successful of the Geneva agreements. More than 150 countries have signed the 1949 agreement, but not many more than half of those have agreed to the 1977 additions (the United States is one of the countries that signed the 1949 conventions but not the 1977 protocols).

The net result of the Geneva Conventions has not been to limit the conduct of war but rather to limit the targets of war's violence. The conventions removed wounded soldiers and the personnel who cared for them from within the boundaries of violent conflict: A wounded soldier was to be considered a neutral bystander, not an enemy, and all wounded soldiers were to be treated with equal care. Similarly, prisoners of war were to be treated as something less than active enemies. Their freedom could be restricted, but their basic humanity was not to be violated. If the Geneva Conventions were not universally followed, in those places where they were obeyed, they did succeed in reducing some of the brutalities of war.

The Peace Conferences

The Geneva Conventions assumed that war would exist, but tried, with some success, to lessen its ill effects. The late nineteenth and early twentieth centuries also saw a series of conferences with more radical agendas: the reduction of arms stockpiles and the eventual elimination of war entirely.

In 1899 and 1907, two international conferences were held at The Hague in the Netherlands in an attempt to limit both weapons of war and the size of armies. Both conferences had only moderate success. Too many countries were unwilling to limit their military power for the sake of general humanity; the United States, for example, was reluctant to forgo the use of expanding (dumdum) bullets, because they were useful in putting down the Philippine insurrection. The Hague Peace Conferences did create a set of agreements concerning the rights of neutral countries during war and the dropping of explosives from balloons. They also laid the groundwork for creating the Hague Tribunal, an international court of arbitration.

In the years after World War I, disgust at the casualties caused by modern weaponry helped to fuel a strong pacifist movement in Europe and the United States. The result was a series of arms limitations treaties, the most successful of which were the Washington Naval Conference of 1921–1922 and the London Naval Conference of 1930, both of which limited the size of the world's five largest navies. The Kellogg-Briand Pact of 1928 went further and outlawed aggressive war. Created by the American secretary of state, Frank Kellogg, and the French foreign minister, Aristide Briand, the pact's signatories promised to abjure war as a means of settling disputes. Although signed by sixty-two nations, it was not taken seriously by most of the signatories and did nothing to prevent the onset of World War II.

The pacifist idealism that had followed World War I was destroyed by World War II. The idea of complete disarmament was an impossibility. The post–World War II world was divided between two power blocs: that of the Soviet Union and its allies facing the United States and the West. Demobilization immediately followed the war's end, but was reversed in the 1950s as both sides in this "cold war" jockeyed for advantage. Rather than tanks and planes, the most important weapon of the cold war was the atomic bomb, and both the United States and the Soviet Union raced to increase the size of their nuclear stockpiles. The nature of the cold war made arms control a difficult goal

to achieve; with the existence of nuclear weapons, an agreement of some kind began to seem a necessity if the human race was to survive beyond the twentieth century.

Nuclear Weapons

The dropping of atomic bombs on Hiroshima and Nagasaki (August 6 and 9, 1945) unleashed previously unimaginable forces on the earth. The Hiroshima bomb released energy equivalent to 15 kilotons (15,000 tons) of chemical dynamite and killed at least 80,000 civilians and soldiers. By the 1960s, the United States and the Soviet Union had weapons in their arsenals which would release the equivalent of more than 15 megatons (15 *million* tons) of dynamite, and at the height of the cold war both sides had approximately 30,000 nuclear warheads each. This gave them the capacity to kill every human being on the planet many times over. With Armageddon a possibility, leaders in both the United States and the Soviet Union stated their willingness to engage in some form of arms control. Political and military realities, however, interfered in the signing of arms control or disarmament treaties.

First, neither side trusted the other. Cold war propaganda reflected this paranoia: The Soviet Union accused the United States of being an imperialistic power bent on economic domination of the world; the Soviet Union was portrayed by the West as being dedicated to converting the world to totalitarian communism. With this level of suspicion, it was difficult for either side to have confidence in the other's sincerity. An early attempt at nuclear disarmament, the Baruch Plan (1946), collapsed in the face of this mutual suspicion and mutual insincerity.

Second, the difficulties of verification made arms control treaties difficult to agree upon. Both sides kept weapons construction as secret as possible and there seemed to be no guarantee that an agreement once reached would be abided by—neither country was willing to let inspectors wander its territory looking for weapons. (The lack of trust between the two superpowers was proved reasonable by events; the Cuban missile crisis arose because the Soviet Union was able to secretly deploy missile delivery systems to Cuba, in spite of its leaders' assurances to U.S. President John F. Kennedy that it would never do so.) This difficulty was eventually partially overcome by the development of effective observation satellites during the 1960s. With these eyes-in-the-sky, the United States and the Soviet Union had the ability to observe each other's weapons systems and determine whether or not an agreement was being kept. Treaties, therefore, tended to be restricted to those weapons systems that could be easily observed: anti-ballistic missiles (ABMs), submarine-launched ballistic missiles (SLBMs), and intercontinental ballistic missiles (ICBMs) were regulated by these nuclear treaties; tactical nuclear weapons were not.

Third, the lack of nuclear parity made negotiating nuclear arms control treaties difficult. The Soviet Union, which remained "behind" for much of the nuclear arms race, argued that arms control agreements should require the United States to reduce or eliminate its existing stockpiles to reach parity with Soviet levels. The United States preferred nuclear "freezes," in which both sides would stop building weapons—a situation that would clearly favor the United States with its larger stockpile. (The United States was reluctant to lose its nuclear advantage, because it helped to offset the Soviet advantage in conventional forces; the only effective means the Americans had to stop a large-scale Soviet invasion of Western Europe was to strike the advancing Soviet tanks with a nuclear barrage.) It was not until the 1960s, when the two countries' nuclear arsenals approached approximate parity, that nuclear arms limitation treaties began to be negotiated.

Finally, nuclear negotiations became more complicated as other powers joined the nuclear club. The Soviets tested their first nuclear weapon in 1949. The British tested a device in 1952, the French in 1960, and the Chinese in 1964. In 1998, both India and Pakistan tested nuclear devices. (India had detonated a bomb in 1974, but had not created a nuclear stockpile at that time.) Israel was and is strongly suspected of having a nuclear stockpile, while Iraq, Libya, and North Korea have been accused of trying to acquire one. The steady widening circle of nuclear-equipped nations has made regulating nuclear weapons increasingly problematic. (Although the stockpiles of a few dozen warheads possessed by these secondary nuclear powers were dwarfed by the thousands of warheads controlled by the two nuclear superpowers.)

Nuclear Weapons Treaties

A first step toward arms control was taken with the Partial Test-Ban Treaty of 1963. The pressure to create the treaty was motivated in part by widespread fears in the United States and Europe of the threat of nuclear radiation spread by atmospheric tests. Growing scientific evidence demonstrated that above-ground tests spread irradiated dust particles throughout the world. An explosion in Siberia might lead to radiation in Australia. To quiet these fears, both the United States and the Soviet Union discussed limiting above-ground testing. In 1959, both nations voluntarily suspended above-ground nuclear tests, but resumed them as cold war tensions continued to inspire distrust. Negotiations over a test-ban treaty finally reached fruition in 1963. The Partial Test-Ban Treaty was signed by the United States, the Soviet Union, and Great Britain on August 5, 1963, in Moscow. All tests on the surface, under water, or in outer space, were forbidden; only underground nuclear tests were permitted.

Most of the world's governments signed the Partial Test-Ban Treaty. Two exceptions were France and Communist China, which continued to test their nuclear weapons above ground. The Chinese tests at their Lop-Nor facility and the French tests on the Mururoa atoll in the South Pacific continued to arouse worldwide condemnation. (In 1985, the French tests led to a confrontation with the environmentalist group Greenpeace: French secret service agents blew up the Greenpeace protest vessel *Rainbow Warrior*, berthed in Auckland, New Zealand, killing one crewman. The controversy surrounding this violation of the Partial Test-Ban Treaty was one of the factors that led New Zealand to withdraw from the ANZUS alliance.) Anti-nuclear activists had hoped that the Partial Test-Ban Treaty would be a first step toward banning all nuclear tests, but attempts to create a Comprehensive Test Ban Treaty (CTBT) have collapsed, largely because of American doubts regarding the difficulties of detection and verification of compliance. As of June 1998, only thirteen nations have fully ratified the CTBT.

Less controversially, on July 1, 1968, a Nuclear Non-Proliferation Treaty (NPT), negotiated by the United Nations, was signed by almost 100 nations, including the United States, Great Britain, and the Soviet Union. The treaty called for nuclear-equipped states to work to prevent non-nuclear states from obtaining nuclear technology and for non-nuclear states to refrain from attempting to gain nuclear technology for themselves. The treaty provided for a system of inspections to guarantee that a non-nuclear state remained nuclear free. In effect, the treaty divided the world into three groups: a small group of nuclear-equipped powers (the haves), consisting of the United States, the Soviet Union, Britain, France, and China; a much larger group of nations who pledged to never acquire nuclear weapons (the have-nots); and a small group of nations who refused to sign the NPT (the might-wants), consisting of, in 1998, India, Pakistan, Israel, Brazil, and Cuba. The NPT was designed to preserve the status quo.

Coming into effect in 1970, the NPT was eventually ratified by most of the world's nations, including (in 1992) China and France. However, while the treaty may have retarded the spread of nuclear weapons, it did not prevent it. In 1998, both India and Pakistan set off nuclear explosions, signaling their entry into the nuclear club of nations, and other nations, such as Israel, almost certainly have the capacity to create nuclear weapons. Nevertheless, some states that wished to gain a nuclear capability had been unable to do so, perhaps in part because of the NPT (prominent among these nuclear aspirants were Iraq, Iran, and North Korea—all of whom had signed the treaty). The NPT also provided a framework for South Africa to bow out of the nuclear club, dismantling its six nuclear devices and opening its doors to international inspections. (The devices had been built by South Africa's white government, whose policies were repudiated by President Nelson Mandela when he took power in 1994.) Critics of the agreement have pointed out that its emphasis on voluntary compliance allowed Iraq and North Korea to come close to being able to build their own nuclear weapons.

The first successful negotiations to limit nuclear arsenals—rather than their testing or spread—were the Strategic Arms Limitations Talks (SALT), which were begun in 1969 in Helsinki. The first treaty (SALT I) was signed by U.S. President Richard Nixon and Soviet General Secretary Leonid Brezhnev in Moscow on May 26, 1972. SALT I limited the ABM arsenal of both countries to two deployment areas and 100 missiles. The purpose of the ABM limitations was to ensure that each side remained vulnerable to the other's nuclear strike; the hope was that, as long as both sides feared a nuclear strike, neither would began a nuclear war. SALT I also froze the number of ICBMs and SLBMs at their existing levels for five years.

SALT I was a landmark treaty. For the first time American and Soviets were negotiating limits on their nuclear arsenals. Nevertheless, it had many critics. Some politicians did not like that it froze the Soviets' numerical advantage in ICBMs. Disarmament advocates pointed out that the treaty froze only the number of missiles but did nothing to stop the creation of multiple independently targetable re-entry vehicles (MIRVs). By using this technology, both countries could (and did) continue to increase the total number of missile-launched warheads at their disposal. SALT I slowed the arms race; it did not stop it.

SALT II negotiations began in 1972 and continued until 1979. Disagreements over methods of weapons limitation and verification contributed to the long gestation of an agreement. The final treaty, signed in Vienna on June 18, 1979, by Brezhnev and U.S. President Jimmy Carter, put limits on the number of MIRVs, the number of nuclear-equipped bombers, and the number of ICBMs allowed in each superpower's arsenal. Because of fears among some American hawks that the United States had given away too much in the treaty, the Senate hesitated to ratify it. The 1979 Soviet invasion of Afghanistan raised tensions between the Soviet Union and the United States and guaranteed that the Senate would refuse to endorse SALT II. Nevertheless, both sides agreed to voluntarily follow its provisions during the 1980s. Despite their limited achievements—slowing weapons growth rather than reducing weapons stockpiles—the SALT agreements should be viewed as modest successes: They not only put limits on superpower arsenals, but by slowing the arms race, they also helped to reduce tensions and perhaps pave the way for the end of the cold war.

The Strategic Arms Reduction Talks (START) were an attempt to expand on the successes achieved in SALT I and II. The talks were begun in 1982 with U.S. President Ronald Reagan proposing extensive reductions in the arms stockpiles of both superpowers. The talks, which in their various forms discussed both strategic and European-based regional weapons, stalled from 1983 to 1985. One of the stumbling blocks to an agreement was the existence of the nuclear forces of France and Great Britain, which the Soviet Union insisted should be included in any treaty governing weapons systems based in Europe. The United States, however, did not wish these weapons (which it had no control over) to be included in negotiations. In fact, rather than thinking that the British and French missiles gave them an advantage, American planners argued that they were at a missile disadvantage in Europe; for this reason, Reagan ordered the deployment of Pershing II IRBMs (nuclear missiles with a range greater than 500 but less than 5,500 kilometers) and cruise missiles to Western Europe, further angering the Soviets.

The START talks were resumed with the rise to power of Soviet reformer Mikhail Gorbachev, who was eager to cut military spending in order to have sufficient resources for his domestic reforms. The first product of these negotiations was the 1987 Intermediate-Range Nuclear Forces (INF) Treaty, which eliminated all Soviet and American IRBMs—an amazing result when compared to the limited successes of the SALT negotiations. In July 1991, the main START agreement was signed by Gorbachev and U.S. President George Bush. The agreement significantly reduced the number of strategic nuclear warheads in their countries' arsenals. START cut the Soviet arsenal from approximately 11,000 to 6,000 strategic warheads and the Americans stockpile from 12,600 to 8,500. In 1993, with the Soviet Union dissolved, the United States signed a START II agreement with Boris Yeltsin, the new leader of the Russian Federation. START II reduced the Russian strategic arsenal to 3,000 warheads and the American arsenal to 3,500, as well as eliminating MIRVs. START, unlike SALT, actually succeeded in reducing nuclear weapon stockpiles—a result that was made possible by the ending of cold war tensions. A third START agreement was proposed in March 1997, which would reduce Russian and American nuclear stockpiles even further, perhaps to a number just more than 2,000 warheads per nation.

In addition to nuclear treaties between the great powers, regional groups and individual countries have announced the existence of nuclear-free zones. The Treaty of Tlatelolco (1967), for example, bans nuclear weapons from Latin America. These treaties have a largely symbolic value, condemning nuclear weapons while having little practical effect. Their creation also had the potential for causing strains between nuclear and non-nuclear powers, as was the case when New Zealand banned nuclear weapons from its harbors in 1985 and thereby excluded much of the American navy.

Conventional Treaties

The focus of post-war disarmament talks has been on controlling or reducing stockpiles of nuclear weapons, but two other war-making tools, chemical and biological weapons, also have the potential of causing massive numbers of military and civilian casualties, and so have been targeted by their own weapons treaties. Often the three weapons systems are linked together under the rubrics ABC weapons (atomic, biological, and chemical) or WMD (weapons of mass destruction). According to a 1994 Janes Intelligence Review report, more than twenty-five nations "may have, or be in the process of developing, WMD and the means to deliver them."

Biological weapons, which include microbes, viruses, and bacteria, are particularly threatening because of their insidious method of attack (a bomb containing deadly viruses exploded over a city could have the potential of silently killing most of its population) and because they contain the possibility of starting a pandemic. The vision of a genetically engineered anthrax or bubonic plague virus spreading across a city's skies has given many arms control negotiators nightmares. A Prohibition of Biological and Toxin Weapons Convention (BWC), negotiated by the United Nations in 1972, binds all signatories to never produce, acquire, or use biological weapons (although they may continue to research the use of such weapons). The BWC went into effect in 1975, and as of June 1998, it had been approved by more than 130 countries, including the United States. Because of their nature, however, it is difficult to verify the presence of biological agents. Only after the Persian Gulf War, it was discovered that Iraq, a signatory, had produced and accumulated stockpiles of biological agents, including anthrax.

Chemical weapons do not have the same potential for mass slaughter as do biological or nuclear attacks, but their gruesome method of killing has led to a general turning away from their use. The chemical weapons developed during World War I were blistering agents, such as mustard gas, designed to raise blisters on the skin and, if breathed, within the lungs—the latter causing the victim to suffocate to death. Modern chemical agents, such as the organophosphorus nerve gases, are much more deadly and can kill by being inhaled or absorbed through the skin. In 1995, Sarin—one of the organophosphorus agents developed by the United States for its chemical weapons arsenal—was used in a terrorist attack by the Aum Shinrikyo religious cult on the Tokyo subway. The attack, which used a diluted form of Sarin, killed twelve people and injured more than 5,000. Since 1972, the United Nations has attempted to bring about an agreement that would ban chemical weapons, but was prevented by disagreements between the Soviet Union and the United States. In January 1993, with the cold war over, the Chemical Warfare Convention (CWC) was signed, outlawing the production, acquisition, or use of chemical weapons. Existing supplies must be destroyed by the year 2005. The treaty came into effect in 1997. India, South Korea, the United States, and Russia have all agreed to

destroy their chemical stockpiles. As of June 1998, 110 countries had signed the CWC.

The end of the cold war led to discussions of treaties designed to limit more than just the ABC family of weapons. One particular target has been the land mine. Land mines pose a particularly devastating human health hazard because of their indiscriminate destructive potential. They are cheap to deploy—some models only cost a few dollars each—and so have been used extensively in conflicts throughout the world. Once deployed, however, a land mine will kill a civilian as easily as a soldier and its destructive potential will last long beyond the war it was originally deployed to win. Some countries—such as Cambodia with 6 million land mines, Angola with 9 million, and Afghanistan with 10 million—will spend decades deactivating the land mines that remain hidden in their forests and fields; until the mines are removed, peasants will continue to be killed or lose limbs (in Angola, 5,000 artificial limbs are needed each year). The expense of land mine removal is far greater than deployment; the United Nations estimates that land mine clearance costs between $300 and $1,000 per mine.

In 1997, the ugly effects of land mines led many to advocate a complete ban on the production, distribution, and use of anti-personnel land mines (a proposal that achieved popular awareness in part because of the support it received from the late Princess Diana of Britain). In December 1997, more than 100 nations met in Canada to sign the Ottawa Convention, banning all use of anti-personnel land mines. The United States was among the few nations to publicly oppose the proposed land mine ban. American generals, supported by President Bill Clinton, argued that land mines were an important part of America's defensive arsenal, particularly in Korea, where a large North Korean army faces a smaller American–South Korean army. Without land mines, these generals argued, American troops would be vulnerable. (Other generals, however, including Norman Schwartzkopf, the commander of allied forces during the Persian Gulf War, signed an open letter to Clinton in support of a land mine ban.) In 1998, the United States agreed to end all use of mines outside Korea by 2003, but refused to give up the mines in Korea without finding a suitable substitute. It was unclear whether American intransigence would stand in the way of a successful implementation of the Ottawa Convention.

Beyond attempting to eliminate specific weapons systems, post–World War II negotiations were also directed toward limiting the risks and scope of conventionally equipped armies. During the cold war, however, attempts to limit the size or area of deployment of other conventional armies foundered on cold war distrust. The main proponent of such plans, the Soviet Union, advocated creating a demilitarized zone in Central Europe (the Rapacki Plan). This would have meant disarming West Germany, a key member of the NATO military alliance, and so these plans were rejected by the United States and its allies. Attitudes shifted with the end of the cold war. The 1990 Conventional Forces in Europe (CFE) treaty—signed by the member states of the NATO and Warsaw Pact alliances—reduced the numbers of troops deployed by both the Soviet Union and the West. Further reductions became moot as Gorbachev's Soviet Union collapsed and was replaced by Yeltsin's less-threatening Russian Federation. The end result has been a great decrease in the numbers of troops active in Europe.

Conclusion

War and weapons conventions fall into a number of categories: treaties designed to limit future weapon numbers or deployment (arms control treaties), treaties designed to reduce the total numbers of weapons (disarmament treaties), and conventions designed to ameliorate the damages of war (human rights conventions). There is some crossover between the three (the Ottawa Convention on Land Mines is both a disarmament treaty and human rights convention). In all three categories, the post–World War II world has achieved moderate successes.

The Geneva Conventions ratified in 1949, although rooted in the original 1864 convention, broke new ground by providing clear guidelines for how wounded soldiers and prisoners are to be treated during the course of a war. Although they have been ignored more often than obeyed, they provide a standard by which a nation's behavior may be judged. (Violation of the Geneva Conventions provides a justification for outside intervention, as occurred after Iraq's mistreatment of the Kurds and after the Bosnian Serb attacks on the Bosnian Muslims.)

In many ways the disarmament and arms control processes have been more successful than human rights conventions. In a world where strategists on both sides seriously considered the means by which a "limited" nuclear war might be fought, the arms control process helped to slow the speed of the arms race and create an atmosphere of reduced tension. It also created a context from which—with the end of the cold war—it was possible to implement the START reductions. The CWC and BWC agreements have also helped to reduce—but not eliminate—the danger that a nation will use chemical or biological weapons of mass destruction.

The success of the United States and Russia in reducing their nuclear arsenals with the START treaties has helped to reduce world tensions, and the CWC and BWC have limited the spread of non-nuclear threats. Unfortunately, the failure of the Non-Proliferation Treaty has undercut much of the good done by these achievements. With seven official nuclear states—the United States, Russia, China, Britain, France, India, and Pakistan—and one very unofficial state—Israel—the difficulty of negotiating limitations on nuclear weapons increases. The increase in the number of nuclear-equipped nations also increases the possibility that one of them will use a nuclear weapon to defend its perceived interests, and by doing so may set off a chain reaction of nuclear destruction. The spread of chemical and biological weapons is perhaps less threatening, but is also much more difficult to detect and prevent.

Post-war agreements have succeeded in limiting the threat of weapons of mass destruction, but not eliminating them.

Carl Skutsch

See also: Cold War Confrontations; United Nations.

Bibliography

Best, Geoffrey Francis Andrew. *Humanity in Warfare.* New York: Columbia University Press, 1980.

———. *War and Law Since 1945.* New York: Clarendon Press, 1994.

Detter Delupis, Ingrid. *The Law of War.* New York: Cambridge University Press, 1987.

Draper, G.I.A.D. *The Red Cross Conventions.* New York: Praeger, 1958.

Dunbabin, J.P.D. *The Cold War.* New York: Longman, 1994.

Greenspan, Morris. *The Modern Law of Land Warfare.* Berkeley: University of California Press, 1959.

McCoubrey, H. *International Humanitarian Law: Modern Developments in the Limitation of Warfare.* Brookfield, VT: Ashgate, 1998.

CONFLICTS

AFGHANISTAN:
Soviet Invasion, 1979–1989

TYPE OF CONFLICT: Cold war confrontation
PARTICIPANT: Soviet Union

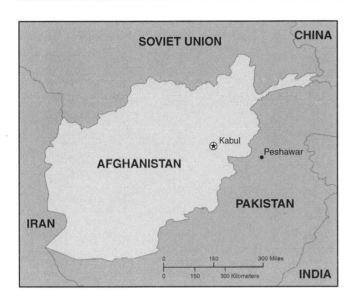

Historical Background

The Soviet invasion of Afghanistan in 1979 had its roots in sixty years of close Afghan-Soviet relations. In early 1919 Afghanistan was the first nation to recognize the new Communist state in Russia, and this recognition helped to create a "special relationship" between the two countries which was to last until it was destroyed by the Soviet invasion. Afghanistan's initial reason for allying itself to the Union of Soviet Socialist Republics (the name the Russian communists adopted for their nation in 1922) was to counterbalance the power of the British to the south. Rulers of the entire Indian subcon-

tinent, the British had often threatened Afghanistan's autonomy, invading twice in the nineteenth century. Playing the Soviet Union to the north against the British Empire in the south allowed Afghanistan to remain independent of them both. After World War II, however, the withdrawal of the British from India left the Afghans facing the Soviets alone.

In the 1950s, Afghanistan—still a monarchy—established limited economic and military ties with the Soviet Union. This policy was partly motivated by the United States' refusal to offer military assistance to the Afghans. The United States saw Afghanistan as irrelevant to its cold war calculations, and was worried that any aid to Afghanistan might alienate neighboring Pakistan, a country with which the Americans were more eager to maintain good relations. In spite of their Soviet ties, and American neglect, Afghanistan tried to remain neutral in the cold war, attempting to maintain good relations with both East and West.

A 1973 coup (carried out while the king of Afghanistan was vacationing in Italy) brought the country still closer to the Soviet Union. Led by a former prime minister, Mohammed Daoud, the coup was supported by leftist military officers and members of the Peoples' Democratic Party of Afghanistan (PDPA), a Marxist party founded in 1965.

Daoud himself was not a communist, but he did initiate some social reforms and accept Soviet military aid. He was not, however, a Soviet puppet. On the contrary, he attempted, with moderate success, to improve relations with Pakistan and other Western-aligned nations, gradually replacing communist sympathizers in his government with more traditional, conservative politicians. Daoud, while still maintaining good relations with the Soviet Union, was clearly bent on creating a nationalist dictatorship that would both keep Afghanistan neutral and Daoud in power. These actions pleased neither the communists who had supported his coup nor the Soviets who had thought that he would be a more cooperative leader. During Daoud's five years in power, he faced increasing opposition. His drift to the right angered those elements of the PDPA which had initially supported his coup, his strong-arm methods disturbed those who wished to see a more democratic Afghanistan, and the immoderate nepotism of his administration alienated those Afghans who were not in his circle of family and friends.

Pro-Soviet Coup

Discontent with Daoud's rule flared into open revolt following the April 1978 murder of Mir Akbar Khyber, a prominent member of the Parcham (Banner) wing of the PDPA. Although some Afghans later suggested that the murder had been carried out by rivals from the competing Khalq (People's) wing, most blamed Daoud and his increasingly repressive secret police. Mobs of anti-Daoud demonstrators thronged the streets of Kabul, Afghanistan's capital. By the time Daoud realized his danger, it was too late: the orders to arrest the PDPA leadership did not come in time to stop Hafizullah Amin, a Khalq

leader, from organizing an attack on the Presidential Palace with the aid of sympathetic military units (including bombing attacks by Soviet-built MiG fighters). Daoud was killed early on April 28, 1978, and the PDPA, led by its founder Nur Mohammed Taraki, took control of the new government.

It is unclear whether the Soviets knew about the PDPA coup in advance, but they certainly helped it to prevail—Soviet advisors helped orchestrate the rebel air attacks and accompanied some of the tank columns that rode through Kabul—and they benefited from its success. Even though Taraki denied that his was a Communist government—communism was viewed with hostility by most religious Muslims in Afghanistan—it was clear that he and his associates saw themselves as socialists in the Marxist tradition. Afghanistan's neighbors also had few doubts about the nature of the new regime: both the Shah of Iran and General Mohammed Zia of Pakistan claimed that Afghanistan had become a client of the Soviets. Overall, therefore, the coup seemed a propaganda victory for the Soviet Union.

The Soviet victory soon began to turn sour. After a brief honeymoon of popularity, the harsh measures of the new government soon made it even more disliked than that of Daoud had been. Despite Taraki's denials, his government was viewed both as communist and as a tool of the Soviet Union. This damaged its credibility in the eyes of the Afghan people. The PDPA also suffered a split within its own ranks. The hard-line Khalq faction, to which Taraki belonged, became increasingly dominant, while members of Parcham were forced to go into exile as ambassadors. Opposition to the regime increased.

In an attempt to crush the opposition, thousands of Afghans were arrested. Hundreds, perhaps thousands, were killed. The educated elites of Kabul were decimated. These attacks on the educated classes of Kabul made it difficult to find enough qualified people to work for the government; the PDPA leaders, therefore, became even more dependent on Soviet advisors, whose numbers had risen to over a thousand within three months of the coup. This influx of outsiders helped to alienate even further the more traditional groups of Afghan society.

Afghanistan is primarily a nation of small villages, traditionally led by mullahs—religious teachers. The mullahs looked with suspicion on a government that seemed to be advocating godless communism. That the new rulers were primarily members of an urban minority who looked down upon the rural masses did nothing to aid relations between Kabul and the countryside. Encouraged by their mullahs, Afghan men began to take up arms against the PDPA government. By March 1979 these rebels were strong enough to briefly seize control of Herat, the administrative center of western Afghanistan, before being forced out by government reinforcements.

The PDPA responded to the unrest by making Hafizullah Amin the new prime minister of Afghanistan. Amin, who had received a master's degree from Columbia University, was a Khalq hard-liner who was determined to crush the rebels. He asked for and received increased amounts of Soviet military aid, including advanced helicopter gunships and jet fighters. The new weapons were accompanied by substantial numbers of Soviet troops; many of these troops went beyond advising Afghan troops and began to fly combat missions on their own.

As the Soviets became more involved in the day-to-day direction of anti-guerrilla operations, they became increasingly dissatis-fied with Amin's leadership. Amin's troops behaved with excessive violence, destroying villages and murdering opponents, both among their fellow leftists and among the mullahs of the countryside. Their actions had the paradoxical effect of increasing the resistance they were trying to suppress. The situation was exacerbated by a high rate of desertion from the Afghan army, whose peasant draftees were reluctant to fire on the rebels.

The situation in Afghanistan reached a climax in September 1979, when Amin had former president Taraki arrested and shot. Amin claimed that Taraki had been planning to assassinate him and take power with Soviet help, and that he only acted out of self-defense. Over the next few months, as part of this program of self-defense, Amin ordered the arrest and execution of at least hundreds, perhaps thousands, of Afghans whom he suspected of plotting against him. Whether or not the Soviets had actually planned to replace Amin with Taraki, Amin's actions subsequent to Taraki's murder convinced them that Amin had to be replaced if they did not wish to see their client state overwhelmed by the growing opposition.

The Invasion

On December 24, 1979, Christmas Eve, the Soviets began flying elements of the 105th Airborne Division into Kabul International Airport; other airborne units landed at Bagram, Shindand, and Herat. Although the buildup was portrayed as a military exercise, it soon became clear that Soviets intended to remove Amin by force. Fighting broke out on December 27; by the following day Amin was dead and the Russians were in control of Kabul. That same day, four motorized rifle

Defectors from the Afghan army firing a captured Soviet cannon at government positions near Kabul, the Afghan capital, in September 1979. *(Associated Press/Wide World)*

divisions began crossing the Soviet border into Afghanistan.

Officially the fighting in Kabul and the Soviet cross-border troop movements were not part of an invasion, but rather were a response to an Afghan request for support. On the day the fighting began, the Soviets had broadcast via radio a recording from exiled PDPA leader Babrak Karmal, one of the leaders of the more moderate Parcham wing of the party. In the recording, Karmal announced the defeat of Amin and asked Afghans to rally to his cause. The following day, Kabul radio, now under Soviet control, issued a demand that "the USSR render military aid to Afghanistan." The Soviets happily obeyed this orchestrated "demand."

Within one month the Soviets had 40,000 troops in Afghanistan and had occupied all its major cities.

If the Soviets had expected Afghanistan to calmly accept Karmal as its new ruler, they were to be disappointed. In January, in his first public appearance after gaining power, Karmal called on the people of Afghanistan to "come together and support our glorious revolution." Instead, they came together in an attempt to kick Karmal and the Soviets out of the country. Resistance to the central government became even more widespread than it had been under Amin. The Afghan army, already badly damaged by desertions, almost completely disappeared as an effective fighting force: some troops simply refused to fight for what they perceived as Soviet conquerors; others deserted directly to the rebels, bringing with them valuable weapons and supplies. By the end of 1980, the government could count on only some 30,000 troops, and no more than half of these were considered reliable.

The rebels, on other hand, saw an explosion in strength and support. Simmering unrest was transformed into nationwide guerrilla war. Every province of Afghanistan contributed soldiers to this war, with the result that Soviet and Afghan government control did not reliably extend outside the major urban areas. The Afghan freedom fighters took upon themselves the name *mujahideen*, or holy warriors. Despite being divided among four major ethnic groups and two different brands of Islam, the *mujahideen* were united in wanting the Soviets to leave. Given the informal nature of their recruitment, the *mujahideen* were difficult to count, but it seems certain that there were at lest 100,000 involved in the war against the Soviets, and at times—during the summer campaigning season—their numbers might have risen to at least twice that figure.

The Struggle

Unwilling to abandon Karmal, the Soviets responded to Afghan resistance by steadily increasing the number of Soviet soldiers in the country. By the end of 1980 they had 80,000 troops in Afghanistan, and that number would rise to over 100,000 by the end of 1981. At its height, the Soviet occupation force probably included 120,000 soldiers.

At first this increased Soviet presence had only a marginal effect on the resistance. The rough mountainous Afghan countryside made conventional Soviet tactics ineffective. Soviet armored columns could sweep through Afghan valleys with ease, but the

mujahideen would simply retreat up into their mountain strongholds; as soon as the Soviets had departed, the *mujahideen* would return and retake control. Afghanistan's 15,000 villages, therefore, remained dominated by the rebels. Even the major cities were not completely under Soviet control; the *mujahideen* were able to infiltrate units into Kabul and other major cities to carry out assassinations of Afghan and Soviet officials. The rebels also used Pakistan as a base of operations, crossing the border to raid Soviet outposts, and then retreating back to Pakistan—with the permission of the Pakistani government— for supplies and reunions with their families, who had resettled in refugee camps on the Pakistani side of the border.

In 1981, accepting the impossibility of controlling rural Afghanistan, the Soviets changed their strategy. Concentrating most of the troops in the cities, they used special mechanized and airborne units to carry out hit-and-run raids on rebel supply lines leading from Pakistan and to attack those villages that continued to support the *mujahideen*. Since most villages at least tacitly supported the *mujahideen*, this meant that almost all of rural Afghanistan became a free-fire zone. Because they could not control the villages, the Soviets seemed intent on destroying them. The result of this new strategy was to force millions of Afghan farmers to flee, either to the cities where the Soviets could more easily control them, or outside the country, to Iran or Pakistan. By 1985 one-third of Afghanistan's 15 million people were refugees or internally displaced: 3 million in Pakistan, 1 million in Iran, and 1 million in the major cities of Afghanistan itself. In the face of these tactics, with no safe areas in the countryside, the *mujahideen* found it extremely difficult to operate.

The *mujahideen* also found it difficult to counter superior Soviet weaponry. Soviet air strikes could hit *mujahideen*-controlled villages with little risk of counterattack. Particularly deadly was the Soviet Mi-24 Hind helicopter gunship; equipped with machine guns, rockets, and anti-tank missiles, the armored Hind could hover above a rebel force and destroy it while being in very little danger from Afghan small-arms fire. A 1982 *New York Times* reporter quoted a *mujahideen* leader as saying, "We are not afraid of the Russians, but we are afraid of their helicopters."

Afghan difficulties were exacerbated by the lack of coordination between the various *mujahideen* groups. At least six major and numerous minor groups were fighting against the Soviet presence. Shi'a Muslims and Sunni Muslims fought under separate banners. Traditionalists did not wish to fight alongside Western-oriented leftists. Units led by a Pashtun leader might not include Tajik, Uzbek, or Hazara soldiers (the Pashtun were the largest ethnic group in Afghanistan; most *mujahideen* groups were dominated by the Pashtun). This disunity made cooperation against the Soviets difficult. Occasionally rebel groups would even fight each other.

By 1985 Soviet scorched-earth tactics and sophisticated technology, aided by Afghan disunity, had badly crippled the *mujahideen* resistance.

Foreign Reaction

As a counterbalance to Afghan disunity, there was the nearly universal condemnation with which the international community received the Soviet invasion.

American President Jimmy Carter, even though distracted by the Iran hostage crisis, vigorously denounced the invasion, calling it "the greatest threat to peace since the Second World War." Carter imposed a grain embargo and ordered U.S. athletes to boycott the Olympics games, which were to be held in Moscow in 1980. The U.N. General Assembly followed Carter's lead and voted for a resolution demanding that all foreign troops withdraw from Afghanistan. Afghanistan's regional neighbors were equally hostile, with General Mohammed Zia al-Huq of Pakistan immediately condemning the invasion. Iran, distracted by its hostility to America, at first seemed willing to turn a blind eye to the invasion, but by March 1980 the Ayatollah Khomeini was condemning "the brutal intervention in Afghanistan by looters and occupiers," saying that the Soviet Union was as bad as the United States.

Verbal condemnation was followed by military support. The United States, Iran, China, and many Middle Eastern Arab states, particularly Saudi Arabia, attempted to funnel supplies and weapons into Afghanistan. At first these supplies were limited to small arms, but, as the war went on, the types of weapons being supplied expanded to include anti-aircraft guns and Soviet-designed surface-to-air missiles (donated by the Egyptians from their stockpile of Soviet-supplied weaponry). The Arab states also sent 6,000 volunteers to join the jihad against the Soviet invader.

Finally, in 1986, the United States began supplying the *mujahideen* with one of the best weapons in its arsenal: Stinger surface-to-air missiles. The Stinger was a shoulder-launched missile that weighed only 34 pounds but could reach speeds of more than a thousand miles an hour. With the Stinger in their hands, the *mujahideen* began to shoot down Soviet planes and helicopters at the rate of more than one a day. This made the battlefield much more dangerous for Soviet aircraft and therefore forced the Soviets to cease their indiscriminate attacks upon *mujahideen* strongholds. Under the umbrella of the Stinger, rebels began to operate much more freely.

The *mujahideen* also made innovative use of non-military equipment. Piling their weapons on top of four-wheel-drive Toyota pickup trucks, they were able to travel roads that were too difficult for the slower and more cumbersome Soviet tanks and armored personal carriers. Looking back from 1992, one *mujahideen* leader said, "Stingers and Toyotas helped us win the war."

Soviet Withdrawal

Along with better weapons came more cooperation. In May 1985 the major rebel groups based in Pakistan agreed to work as a united front. While this only had a theoretical effect on the behavior of fighters in Afghanistan— the political groups in Pakistan had little control over the military leaders in Afghanistan— it did help to streamline the weapons supply process, and it was matched by increased cooperation in the field.

The year 1985 also saw changes in the Soviet Union. With the coming to power of Mikhail Gorbachev, Soviet policies began to alter. Gorbachev's introduction of *Glasnost* (openness) to Soviet public life was designed to shake up the overly rigid Soviet society, but it also had the effect of opening up the regime to public criticism, and one of the things most criticized was the war in Afghanistan. Mothers complained about sons coming home in body bags, or coming home alive but burdened with drug or psychological problems. Public opinion was becoming

important in the Soviet Union, and it was increasingly opposed to keeping Soviet troops involved in the Afghan war.

In 1986 the Soviet war effort was somewhat reinvigorated when Karmal, who had become an alcoholic embarrassment, was replaced by the much more competent Mohammed Najibullah, the former chief of political police, and, like Karmal, a member of the moderate Parcham wing of the PDPA. Najibullah attempted to revitalize the government by inviting in ministers from other political parties and attempting to distance himself as much as possible from his Soviet backers. His attempts to portray himself as an Afghan nationalist first, and a communist second, were somewhat successful. Under Najibullah's command the Afghan army was rejuvenated and was able to win some battles in late 1987 and early 1988.

This success, however, came too late for the Soviets. In February 1988 Gorbachev announced on Soviet television that he was willing to withdraw all Soviet troops from Afghanistan. Negotiations between the Soviet Union, the United States, Afghanistan, and Pakistan—which had been dragging on slowly for the previous few years—suddenly took on a new urgency. An international agreement was signed in April and the troops began leaving in May. The last Soviet soldier left Afghanistan on February 15, 1989.

In spite of the Soviet troop withdrawal, Najibullah, still receiving Soviet economic and military aid, was able to hold on for three more years. He was helped by the rebels' inability to agree on a consistent or coordinated strategy. However, with the collapse of the Soviet Union in 1991, his regime was doomed. In April 1992 a combined *mujahideen* army marched into Kabul and

Najibullah sought sanctuary in a U.N.-controlled compound. Four years later he would be dragged out and executed. The government which the Soviets had created was gone and the war they had begun was over—even as a new war, this one between the various *mujahideen* factions, was just starting.

Approximately 1 million Afghans had died during the war, along with 15,000 Soviet soldiers.

Aftermath

Although the Soviets left Afghanistan in 1989, the effects of their invasion continued to be felt long after.

The Soviet Union itself was the one of the worst hurt by its own invasion. The war cost it dearly in economic terms and in prestige. The inability of the huge Soviet empire, containing 265 million citizens, to defeat 15 million Afghans was damaging to opinion at home and abroad. The defeat in Afghanistan probably accelerated the fall of Gorbachev's regime and helped to bring an end to seventy years of communist rule in Russia.

In Afghanistan itself, the fighting continued even after Najibullah's defeat. The *mujahideen* coalition split along ethnic and religious lines and immediately began to struggle for control of the capital Kabul and the country. That fighting has continued to the present day.

Islamic fundamentalism also received a boost from its success in Afghanistan. Many young men from the Islamic world who went to Afghanistan to fight as *mujahideen* returned to their home countries eager to continue the fight—this time, however, in opposition to their own governments. Egypt, Algeria, and Saudi Arabia have all had difficulties with these "Afghanis." Other Afghanis went on to Bosnia and contributed to the violence there. The bombers of the World Trade Center in New York City and the U.S. embassies in Kenya and Tanzania were also alleged to have had Afghani connections.

Finally, many of the weapons that were supplied to the *mujahideen* have since found their way into other hands, becoming part of the worldwide trade in black market arms. This is particularly disturbing in the case of the Stinger missile, whose 5-mile range would make it ideal for any terrorist group wanting to shoot down a passenger airliner. It is estimated that at least 200 Stingers exist in secret arms caches. Among those rumored to have Stingers in their possession are the Iranian Revolutionary Guards, as well as rebels in Algeria, Angola, Lebanon, and Turkey.

Carl Skutsch

See also: Afghanistan: Civil War, 1989.

Bibliography

Bradsher, Henry. *Afghanistan and the Soviet Union.* Durham, NC: Duke University Press, 1985.

Galeotti, Mark. *Afghanistan, the Soviet Union's Last War.* Portland, OR: Frank Cass, 1995.

Hyman, Anthony. *Afghanistan under Soviet Domination.* New York: St. Martin's Press, 1992.

Kakar, M. Hassan. *Afghanistan: The Soviet Invasion and the Afghan Response, 1979–1982.* Berkeley: University of California Press, 1997.

Roy, Olivier. *Afghanistan: From Holy War to Civil War.* Pennington, NJ: Darwin Press, 1995.

Rubin, Barnett R. *The Search for Peace in Afghanistan: From Buffer State to Failed State.* New Haven, CT: Yale University Press, 1995.

AFGHANISTAN: Civil War, 1989

TYPE OF CONFLICT: Ethnic and religious

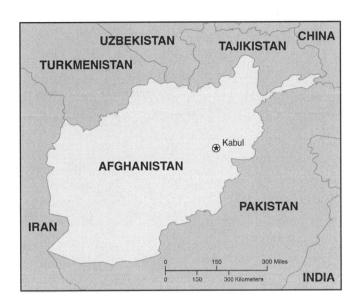

Historical Background

Afghanistan's current troubles began with the 1979 invasion by the Soviet Union. The Soviets had sent their troops into Afghanistan in an attempt to maintain the puppet Communist government, which had been in danger of being overthrown by Muslim rebels. Angered by the presence of foreign troops on their soil, the Afghan people rose up in a ten-year-long war dedicated to expelling the Soviets. In February 1989, the Soviet Union decided that it could not win the war and withdrew all its soldiers from Afghanistan.

The Soviet withdrawal, however, did not end the fighting. Although the rebels dominated the rural areas, the major cities were still controlled by the Communist government of Mohammed Najibullah, which continued to receive economic and military aid from the Soviets. It would take the Afghan rebels, known as *mujahideen* (holy warriors), three more years to defeat Najibullah.

Najibullah was able to hold on to power partly because of his own talents, but mostly because of the division of his opponents. In the war against the Soviets, the *mujahideen* had been divided into a half-dozen major groups and numerous minor ones. These rebel groups were often separated by ethnicity, religious affiliation, or simply the animosity of individual leaders toward each other. During the war against Najibullah, these divisions made cooperation difficult (as they had during the war against the Soviet occupiers), and opposing *mujahideen* would occasionally fight one another. After Najibullah's defeat, these occasional skirmishes were transformed into full-scale war, as the *mujahideen* fought to determine who would rule over post-war Afghanistan.

Hence, the civil wars in Afghanistan break into at least two distinct phases. The first is the war against Najibullah, who was attempting to legitimize his regime in the eyes of the Afghan people, while the *mujahideen* spent most, but not all, of their energies attempting to defeat him. The second phase began with the fall of Kabul, Afghanistan's capital, and the defeat of Najibullah, whereupon the various *mujahideen* groups turned on each other and began the fight for Afghanistan which continues to the present day.

Mohammed Najibullah

In 1986, after he replaced Babrak Karmal as the leader of Afghanistan's Communist government, Najibullah began a radical series of policy shifts designed to strengthen his position in the country. These new policies centered on Najibullah's attempts to distance himself from his Soviet patrons by demonstrating that he was more of an Afghanistan nationalist than he was a communist. He brought non-communists into his government and, unlike his predecessors, showed himself willing to accept a limited amount of criticism from the press. These policy changes were accelerated after the Soviets withdrew in 1989. By 1991, a majority of Najibullah's cabinet were non-communists.

Najibullah also worked to gain support among progressives in Afghanistan. Women, for example, were treated as equals—a radical departure from traditional practice in Islamic Afghanistan—and even served in Najibullah's cabinet. While this appealed to those who admired the West, it also further alienated traditional Muslims, who did not believe women had a place in political life.

Finally, Najibullah also improved the pay and training of his army, turning it into a relatively efficient fighting force.

The success of Najibullah's policies led some of the mujahideen to question whether or not they could actually succeed in overthrowing him, particularly as long as he continued to receive aid from the Soviet Union. By the end of 1991, Iran and Pakistan, which had supported the war since the 1979 invasion, were urging the *mujahideen* to make peace with Najibullah. In return for small subsidies and local autonomy, some *mujahideen* groups began to sign ceasefire agreements with the Afghan government.

In 1992, however, the possibility of a Najibullah victory was ended by the collapse of the Soviet Union and the consequent cessation of Soviet aid for Najibullah's regime. Despite his success at forging home-grown support, he could not survive this drying up of equipment and supplies. The rebels began their final advance on Kabul.

The *Mujahideen*

The war against Najibullah, like that against the Soviets before him, was complicated by the divided nature of the *mujahideen* movement. The rebel *mujahideen* were divided into a half-dozen different major factions, each with dozens of independent minded local leaders.

The divisions within the *mujahideen* arose from Afghanistan's extremely complex ethnic and religious makeup. Afghanistan has four major ethnic groups, Pashtuns, Tajiks, Uzbeks, and Hazaras. Pashtuns make up slightly less than half the population, followed in numbers by Tajiks. The country is also split religiously: about 15 percent of the population follows the Shi'a branch of Islam, while the remainder are Sunni Muslims. Finally, Afghans are divided between those who favor the creation of an Islamic state, those who are ethnic nationalists, and those who believe in a pan-Afghan nationalism. The hostilities that resulted from this patchwork mix of identities made cooperation difficult and contributed to Najibullah's surprisingly long stay in power.

Still, by 1992 two major Afghan leaders

Radical fundamentalist fighters guard a checkpoint in Kabul, the Afghan capital, in April 1992. Behind them is a picture of the Iranian leader Ayatollah Ruholla Khomeini. (*Associated Press/Wide World*)

had managed to create coalitions of *mujahideen* that were able to face Najibullah's weakening army on better than equal terms.

The first was Ahmad Shah Massoud, known as the Lion of Panjshir because of his longtime dominance of the Panjshir valley area (located northeast of Kabul). Massoud was the military leader of the Jamiat-i-Islam faction, whose political leader was Burhanuddin Rabbani—an Islamic scholar who left the business of leading Jamiat-i-Islam to Massoud. Jamiat-i-Islam drew its support primarily from the Tajiks of the north (both Massoud and Rabbani were Tajiks) as well as from some Hazaras, Uzbeks, and Persian-speaking Pashtuns. (Dari Persian is the dialect of Tajiks, Hazaras, and many urbanized Pashtuns; Pashtu is the language of most Pashtuns.) While Massoud and Rabbani were believers in an Islamic state, they were considered more moderate than their rivals, and were therefore regarded with greater favor by the Western countries that had helped supply the *mujahideen* during the war against the Soviets.

The second *mujahideen* leader was Gulbuddin Hekmatyar, head of the Hizb-i-Islam faction. Hekmatyar is an ethnic Pashtun who follows an extremely fundamentalist brand of Islam and advocates the creation of an Islamic state. (As part of his defense of Islamic values, it is said, Hekmatyar threw acid on unveiled Afghan women in the 1970s.) During the war against the Soviets he received aid from Pakistan and Iran and had ties with the extremist Muslim Brotherhood. His support came primarily from the Pashtuns of the south and west.

A third successful, although smaller, group was the Hizb-i-Wahdat-i-Islam. Made up of Shi'a Muslims, the faction drew its strength mainly from the Hazara ethnic minority. (Most Shi'a Muslims in Afghanistan are Hazara.)

Najibullah Overthrown

In early 1992, with Soviet aid cut off, the Najibullah regime began to fall apart under *mujahideen* pressure.

The collapse was accelerated in March 1992 when General Abdul Rashid Dostam, one of Najibullah's most important supporters, decided that the regime was doomed and switched to the side of the *mujahideen.* Dostam was an Uzbek with strong support within that ethnic group. Between them, the three main opponents of Najibullah—Massoud, Hekmatyar, and Dostam—had enough strength to force their way into Kabul. In April 1992 Massoud and Dostam did exactly that. As the *mujahideen* entered the city, Najibullah went into hiding, eventually finding refuge in a U.N. compound (where he would spend the next four years, unable to leave the country).

However, even though Najibullah had been defeated, the civil war did not end. The rivalries that had simmered during the war against Najibullah boiled over into open conflict. The personal hostility between Hekmatyar and Massoud was particularly strong (in 1976 followers of Hekmatyar had tortured and killed a friend of Massoud's during a political struggle between the two men's factions). When the forces of Hekmatyar were prevented from entering the city, they began to drop artillery shells on Kabul.

War Between the *Mujahideen*

Broken up by intermittent peace talks, the shelling went on into 1993. In an attempt to create a stable Afghan government, Massoud and Dostam managed to get a number of *mujahideen* commanders to support a new government in which Rabbani would be president, with Massoud as his minister of defense. This government took office in December 1993, but Hekmatyar refused to accept the agreement. Arguing that he could not work with a government that included General Dostam among its supporters, he continued to shell Kabul from his mountain strongholds, while attempting to cut the city off from outside supplies.

Many Pashtun leaders supported Hekmatyar on ethnic grounds. Even though Rabbani and Massoud claimed to be Islamicists first and Tajiks second, they were accused by their opponents of trying to set up a Tajik-dominated Afghanistan. This was particularly galling to Pashtuns, who had traditionally been, until the invasion of the Soviet army, the dominant ethnic group in the country. Some Pashtuns went so far as to say they would refuse to support a government that was led by a non-Pashtun. These attitudes increasingly helped to make the conflict one of ethnic rivalry, with Pashtuns of the south supporting Hekmatyar, while Tajiks, Hazaras, and Uzbeks supported Tajik, Massoud, and his Uzbek ally, Dostam.

In some ways, the fall of Najibullah marked the end of a Pashtun-dominated Afghanistan, and introduced a new era in which the minorities of the north would have an equal, or perhaps even a greater, say in how the country was to be governed.

The patchwork nature of Afghan loyalties, however, made it impossible to characterize the fighting as merely ethnic based. Many Pashtun, particularly Persian speakers, supported Massoud, or simply refused to help Hekmatyar, while not all Tajiks were loyal to Massoud. In addition, Hekmatyar also received help from the Shi'a Wahdat faction, a Hazara group. So, while the fighting did take on a more ethnic character after 1992, ethnicity was never the sole factor in determining factional loyalty.

In 1993, further attempts at forging an agreement between the three strongmen continued to fail, and the fighting staggered on, with intermittent ceasefires. A March agreement among the three leaders led to the appointment of Hekmatyar as prime minister, but fell apart a few weeks later when Massoud, still minister of defense, again refused to allow Hekmatyar's troops into Kabul. Although Massoud seemed to be the strongest of the three, the balance of power was maintained by General Dostam's repeated switches of loyalty. If Massoud was winning the battle for Kabul, Dostam would join Hekmatyar; and then, when the fighting went in Hekmatyar's favor, Dostam would return to his alliance with Massoud.

Foreign Support

The civil war in Afghanistan was also complicated by the interest of the nations surrounding it. During Soviet occupation (1979–1989), Afghanistan's neighbors consistently supported any *mujahideen* group that was willing to fight the Soviets, but with the collapse of the Soviet Union, loyalties shifted. By 1994, each of the three main Afghan leaders had his own patrons.

Hekmatyar received aid from Pakistan, specifically, from the Pakistani Inter-Services Intelligence Directorate (ISI), which had

backed him since the days of the Soviet war and viewed him as a kind of protégé. The ISI considered Hekmatyar to be the most likely Afghan leader to cooperate with their goal of keeping the Afghan conflict from spilling over into Pakistan itself. (A large Pashtun minority lives in the border regions of Pakistan.)

Massoud drew some support from Russia, which considered him a bulwark against the spread of a more radical Islamic movement. The continued fighting in Afghanistan was bleeding into and helping to destabilize neighboring Tajikistan was a price that the Russians were willing to pay. Massoud also received aid from India, which was probably a reaction to Pakistani aid for Hekmatyar. (Indian and Pakistani rivalry dates back to the birth of both countries.)

Dostam, an Uzbek, received his outside supplies from Uzbekistan, while the Shi'a Wahdat faction received their backing from Shi'a Iran.

The Taliban

In January 1994 the fighting for Kabul continued. On New Years Day, Dostam, again switching sides, attempted a coup d'état against Massoud. (Dostam was supported by both Hekmatyar and the Pakistani ISI.) The coup failed to take Kabul but reignited the war in Afghanistan. More fighting in Kabul led to thousands of civilian deaths and many more injuries. The fighting spread throughout Afghanistan (most of the battles in 1993 had centered on Kabul) but without substantially changing the battle lines. At the end of 1994, Dostam continued to dominate the northwest, Massoud the northeast, Hekmatyar the south, and the Hizb-i-Wahdat central Afghanistan.

This stalemate began to be overturned in the fall of 1994 with the rise of a new force in the Afghanistan civil war, the Taliban. The Taliban was a movement led by Islamic seminary students and teachers from the schools that dot the Afghan landscape. These religious leaders and their followers were disgusted with the ongoing conflict in Afghanistan and proposed to sweep away the warring factions and create a new, pure Islamic state. Within a few months, starting from a small group of men in the southern province of Kandahar, they had achieved incredible results, conquering most of the southern provinces by January 1995.

The intellectual origins of the Taliban lay in the Deoband Islamic seminary of northern India. The Deoband had been a center of fundamentalist Islamic thought since its establishment in the nineteenth century, and was dedicated to purging Islam of impurities. Its students, taught to hew to the strict letter of Koranic law, had spread throughout the Middle East, including Afghanistan. It was the Deobandis of Afghanistan who came together to form the Taliban in late 1994. And it was the Deoband advocacy of Islamic traditionalism which inspired the new Afghan movement.

The support for the Taliban, however, was not merely religious. While many Afghan *mujahideen* bands surrendered to the Taliban without a fight because of their respect for the Taliban's holy mission, others joined because they saw the Taliban as the one hope for ending Afghanistan's unending wars. And although the Taliban denied being a force for any one ethnic group, they attracted the support of many Pashtun, who were willing to back a movement that looked as if it could counter the strength of the northern Tajiks, Uzbeks, and Hazaras.

Taliban Victorious?

In February 1995, Hizb-i-Islam leader Hekmatyar responded to the growing strength of the Taliban by saying, "In the past twenty-seven years I have been engaged in the struggle to form a true Islamic government for Afghanistan and faced battles people said I would never survive. I am not worried about the Taliban now." The following day the Taliban army overran Hekmatyar's headquarters and the former warlord fled into the countryside, eventually ending up in Iran.

Although the Kabul government of Rabbani and Massoud had at first welcomed this new force, they soon also found themselves under attack. Unlike Hekmatyar's army, Massoud's troops did not simply desert to the Taliban, but they were hard pressed to hold their ground. Massoud and his allies defeated a March 1995 assault on Kabul but lost the western city of Herat in September of the same year. The Taliban's drive was then somewhat slowed, but by September of 1996 they had taken the eastern city of Jalalabad. Later that month, Massoud, his army almost surrounded, pulled out of Kabul and retreated to his northern strongholds. The Taliban followed the withdrawal and seized the city; in two years of fighting they had succeeded in conquering more than two-thirds of the country. (They had also ended the life of former communist leader Mohammed Najibullah: when the Taliban entered the city, they dragged Najibullah out from his hiding place in a U.N. compound and had him executed.)

After the fall of Kabul the Taliban drive slowed to a near halt. Although by March 1998 they controlled 80 percent of the country, a loose-knit Northern Alliance had managed to hold on to the remainder of

Afghanistan. At the center of the alliance was still Massoud's Tajik army. He was joined by Dostam's Uzbeks, the Hazaran Hizb-i-Wahdat faction, and Hekmatyar's Hizb-i-Islam faction. (Hekmatyar, his supporters greatly reduced in numbers, had returned to Afghanistan by early 1998.) Although the Taliban continued its attempts to reunite the country, Kabul was the last important stronghold to be successfully taken by their armies. (Mazar-i-Sharif, the northern stronghold of General Dostam, fell briefly in May 1997, but was immediately retaken.)

Part of the Taliban's later failures are probably attributable to its traditional Islamic approach to governance. Many Afghans were disturbed by the degree of extremism which they saw in the fanatical Taliban forces. Upon taking control of Kabul, the Taliban demanded that women quit their jobs, closed schools for girls, and required women to wear the chador (a traditional black robe that covers the body from head to toe). They also established the Department to Prevent Vice, whose members searched city streets looking for those who were disobeying Islamic law. Men were beaten for flying kites and women for wearing high heels under their traditional robes. This extremism did not fit in with northern Afghanistan's more relaxed approach to Islam, particularly in more cosmopolitan cities such as Kabul or Herat. (When Massoud's troops took Kabul, they forced women to wear less revealing clothing, but did not object if their faces showed or if they continued to work.)

The Taliban's actions also alienated Westerners, particularly the aid workers who were sent to try and put back together the country's shattered infrastructure. Women from international organizations were often attacked by Taliban extremists for violating Islamic morality, and some aid agencies responded by withdrawing their workers from Taliban controlled areas. On the other hand, the Taliban has received substantial support from Pakistan, whose leaders are sympathetic to a Pashtun-dominated regime. (Some senior Pakistanis are also Pashtuns.)

Stalemate

As of early 1998, the Taliban and the Northern Alliance were locked in a stalemate. The Taliban controlled most of the country but were having difficulty advancing further. Still backed by Pakistan, they had also received economic aid from Saudi Arabia. The Northern Alliance was receiving help from a variety of sources that feared an increase in Islamic fundamentalism in the region, including Uzbekistan, Tajikistan, Turkmenistan, and Russia. Iran, although no foe of Islamic movements, opposed the Taliban because its Sunni extremism had led it to attack the Shi'a minority in Afghanistan; Iran, therefore, was supplying arms to the Hizb-i-Wahdat, who were members of the Northern Alliance.

The turmoil in Afghanistan had also spread to surrounding countries. In neighboring Tajikistan the war in Afghanistan had spilled over and merged with an ongoing local civil war. Tajiks from Tajikistan had fought in Afghanistan and had also used Afghanistan as a base for their attempts to defeat the Tajikistan government, which was dominated by old Communist apparatchiks. Pakistan's support for the Taliban also had local repercussions: anti-Shi'a Pakistanis who fought on the side of the Taliban sometimes returned to Pakistan to continue their religious war by targeting Shi'as within Pakistan. (Twenty percent of Pakistan's population are Shi'a Muslims.)

Finally, Iran and Pakistan were still home to millions of Afghan refugees, whose presence had the potential for causing additional instability in the future.

Carl Skutsch

See also: Afghanistan: Soviet Invasion, 1979–1989; Tajikistan: Civil War, 1990s.

Bibliography

Roy, Olivier. *Afghanistan: From Holy War to Civil War.* Princeton, NJ: Darwin Press, 1995.

Roy, Olivier. *Islam and Resistance in Afghanistan.* New York: Cambridge University Press, 1986.

Rubin, Barnett R. *The Search for Peace in Afghanistan: From Buffer State to Failed State.* New Haven, CT: Yale University Press, 1995.

ALBANIA: Civil War, 1997

TYPE OF CONFLICT: Ethnic and religious

Historical Background

Albania was one of the most backward countries in twentieth-century Europe. Before World War II it was a land of clan loyalties and blood feuds. During that war, however, Albania was occupied by German and Italian armies, and Albania united behind the resistance movements that fought to throw the invaders out. After the war, the most powerful of these groups, the Communists, took over Albania's government. Led by Communist dictator Enver Hoxha, Albania became a totalitarian Stalinist state. Until 1985, Hoxha isolated Albania from most of the world. Its borders were closed and almost no one left or arrived. Albania was a sealed box. Even Hoxha's Communist allies were eventually treated as enemies. Hoxha broke with Yugoslavia in 1948, the Soviet Union in 1961, and China in 1976. Albania became the most paranoid country in the world, with no friends, and treated all countries as enemies.

In 1985 Hoxha died, and Albania began slowly to change. Ramiz Alia, a more flexible leader, took control of the country, and began allowing reforms, including greater contact with the outside world. His motive was his desire to strengthen Albania's overly rigid economy, but the result was a rise in demands for more radical changes. The fall of communism in Eastern Europe helped trigger student and worker demonstrations in late 1990. In December 1990, Alia agreed to the creation of a multi-party democracy.

The birth of the new democracy was rocky; Alia and the Communists were reluctant to completely give up power. The year 1991 was filled with disputed elections and civil unrest. Thousands of Albanians fled to Greece and Italy. Finally, in March 1992, Alia resigned and was replaced as president by Sali Berisha of the Democratic party.

An armed masked supporter of President Sali Berisha questions a driver near the port of Durres, March 15, 1997. *(Associated Press/Wide World)*

Corruption and Pyramid Schemes

Berisha immediately set out to bring Albania into the world economy. The door was opened to foreign investment, and Albania's economy slowly began to recover from its long isolation. However, Berisha's commitment to democracy was not as strong as his liking for foreign currency. Keeping a strong hold on the police, army, and media, Berisha worked to keep himself and his party in power.

In late 1995, Berisha forced through a law which forbade former Communist party officials to run for office. This angered the Socialist party, which, as the heir to the old Communist party, was filled with former party officials. The May 1996 elections were preceded by brawls between Democratic and Socialist followers in which some Socialists died. The elections themselves were tainted by vote tampering and voter intimidation by the victorious Democratic party. Unrest followed the fraudulent elections, and Albania remained in turmoil throughout the rest of 1996.

In January 1997, the violence grew worse when a series of get-rich-quick pyramid investment schemes collapsed. The schemes had promised dividends of 30 percent and had done so by paying old investors with the money gained from new investors. When the schemes collapsed, Albanians all over the country lost their life's savings. The anger at Berisha exploded into riots and attacks on government buildings. The government was accused (probably accurately) of having profited from some of the pyramid scams.

Civil War

By March 1997, much of Albania was in revolt, particularly the south. (The Socialist party was strong in the south, while Berisha's support tended to come from a group of clans in his northern homeland.) With many soldiers deserting him, Berisha escalated the violence by having his police hand out automatic rifles and ammunition to any citizen who promised to fight for him. Rebels responded by seizing arms depots. By the end of March, Albania was in anarchy. Rebels controlled some towns and Berisha still held parts of the north, including the capital of Tirana, but in many places the only real authorities were local gangsters (who made their money from drug and gun smuggling).

An April 1997 intervention by a 7,000-strong European security force, mostly Italians, helped provide enough stability to allow the bringing in of food supplies. The European force provided security functions in some coastal cities but had no desire to intervene directly in Albania's tangled political situation. It did, however, agree to help supervise elections in June and July.

Those elections returned a victory for the Socialist party, which replaced Berisha's government. Socialist Fatos Nano became prime minister, while Socialist Rexhep Meidani was chosen to be president. The European expeditionary force left in August 1997.

With the Europeans' departure, chaos returned to Albania. The government was unable to control more than a portion of the country. Most of the army had disappeared and the police were rarely effective. Many parts of the country were controlled by criminal gangs and local militias. The gangs completely dominated some coastal cities, including Vlore, Fier, and Sarande. In many cases the underpaid local police were intimately involved in the gangs' smuggling activities. Albania became the center of the drug trade in Europe; heroin was brought in from outside Europe and then smuggled throughout the continent by the some of the many Albanians who live and work in other European countries.

As of April 1998, there was no civil war, but there was no government control over much of the country. Highway ambushes and robberies were commonplace. Italian advisors had been brought in to try and train a new Albanian army, but it was unclear whether the Socialist government had the necessary support to reimpose some kind of stability in Albania. More than 1,500 civilians had been killed since the violence began in January 1997. An estimated 1 million weapons were in the hands of private citizens, including automatic assault rifles and grenade launchers.

Significance

Albania's lack of a democratic tradition hampered its entry into the modern world. It went from a feudal society based on family and clan to a Communist totalitarian dictatorship. When that dictatorship collapsed, it was not surprising that Berisha's strong arm rule took its place. Once Berisha fell, Albania returned to its feudal roots. Clan loyalties, particularly in the northern part of the country, took priority over loyalty to an entirely discredited central government. In the south, the Socialists had some success in creating a support network but were hampered by the activities of powerful criminal gangs. It remained unclear, as of April 1998, whether Nano's new Socialist government could bring stability to Albania.

The Albanian situation was especially troublesome because of the wide distribution of Albanians in the region. With 2 million Albanians in the Kosovo province of Yugoslavia and 400,000 more in Macedonia, any instability in Albania had the potential of spilling across borders to affect the volatile situations in those neighboring countries. Kosovo already was receiving arms, and perhaps soldiers, from across its porous border with Albania. If the Serbs of Yugoslavia used military force to suppress the Kosovo insurgents, it would be likely that many Albanians in Albania would try and come to the aid of their ethnic cousins. Similarly, any attempt to punish Albania for such intervention would attract the interest of the Islamic world (Albania is the only Muslim state in Europe), which might provide economic and even military aid. Arab states had already shown themselves willing to provide financial assistance to the Muslims of Bosnia.

It was for these reasons that Europe and the United States were continuing to watch the Albanian situation closely.

Carl Skutsch

See also: Serbia: Kosovo Secessionist Movement, 1990s.

Bibliography

Vickers, Miranda. *The Albanians: A Modern History.* New York: I.B. Tauris, 1995.

ALGERIA: War of National Liberation, 1954–1962

TYPE OF CONFLICT: Anti-colonial PARTICIPANT: France

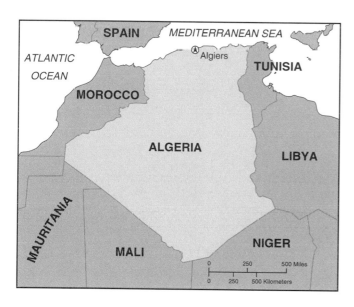

The Algerian war of national liberation from France was among the most significant anti-colonial wars of the twentieth century and represented the longest and most violent revolution in modern Arab history. Over 1 million Muslim Algerians and some 20,000 French soldiers died in the eight-year-long struggle. The ideas and tactics of the National Liberation Front (FLN, its French acronym) served as inspiration and a source of methods for revolutionaries throughout the developing world, as well as among black nationalists in the United States.

At the same time, the war represented a watershed in post–World War II French his-tory. With some 1 million French and other European settlers in Algeria, the French government and French society were ideologi-cally torn apart, as leftists called for withdrawal and rightists demanded the con-tinuation of "Algérie Française." Ultimately, the war brought down the fourth republic and led to the return of Charles de Gaulle to political life and the creation of the execu-tive-dominated fifth republic.

Historical Background

Algerian history has always been dominated by invaders. Between the first millennium B.C.E. and the early nineteenth century A.D., this region of the North African coast has been conquered and occupied by the Phoe-nicians, the Romans, the Vandals, the Byz-antines, the Arabs, the Turks, and finally, the French. Of these various invaders, the two most important, in terms of the legacy they left in Algeria, were the Arabs and the French. The former brought their language and religion; the latter imposed a political system and the rudiments of a modern econ-omy.

Between these two conquerors were the Turks. With the collapse of Moorish Spain in the late fifteenth century, western North Africa faced the threat of Christian invasion. To prevent this, local sheiks appealed to the Ottoman sultan in Constantinople to send forces to the region. This appeal led to three centuries of Turkish domination. As a distant and rather unimportant province of the vast Ottoman Empire, Algeria was divided into four districts, each nominally ruled by sub-governors appointed by the sultan. In fact, however, only the capital, Algiers, and its environs came under direct Ottoman rule. The rest of the country was controlled by local sheiks, who paid nominal tribute and loyalty to Constantinople. This division left a deep, bitter, and lasting hostility between the peasant farmers and herdsmen of the interior countryside, on the one hand, and the merchants and court elite of the coast, on the other.

France's involvement in Algeria began in the early nineteenth century. Angry with Algerian-based privateers preying on European shipping in the Mediterranean and eager to shore up his increasingly fragile rule at home, King Charles V dispatched 37,000 French troops to Algiers in 1830, the last year of his reign. While claiming to liberate Algeria from the increasingly despised Turks, the forces of France brutally attacked and pillaged the city, an action that would be repeated several times during the early years of France's occupation. For the next forty years, Paris moved hesitantly to consolidate its control over Algeria. On the one hand, the French government claimed that its goal was for a "limited occupation" in and around Algiers, and indirect rule elsewhere. At the same time, the French began a policy of settling ex-soldiers and other French pioneers on lands appropriated from Algerian landlords and farmers.

Resistance to French rule began very soon after the initial invasion of 1830, but was hampered by divisions between tribal groups within Algerian society. Gradually, under the leadership of an Arab Emir named Abd al-Qadir—often referred to as Algeria's "greatest national hero"—a united anti-colonial movement began to grow in the 1840s. With Paris's defeat in the Franco-Prussian War of 1870, a massive rebellion spread through much of Algeria in 1871. It took the French over a year and a half to put it down, at a cost of 2,500 European settlers and uncounted thousands of Algerians.

Between 1871 and World War I, the French extended their rule to all of Algeria. This effort involved four distinct elements. First, huge swathes of land were expropriated from Algerians and given to European settlers and landlords at a greatly accelerated pace. Second, the French government passed a series of laws, known as native laws, establishing the primacy of European settlers. Third, there was a conscious effort to divide the minority Berbers from the majority Arabs, by encouraging the assimilation to French ways and offering a superior social status to the former. (Berber and Arab Algerians are identical racially and religiously; the difference is that the lowland Algerians assimilated to invading Arabs of the seventh to tenth centuries, while the highland Algerians did not. The two speak two distinct languages.)

Finally, the French rationalized their rule over Algeria through the propagation of the *misión civilatrice*, or civilizing mission, whereby the Algerian people would be taught French customs and norms for their own good. Ultimately, this policy resulted in the development of a small Algerian elite—called *evolués*, or "evolved ones"—who came to serve French interests and, paradoxically, would come to form the core of the anti-colonial movement of the interwar and post–World War II eras.

Algerian nationalism in this period was nurtured in three spheres: in the mosques, in the expatriate Algerian community in France, and among the French-educated Algerian elite of the coastal cities. The first group, called the Islamic Reform movement, emphasized the return to the roots of Islam, as well as the embrace of Western civilization. Their slogan—"Islam is my religion; Arabic is my language; Algeria is my fatherland"—would be adopted during the revolutionary struggle of the 1950s. The second nationalist element—Algerians in France—coalesced around an organization called the North African Star and its leader Messali Hadj, who helped found the Algerian People's Army and whose slogan was the more radical "Neither assimilation nor separation, but emancipation."

World War II had a galvanizing effect on the Algerian nationalist movement. The collapse of France in 1940 and the Anglo-American invasion of North Africa—as well as the Americans' explicit call for the liberation of colonized people—radically changed the thinking of many Algerian intellectuals. This change was also registered among ordinary Algerians with the great anti-French uprisings in the cities of Setif and Guelma in 1945, both brutally crushed by French forces. Together, these events led to the formation of the Committee of Unity and Action, the precursor to the FLN, which launched the war of liberation in November 1954.

In short, Algerian nationalism passed through several distinct phases between 1900 and 1954: a crusade for equality based on assimilation (1900–World War I); a drive for equality based on cultural distinctiveness (1920s); a political push for autonomy within the French Empire (1930s); and a movement for negotiated separation (1945–1954).

The National Liberation War

While the French security forces in Algeria had suspected throughout 1954 that some kind of guerrilla action was going to take place soon, they were taken by surprise when guerrillas of the FLN launched simultaneous assaults on French army garrisons and dynamited infrastructure projects throughout the country on November 1, All-Saints' Day. At the same time, an announcement went out over Cairo radio, outlining the demands of the FLN and calling for the Algerian people to join the organization in its struggle against the French.

The reaction of French security forces was predictably harsh. Thousands of suspected militants were rounded up in raids throughout the country. These raids also targeted members of the Movement for the Triumph of Democratic Liberties (MTLD), Messali Hadj's new political party. Indeed, the party was banned, its files confiscated, and its leaders arrested. For the *colons* (European or colonial settlers), however, this wasn't enough. They demanded a total crackdown on all Algerian political and social organizations. But while the French sent out forces into the countryside to round up FLN guerrillas, the latter were able to disappear into the mountains of the Aures and Kabyle regions, the latter the heartland of the Berber people. Despite their ability to evade the French, the militants of the FLN were forced to endure a harsh winter with few supplies and few supporters.

Meanwhile, the new French government under Pierre Mendes-France decided to try reform as well as repression to counter the resistance movement. Mendes-France appointed a new governor-general for Algeria. Jacques Soustelle began to try and push the colons to accept the idea of full citizenship for all Algerians. (Under the 1919 Jonnert law, about 500,000, or 10 percent, of the educated Arab- and Berber-speaking Algerians were given citizenship.) At the same time, the French army continued to pursue the indefatigable FLN, which continued to gain recruits disgusted by colon resistance to reform. As the FLN gained experience in guerrilla fighting and established a more structured organization in 1955 and 1956, its attacks on French forces and colon settlements grew more numerous, audacious, and successful. When direct attacks on French forces became more difficult, the guerrillas switched tactics, going after "softer" targets, including Algerian collaborators with the French regime. Similarly, numerous acts of sabotage were carried out against the property of the French government, colon-owned enterprises, and, most commonly, colon-operated farms.

The army reacted to this new aggressiveness by the FLN with a policy of pacification, first developed during the French war against the Vietminh in Indochina from 1945 to 1954. In what was known as the "spreading oil patch" approach, the French army established controlled zones, which served as launching points for incursions into the surrounding countryside in efforts to expand the zones under army domination. But the policy of "limited repression"—that is, attacking guerrillas but leaving civilians alone—confused and frustrated French soldiers, many of whom believed, quite rightly, that the supposedly innocent civilians were actually supporting the guerrillas.

Under pressure from the colons, Soustelle was forced to enact a new, harsher repressive policy of "collective responsibility." If French troops were attacked, nearby village populations would be rounded up, with many of the males detained or put to work on projects for the army or government. In response to the policy of collective responsibility, FLN leaders met in June 1956 and issued a call for reprisals in response to the acts of collective punishment. "To colonialism's policy of collective repression," an FLN manifesto declared, "we must reply with collective reprisals against the Europeans, military and civil, who are all united behind the crimes committed upon our people. For them, no pity, no quarter!"

Thus, reprisals and counter-reprisals escalated, with massacres occurring on both sides, though Algerians tended to suffer more often and more harshly than colons or French troops. In August, the Algerian people themselves rose up in spontaneous rebellions across the country, attacking European civilians at random in urban centers. The response of the French army was immediate and brutal, with troops firing randomly into crowds of Algerian protesters.

Meanwhile, developments were occurring outside the country that would have a major impact on the war. In 1956, France granted the neighboring colonies of Morocco and Tunisia their independence. Unlike Algeria, these two colonies were not legally part of France and had very small populations of French and European settlers. Thus, their independence was achieved peacefully. However, the independence of Morocco and Tunisia meant that the FLN now had rear bases, protected from direct French army attacks and colon reprisals. The following year, however, the French established defense perimeters between Algeria and neighboring Morocco and Tunisia which included minefields, barbed wire, guard towers, and electronic sensors. These measures effectively prevented cross-border raids by the FLN.

In response to the new border defenses and the increasing crackdown on guerrilla forces in the countryside, the FLN embarked on a terrorist bombing campaign in the coastal cities, including the capital Algiers, in late 1957 and early 1958. Often using European-looking Algerian women to place the devices in French cafes and restaurants, the bombing campaign was successful in shaking the confidence of the colons. But it also inflamed their passions and led to increasing frustration in the army, many of whose officers believed they were not receiving the kind of support they deserved from the government in Paris.

Meanwhile, both the army and the colons were feeling increasingly isolated internationally and within the French political environment. While leaders of the socialist bloc countries and newly independent states in the developing world had long called for France to give up Algeria, these voices were joined by Western ones, including that of John Kennedy in America. At the same time, suspicions were growing among the French colons and the army in Algeria that Paris was prepared to negotiate an end to the war with the FLN, by freeing Algeria.

Together these pressures and fears led to an army uprising that would bring down the fourth republic in France itself in May 1958. The events of that spring began when the army, supported by right-wing forces in France, sent tanks into the streets of Paris in an attempted coup. Only the return of World War II hero Charles de Gaulle prevented the military from taking power. De Gaulle demanded and got a revised constitution granting extraordinary power to the executive. In response, the Algerian nationalists, under the leader of long-time political activist Ferhat Abbas, formed a free Algerian government-in-exile.

De Gaulle was acceptable to the army and right-wing forces because it was believed he would take a hard line with the rebels in Algeria, a view that he encouraged by the tough-sounding rhetoric of his early days in office. But secretly, de Gaulle had other intentions. Using the newly expanded powers of his office, he opened secret negotiations with the FLN leadership in the Alpine spa town of Evian. Calling for a "peace of the brave," de Gaulle announced the results of the negotiating process in March 1962: Algerians of all backgrounds would vote in a referendum for continued affiliation with France or independence, albeit with French rights to share in the natural gas and oil reserves recently discovered in the Algerian Sahara Desert and to maintain military bases throughout the country. The vote was never in doubt; Algerians overwhelmingly chose independence.

Yet, despite the negotiations and referendum, the war had one final and painful episode to play out. Unrepentant and vengeful army officers and colon leaders formed the Secret Armed Organization and conducted a massive campaign of terror and destruction during 1961 and 1962, destroying key parts of Algeria's infrastructure, killing some 3,000 Muslim civilians, and thoroughly poisoning what little goodwill still existed between the colon community and the Muslim majority.

In all, the war cost as many as 1 million Algerian lives, largely civilians, though the French maintain the figure was more like 200,000. Some 25,000 French soldiers and colons also lost their lives in the fighting, and the cost of the war—about $10 billion 1960 dollars—bankrupted the French treasury. Ultimately, approximately 1 million colons—nearly 100 percent of the population—would flee to France in the months leading up to independence.

The Algerian Side

Throughout Algerian history, the peoples of that land have been divided by clan and tribe. Neither the Arab concept of the Islamic community, the *umma*, nor the Turkish sultanate was able to overcome this centrifugal force in Algerian political life. The French simply ignored it by imposing their own regime. In some sense, the FLN that emerged in the early 1950s and led the nation to independence in the 1960s represented a new clan forged out of that struggle. Educated in French institutions or rising through the ranks of the organization through their talents and commitment, the FLN leaders took a very top-down approach to the liberation struggle, refusing to democratize the movement or open up their decision-making process to the rank and file. As the historian Alistair Horne, author of the definitive English-language book on the revolution, wrote, "the more one studies the Algerian revolution, the more one come[s] to realise how well the F.L.N. leadership succeeded in spinning an impenetrable cocoon of secrecy around the incessant rifts and dissents at the top."

The most significant of these rifts existed between the bureaucratic leadership of the FLN's National Liberation Army, largely isolated in Morocco and Tunisia, and the radical and independent guerrillas fighting inside the country. Ultimately, the former would establish their hegemony over the latter by taking control of the negotiations with de Gaulle's government and then overthrowing the radicals in the first years of independence. In 1965, just three years after independence, the secretive former commander of the FLN forces in Morocco, Houari Boumedienne, would push aside the radical Ahmed Ben Bella in an army coup.

Yet another division within the FLN involved religion, though the full implications of this would not be fully felt until the fundamentalist struggle of the 1980s and 1990s. Since the 1930s, leading Algerian clerics had pushed for a resistance struggle against French rule, seeing the Europeans as infidel invaders. The FLN leadership adopted their call for an independent Muslim Algeria, but never embraced their call for a truly Islamic-oriented state. Indeed, the pan-Arabist wishes of the religious elements within the FLN ultimately lost out to the secular nationalists whose vision for the future revolved around an independent and socialist Algeria.

The French

The French side in the war of national liberation consisted of three elements: the colon settlers, the political right wing in Paris, and the French army. The colons and their right-wing allies were the most adamant in maintaining Algeria as an integral part of France. Throughout the history of the French presence in Algeria, the colons consistently refused to advocate or support any concessions to the Muslim majority, a major cause of the growing frustration and violence of the latter in their evolution toward armed rebellion.

At the same time, the colon members of the French parliament were able to put forward a solid front that prevented such concessions from being enacted over their heads.

French troops on patrol in northeastern Algeria, August 26, 1957. *(Ministry of Defense, France)*

Because the governments of the fourth republic were so weak and divided, any determined bloc within a ruling coalition or even within the opposition could prevent the passage of legislation that it did not approve of. In essence then, long after the majority of the French public had moved from apathy to opposition against the war, the government was paralyzed, held hostage to a minority of colon and right-wing parliamentarians.

The army was more divided than the colons. Many of the officer corps, especially those that came from colon backgrounds or subscribed to right-wing politics, were determined to maintain complete French control of the colony. It was these elements that conducted the coup of 1958 that led to the downfall of the fourth republic and the presidency of Charles de Gaulle. Like other moderates

in the military, de Gaulle gradually came to the understanding that a negotiated settlement was necessary. Indeed, many of these moderates had grown increasingly disillusioned during their stints in Algeria. The inflexibility of the colons, along with the brutal tactics employed by the army, disenchanted them. These elements in the army, along with the mass peace movement emerging in France, were largely responsible for ending the war.

Issues and Tactics

Ultimately, the war in Algeria from 1954 to 1962 was about self-determination versus continuing colonial control. But there were other issues involved. In 1956 and 1957, French geologists discovered vast hydrocarbon reserves in the Algerian portion of the Sahara Desert. Ownership of and access to these reserves became a key demand of the French government in its negotiations with the FLN.

Still, self-determination was the key issue in the war, though it implied different things to the different players of the conflict. Algerian society in the early 1950s was in desperate shape. A rapidly growing Muslim population—benefiting from the advances in medicine brought by the French—was being crowded onto smaller and less productive patches of farmland, with little capital to develop it in ways to compete commercially with colonial farmers. Thus, living standards were low and unemployment was high. Added to this was an insulting array of laws and customs that made Arabs second-class citizens in their own land. Meanwhile, the colons—confident in their control—refused to accept even the slightest accommodation to Algerian demands for a more equal share of economic wealth and political power. Algeria was now a department, or an integral part of France itself, but was largely under the control of the colons in Algiers and the army.

For the colons, the struggle to maintain French control over Algeria was not unlike similar struggles to maintain white rule in southern Africa in the 1970s and 1980s. Having moved to a non-European land where their white skin and European citizenship guaranteed them a standard of living and a social station far superior to what they could probably have achieved in their home countries, the colons were determined to maintain their privileged status at all costs. The main difference with South Africa, of course, is that ultimately the colons did have a country to return to and virtually all did so shortly before independence.

For the French army, the war in Algeria represented a means for them to preserve what little remained of their dignity and effectiveness in the wake of two disastrous losses: their rout by Nazi armies during the 1940 invasion of France and their ignominious defeat by the Vietminh at Dien Bien Phu in 1954. Eventually, however, with the return of General de Gaulle, the army was able to salvage its sense of purpose even as it was withdrawn from Algeria.

The tactics employed by the colons, the French army, and the FLN were typical of struggles for independence in settler societies. The FLN employed several different kinds of tactics. First, there were hit-and-run guerrilla attacks against French army outposts and garrisons, as well as colon settlements. These kinds of attacks continued from the beginning of the war through its conclusion. In order to achieve both the element of surprise and the capacity to avoid French army sweeps, FLN guerrillas came to rely on sympathetic elements among the Algerian civilian population. In response, the French army increasingly came to rely on preventive measures, including population relocation and collective punishment.

In urban areas, the FLN used more terroristic-style tactics, including the planting of bombs in cafes and other spots where European civilians congregated. This kind of tactic was employed only after the French army increased its effectiveness against guerrilla actions in the countryside. A final component of the fighting involved the colon population. Their efforts to put down Algerian resistance also took several forms. This included uncoordinated mob attacks on Muslim civilians, usually in urban areas and almost always following the explosion of an FLN-planted bomb that caused European civilian casualties. At the same time, several secret paramilitary organizations—including the infamous Secret Armed Organization, established toward the war's end—engaged in assassination of FLN leaders and terroristic actions against Muslim civilians.

The End of the War and Its Legacy

More than anything else, it was the failed coup of May 1958 that paved the way for negotiations between the French government and the leadership of the FLN. By thoroughly polarizing the French political scene, the coup eliminated the possibility of a compromise settlement on Algeria, whereby the colony would become an associated part of the French republic. Second, it brought to the fore Charles de Gaulle, whose stature as the savior of France during World War II allowed him a latitude unavailable to virtually any other political figure in France.

By 1960, de Gaulle had become convinced that a negotiated settlement was the only way out of the Algerian quagmire, especially after the mass Muslim rioting of that year proved the lack of support France had among the majority of Algeria's population. At the beginning of 1961, de Gaulle dispatched banker and future president Georges Pompidou to meet secretly with FLN leader Ahmed Ben Bella, who had been imprisoned in a French jail since his capture in 1956, at Evian. To get negotiations going, de Gaulle authorized Pompidou to tell Ben Bella that France would release thousands of Algerian political prisoners and would drop Paris's demand for a ceasefire prior to negotiations, this latter item being the main sticking point for the FLN.

Over the next year or so, the two sides struggled to reach a compromise. Among the items under consideration were the status of the oil and gas fields of the Sahara. France wanted a special status for this region that would give it effective control; the FLN refused. Eventually, a compromise was reached whereby French companies would be given priority in exploration and drilling. In addition, France demanded a military presence at bases in Algeria, which the FLN eventually conceded, though France abandoned the idea shortly after Algeria's independence.

Finally, on March 19, 1962, a ceasefire was declared by both sides. The Secret Armed Organization of reactionary colons violated the pact, leading to retaliation by FLN and other Muslim forces, and ultimately to the mass exodus of the European population in the months leading up to independence in July 1962.

Algeria's war of national liberation established significant legacies in both Algeria and France. In the latter, of course, it caused the collapse of the fourth republic and the establishment of the more stable and executive-empowered fifth. It also helped precipitate a new French policy toward colonial possessions and shape the country's role in the superpower confrontation of the cold war. Rather than attempting any more rear-guard efforts to preserve its colonial holdings, France embarked on a more conciliatory policy toward its former colonies, though many critics point out that Paris merely employed more subtle forms of economic control, political pressure, and cultural domination.

For Algeria, the impact of the war was naturally even more profound. The gradual conversion of the FLN from a ragtag rebel movement to a highly bureaucratic organization, with its own army and government-in-exile, would lead to a struggle between the forces of radical, democratic socialism and an FLN leadership that emphasized top-down bureaucratic control and centralized economic planning. The secretive nature of the FLN, itself a legacy of the war, ultimately resulted in corruption, incompetence, and nepotism at the top.

These elements would come to alienate the Algerian people, especially after the drop in gas and oil prices in the 1980s, when the government could no longer buy the populace's allegiance to an undemocratic, elitist government with well-funded social welfare programs and padded payrolls at state-owned enterprises. Ultimately, opposition to the FLN would be channeled into the only institution that remained independent of FLN control, the network of free mosques established by radical clerics in the 1970s and 1980s. These mosques and clerics would form the core of the fundamentalist challenge to FLN rule that would explode into civil conflict in the 1990s.

James Ciment

See also: Algeria: The Fundamentalist Struggle Since 1992; Vietnam: First Indochina War, 1946–1954.

Bibliography

Bennoune, Mahfoud. *The Making of Contemporary Algeria, 1830–1987: Colonial Upheavals and Post-Independence Development.* New York: Cambridge University Press, 1988.

Entelis, John, and Philip Naylor, eds. *State and Society in Algeria.* Boulder, CO: Westview Press, 1992.

Fanon, Frantz. *A Dying Colonialism.* New York: Grove Press, 1965.

Horne, Alastair. *A Savage War of Peace: Algeria, 1954–1962.* New York: Penguin, 1987.

Ottaway, David, and Marina Ottaway. *Algeria: The Politics of a Socialist Revolution.* Berkeley: University of California Press, 1970.

Ruedy, John. *Modern Algeria: The Origins and Development of a Nation.* Bloomington: Indiana University Press, 1992.

Tlemcani, Rachid. *State and Revolution in Algeria.* Boulder, CO: Westview Press, 1986.

ALGERIA:
The Fundamentalist Struggle Since 1992

TYPE OF CONFLICT: Ethnic and religious

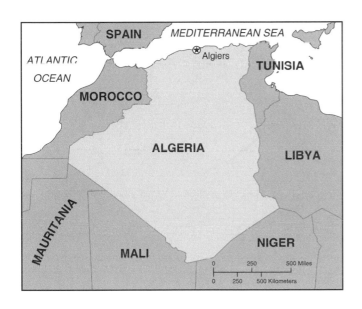

Introduction

The civil war between fundamentalist Islamic forces and the government of Algeria that began in 1992 represents one of the longest and certainly one of the bloodiest religious struggles in the Islamic world of the post–World War II era. While no hard figures on casualties are available, it is nevertheless estimated that over 100,000 persons—largely civilian—have died in the conflict.

The immediate cause of the war was the canceled general elections of 1992, elections that the Islamic Salvation Front (FIS, its French acronym) was poised to win by a landslide. Fearing for the future of a secular Algeria and their own perquisites of power, the military usurped power and immediately began a massive repression of Islamist leaders and supporters, sparking a bitter underground rebellion.

As the war continued, leaders on both sides began to lose control of their forces, leading to acts of wanton violence, torture, and terrorism. Having thoroughly demonized each other, neither side—especially the military-dominated government—has been willing to negotiate in good faith with the other.

Social and Economic Causes

Following a brutal eight-year-long war of national liberation against France, the colonial master of Algeria since 1830, the leaders of the National Liberation Front (FLN) took power in a negotiated settlement in Paris. They inherited a country purposefully underdeveloped. Algeria had a colonial economic infrastructure—largely geared to serve the needs of metropolitan France—and a primitive health and education system. Moreover, virtually the entire technical and professional class—almost all of whom were members of the European settler community—fled the country shortly before independence.

The FLN struggled mightily to overcome these handicaps in the first two decades of independence, aided by revenues generated from the huge natural gas and oil fields of the Sahara. The state lavished much of this revenue on industrial development, with an emphasis on heavy industry. It also invested heavily in social welfare, health, and educational programs, raising Algeria to the top ranks of the developing world in these indexes.

Deeply influenced by the command-economy model of the socialist world, the FLN government also adhered to a radical foreign policy. It supported revolutionary movements throughout the world and offered refuge to political exiles from both the developing and the developed worlds. Indeed, several members of the Black Panthers settled there after being indicted in the United States.

At the same time, however, the FLN nurtured an oppressive political environment at home. Following a brief experiment with *autogestion* (self-development), which included worker and peasant councils, the FLN government soon turned to more bureaucratic economic and political structures, especially after the 1965 coup that put former Algerian Liberation Army commander Houari Boumedienne in power.

Under the Boumedienne regime, virtually all the once-independent worker, peasant, youth, and women's councils were placed under state control. Rather than serving as democratic forums, the various unions served as means to propagate and enforce policies enacted by a small elite of political and military leaders. Moreover, worker and peasant democracy was forgone in favor of rapid, state-sponsored, and state-directed economic development. Increasingly, the French-speaking elite of Algiers lost touch with the wants and needs of the masses of Algerians.

Many of these growing contradictions between rulers and ruled were smoothed over and masked by the fact that the government, with its hydrocarbon revenues, was able to improve the standard of living and social indexes of the masses, especially after the huge jump in oil prices in the early 1970s.

Yet within that price hike and the enormous wealth it created were the seeds of future problems. State-owned enterprises—many of them unproductive and highly protected from international competition—expanded rapidly, hiring tens of thousands of new workers, many of whom were redundant. In addition, the mass of petrodollars flowing into the country fed enormous levels of corruption at the top.

With Boumedienne's sudden death in 1978 and, more important, because of the collapse of oil prices in the mid-1980s, the contradictions within *boumediennisme* began to become apparent. Under the regime of his successor Chadli Benjedid, several major policy changes were undertaken. First, significant cutbacks were made in the provision of social services. More important, an effort was made to make the huge state industrial enterprises more productive. This largely involved breaking them up into smaller units and giving managers more leeway to make policy decisions at the factory level. Finally, the heavy tariffs on imported goods, partly instituted out of the revolutionary impulse to make Algeria independent of outsiders and partly to protect the country's fledgling industries, were lifted.

The results of these reforms proved disastrous. Given more freedom to run their enterprises—but shielded from the consequences of their actions by being part of the protected elite—the new managerial elite rewarded themselves with the increased profits generated by firing thousands of workers, rather than reinvesting the revenues to increase productivity. Moreover, with many more smaller firms, the ranks of the managerial elite—largely members (or offspring of members) of the former revolutionary cadres of the FLN—grew in number.

Their incomes grew rapidly in the 1980s as well and they spent the money on luxury imports, long denied them by the country's once high tariffs. The cities of Algeria during this period saw a proliferation of fancy cars, restaurants, villas, and boutiques. The increasing discrepancy between the profligate lifestyles of the rich and well-connected versus the average Algerian—increasingly unemployed or under-employed—became apparent to all.

Other problems confronting Algerian society in the 1980s grew, ironically, out of the very gains achieved by the FLN. Having expanded the health care system, the government had effectively lowered the death rate to near first-world levels, even as it encouraged Algerians to keep to their tradition of large families. The population exploded, particularly in the cities, since the FLN had largely neglected agricultural and rural development, which helps explain how a food exporter in colonial times had to spend billions of dollars in hard currency by the 1980s to import more than half the basic foodstuffs required by the population. At the same time, millions of Algerian peasants flocked to the coastal cities, where they were greeted by serious housing shortages, traffic jams, and deteriorating environments, by-products of the government's overemphasis on heavy industry over consumer goods production and basic infrastructure development.

Moreover, the population was growing increasingly younger and better educated. By the early 1990s, over 75 percent of the population was under the age of twenty-one and most young people had high school diplomas. But cronyism at the top and shrinking payrolls denied them the opportunities they had come to expect. Meanwhile, the lack of housing forced many to put off marriage, compounding the frustration of unemployment and idleness. In addition, as the population grew younger, memories of the revolution—the basis of the FLN's legitimacy—became dimmer.

In October 1988, these frustrations exploded in nationwide rioting over rising food prices, lack of housing, growing unemployment, and corruption. The government panicked. After several days of violence, it sent troops in to quell the riots. The troops opened fire on demonstrators, killing anywhere between 200 and 1,500 persons. The event shocked both the government and the Algerian people. The former tried to calm popular passions by inaugurating a policy of democratization. The press was unshackled from censorship, political parties and independent organizations were legalized, and elections—first at the municipal and then at national levels—were scheduled.

Competing in the municipal elections of 1989 and the first round of the national elections in December 1991 were the FLN, the Berber-based Socialist Forces Front (FFS), dozens of small parties, and the Islamic Salvation Front (FIS), an avowedly fundamentalist party. While the FFS garnered 20 percent of the voters who were Berber, the FIS took the lion's share of the rest, making it the dominant party in the country.

With the second round of the national vote scheduled for January 1992, and the FIS poised to win more than the two-thirds of the assembly seats needed to amend the national constitution, the army moved in. It dissolved the government of Chadli Benjedid, forcing the president to humiliate himself by resigning on national television. It canceled the second round of voting; outlawed the FIS; and declared martial law, rounding up thousands of FIS leaders and supporters in the process. The army claimed it was protecting Algeria's fledgling experiment with democracy. As Liamine Zeroual, the defense minister and leader of the new ruling junta put it, an FIS victory would mean "one man, one vote, one time." The fundamentalists were outraged; it was we, they said, who played by the democratic rules and the army that violated them.

Despite the FIS's impressive electoral showing, most foreign and domestic experts on the Algerian political scene agreed that perhaps one-fourth of the country's electorate could be called fundamentalist in their ideological orientation. So why had the party garnered such a huge vote?

The Rise of Fundamentalism

Invading Arab armies brought Islam to Algeria in the eighth century A.D. Under the Turks, who ruled the region from the fifteenth to the early nineteenth centuries, the practice and organizational structure within Algerian Islam split into two. An educated clergy, serving the court and the commercial elite, developed in the coastal cities. In the mountainous Berber areas and in the peasant farmlands of the interior, a more popular form of Islam known as *mahgourism* (similar to Sufism in the Arab east), based on the worship of popular sheiks and situated around their burial sites, developed.

As in other Islamic lands, the arrival of conquering Europeans in nineteenth-century Algeria sparked a religious reaction. Under the charismatic sheik Abd al-Qadir, a rural revolt exploded across the country that took the French more than a year to quell. But this kind of uncoordinated and unorganized reaction soon died out. In its place arose a new kind of Islamic thinking, though, in Algeria, it was largely borrowed from the Muslim Brotherhood of Egypt and other out-of-country sources.

The Brotherhood and other groups of the Islamic renaissance sought to find a way to learn from the Europeans, even as they adapted Western ideas to an Islamic setting and laid the foundations for the ultimate ejection of westerners from Islamic lands. And while the FLN's revolution against the French was largely secular in orientation, its appeal to the masses was largely based on Islam.

Following independence, the ruling FLN did what the Turks and French had done before them: they established control over the Muslim clergy and the mosques through official appointments and funding. This was part of the above-mentioned FLN strategy of yoking all institutions in the country to the ongoing FLN-led revolution. They called it Islamic socialism or, alternatively, socialist Islam.

In either case, it deeply offended many Muslims, who saw in the revolutionary ideology—and its insistence on a society based on individual rights rather than patriarchal family-centered values—an anti-Islamic bent. To counter this, they drew upon Islamic teaching that advocated rebellion against heretical rule. At the same time, they began to develop a network of free mosques, especially in the growing shantytowns and slums of the major cities, which were free of official control. There they preached a return to fundamental Islamic values and offered the only independent organization for Algerians frus-

Riot police outside a mosque in Algiers guard against demonstrations by Islamic Fundamentalists, January 1992. *(Associated Press/Wide World)*

trated with the economic decline and corruption gripping the country.

As noted above, when the Algerian people were given the chance to express their feelings about the ruling FLN elite at the ballot box, they rejected them outright by voting for the only opposition party with a national base and infrastructure, the FIS.

The War

On January 11, 1992, President Chadli Benjedid went on national television and announced his resignation. Formation of the High Council of State (HCE) was announced the next day. While it included government and civic leaders, the military was the dominant player. After canceling the second round of elections, they recalled Mohammed Boudiaf, one of the *chefs historique,* or historical leaders of the revolution, from twenty-seven years of exile in France, to give the new body legitimacy. While the FIS and even the now-deposed FLN condemned the coup, the FIS urged calm on its followers, fearing a bloodbath as in 1988.

The general quiet was a false one. Militants within both the FIS and the military were maneuvering toward an escalation. The military moved first, beginning with a crackdown on free mosques; illegal demonstrations, and the arrests of, among others, the FIS's two best-known leaders, Ali Belhadj and Abbasi Madani, one the representative of the old Islamic guard and the other a spokesmen for younger, more technocratically oriented Islamists.

The FIS militants reacted to this persecution with a disorganized assassination campaign aimed at security personnel. In June, the hardliners in the military turned on their own, allegedly assassinating Boudiaf for making overtures to the FIS. (The word "allegedly" is used because Boudiaf was killed by a military marksman who had suspected but never proven links to the hardliners in the army.) The following month Belhadj and Madani—neither of whom would appear in what they considered to be a kangaroo court—were convicted of breaking aspects of the Emergency Law—passed in January—and sentenced to fourteen years in prison. The imprisonment of these leaders, say many experts, intensified the war. As they were advocates of the electoral process for Islamizing Algerian politics and society, their absence left a vacuum that more militant FIS leaders took advantage of.

Meanwhile, the military continued its crackdown through early 1993, arresting no less than 10,000 suspected FIS militants; many of them were sent to horrific prison camps in the Sahara, which had been first built and used, ironically, by the French in their war against Algerian independence fighters thirty years before. Most of those arrested in 1992 and 1993 were not guerrilla fighters or assassins. Indeed, like most religious-oriented political organizations in the Islamic world, the FIS was a hybrid, being both political party and social welfare organization. The hardliners in the military made little effort to differentiate between these two elements, holding many innocent people without trial and torturing hundreds of prisoners, according to Amnesty International.

Militants from the FIS, many of them having left the organization for the more radical and violent Armed Islamic Group (GIA), began an extensive campaign of assassina-

tions, targeting government-appointed religious officials, security forces, bureaucrats, anti-Islamic intellectuals, and journalists. Attempting to isolate the regime from international supporters, especially France, the GIA issued a warning to all foreigners in the country in September 1993 to leave or risk being murdered.

Both sides increased the vitriol in their rhetoric as well. The FIS continued to deny the legitimacy of the HCE, denounced its repressive tactics, and claimed that it did not have the support of the Algerian people. For its part, the government insisted, not without foundation, that the majority of Algerians did not want a fundamentalist state but had voted for it out of sheer frustration with the ineffectual rule of the FLN.

The two sides also charged one another with serving foreign interests, a harsh indictment in a country that prided itself on its nationalism and its independence from foreign domination. The FIS said the HCE were the tools of France; the government insisted that the FIS and the GIA were both supported by fundamentalist forces from Saudi Arabia and had the backing of the United States, which, it was said, was eager to back the pro-market fundamentalists as a way to earn points in the Arab world. These mutual recriminations made negotiations virtually impossible, especially since the government simply refused to accept the FIS as a negotiating partner, even though the Islamists had, by 1994, formed an opposition alliance with the major secular parties in Algeria.

Moreover, forces on both sides were beginning to spin out of control. The government set up an anti-terrorist police force, known popularly as the "ninjas" because of their black outfits and balaclava hoods. Secular death squads, many of them with connections to the security forces, began to attack both Islamist supporters and guerrillas in retaliation. On the Islamist side, the more politically oriented FIS leadership found itself in prison or in exile, with little control over its militant members and virtually no authority over the GIA.

As the government began to take measures to protect its own personnel, the GIA began going after softer targets. Women were particularly vulnerable. Like other fundamentalists, the GIA had strong and reactionary views on the role of women in Islamic society. A campaign—if such a purposeful-sounding word can be used for a virtually leaderless network of guerrilla cells—began, to force women to wear the veil, through rape, beatings, and even assassination. In addition, the GIA acted on its warning against foreigners in July 1994 by murdering seven Italian seaman aboard their ship in the port of Djedjen, 200 miles east of Algiers. In December, GIA militants hijacked a French jet in Algiers, intending to fly it over Paris and then blow it up. They were gunned down by a French anti-terrorism squad while the jet was parked on a tarmac at Marseilles airport.

Rather than negotiating, the government decided to hold new presidential elections in 1995, though without the participation of the FIS. Zeroual was elected president. Most major parties boycotted the elections. Elections for the national assembly followed in late 1996, with a high voter turnout, a fact which the government claimed showed its own legitimacy and the basic distaste most Algerians had for fundamentalist politics. At the same time, Algiers continued to insist that negotiations with "terrorists" remained out of the question. It also established such a strong security presence in the major urban areas that bombings and assassinations of government officials tapered off. The government began to claim it was winning the war.

These assertions were not without an element of truth. The GIA, growing more isolated, was forced into taking more drastic actions. It planted a series of bombs in the Paris metro, in order to force France to drop its support for the Algerian government. France, fearing a wave of unwanted immigration from Algeria should the Islamists win, made no secret which side it supported in the war.

But the real escalation of the GIA's war was occurring in the suburbs and towns south of Algiers, an area that the local press had come to call "the triangle of death." In a series of attacks designed to disrupt elections and then the celebration of the holy month of Ramadan, the GIA in both 1997 and 1998 carried out bloody massacres of villagers and townspersons, killing some 1,000 or more people in January 1998 alone. The GIA and some of the FIS claimed the government was responsible, pointing out that many of these villages and towns had once voted heavily for the FIS. The seemingly senseless attacks that the government blamed on the GIA were aimed, they said, at Algerian public opinion. For many Algerians, and most outside observers, it is difficult to tell who is responsible. Both the government and the Islamists share an Algerian penchant—formed over a century of opposition to French rule and sharpened in the eight-year-long war for independence—for secrecy.

As of this writing, the war in Algeria continues. Firm estimates of the war's victims are impossible to obtain; the government says about 50,000 have died, while many non-governmental Algerian and international experts put the figure at double that.

James Ciment

See also: Algeria: War of National Liberation, 1954–1962.

Bibliography

Burgat, François, and William Dowell. *The Islamic Movement in North Africa.* Austin: Center for Middle Eastern Studies at the University of Texas, 1993.

Ciment, James. *Algeria: The Fundamentalist Challenge.* New York: Facts on File, 1997.

Kelsay, John. *Islam and War: A Study in Comparative Ethics.* Louisville, KY: Westminster/John Knox Press, 1993.

Lazreg, Marnia. *The Eloquence of Silence.* New York: Routledge, 1994.

Roy, Olivier. *The Failure of Political Islam.* Cambridge, MA: Harvard University Press, 1994.

Ruedy, John. *Islamism and Secularism in North Africa.* New York: St. Martin's Press, 1994.

Stone, Martin. *The Agony of Algeria.* New York: Columbia University Press, 1997.

ANGOLA:
War of National Liberation, 1961–1974

TYPE OF CONFLICT: Anti-colonial **PARTICIPANT:** Portugal

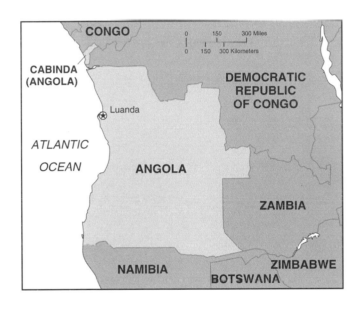

Historical Background

Angola, one of the first territories to be incorporated into a European Empire, had been a Portuguese colony since the late fifteenth century, when explorers looking for an all-sea route to India and China established trading posts and forts near the mouth of the Congo River and the present-day capital of Luanda. Nevertheless, Portuguese efforts to penetrate and establish hegemony over the interior of the colony were sporadic and largely ineffectual until the twentieth century.

That is not to say, however, that the Portuguese soldiers, traders, and settlements did not have an impact far outweighing their limited numbers and limited geographical penetration. Many of the settlers took Angolan wives, gradually establishing a population of mixed Afro-Portuguese in Angola. This group of people established themselves as a class of commercial intermediaries between the European traders of the coast and the African nations of the interior. These creoles spoke Portuguese, but blended European and African customs to create a unique culture that would eventually become the dominant one among Angola's elite. At the same time, these creoles would play the leading role in their nation's struggle for independence from Portugal in the mid-twentieth century.

The Afro-Portuguese defended their position by balancing the interests of the Europeans and the Africans, preventing either from coming into contact with one another or growing too powerful. This balancing act allowed them to maintain their role as the irreplaceable middlemen of Angolan trade, including its most lucrative commodity, human beings. It has been estimated that fully 12 million Africans from lands south of the equator were forcibly shipped to the Americas, and the bulk of these were captured in or transported through Angolan territory.

But several factors in the late nineteenth century undermined the position of the Afro-Portuguese. The outlawing of the international slave trade eliminated a valuable commodity. The Berlin Congress, which divided Africa up into European colonies, forced Portugal to begin asserting its claims for territory by demonstrable efforts to suppress indigenous peoples. And finally, the presence of the British in the interior of southern Africa led to new trading patterns and competitors.

The Afro-Portuguese in the cities faced their own problems. By the turn of the century, more and more impoverished whites were emigrating to Angola, many encouraged by the government. Lisbon hoped to solve several problems through immigration to Africa. First, it would relieve population pressures in one of the most crowded and poorest countries in Europe. Second, it would provide a white bulwark in the colonies as defense against both rebellious Africans and covetous Europeans in neighboring colonies. Third, it was hoped, the new farmers would raise valuable tropical products that would bring revenue to both colonial and metropolitan treasuries. The policy largely failed. The farmers, usually the least educated and most unsuccessful in Portugal, could not make a go of it in the harsh wilds of Angola. Most drifted to Luanda or the provincial capitals, where they increasingly competed with the Afro-Portuguese for civil service and commercial positions. They pushed the government to defend their own interests with a series of racist edicts, favoring whites over Africans, even the creoles.

The situation intensified after the rise to power in Lisbon of the Antonio Salazar dictatorship in the 1920s. Like Mussolini in It-aly, the fascistic Salazar was eager to revive a glorious national past, in this case by building what was called a Lusotropical (Luso is the adjective for Portuguese) empire in Africa, Asia, and even Brazil. Settlement of white farmers in Angola was again encouraged, but this time with better effect. Better roads, more capital, and more effective medicines against tropical disease allowed many white farmers to succeed. Most important, Portugal's neutral status in World War II put it in an ideal situation for producing and selling critical tropical products to both Allies and Axis powers. Angola flourished and more white settlers poured in, though most of them still ended up in the cities.

The decades following the end of World War II saw much of the same, but at an even more accelerated pace. In the great capitalist expansion of the 1950s and 1960s, Angola's products—including cotton, coffee, ivory, diamonds, gold, and increasingly oil—were in high demand. By the early 1970s, several hundred thousand whites—mostly Portuguese, but also Spanish and Italian—lived in Angola. Many remained poor, living in conditions little better than the creoles and often competing for the same jobs.

At the same time, however, the winds of decolonization were sweeping across sub-Saharan Africa, beginning in Ghana in 1957 and spreading to virtually the entire continent from the Congo River basin north. Southern Africa, however, remained in the grip of white control, in the form of settler republics in Rhodesia and South Africa and continued colonization in the case of Mozambique and Angola. Lisbon had several reasons for resisting the so-called winds of change in Africa. For one, the colonist population insisted they remain under Portuguese rule. They and Lisbon even developed a rationale for continuing occupation in an age of decolonization. The Portuguese, it was argued, had developed a non-racial form of cooperation with the Africans, unlike the racist apartheid regimes in South Africa and Rhodesia. The races socialized, worked, and married together, creating a unique Luso-tropical civilization.

There was a kernel of truth to these assertions. The Portuguese did not seem quite so obsessed with maintaining the separation between the races; there was a far more relaxed social atmosphere in Angola and Mozambique than in neighboring Rhodesia and South Africa. But this kernel of truth was wrapped in layers of hypocrisy. Angolan society was stratified by race, with white colonists in near total control of the political and commercial scene. For Africans and creoles, there was more than just poverty to bear; there was a repressive police state designed to break any attempts to organize or demonstrate for improved economic conditions or true political equality.

But the real reason Portugal was unwilling to free its colonies in Africa was a much simpler one. The colonies were immensely profitable. Unlike France and England, the two other great colonial powers in Africa, Portuguese capitalists did not have the means to compete in the international marketplace. That is to say, they knew that if they lost political control of their colonies, they could not maintain their economic hegemony against the encroachments of other Europeans and South African whites. They could not, as England and especially France did, maintain a kind of neo-colonialist system in their former African possessions.

Angolan Society

On the eve of the national liberation struggle in Angola in the early 1960s, Angola was a complex society. Stratified by race and class, it had a small elite of administrators, businesspeople, and planters. Beneath the elite was a middle class of professionals, retailers, and civil servants, largely white but including the occasional *assimilado,* the official designation for the Afro-Portuguese and other educated and acculturated Africans. Beneath the middle class were the masses of workers in the cities, largely black, and farmers in the countryside.

This group, representing the vast majority of Angolans, was itself divided by ethnicity and economics. The indigenous African people of Angola were largely divided into three distinct ethnic and linguistic groups: the Ovimbundu in the south and central parts of the country, the Kimbundu along the coast, and the Kikongo in the northeast. Moreover, each of these different peoples played a different role in the country's economy and was, in turn, shaped by that role. Many of the Ovimbundu worked for the cotton planters of the Central Highlands, but others had migrated or been transported to the north to work on the coffee plantations. This put them into a fierce rivalry with the Kikongo, who resented their access to jobs and who held them in contempt for being under the thumb of white planters. Meanwhile, the Kimbundu of the coast dominated the African neighborhoods of the major cities and were increasingly resented by the Kikongo and Ovimbundu for their street-smart ways and their control of the job market in the port cities.

The War for Independence

Just as the late nineteenth-century scramble for European control of sub-Saharan Africa—and with it Portugal's first real efforts to assert administrative control over its colonies

Troops of the Angolan National Liberation Army communicating by radio to other units in September 1964. (*United Press International/Corbis-Bettmann*)

there—was initiated by Belgian King Leopold II's aggressive forays into the Congo, so the beginnings of the resistance movements against Portuguese rule can be traced to the sudden decolonization of the Belgian Congo. In 1959, Brussels agreed to a four-year decolonization plan, but then abruptly changed its mind, giving Congo independence in 1960. Ill prepared, the country was immediately embroiled in a multi-sided struggle for power between right- and left-wing elements, as well as separatists in different provinces of the vast new country.

The conflict in the Congo worried the authorities in Angola since the two shared a border more than 1,000 miles long. More ominous was the large Kikongo population in the Congo, many of whom drifted back to their homes in Angola after the Belgian-

owned plantations where they worked closed down. Even before the war, the Kikongo had taken the lead in pushing for autonomy. Under the leadership of Holden Roberto, they formed the Union of the Peoples of Northern Angola (UPNA, later the UPA) in 1957, a largely ethnic-based, rural organization. Its leadership largely made up of small commercial farmers and small-time urban entrepreneurs, the organization took on a strongly anti-communist ideology.

Meanwhile the Kimbundu people in Angola were also getting organized, having formed the Popular Movement for the Liberation of Angola (MPLA, its Portuguese acronym), under the leadership of an *assimilado* doctor named Agostinho Neto. Like Neto himself, the MPLA was cosmopolitan in outlook and socialist in its political orientation, quite unlike the UPNA. In June 1960, colonial police arrested Neto, setting off riots in Luanda that resulted in the deaths of several unarmed demonstrators. Then, in an entirely separate incident, thousands of Kimbundu cotton farmers in the Malange province 400 miles southeast of Luanda rose up in an armed uprising (the arms were machetes) over falling prices, destroying colonial livestock and property before being brutally suppressed by soldiers. It is estimated some 7,000 farmers were killed. The incident, so distant from the capital, went largely unnoticed.

Then, in February 1961, hundreds of African Luandans, angered at police brutality and arbitrary arrests, stormed the city's prisons, freeing dozens of militants along with petty criminals. While the MPLA claimed credit, most historians believe it was a spontaneous affair. In either case, the uprising fueled a violent reaction among the city's whites, who brutally killed hundreds of unarmed blacks in retaliation. This particular incident officially marked the beginning of the war of liberation and is celebrated today as Angola's major national holiday. A month later, the Kikongo of the north rose up under the loose control of the UPNA, now renamed the National Liberation Front of Angola (FNLA). Again, the Portuguese forces reacted brutally, killing some 20,000. These repressive measures were largely effective against the FNLA. Within a couple of years, the organization was limited to ineffective raids across the border from its sanctuary in the now-independent Congo.

Even more destructive for the cause of Angolan independence was the growing animosity between the rightist, rural, Kikongo-based FNLA and the socialist, urban, and cosmopolitan MPLA. Indeed, as early as October 1961,

FNLA partisans were attacking MPLA guerrillas, a harbinger of much worse to come. Adding to the latter's woes, they were evicted from the Congo by the right-wing dictator, Joseph Mobutu (later Mobutu Sese Seko), and were forced into Congo-Brazzaville, which shared no border with Angola outside the enclave of Cabinda. This made it difficult to attack inside Angola and, indeed, not until part of the MPLA relocated to Zambia, on Angola's eastern border, in 1966 did MPLA guerrillas again engage colonial forces in battle. Despite these setbacks, the MPLA, with its more left-wing politics and non-tribal inclusiveness, attracted the lion's share of recruits to the rebel cause.

The move to Zambia, while strategically appealing, put the MPLA into conflict with yet another rebel movement, that of Jonas Savimbi's Union for the Total Independence of Angola (UNITA). Savimbi, once a leader in Roberto's FNLA, had left that organization because of its timidity and its ethnic exclusiveness. Savimbi was a well-educated and highly ambitious Ovimbundu man who felt that his own career and the interests of his people were better served by their own organization. In 1966, he formed UNITA. From the beginning, however, the MPLA had suspicions about the organization. They said it was really a front set up by the Portuguese, to engage the MPLA in battle and keep the Ovimbundu in line. These accusations were later corroborated from the files of the Portuguese security forces, opened after a coup in 1974 toppled the dictatorship in Lisbon.

Meanwhile, the Portuguese military began employing the anti-guerrilla strategy developed by its NATO ally and main weapons provider, the United States. All the tactics used in Vietnam were copied on a smaller scale in Angola, including search-and-destroy missions, helicopter-aided mobility, the establishment of village militias, and even the use of napalm to deny the rebel forces jungle cover. Ovimbundu peasants were herded into relocation camps, to keep them from providing aid to the rebels. Because of the vast reaches of the country and the relatively small areas in which the Portuguese planters and urban population lived, the army was able to keep the guerrilla war largely out of sight and out of mind. But the effort was costly, in both financial and political terms.

Independence and Internecine Fighting

Trying to suppress rebellions in several of its colonies—Angola, Guinea-Bissau, Cape Verde Islands, and Mozambique—put too much of a strain on the impoverished and politically stagnant metropolis. In February 1974, a group of centrist and left-wing military officers overthrew the dictatorship of Marcello Caetano, the man who had acceded to power after Salazar's death in 1968. For a time, the new government, under the leadership of war hero Antonio de Spinola, tried to find a way to maintain some kind of political union with the colonies. But in October, Spinola was forced out by more left-wing officers, who immediately declared their intention to free Portugal's colonies forthwith.

The news caught the different rebel groups and the colonial leadership in Angola by surprise. The MPLA, its Luanda and eastern factions locked in a power struggle, were suspicious. The FNLA, backed by Zaire and Mainland China, believed it was in the best position to assume power. It welcomed negotiations with Lisbon, as did the more isolated UNITA in the south. Meanwhile, the whites of

Angola were, not surprisingly, filled with trepidation about the unfolding events in Lisbon. Riots, largely instigated by whites, broke out in the capital. The whites talked about a unilateral declaration of independence, much as Rhodesian whites had done when Britain talked of black rule there in 1965.

Arms began to flow into the country as the Portuguese prepared to pull out. The FNLA was supplied with weapons by China and, oddly, by the CIA as well, both countries using Mobutu's Zaire as their conduit. This case of strange bedfellows can be explained by Beijing and Washington's mutual suspicions of the Soviet-backed and -armed MPLA. By November 1974, when representatives of the three rebel groups met with Portuguese officials in the Lisbon suburb of Alvor, Angola was slipping into a foreign-aided civil war. While the Alvor accords promised elections following Angola's formal independence on November 11, 1975, few observers believed the situation would be solved off the battlefield.

In March 1975, the well-armed FNLA in the northeast marched on Luanda, hoping to capture the strategic junction at Caxito just north of the city. In response, the Soviets and Cubans began a major arms shipment to the MPLA, via Congo-Brazzaville. The fighting escalated through the summer, causing the vast majority of Portuguese colonists to flee, though not before acting out vengefully by destroying whatever property they could not take with them. In mid-September came the inevitable showdown between the FNLA and the MPLA. Utilizing rather ineffective but terrifying World War II–vintage Soviet rocket launchers—popularly known as "Stalin's Organs"—the MPLA routed the FNLA. Roberto's liaisons with the Central Intelligence Agency (CIA) from the United States advised him to retreat and regroup, but the

FNLA leader insisted on pushing on toward Luanda. The FNLA forces arrived in the suburbs of the capital on the eve of independence, but were again turned back by MPLA and Cuban forces, this time for good.

Meanwhile, the war was heating up in southern Angola. By August, UNITA had formed a strategic alliance with the government of South Africa, the latter fearing an Angola ruled by the socialist and militantly anti-apartheid MPLA. On October 16, the South African Defense Forces (SADF) invaded Angola in order to back UNITA's push on Luanda, only to be pushed back by a Cuban and MPLA counter-offensive in mid-November. The SADF soon retreated to South African–controlled Namibia, Angola's neighbor to the south.

By the end of the year, the MPLA was in firm control of most of the country. The FNLA, having pulled back to Zaire, largely collapsed, especially after the U.S. Congress passed a law forbidding CIA intervention in Angola, and Beijing decided it needed to find a modus vivendi with the victorious MPLA government. UNITA was a different story. A more effective strategist and leader than Roberto, Savimbi led the remnants of his forces on a "long march" into the bush of southern Angola, determined to fight on another day.

James Ciment

See also: Angola: First War with UNITA, 1975–1992; Angola: Second War with UNITA, 1992–1998; Congo (Zaire), Democratic Republic of: Post-Independence Wars, 1960–1965.

Bibliography

Bender, Gerald. *Angola under the Portuguese: The Myth and the Reality.* Berkeley: University of California Press, 1978.

Ciment, James. *Angola and Mozambique: Postcolonial Wars in Southern Africa.* New York: Facts on File, 1997.

Davidson, Basil. *In the Eye of the Storm: Angola's People.* Garden City, NY: Doubleday, 1972.

Marcum, John. *The Angolan Revolution: Volume 1: The Anatomy of an Explosion.* Cambridge: MIT Press, 1969.

———. *The Angolan Revolution: Volume 2: Exile Politics and Guerrilla Warfare.* Cambridge: MIT Press, 1978.

Minter, William (ed). *Operation Timber: Pages from the Savimbi Dossier.* Trenton, NJ: Africa World Press, 1988.

Stockwell, John. *In Search of Enemies: A CIA Story.* New York: W.W. Norton, 1978.

ANGOLA:
First War with UNITA, 1975–1992

TYPE OF CONFLICT: Cold war confrontation; Ethnic and religious
PARTICIPANTS: Congo (Zaire); Cuba; South Africa; Soviet Union; United States

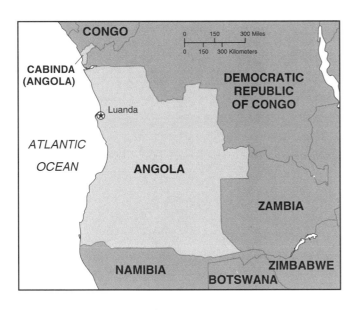

Historical Background

On November 11, 1975, Angola held what may be the strangest independence day in African history. As Portuguese Admiral Leonel Cardoso lowered his country's flag over the capital city of Luanda, artillery could be heard in the background. While the left-wing Popular Movement for the Liberation of Angola (MPLA, its Portuguese acronym) took the reins of power, a rival group, the CIA-backed National Front for the Liberation of Angola (FNLA), was marching on the city. Meanwhile, in the southern provincial capital of Huambo, a third liberation force, the South African–assisted Union for the Total Independence of Angola (UNITA), was conducting its own independence celebration and getting ready to launch a military drive on the capital hundreds of miles to the north.

Within a few months, however, MPLA forces, backed by Soviet arms and augmented by Cuban troops, would crush both the FNLA and the UNITA in battle, sending the former into oblivion and the latter on its famous "long march" into the southern Angolan bush, to prepare for yet another round of fighting.

In the capital, the leadership of the MPLA moved on its political enemies. Both UNITA and the FNLA were outlawed, and what few supporters remained in Luanda were rounded up. Some thirteen FNLA mercenaries, mostly Americans and Britons, were convicted of various crimes, and four were executed. Even dissidents with the MPLA felt the post-war wrath. Two top advisors to

President Agostinho Neto were arrested for organizing opposition within the party.

Meanwhile, the MPLA tried to establish its international credentials. Strong-arming neighboring Zaire and Zambia, both dependent on Angolan railroads and ports for the bulk of their international trade, Luanda won agreements that neither country would sponsor rebel movements within Angola. While leaning toward the socialist bloc countries— for both ideological and military reasons— the MPLA government also tried to reach out to the West, knowing that only the big oil companies could provide the expertise and capital necessary to fully exploit the country's vast reserves.

MPLA spokespersons refused to see any contradiction in establishing a socialist government even as they opened up the country to capitalist investment. This contradiction was made possible by the general political tenor of the times. Having defeated the United States in Southeast Asia—as well as taking power in Angola, Ethiopia, and Mozambique—the socialist bloc was confident and assertive. At the same time, both the South African government under Prime Minister John Vorster and the U.S. government under President Jimmy Carter were in periods of foreign policy retrenchment, both having been burned in Angola by backing the losing side.

Despite this auspicious beginning, the MPLA began making mistakes in its administration of the Angolan economy. Rather than attempting true land reform, the government continued the hated agricultural policies of the Portuguese, forcing small farmers to sell their crops at below-market rates to government purchasing boards. To guarantee stability in the countryside, the government often used holdovers from co-

lonial times, many of them chieftains and labor bosses who had worked with the Portuguese. And on top of all this, the MPLA laid down an enormous bureaucracy to institute a centralized, command economy on the lines of its mentors, the Soviet Union and Cuba.

This sparked a coup in 1977 among more radical members of the MPLA like Nito Alves, who had been put in charge of organizing Luanda's citizens into *poder popular* (people's power) committees during the late stages of the national liberation war. While the coup was easily crushed and the committees were hounded out of existence, it left a residual bitterness among the Angolans and killed any possibility of a diplomatic opening to the United States or South Africa. Of course, it should be noted, both Carter in the United States and Vorster in South Africa were coming under increasing pressure from their respective right wings and both would be ousted from power—Vorster in a constitutional coup in 1978 and Carter in the elections of 1980.

The Rise of UNITA

Following his defeat in 1975, UNITA leader Jonas Savimbi maintained a low profile in a redoubt hidden in the southern Angolan bush, an area the Portuguese had aptly named "the land at the end of the earth." His main backer, South Africa, had largely abandoned him and a potential backer, the U.S. government, was legally mandated by an act of Congress to stay out of Angolan affairs. Still, by 1977, Savimbi felt confident enough to begin launching hit-and-run attacks on isolated MPLA outposts and infrastructure targets, the latter mostly confined to the Benguela rail line between the Atlantic port of that name and the copper belt of Zambia. By 1980, however, UNITA had grown significantly, both in numbers and in military potential, and was now capable of hitting the railroad at almost any point along its 700-mile length in Angola.

How UNITA grew so fast is a matter of some controversy. Its supporters say that it appealed to disenchanted Ovimbundu farmers—Savimbi, himself, was an Ovimbundu and appealed to ethnic solidarity—upset by the government's agricultural policies, which included the consolidation of villages into farming cooperatives under the control of bureaucrats from Luanda and local chieftains, many of them quite unpopular. UNITA offered them a way to fight back.

The organization's opponents say that UNITA's forces improved only after the right-wing "coup" by South African Defense Minister P. W. Botha, who had made support of anti-communist rebel movements in southern Africa a key part of his strategic defense of the apartheid regime. The policy, known as "total strategy," was intended to make these countries ungovernable and to portray black majority rule as incapable of bringing peace and prosperity, while at the same time strong-arming the new independent black states into giving up any tacit support for the African National Congress, itself fighting for an end to apartheid in South Africa.

With the election of Ronald Reagan in 1980, Botha now felt he had a kindred spirit in Washington. So too did Savimbi, who was quoted as saying that Reagan's election was "the best news since the beginning of the war." Indeed, the assistant secretary of state for African affairs, Chester Crocker, outlined his "constructive engagement" policy toward South Africa and insisted on a new linkage of southern African issues: specifically, South Africa should only pull out of its illegal colony in Namibia if and when Cuban troops abandoned Angola.

South Africa Invades

With the green light on in Washington, South Africa stepped up its support for UNITA dramatically. In 1981 alone, the South African Defense Forces (SADF) conducted over 1,000 bombing missions and fifty ground assaults, including the massive Operation Protea, in which a 5,000-man force occupied the southern Angolan province of Cunene for several weeks. The declared rationale was to eliminate Southwest African People's Organization (SWAPO) forces, fighting for the liberation of Namibia from South Africa. Eventually, the Angolan forces, with Cuban support, halted the advance sixty-five miles north of the Namibian border.

UNITA, now a well-armed and formidable force of its own, had canceled the MPLA government's writ in much of southern Angola, as well as in the Ovimbundu homeland in the central highlands. Still, it was always at a disadvantage vis-à-vis the MPLA, which had an enormous war chest paid for by its substantial oil revenues. The MPLA had more soldiers, more arms, and virtually total control of the skies, except when South African forces invaded, as they did once more with Operation Askari at the end of 1983. Initially, Askari was not meant to be a mere attack on southern Angola, as Protea had been, but an all-out invasion intended to put Savimbi and UNITA in power in Luanda. But when military satellites revealed the extent of the South African buildup, the Soviet Union issued stern warnings, forcing Pretoria to scale back its plans.

With anti-apartheid sentiment growing in the United States in the election year 1984, the Reagan administration temporarily backtracked, pushing negotiations on all parties to the conflict. An accord signed in the Zambian capital of Lusaka included a ceasefire and assurances that neither UNITA nor SWAPO take advantage of a SADF pullback from southern Angola. But, as with the roughly contemporaneous Nkomati Accords in the Mozambican War, Pretoria had no intention of honoring its word, a fact made plain when a group of South African commandos were captured while attempting to blow up oil facilities in the Angolan enclave of Cabinda far to the north.

On the eve of Angola's tenth anniversary of independence, both UNITA and the MPLA were growing weary. The MPLA was alarmed at the SADF's capacity to attack anywhere in the country, and UNITA was worried, for a time at least, that Lusaka might mean an end to South African aid. But rather than encouraging peace, the mutual weariness led to increasingly brutal tactics by both sides, though UNITA was portrayed—and not without reason—as the worst offender by human rights organizations. Savimbi's forces intent was to make the country ungovernable. And to do this, they engaged in a reign of terror, murder, and destruction. They attacked and destroyed cooperative farms and forcibly recruited villagers to serve as porters, servants, farmers, and soldiers in the UNITA cause.

For its part, the MPLA considered almost any Ovimbundu person to be a potential supporter of UNITA. This thinking led to mass arrests and confinement for thousands of Ovimbundu peasants in camps that bore a striking resemblance to the fenced-in, prison-like strategic hamlets of the U.S. war in Vietnam. Thus, UNITA was not always required to forcibly recruit new soldiers; MPLA tactics did much of this work.

Nor did war weariness encourage any of the warring parties to scale back their operations. Indeed, the year 1986 represented a watershed in the war, as UNITA, the MPLA, and their respective allies prepared for what they all saw as the decisive showdown in the now almost decade-long conflict. The flood burst the following year in the great land battles of Mavinga and Cuito Cuanavale, the largest military engagements in the history of sub-Saharan Africa.

The precipitating event, typically, was the result of the MPLA's military edge over UNITA. Having installed air defense systems capable of keeping the South African air force out of Angolan skies, the MPLA had been ruthlessly tracking down and bombing UNITA forces. Fearing defeat, Savimbi appealed to Pretoria which then launched a massive 10,000-man assault first on the town Mavinga, then on the fortified city of Cuito late in 1987. With supplies running low, the MPLA turned to its patron, Cuba, which came to its aid with some 50,000 troops. A successful Cuban-MPLA assault on the SADF's rear placed the South Africans in dire straits, pummeled by the Angolan air force and unable to retreat. Fearful of a mass surrender, and facing increasing protests at home, Pretoria agreed to pull out of Angola and sit down to negotiate an end to its war in Angola.

The End of the War

The defeat was not just a watershed moment in Angolan history, but also for South Africa itself. Many students of apartheid believe that the Angolan defeat represented a critical blow to both the "total strategy" policy and the Botha administration. Within two years

UNITA guerrillas armed with rocket-propelled grenades defending the Mavinga region in southeastern Angola, January 1990. (*Associated Press/Wide World*)

of the Cuito defeat, a new and more conciliatory South African government under F. W. de Klerk had legalized the African National Congress (ANC) and set the country on the road to racial reconciliation. South Africa also agreed to free Namibia before the Cubans pulled out of Angola, one of the sticking points in earlier negotiations. Indeed, Namibia held elections in 1989 and 1990, leading to independence and the victory of SWAPO as the country's ruling party. Cuba lived up to its word and pulled its troops out of Angola by the May 1991 deadline in the accords, which were signed in New York in 1988.

Savimbi was distraught by these developments, and by the knowledge that the Reagan administration was coming to an end. But with the election of George Bush, direc-

tor of the CIA during that agency's earlier foray into Angola in 1975, Savimbi was assured of American support, since the congressional act banning aid to the parties in the Angola conflict had expired in 1986.

In 1989 and 1990, both the war and negotiations to end the war sputtered on. The U.S. government, taking up the slack left by the departing South Africans, pumped millions into UNITA coffers, making biweekly flights to UNITA's headquarters at Jamba, in southeastern Angola, from bases in Zaire. And despite its ongoing collapse, as well as the scheduled departure of their Cuban allies, the Soviet Union did the same for the MPLA government, not only providing much-needed weapons, but rescheduling some $2 billion in loans owed to Moscow.

Still, both the military and the political situations had changed dramatically since the signing of the New York Accords. Gone were the days of major land battles. Instead, the war returned to the course it had taken in the early 1980s, in which the MPLA and UNITA engaged in guerrilla attacks and counter-attacks, with the civilian population caught in the middle. Meanwhile, the departure of the Cubans and South Africans had pulled the ideological rug out from under the feet of both parties to the conflict. With Havana gone and the cold war ebbing, Savimbi could no longer portray himself as the bulwark against the spread of communism in southern Africa. And with Pretoria's withdrawal, the MPLA lost its most compelling rationale for all-out war against UNITA. Thus, both sides were more willing to negotiate, even if talks served as a cover for their continuing efforts to settle their struggle for power on the battlefield.

In June 1989, Zairean dictator Mobutu Sese Seko invited both sides to talk at his presidential compound in Gbadolite. Mobutu, however, proved himself a disingenuous intermediary, even if his less-than-covert aid to UNITA is discounted, by promising mutually exclusive things to the MPLA and UNITA, telling one or the other that Savimbi would either go into exile or be guaranteed a role in a government of national reconciliation. Not surprisingly, the talks went nowhere and both sides dug in their heels. Many in Luanda felt that Savimbi had been South Africa's puppet and, with aid from Pretoria drying up, he could be easily defeated. For his part, Savimbi ruthlessly purged his ranks of pro-conciliatory elements, such as his chief lieutenant Tito Chingunji.

Meanwhile, UNITA was coming under increasing fire from human rights organizations, who accused it, among other things, of using food relief as a weapon. That is to say, since 1990, it had blocked U.N. convoys from delivering much-needed foodstuffs to Angolan peasants, who were suffering both from disruptions caused by the war and from the extended drought that hit southern Africa in the late 1980s and early 1990s.

As 1990 drew to a close, both the war and the talking—the latter, this time, under the aegis of the Portuguese—accelerated. In December, the MPLA launched its long-expected assault on Jamba. But instead of defending his headquarters, Savimbi outflanked the government forces and took his army to the north and east. It was a clever tactical move. Without the support of the SADF, Savimbi knew he could not beat the MPLA in a head-on conflict. Instead, he adopted a more mobile strategy, employing hit-and-run tactics. In addition, he sought to entrench himself in the diamond-mining areas near the country's northeastern frontier with Zaire, thereby assuring himself of a steady source of revenues and access to U.S. arms.

By spring 1991, the war had again stalemated, with neither side able to deliver the knock-out blow against the other. This situation, however, benefited Savimbi who, by the oldest rule of guerrilla warfare, simply had to survive in order to win, which is exactly the way he liked it. The UNITA leader had always made it clear that he did not like to negotiate from a position of weakness. In May, the two sides finally signed onto a deal that seemed to promise an end to hostilities. Under the so-called Bicesse Accords, named after the Portuguese resort town where they were signed, both sides agreed to an in-place ceasefire within one month, a U.N.-monitored election and demobilization of both forces, a joint commission to draw up a new constitution—overseen by the three Bicesse guarantors: the Soviet Union, the United States, and Portugal—and an integrated 50,000-man army.

The treaty could not have come a moment sooner. In the fifteen years since independence, war had engulfed the country and brought appalling losses in its wake. Some 100,000 Angolans had died in battle, while another 700,000 died from disease and malnutrition directly related to the war. Approximately 30 percent of the nation's 10 million citizens had been displaced and over 6 million landmines laid, leaving Angola—alongside Cambodia—as a world leader in amputees. It is estimated that between them, the MPLA and UNITA spent $10 billion prosecuting the war, with a further $2 billion pumped in by both the Soviet Union and South Africa, and with several hundred million provided by the United States. Cuba had committed no less than 100,000 troops over that same period of time. It was, by all accounts, the bloodiest war in the history of southern Africa.

The Participants

Despite its claims to being the most inclusive of Angola's three major political movements of the pre-independence period, the MPLA had a leadership largely composed of urban intellectuals. Both Neto and Jose Eduardo dos Santos—who led the MPLA from its inception in 1956 through today—hold advanced degrees. A further contradiction in the makeup of the party is its factionalism. While the leaders share similar backgrounds, the infighting among them has often been intense. Both Daniel Chipenda and Nito Alves, among the leading figures in the movement

before independence, were ruthlessly purged when their radical politics ran afoul of the bureaucratic and centralized dictates of Neto and dos Santos.

The MPLA has been heavily criticized on several counts, and not just by supporters of UNITA. First, its urban leadership, many say, has failed to understand the needs of the vast majority of Angolans who remain in the countryside. Its push to communalize holdings offended many tradition-bound farmers, while its support of purchasing boards run by local strongmen seemed too akin to Portuguese practices. Finally, its army—often forcibly recruited, poorly trained, and underpaid—tended to act like an army of occupation rather than as a defense against rebel attacks.

In several ways, UNITA has been the mirror opposite of the MPLA. Where the MPLA liked to portray itself as an inclusive party representing all Angolans, Savimbi did little to dispute the charges that UNITA was nothing more than an Ovimbundu political and military front. Yet while the MPLA leadership remained in Luanda, almost entirely out of touch with the Angolan peasantry, Savimbi remained in the bush, and sought to retain a close rapport with the peasant farmers in his area of control.

At the same time, however, UNITA has largely been a creation and tool of Savimbi's own ideological thinking and his abundant ambition. Savimbi has been a very effective military and political leader, resurrecting an almost totally destroyed or outnumbered force on at least two occasions through his ruthless and charismatic leadership. A chameleon-like political figure, Savimbi has espoused a cross-section of doctrines and won accolades from an odd cross-section of admirers that, over the years, has included such disparate figures as Ronald Reagan and Mao Zedong.

Issues and Tactics

Like many civil conflicts, the post-independence war in Angola was sparked by one set of issues but became bogged down in other disagreements as it continued on for fifteen years. As a self-proclaimed Marxist-Leninist organization, the MPLA instituted a bureaucratic centralized state, with forced communalization of the countryside, state-run agricultural purchasing boards, single-party politics, and a repressive political apparatus. In essence, the MPLA tried to create a Soviet-bloc–style state in a country whose economy, outside of a few key sectors, was dominated by subsistence farmers.

This is what Savimbi and UNITA said they were fighting against. Savimbi made it clear that he believed that a free market economy and a non-intrusive state were what Angolans wanted and needed. His rhetoric included frequent references to the use of Angolans as guinea pigs in a misguided experiment to impose a command-style economy on a people with a free enterprise tradition. But his chameleon-like ways often made his criticisms seem suspect. Having once trained in mainland China, Savimbi began his career as a Maoist believer in peasant revolution. When the cold war heated up, he changed his tune, emphasizing his anti-communist credentials. And when the cold war ended, he renewed himself once again, this time as a defender of democracy.

As the war continued, however, new issues came to the fore. Most important among these was foreign involvement. By appealing for aid from South Africa, Savimbi lost a great deal of credibility with the Angolan people and leaders throughout Africa. At the same time, the MPLA constantly charged that UNITA was a mere tool of reactionary white regimes, in both Pretoria and Washington, determined to prevent the establishment of a truly revolutionary state in southern Africa. UNITA countered with charges that the MPLA was little more than a tool of Soviet expansionists and their Cuban allies.

Because of its length, intensity, and wide array of outside interests, the MPLA war with UNITA saw virtually every tactic of modern warfare employed during the fifteen years from independence to ceasefire. This included guerrilla warfare in the bush as well as house-to-house urban fighting. There were great land battles and lengthy sieges. Aside from the massive amount of weaponry employed, the only constant during the war was the suffering of the civilian population caught in the middle.

Both sides also engaged in egregious human rights violations, not as a by-product of the war but as a conscious tactic to win. Aiming to overthrow the MPLA government, UNITA tried to undermine the government's writ in the countryside by destroying infrastructure and murdering civilians, both tactics aimed at showing the peasantry that the government could not effectively defend them. As for the MPLA's forces, their mission to uproot a largely Ovimbundu army in Ovimbundu territory led to a military mindset in which every Ovimbundu-speaking person was a potential enemy.

Negotiations

The long post-independence war between the MPLA and UNITA saw no fewer than four separate attempts to find a negotiated settlement. The first were the 1984 Lusaka Accords.

A complete failure, the accords were meant to disengage South African, Cuban, and Angolan forces in the southern part of the country. They lasted less than six months, when the MPLA government discovered that both South Africa and UNITA were engaging in illegal sabotage. The second set of negotiations in 1988 led to the only permanently successful agreement of the war. With the New York Accords, both South Africa and Cuba agreed to pull their forces out of Namibia and Angola, respectively, with the former country being granted independence. Both Cuba and South Africa lived up to the letter and spirit of the accords in full.

The final two sets of negotiations—those conducted under Zairean aegis in 1989 and those held in Portugal in 1991—concerned the two Angolan antagonists. The Zairean talks utterly failed, undermined by the mutually exclusive promises Mobutu made to each side. The Bicesse Accords of 1991—with the United States, the Soviet Union, and Portugal as guarantors—was nominally more successful, though it too would prove temporary. With its strict deadline and demobilization deadlines, the Bicesse Accords did not allow enough time for the tensions between the two sides—built up over fifteen years of bitter and bloody fighting—to subside sufficiently to conduct such delicate procedures. They too would break down, leading to a second and even fiercer war between the MPLA and UNITA.

James Ciment

See also: Angola: War of National Liberation, 1961–1974; Angola: Second War with UNITA, 1992–1998; Mozambique: Renamo War, 1976–1992; South Africa: Anti-Apartheid Struggle, 1948–1990; Zimbabwe: Struggle for Majority Rule, 1965–1980.

Bibliography

Bridgland, Fred. *Jonas Savimbi: A Key to Africa.* Edinburgh: Mainstream, 1986.

Ciment, James. *Angola and Mozambique: Postcolonial Wars in Southern Africa.* New York: Facts on File, 1997.

Minter, William. *Apartheid's Contras: An Inquiry into the Roots of War in Angola and Mozambique.* London: Zed Books, 1994.

Ohlson, Thomas, and Stephen Stedman. *The New Is Not Yet Born: Conflict Resolution in Southern Africa.* Washington: Brookings Institution, 1994.

Saul, John. *Recolonization and Resistance in Southern Africa in the 1990s.* Trenton, NJ: Africa World Press, 1993.

Seidman, Ann. *The Roots of Crisis in Southern Africa.* Trenton, NJ: Africa World Press, 1985.

Spikes, Daniel. *Angola and the Politics of Intervention.* Jefferson, NC: McFarland, 1993.

Vines, Alex. *Angola and Mozambique: The Aftermath of Conflict.* Washington: Research Institute for the Study of Conflict and Terrorism, 1995.

ANGOLA:
Second War with UNITA, 1992–1998

TYPE OF CONFLICT: Ethnic and religious

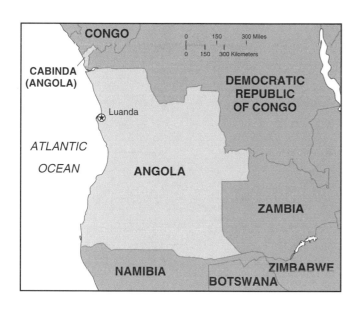

Historical Background

With the Bicesse Accords of May 1991, the first post-independence war between the Popular Movement for the Liberation of Angola (MPLA) government in Angola and the U.S.-supported rebel forces of the National Union for the Total Independence of Angola (UNITA) came to a gradual end, though sporadic fighting between the two groups continued through 1992. Under the Bicesse Accords, named after the Portuguese resort town where the accords were signed, both sides agreed to the following: an in-place ceasefire within one month, national elec-

tions by September 1992, and the demobilization of both forces and their integration into a 50,000-man national military force by the same time. A multinational U.N. force was supposed to monitor all these activities.

The problems began here. The United Nations committed neither the money, the personnel, nor guidance in the complicated and sensitive procedures required. First, the United Nations budgeted about $130 million and dispatched 500 peacekeepers and election monitors to disengage and demobilize two large and hostile armies scattered over a terrain twice the size of Texas, while simultaneously registering millions of voters, albeit with the help of both government and UNITA officials, and setting up some 6,000 polling stations.

Mistaken assumptions and expectations compounded these massive logistical problems. Like most outside observers, and indeed like most Angolans, the U.N. force by and large expected UNITA leader Jonas Savimbi to win the elections handily, given the rotten shape of the Angolan economy and the widespread criticism U.N. officials were hearing from the Angolan people about the MPLA. Thus, when journalists and human rights activists pointed out the egregious campaign irregularities and intimidation of voters occurring in the zones under UNITA control, the United Nations turned a blind eye, since it expected Savimbi to win anyway. In addition, U.N. peacekeepers largely ignored the fact that only the Angolan army was effectively demobilizing, while UNITA was merely handing over its most out-of-date weapons, keeping its more modern armaments and best-trained men in reserve in bush camps.

The United Nations was not wholly at fault. Fearful of infringements on its sovereignty—a not-surprising attitude given its experience with foreign interference since independence—the MPLA insisted on keeping the U.N. force as small as possible, and giving it as little freedom of action as it could. For example, U.N. monitors could do nothing to stop violations of the Bicesse Accords; they could only take notes and make their reports.

Electoral predictions, however, did not turn out as anyone expected. Instead of awarding a landslide victory to UNITA, Angolan voters—fearing the harsh, ethnically charged rhetoric coming from that camp—chose the MPLA. As campaign graffiti on the walls of Luanda put it: "The MPLA steals; UNITA kills." Voters preferred thieves to murderers and gave the MPLA 129 out of 220 seats in the national assembly. They also opted for MPLA leader Jose dos Santos over Jonas Savimbi as president. UNITA garnered just seventy seats, with the vast majority of its votes coming from areas under its own control.

The troubles began on September 30, 1992, the second and final day of voting. Both sides had suspicions about voter fraud and intimidation. But UNITA was particularly upset at the fact that MPLA-controlled radio and TV announced the government party's victory even before the polls had closed. Adding to the problem was the fact that neither the Angolan parties nor the United Nations had thought much about what would happen after the elections. That is to say, all parties were so concerned with the electoral process itself that they did not concern themselves with questions about what kind of government was going to exist after the elections and what role the opposition would play in that government.

The War

Within days, angry rhetoric had degenerated into violence. As UNITA troops began to drift out of the demobilization camps, others in the south launched their first attack against a government-controlled town in mid-October. At the same time, riots broke out in the capital. Both government troops and civilians began to attack UNITA supporters, ultimately killing over 1,000 of them, including UNITA vice-president Jeremias Chitunda, who was gunned down as he tried to flee the city. Savimbi, meanwhile, fled the provincial capital and Ovimbundu's stronghold of Huambo. His return to the bush portended ominous things, given his past record of regrouping and retaliation.

At first it seemed, Savimbi had made a gross error in judgment. Usually an astute reader of the American political scene, the UNITA leader had banked on support from past patron George Bush, whom he expected to win the American elections that were held just over a month after the Angolan ones. But, of course, Bush lost to Bill Clinton, who made it clear that America was not going to support a relic of the cold war, especially one that apparently refused to play by the rules of the electoral game.

Recent recruits in the Angolan government army, February 1993. *(Associated Press/Wide World)*

Though now lacking a superpower patron, UNITA nevertheless had the advantage over the MPLA on the battlefield, which had effectively demobilized in the months leading up to the election. By the middle of November, UNITA forces were on the offensive, having captured some 57 of Angola's 164 official municipalities, including three provincial capitals, in both the north and the south of the country, as well as the port of Lobito in the south. A brief government offensive stalled in December and Savimbi, sensing the tide was going with UNITA, kept the military pressure on.

Using his diamond resources, mined in his stronghold in the northeast of Angola, Savimbi went on a buying spree in the international arms market, importing, via Zaire, some $100 million in weapons from Israel and the South African homeland of Bophutswana. Caxito, a major hydroelectric station, was captured, leaving the capital of Luanda without electricity and water. But Savimbi's main targets were the central highlands cities of Huambo and Cuito, both of which came under lengthy and bloody sieges through much of 1993. After nearly two months of fighting, both fell to the rebels. A civilian exodus from Huambo, however, could not completely prevent mass executions by UNITA forces, including wounded civilians and soldiers in the town's hospital.

It took some six months for the MPLA forces to get back on their feet, aided by more than $3.5 billion in weapons purchased from oil revenues in late 1993 and early 1994. Reorganized and rearmed, the Angolan army went on the offensive, sweeping UN-

ITA forces off the coast and into the interior. Both Huambo and Cuito came under heavy aerial and artillery bombardment which killed thousands of civilians. Huambo returned to government control in January 1994 and, after months of block-to-block fighting, so did Cuito. With both armies poorly provisioned, soldiers and rebels alike took turns hijacking U.N. food convoys and seizing food drops from the air.

As he had done after his defeat in 1975, Savimbi took the still substantial remnants of his army deep into the Angolan bush, though this time he headquartered himself in the east and northeast of the country, the latter region being the source of his diamond revenues and his access to airfields in Zaire. Despite international sanctions, Savimbi appeared to have few difficulties in securing the weapons he needed on the international arms market and getting them to his troops over the porous border with Zaire. Indeed, the Zairean dictator Mobutu Sese Seko turned a blind eye to planes trans-shipping arms through his country to UNITA. By the end of 1993, when a new round of talks between the MPLA and UNITA began in the Zambian capital of Lusaka, the war seemed to be returning to a familiar stalemate.

Negotiators at Lusaka, under U.N. aegis, were far more careful, patient, and sober than they had been at Bicesse three years earlier. Having learned the lesson the hard way, all sides were willing to take their time in hammering out a set of accords that would work. It took them nearly a year. The Lusaka Accords of November 1994, though similar in content to those of Bicesse, were far more flexible in terms of implementation. Gone were the strict deadlines for demobilization and elections. Instead, all sides agreed to let these processes occur under their own momentum. And this time, the United Nations committed the necessary resources, including over $1 billion and several thousand peacekeepers.

From 1995 to 1998, the United Nations set up demobilization camps throughout the country, though it took well into the latter year before it could declare that the process was nearly complete. In the meantime, there were sporadic armed confrontations between UNITA and the MPLA, as well as several incidents in which U.N. peacekeepers and monitors were attacked, usually by UNITA forces. In March 1998, UNITA officially disbanded as a military force and reorganized itself as a political party, with Savimbi as its leader. As of this writing, a permanent power-sharing arrangement between the MPLA and UNITA had yet to be worked out, though a number of UNITA officials had settled in the capital. Elections had yet to be scheduled. By late 1998, fighting had again broken out between the MPLA and UNITA.

James Ciment

See also: Angola: First War with UNITA, 1975–1992.

Bibliography

Bayer, Tom. *Angola. Presidential and Legislative Elections, September 29–30, 1992. Report on the IFES Observation Mission.* Washington: IFES, 1993.

Human Rights Watch/Africa. *Angola: Arms Trade and Violations of the Laws of War Since the 1992 Elections.* New York: Human Rights Watch/Africa, 1994.

Knudsen, Christine, and I. William Zartman. "The Large Small War in Angola." *Annals of the American Association of Political and Social Sciences* (September 1995).

Pereira, Anthony. "The Neglected Tragedy: The Return to War in Angola." *The Journal of African Studies* (Winter 1994).

ARGENTINA:
Dirty War, 1960s–1970s

TYPE OF CONFLICT: Terrorism

Argentina is a huge country covering 1,073,399 square miles and with a population of approximately 37,000,000. The capital, Buenos Aires, has over 10 million people,

and is also the center of industry and finance. Geographically, Argentina is defined by the huge plains, *pampas,* which support its traditional activities of stock raising, particularly beef cattle and sheep, and wheat growing on huge ranches or *estancias.* The population is almost entirely European, principally of Spanish and Italian descent.

During the colonial period most of Spain's imperial trade was with Mexico, through Vera Cruz, and Peru, via the Isthmus of Panama. In the eighteenth century, Spain liberalized its trade policies, and Argentina's salt beef and leather were shipped to Europe from Buenos Aires, giving the city a European orientation and a culture quite different from the interior, which was ruled by provincial cattlemen, *caudillos,* employing private armies of gauchos and with an economy traditionally linked with Peru.

Historical Background

This distinction between the interior and the port provided the dynamic for much of Argentina's nineteenth-century history. By the 1850s, Buenos Aires established political control over the interior and there was a rush to modernization. Railroads were built, and with the development of the refrigerator ship in the 1870s, an enormous export trade in beef with Europe, particularly England, emerged. Cattlemen, and later, wheat grow-ers and sheep ranchers, owning tens of thousands of acres of land were able to amass huge fortunes. By the turn of the century, Argentina's economy was estimated to be among the top fifteen in the world. Buenos Aires had become a cosmopolitan city of over a million people, and immigrants—principally Italian—were pouring in by the hundreds of thousands, forming a new urban working class, many of whose members espoused Marxism or anarcho-syndicalism.

Politically, Argentina was an oligarchy with a severely restricted suffrage. A growing middle class, organized as the Radical party, protested the system and boycotted the elections until 1916 when universal male suffrage was introduced.

The Radical leader, Hipolito Yrigoyen became president in 1916 and was re-elected in 1928. A master political intriguer and organizer, Yrigoyen unfortunately had no coherent legislative program and was an abominable administrator. When the world depression struck he was at a loss. The country was essentially leaderless and the constitutional political process discredited. At this point two army leaders, Generals Jose Uriburu and Agustin P. Justo, both with close links to the old oligarchy, overthrew the aged Yrigoyen.

Uriburu served briefly as provisional president, and in 1932, Justo was elected for a six-year term. In 1938 Justo imposed a successor, a civilian lawyer named Roberto Ortiz who died in office to be replaced by Ramon Castillo, a notoriously corrupt provincial politician. Although electoral forms had been followed, the existing political system seemed worn out, incapable of dealing either with the economic crisis or the immense social changes arising from the enormous migration of impoverished peasants and small

farmers from the countryside into urban slums.

The Rise and Fall of Peron

As Castillo's term came to an end in 1943 he tried to impose a successor, one Robustiano Patron Costas, a notoriously corrupt politician and an immensely wealthy sugar plantation owner infamous for his atrocious treatment of labor. A young colonel named Juan Domingo Peron organized the Group of United Officers (GOU) with the aim of preventing this. Another set of officers under General Arturo Rawson was also working toward the same end. Together they removed Castillo on June 3, 1932, and established a military government, the first in Argentina's history.

The coup had been carried out in haste, and most of the officers had no goal beyond blocking Patron Costas. The ambitious Peron, though, much influenced by Mussolini, believed the answer to Argentina's future, and his own, was a social revolution based on a military–working-class alliance and took the post of Minister of Labor. A genius at organizing and a master of public relations, Peron overcame traditional labor-military hostility, eliminated Communist and Socialist union leadership, and built a powerful working-class political base.

In 1945 the military government decreed new elections. Peron, who during this period had met and married his second wife, a radio actress named Evita Duarte, became the candidate of a Labor party and Radical coalition. Holding elections was not easy. The United States had identified Peron as the dominant figure in the military government which it disliked tremendously because of its generally pro-Axis neutrality during the war. U.S. Ambassador Spruille Braden mounted an all-out public campaign against Peron's candidacy. Many Argentine conservatives, both in and out of the military, also feared Peron and his underclass constituency. Shortly before the election senior officers arrested him.

As news of his arrest circulated on October 16, hundreds of thousands of common people, the *descamisados* (shirtless ones), walked into the center of Buenos Aires demanding his release. Faced with this demonstration, Peron's opponents gave way.

The presidential campaign featured extraordinary public attacks on Peron by Braden. These backfired, as Peron used the nationalistic slogan, "Braden or Peron." It was the cleanest election in Argentine history, and Peron won with 52 percent of the vote, despite the almost total opposition of the major newspapers.

Once in office, Peron, ably assisted by Evita who quickly emerged as a dynamic political force in her own right, set about creating an authoritarian, personalistic, populist political system. His Peronist party was highly disciplined and instilled with devotion to Peron personally. A new constitution granted the right to vote to women, and Evita organized a Peronist Women's Party that quickly became the second largest political organization in the country. Through the ostensibly private Eva Peron Foundation she managed a highly effective extra-governmental welfare system whose clientele was rabidly loyal to her and Peron. She was also the directing force in the national labor organization, the CGT (Confederacion general de los trabajadores).

The years 1946 to 1948 were flush times economically. Argentina's exports brought in huge quantities of foreign exchange, and the absence of competition from Europe's ruined economies allowed Argentina's industries to flourish. Peron and Evita saw to it that the workers got their fair share of the wealth. Relations with the United States improved, as Washington now saw Peron not as pro-Axis but anti-Communist. In fact, as the United States itself now embraced former Nazis as allies against Moscow it used Argentina as a convenient refuge for useful members of the Hitler regime.

Peron's nationalism led to one major economic error. It was a matter of pride to recover for Argentina the railway lines and electric power companies owned by Great Britain. Unfortunately, Peron paid inflated prices for outdated and broken-down plants and equipment, which the state then ran at tremendous losses. All this contributed to the end of the economic boom in 1949 and a rise in inflation that largely destroyed the value of the wage increases workers had received after 1946.

Elections were scheduled for 1951, and Evita by genuine popular demand was persuaded to run for vice president. The elections produced a 61 percent vote for them. However, Evita was already dying of cancer, barely surviving until inauguration day.

Peron failed to understand how the growing cult of Evita, in which she was compared to the Virgin Mary, offended the Catholic Church and outraged conservative Catholic laymen. Moreover, he upset nationalist sentiment when he agreed to allow U.S. oil companies to operate in Argentina. It did not help his standing with the military or the upper classes that he took a teenage mistress, Nelly Rivas, and zoomed around Buenos Aires on his motorcycle.

In June 1955 a crowd of Catholic fanatics ran the Vatican flag up over the Congress building, crying "Death to Evita" and destroying her memorials. Peron ordered two bishops into exile and, in turn, was excommunicated. Admiral Toranzo Calderon, who had been plotting a coup, launched a naval air strike and a marine assault on the Presidential Palace, killing over 200 people. The next day, despite Peron's call for calm, Peronista mobs took their revenge by burning the cathedral and a dozen other churches. Tension continued, and in September, army units under General Eduardo Lonardi joined Admiral Isaac Rojas in a combined attack against troops loyal to Peron. Rojas's cruisers shelled oil storage facilities and threatened to destroy the main oil refinery if Peron did not step down. On September 20 he took asylum in the Paraguayan embassy.

Peron's Exile

Peron's descamisados had called for weapons to defeat the coup, and loyal army units were heading for Buenos Aires when he agreed to resign. His reasoning was that he did not want to submit the country to civil war and revolution. However, many of the Peronist rank and file began to organize for an underground struggle against the new military rulers.

General Pedro Aramburu succeeded Lonardi, Peron's successor, as president in November, initiating a wave of repression. Congress was closed and all the Peronist deputies arrested on charges of treason. The memorials to Evita were destroyed, and her embalmed body was secretly taken out of the country and reburied in Italy. The trade union political organizations were disbanded. In June 1956 a retired Peronist general, Juan Jose Valle, tried to organize an uprising. It failed, but Aramburu shocked the country by sending twenty-seven of the participants before a firing squad, something previously unheard of in Argentina.

Despite all this, the Peronists remained the largest political force in the country. This inspired Arturo Frondizi, leader of one branch of the Radical party, to seek Peronist backing for his election in 1958. However, his efforts to work with the Peronists resulted in his ouster by another military coup in 1962.

In the meantime, the Peronists, denied open participation, used tactics of resistance—protests and industrial sabotage. Participants formed a left wing of *peronismo*, student groups and union *combativos*, who united with the remnants of the old marxist left and prepared for revolution as the only way to bring back Peron and create a new political order they called the "justicialist" state. Peron, who eventually settled in Spain with his third wife, Isabel (Maria Estela Martinez), was aware of these activities and encouraged them to the extent that they might help his return. The resistance became an essentially messianic movement believing simply that Peron was the answer to every problem.

Elections in 1963 produced another minority president, Arturo Illia. In June 1965 with the country still politically paralyzed, the army moved again, establishing an openly military government that was to stay in power for at least fifteen years in order to completely remake Argentina as a moral society based on pre–Vatican II Catholic values.

Beginning of Violence

Unfortunately for the new president, General Juan Carlos Ongania, the appeal to Catholic values came at a time when the Latin American Church was moving toward the left, even admitting that armed revolution might be necessary to correct deep-rooted social injustice. The combination of Catholic Action and the emerging underground Peronist

Following the overthrow of the government of Isabel Peron in March 1976, the military patrols the streets of Argentina's capital, Buenos Aires. *(Associated Press/Wide World)*

Revolutionary Movement (MRP) was to prove explosive. In the late 1960s various groups, using such names as the Peronista Armed Forces (FAP) and the Revolutionary Army of the People (ERP), with roots in the old Trotskyite movement and the Descamisado Command, originating in the Christian Democratic youth movement, appeared. In 1968, Mario Fermenich, a young leader of the social movement Catholic Action, organized the most important of the armed revolutionary groups, the Montaneros. As the resistance grew during the next few years the various groups coalesced under the general leadership of the FAP.

At first these were largely spontaneous movements of young people responding to Ongania's assaults on the universities, regarded as hotbeds of subversion and immorality. On July 29, 1966, the "night of the long batons," police and military forces invaded campuses all over the country, beating and arresting students and faculty members. By May 1969, a time of student unrest throughout the world, Argentine students were marching and demonstrating. In Cordoba, on May 29, students joined workers at the local Renault factory protesting layoffs. There was rioting and destruction of property. Then Ongania sent the army in. Fourteen demonstrators were killed. The military government closed the university and court-martialed the rioters. This action, known as the *cordobazo*, did much to discredit the military rulers and help justify armed action against them.

Ongania was forced to resign, but his successors were just as heavyhanded. In 1970, there was a sitdown strike at the Fiat plant in Cordoba. Again the military moved in. The result was 2 deaths, 30 injuries, and over 300 arrested.

The growing underground armed opposition was not idle, either. When Nelson Rockefeller, visited Buenos Aires in June 1969, members of the FAR burned fifteen Mini-Max stores, part of a Rockefeller-owned grocery chain. On June 30, a hit squad from the Descamisado Command murdered Agusto Vandor, a CGT official accused of cooperating with the military. In May 1970, two Montaneros, disguised as military officers, came to the Buenos Aires apartment of General Arumburu, who was blamed for taking the body of Eva Peron; they captured and executed him. In the next two months, eluding the 22,000 troops sent to capture them, the Montaneros carried out two more spectacular actions. In one they took over the town of La Calera, robbing the bank and capturing the weapons in the police station. However, two were captured, and the information they supplied caused the group to return to basically political action. In fact, this was the beginning of successful military intelligence penetration of the guerrilla forces resulting eventually in effective manipulation of those forces for political reasons.

Throughout the late 1960s the pace of guerrilla action quickened. In 1969 there were a reported 114 armed actions; there were 434 in 1970, and 654 in 1971. The political impact was heightened by the fact that the majority of members of the groups came from middle- and upper-class families, including children of military officers. Public opinion polls taken at the time showed half the Argentine people believed armed revolutionary action was justified and that a clear majority of the middle and upper classes supported that view.

Peron Returns to More Violence

In March 1971 another strike in Cordoba was bloodily put down, causing another military president to resign and another general, this time Alejandro Lanusse, to take his place. Lanusse concluded that the only way to end the violence was to bring Peron back and restore the alliance between the right-wing Peronists and the military. He began secret negotiations with him in Madrid and returned Evita's mummified body—which had been concealed in an Italian cemetery—to Peron as a sign of good faith.

At the same time, Lanusse, relying on military intelligence penetration, began to hurt the guerrilla organizations severely. In 1972 there were only 352 armed actions, and a significant number of guerrillas were killed and captured. Special prisons were established for prisoners where they were subjected to physical and psychological torture to provide information. On August 17, 1972, the guerrillas responded by staging a raid on the Rawson Maximum Security Prison and rescuing 100 prisoners. A hijacked plane was waiting at a nearby airfield to transport them to Chile, but before all the escapees could board, security forces moved in. Six of the leaders were able to take off. Nineteen others were recaptured and killed "trying to escape." The killings were part of a deliberate campaign of ruthlessness designed to intimidate not only the guerrillas, but all who might be thinking of joining them. Within the next few weeks guerrillas killed the chairman of the Joint Chiefs of Staff and two ranking military intelligence generals in reprisal.

While Peron pretended to support the armed resistance, he and Lanusse quietly worked out a political deal. The Peronist parties could run in elections scheduled for March 1973 and Peron could return. Peron would claim that the goal of the armed resistance had been achieved and would work with the military to suppress any further guerrilla action.

For the elections, the Peronists united to form the Justicialist Liberation Front and won convincingly. Their candidate, Hector Campora, took office in May and surprised both Peron and Lanusse by aligning himself with the Peronist's so-called Revolutionary Tendency party. He established diplomatic relations with Cuba, North Vietnam, and North Korea, and closed down the federal police intelligence office and ordered its files destroyed. He then pardoned all 371 guerrilla prisoners then in government custody. Lanusse and the military made no objection, simply waiting for Peron, who returned to Argentina on June 20.

A crowd of several million people gathered at Buenos Aires Ezeiza Airport. Security, for some reason, was handled not by the police but by Peronist security forces controlled by a right-wing Colonel Jorge Osinde. As left-wing Peronist columns carrying their banners approached the highway overpass from which Peron was to speak, Osinde ordered them back, and when they kept coming had his men open fire. Before it was over perhaps 200 had been killed and thousands wounded. Peron landed elsewhere and the next day addressed the nation, condemning the left for causing the violence and stressing the need for national discipline and public order.

In a strange and non-constitutional procedure Campora and his vice president resigned in favor of Peron and, as his vice president, Isabel. Isabel Peron had no political experience and was of only modest intelligence. Since Peron was 78 years old and in poor health, this should have caused con-

cern. However, the national rapture at the return of Peron overcame everything else. Isabel was completely controlled by the man she had made Peron's private secretary, Jose Lopez Rega, a believer in the occult. Lopez Rega was also a member of the notorious P-2 Masonic Lodge in Milan, Italy, a center of far-right-wing activity connected with both Italian and U.S. intelligence agencies. One of P-2's directors, Licio Gelli, came to Argentina shortly after Peron returned and helped Lopez Rega organize the Argentine Anti-Communist Alliance (AAA), a death squad largely made up of off-duty policemen and covertly financed by the government.

The true dirty war in Argentina began after Peron's May Day speech in 1974. The left-wing Peronists began chanting that if Evita were alive she would be with them. Peron lost his temper, accused them of being traitors in the pay of foreign powers and promised to eliminate them. With that the guerrillas and their sympathizers, some 60,000 strong, marched out of the plaza, their illusions about Peron now completely destroyed, and resolved to renew the armed struggle.

The Dirty War

Within two months Peron was dead. Isabel was president, but Lopez Rega, holding the office of social welfare minister, was actually in control. Peron, before he died, had suppressed the publications of the left Peronist groups, dismissed governors believed to be tolerant of them, and issued harsh new laws against terrorism. The AAA went into action. During the first two weeks of 1974 there were twelve assassinations, and two dozen left-wing Peronist offices were destroyed.

The Montaneros and other groups mobilized. By the end of 1973 they had an estimated 5,000 men and women in arms. Between 1973 and 1975 they financed themselves with a series of kidnappings for ransom that netted an astonishing $105 million.

While the AAA could kill leftists—by 1976 a political assassination was reported every five hours—it could not destroy the main guerrilla forces. The army, which under Lanusse had hoped that the return of Peron would lead to peace, now saw the situation as worse than it had been in 1973. On March 25, General Jorge Videla formed a junta that arrested Isabel—and established yet another military government, which began what was euphemistically called the Process of National Reorganization.

This time the military leadership was determined to eliminate not only those in arms but all those who supported them either materially or intellectually and to use every means at their disposal without regard to law. The AAA now came under direct and open military control. By the end of 1976 an average of fifteen people a day "disappeared." Secret prisons were established, and torture was routinized. The most notorious of detention centers was the Naval Mechanics School. Victims were buried in mass graves or simply thrown out of airplanes, alive or dead, into the Atlantic. The idea, very simply, was to destroy absolutely and pitilessly, the social base on which the guerrillas depended.

On the purely military front, the Montaneros—which by 1976 had incorporated almost all the other armed factions—engaged in some spectacular battles with regular army units. However, they paid a heavy price; 100 were killed in a single assault on the Monte Chingolo barracks near Buenos Aires in December 1975. This was their last major offensive military action. One guerrilla survivor estimated that of the 5,000 mobilized in 1975, 4,000 died during the next year. According to one theory, the Argentine army had placed many of its own operatives in guerrilla leadership positions, inducing the Montaneros, to carry out suicidal attacks and also, by continuing their guerrilla activity, to justify the continuation of military rule.

The End of the War

By 1979 the Argentine politico-military struggle that had begun with the emergence of Juan Peron and the GOU in 1942 was essentially over. Peron himself, and his legend, had been almost totally discredited except among a few faithful labor diehards. The messianic hopes he had raised for creating a new, socially just and vital Argentina had been dashed. However, in the process of defeating peronismo, the victors—the military and the economic elites—had established a terrorist regime, and even though the majority of Argentines had acquiesced in its establishment or even supported it, public morale was destroyed. Almost 2 million Argentines emigrated during the 1960s and 1970s.

Nor had the generals been able to resolve the economic malaise that had turned Argentina into a third-world country. Videla's economics minister, Jose de la Hoz, a strict conservative, succeeded in bringing inflation under control in 1976 and 1977, but by 1980 the economy was once again on the point of collapse.

There was growing public demand for an accounting of the 9,000 to 30,000 who had disappeared and discontent with the continuing suppression of civil and human rights. Something had to be done to restore the prestige of the military government and the honor of an army now associated with the perpetration of atrocities. Likewise something had to be done to take people's minds off the dreadful state of the economy. Thus, under the third military president directing the Process of National Reorganization, Leopoldo Galtieri, the decision was made to invade the British-held Falkland Islands, territory long claimed by Argentina.

The resounding defeat suffered by the Argentine armed forces in June 1982 brought the whole structure crashing down. Civil government was restored, but the process of accounting for the victims of the dirty war and dealing with its perpetrators continues to dog Argentina to the present.

David MacMichael

See also: Argentina: Falklands/Malvinas War, 1982.

Bibliography

Andersen, Martin Edward. *Dossier Secreto: Argentina's Desaparecidos and the Myth of the "Dirty War."* Boulder, CO: Westview Press, 1993.

Crassweiler, Robert. *Peron and the Enigmas of Argentina.* New York: Norton, 1987.

Moyano, Mario Jose. *Argentina's Lost Patrol: Armed Struggle 1969–1979.* New Haven: Yale University Press, 1995.

Poneman, Daniel. *Argentina: Democracy on Trial.* New York: Paragon, 1987.

ARGENTINA: Falklands/Malvinas War, 1982

TYPE OF CONFLICT: Invasions and border disputes
PARTICIPANT: United Kingdom

The Falkland Islands (as they are called by the United Kingdom), or the Malvinas (as they are called by Argentina), are a group of approximately two hundred islands in the South Atlantic about 400 miles northeast of Tierra del Fuego, the southern tip of South America. The possession of the islands has been disputed historically by England and Argentina. There are two main islands, East Falkland and West Falkland, and the whole group has an area of about 4,700 square miles. The population is about 5,000, mostly people of Scotch or Welsh descent. The capital, Port Stanley, is on the south coast of East Falkland.

The only economic activity on the treeless islands is sheep raising. The Falkland Islands Company owns most of the grazing land, and the majority of islanders are employees of the company.

Historical Background

Which European explorer first discovered the barren and unpopulated islands is a matter of historical dispute. During the sixteenth, seventeenth, and eighteenth centuries, Spain, France, and England all claimed them, principally for their presumed strategic situation guarding the approaches to Cape Horn and the Straits of Magellan. From time to time, each would establish a colony or a small naval station, only to abandon it. A British navy captain named the islands Falklands for the then commissioner of the admiralty in 1690; French settlers called them the Malouines, after St. Malo in France. The Spanish, after purchasing the islands from France in 1767, used a Spanish version of the French name—Malvinas. Despite the sale, the British still maintained their claim.

After declaring independence from Spain in 1816, Argentina promptly declared the Malvinas their territory and in 1823 established a settlement there to exploit the fisheries. In 1831 the Argentine governor seized two American sealing vessels and charged their captains with poaching. In retaliation, the USS *Lexington,* which was nearby, bombarded the settlement, razing it to the ground, they took all the inhabitants prisoner and declared that the United States recognized no government there. A year later, as Argentina was in the process of rebuilding the settlement as a penal colony, a British naval ship arrived, ordered the Argentines off, and took possession for England. Argentina protested in vain, beginning an argument that was to last for 150 years.

The Effort for a Diplomatic Solution

In the years after World War II, as the United Kingdom divested itself of its empire, Argentina pressed its case in the United Nations and in direct negotiation with England. The Falklands, 8,000 miles from London and essentially an enormous sheep ranch, were of insignificant strategic or economic value to the British government, and certainly of little concern to the British public. For Argentina,

however, the Malvinas were, however irrationally, a matter of enormous national interest. The British seizure of the islands was cited in school textbooks as an intolerable insult to national pride and, especially in the 1930s and during World War II, when resentment of British economic dealings with Argentina was a continuing theme in the country. Recovery of the islands became an important and highly emotional goal.

England made it clear during negotiations with Argentina that it was prepared to relinquish the territory. The problem was the people living in the islands. They were all British subjects—there was no indigenous population—and objected strenuously to any idea of their becoming Argentine citizens. The directors of the Falklands Company also were opposed to coming under Argentine control and maintained a strong political lobby in England. Nor was the Argentine cause helped in England during the 1970s, when Argentina's military government became an international pariah because of its suppression of dissidence through state terror.

However, in 1980, the government of General Roberto Eduardo Viola stepped up the campaign for recovery of the islands. He and his successor, General Leopoldo Galtieri, believed conditions favored them. Argentina had become the favorite Latin American ally of the Reagan administration in the United States. It was providing military trainers and other support for U.S.-backed contra rebels attacking the Sandinista government in Nicaragua. In addition, Argentina was a key factor in U.S. global strategy. There were plans for a combined Argentine–South African–U.S. naval force to control the "South Atlantic Narrows"—the area between Cape Horn and the Cape of Good Hope. Moreover, Argentina had a powerful friend in Jeane Kirkpatrick, the new U.S. ambassador to the

United Nations, who made no secret of her preference for strong authoritarian regimes. Under the circumstances, Galtieri convinced himself that the United States would pressure England to cede the islands or, if Argentina resorted to force, that Washington, owing Buenos Aires favors for Argentine assistance in Central America and mindful that much of the rest of Latin America was opposed to U.S. policy in Central America— which was seen as Yankee intervention— would side with Argentina. There was also the Monroe Doctrine to consider, with which the United States had pronounced itself opposed to European colonial holdings in the Americas. A bonus for Argentina would be its own restoration to good graces in Latin America, where many disliked not only its repressive domestic policies but also its intervention, with and without U.S. participation, in neighboring countries.

There was one other factor pushing the Argentine military government to take drastic action in the Malvinas. The generals knew they had little support among the Argentine people and that they controlled only through fear. In addition, the economy had collapsed in the late 1970s. Inflation was running at 150 percent a year, and unemployment was high and growing. Playing the patriotic card, they believed, would rally the people behind them, make them forget their economic problems, and restore the prestige of the armed forces. Moreover, Argentina had just suffered a significant diplomatic setback when international arbitration had ruled against it in its dispute with Chile over the Beagle Islands in the Strait of Magellan, a dispute that had almost escalated into war. This recent failure made a victory in the Falklands all the more necessary, and in fact influenced the conduct of the war. Argentina, fearing that Chile might attack while its forces were oc-

cupied in the Falklands, kept some of its best troops near the disputed Beagle Channel to defend against a possible Chilean attack.

The generals were further encouraged by British policy. By 1980, the British government, without real interest in the Falklands and finding that the maintenance of a government and security and naval forces there, albeit small ones, was an unnecessary expense, was prepared to acknowledge Argentine sovereignty, but to continue to administer the islands under a long-term lease, at the expiration of which Argentina would take full possession. This was a solution that should have pleased everyone: Argentine sovereignty was recognized; the islanders (few of whom owned anything on the islands; they were almost all employees of the Falkland Islands Company) would have twenty-five to fifty years either to adjust to the new situation or to leave; and England would be rid of a nagging controversy that affected important economic interests in Latin America and elsewhere in the third world and held potential for conflict with her most important ally, the United States.

The Argentine Invasion

Argentine navy chief Admiral Jorge Anaya had been particularly unhappy with the resolution of the Beagle Channel matter and was eager for direct action in which the Argentine navy would reap glory. His counterpart in the air force, General Basilio Lami Dozo, had developed a modern force built around missile-firing U.S.-supplied Skyhawk jet fighters and the even more modern French-supplied Mirage. They were armed with the French-built Exocet, considered the best air-to-ground missile in the world. The pilots had been trained in the United States, France, and Israel and were superbly confident. England was 8,000 miles away and had no way to prevent a takeover. Once the seizure had taken place, while London might protest, the odds were that the United Nations would support Argentina—which did have a recognized legal claim—and that the matter would be a fait accompli. A purely military factor in Argentina's favor was that in April the Antarctic winter would arrive in the South Atlantic, something that would make naval and amphibious operations almost impossible, and the British had no operations base in the region. The nearest British possession, now that South Georgia to the southeast had been taken by Argentina, was Ascension Island, a tiny speck of land 4,000 miles north.

Argentine troops landed on the Falkland Islands on April 1, 1982, and seized Port Stanley. They were essentially unopposed by the forty-odd Royal Marines that composed the British security force, although three Argentine commandos were killed when they broke into the British governor's house. A week earlier, Argentine marines had landed on South Georgia, an almost uninhabited island about 800 miles east of the Falklands, where Great Britain maintains an Antarctic research station, ostensibly to protect the salvage operations of an Argentine businessman. With the invasion of the Falklands, the Argentines raised their flag and claimed South Georgia, too. The squad of Royal Marines there put up a futile resistance, killing four of the invaders, downing a helicopter, and damaging an Argentine naval frigate before surrendering.

While the Argentine forces were consolidating their hold on the Falklands and crowds were celebrating the triumph in Buenos Aires, the British government, taken by surprise by the suddenness of the Argentine action, debated a response. Argentine

expectations that Britain would accept the fait accompli were dashed. Both sides in the British parliament were outraged and demanded military action to retake the islands. The foreign minister, Lord Carrington, was forced to resign for failure to foresee the invasion and take effective steps to prevent it. Orders went to the Defense Ministry to prepare the largest military force Britain had deployed since the Suez invasion in 1956.

In the United States, the Reagan administration was torn. President Reagan had a long and inconclusive telephone conversation with Galtieri. U.N. Ambassador Kirkpatrick seemed clearly on the Argentine side when she not only attended a banquet at the Argentine embassy on April 2 but excused her abstention on the U.N. Security Council vote on Resolution 502 (which called on Argentina to withdraw) in a television interview in which she said that because of Argentina's legal claims to the Falklands its landing of troops was not technically an invasion. Secretary of State Alexander Haig, although relying on the Argentines for help in the conduct of U.S. Central American policy and personally friendly with Galtieri, was a former NATO commander and very concerned about adverse effects on relations with Britain if the United States did not back its NATO ally—especially since British resentment over U.S. failure to support it at Suez in 1956 still rankled.

Even while England was assembling its forces for re-taking the Falklands, Haig, accompanied by Assistant Secretary of State for Inter-American Affairs Tom Enders and Ambassador-at-Large Vernon Walters (a former deputy director of central intelligence and a key figure in Latin American operations) flew back and forth between London and Buenos Aires seeking a compromise. British Prime Minister Margaret Thatcher was not

A British paratrooper guards a captured Argentinean soldier, May 23, 1982. *(Associated Press/Wide World)*

inclined to compromise, and if she had, given the public and parliamentary mood, she would have been out of office. In Buenos Aires, a combination of military confidence, particularly on the part of Admiral Anaya and General Lami Dozo, and the patriotic fervor that Galtieri kept stirring up with his public speeches made it impossible for the Argentines even to consider withdrawal or negotiations. If war came, they believed, they would win. The U.S. effort at mediation failed, a diplomatic disaster that caused Haig's resignation as secretary of state.

Still Kirkpatrick argued for a U.S. position of "public neutrality." She was overruled, and the Reagan administration joined Britain in denunciation of Argentine "aggression" and applauded its military effort. It embargoed arms deliveries to Argentina and withdrew its military advisors. (The U.S. air force advisor remained in Buenos Aires and during the fighting helped the Argentines correct problems they were having with U.S.-supplied aircraft.)

The Empire Strikes Back

By April 9, the advance elements of the British task force were already at sea. On April 25 a British Royal Marine unit of 110 men, supported by air strikes and naval gunfire, went ashore in severe winter weather on South Georgia. The Argentine garrison promptly surrendered, and an Argentine submarine caught on the surface was destroyed. There were few casualties on either side.

The news caught the overconfident Argentine military leaders by surprise. Galtieri wanted to accept U.N. Resolution 502 and withdraw. Anaya and Lami Dozo would not hear of it. They argued that if the troops were withdrawn, they would be overthrown by a popular revolution.

The South Georgia operation had relatively little military significance. It was designed as much to boost public morale (and public support for the Thatcher government) in England as to provide a base for operations against the Falklands. On April 28 the real war got under way. The British military command was concerned about the Argentine air threat to their invasion fleet. Raids on Argentine mainland bases were ruled out. This was partly due to the risk of heavy losses but also because the mainland bases were themselves so far from the Falklands that Argentine pilots flying from them would have little fuel left to conduct attacks once they reached the battle area. The primary target, then, was the airfield at Port Stanley. Thus, while the main task force was steaming toward the Falklands, British long-range bombers took off from Ascension Island and, refueling in the air to complete the longest combat flight in history, attacked Port Stanley, severely damaging the airfield.

There was also concern about the Argentine navy. On May 2, the British nuclear-powered submarine HMS *Conqueror*, patrolling off the Argentine coast, spotted the cruiser *Belgrano* and its two destroyer escorts. She put two torpedoes into the *Belgrano*, which went down with the loss of 368 crewmen. The action was controversial because it took place several hundred miles from the Falklands and in or close to the so-called exclusion zone. The British were unapologetic, though, and for all Anaya's bravado, the Argentine fleet did not venture out of port again.

Argentine naval aircraft did, though. On May 4, an Argentine Étandarte, one of the French-supplied attack planes, sank the destroyer HMS *Sheffield*. Argentine morale soared, but in England both public and official determination only increased. In fact, the two naval actions sank not only ships but the last chance to end the fighting by diplomacy.

The U.N. secretary-general, the Peruvian Javier Pérez de Cuéllar, after consulting with Haig, proposed a cease-fire, the mutual withdrawal of forces, U.N. administration of the Falklands/Malvinas with British and Argentine participation, and good-faith negotiations to be completed by the end of 1982. The British were noncommittal, and Argentina, angry over the loss of the *Belgrano* and made overly confident by their sinking of the *Sheffield*, rejected the plan on May 18. Even Jeane Kirkpatrick, who pleaded with her Argentine friends to accept, called the rejection "sheer madness."

Already on May 1, the first British amphibious reconnaissance patrols had gone ashore at the proposed landing site at San Carlos, 65 miles from Port Stanley on the opposite side of East Falkland Island. On May 11 a commando raiding party had destroyed eleven Argentine aircraft on Pebble Island without losing a man. On May 21, after the Argentine rejection of the peace plan, a regiment-sized (3,000-man) British force—principally Royal Marine commandos and paratroopers—landed at San Carlos, meeting very light resistance and losing two helicopters in the process. The next day, Lami Dozo's pilots carried out mass attacks on the British fleet. They sank the destroyer escort HMS *Antrim*, severely damaged HMS *Argonaut*, and would have sunk three other destroyers except that their overage U.S.-supplied bombs failed to explode when they hit their targets. Two days later, another Argentine air attack sank HMS *Antelope*, and the day after that (May 25), Argentine

planes damaged the landing ships *Sir Galahad* and *Sir Lancelot*. They were not done yet. On May 26, they sank the destroyer HMS *Coventry*, killing nineteen British sailors, and the supply ship and reserve aircraft carrier *Atlantic Conveyor*, which was a heavy logistical blow, as it carried ten helicopters that were to have transported the landing force from San Carlos to Port Stanley. The result was that the British troops had to march across the island.

There was momentary panic in London. If the losses continued, and especially if the British flagship, the aircraft carrier HMS *Invincible*, was lost (and there were rumors that it had been), the whole expedition might have to be called off.

The British now began their attack on Port Stanley. Except at Goose Green, there was little resistance from the 10,000 Argentine ground troops. They were ill-trained and poorly equipped for the bitter winter weather. Even at Goose Green, where there were a few hours of stiff resistance, both from artillery and attacks by the Argentine light Pucara close-air-support planes, the issue was never in doubt; over 1,600 demoralized Argentine draftees surrendered to the 450 British attackers.

The British were to suffer further losses from air and missile attacks, though. HMS *Galahad*, previously damaged by a bomb that failed to explode, was transporting Welsh Guardsmen for a landing at Bluff Cove, 10 miles southwest of Port Stanley, when it was hit again; fifty-one British soldiers and sailors died and another forty-six were wounded. The ship was lost, and another landing ship, HMS *Tristram*, was also hit and suffered two dead. The following day, a shore-based Exocet missile hit the destroyer HMS *Glamorgan*, killing thirteen crewmen.

On June 12, the main British force, now consisting largely of regular infantry and Guards battalions, began the advance on Port Stanley from the heights above, captured after some resistance that had taken about thirty British lives. That was the last serious resistance. On June 14, the Argentine commander, General Mario Benjamin Menendez, surrendered his remaining 9,000 demoralized soldiers, and the fighting part of the war was over.

The British victory was an enormous boost for Margaret Thatcher's government. It was also, though, a sobering warning to the major powers about the effect high-technology weapons could have in the hands of third-world countries, and it provided lessons that were later applied in the Gulf War.

The most dramatic result of the war was the total discrediting of the Argentine military and military government. Within a month, the military junta had been overthrown, and angry crowds were threatening to attack the barracks.

David MacMichael

See also: Argentina: Dirty War, 1960s–1970s.

Bibliography

Ethell, Jeffrey, and Alfred Price. *Air War South Atlantic.* New York: Macmillan, 1983.

Hastings, Max, and Simon Jenkins. *The Battle for the Falklands.* New York, London: W.W. Norton, 1983.

London *Sunday Times* Insight Team. *War in the Falklands: The Full Story.* London: Times Publishing Company, 1982.

ARMENIA: Nagorno-Karabakh Conflict, 1990s

TYPE OF CONFLICT: Ethnic and religious; Invasions and border disputes
PARTICIPANT: Azerbaijan

The breakup of the Soviet Union in 1991 generated many demands for self-determination. Many of the fifteen republics in the Soviet Union had territorial boundaries that were drawn in an arbitrary fashion. Soviet dictator Josef Stalin redrew boundaries for basically political reasons. He often scattered members of the same ethnic group in different geographical areas. This was part of his policy of divide and rule.

When Mikhail Gorbachev came to power in 1985, he was determined to bring about fundamental changes in the Soviet political system. To achieve his goal of reforms, he instituted the policies of *glasnost* and *perestroika*. The purpose of glasnost was to end the Soviet penchant for secrecy. Gorbachev wanted policies and data to be more transparent than in the past. Perestroika was a policy of economic and political reform. The first major test of glasnost and perestroika occurred in Nagorno-Karabakh.

Historical Background

The hostility between the Christian Armenians and local Muslim peoples in the area dates back hundred of years. That hostility was exacerbated when the Ottoman Empire broke up after World War I. The Turks drove the Armenians out of Eastern Anatolia and thousands were killed. Armenians refer to this episode as "the Genocide."

In 1923, Stalin made Nagorno-Karabakh an autonomous region within the Azerbaijan Republic. The population of Azerbaijan is predominantly Muslim. The population of Nagorno-Karabakh is predominantly Christian. The Christians outnumber the Muslims by about four to one. In 1988, the Armenians in Nagorno-Karabakh wanted to be incorporated into Armenia, and they began demonstrating to bring this about. The demand for incorporation was complicated by the fact that Nagorno-Karabakh did not share a common border with Armenia.

Gorbachev had a difficult dilemma in dealing with the Armenian demand for self-determination in Nagorno-Karabakh. If he yielded to the Armenian demands, minority groups in other areas would be encouraged to make similar demands. If Gorbachev ordered the military to suppress the uprising, his policies of glasnost and perestroika—his two most important reforms—would be compromised. He also had to contend with the fact that his reforms were opposed by many Soviet leaders. Transparency and democratic freedoms were not characteristic of Soviet rule. Even after the death of Stalin, the Soviet government dealt with demonstrators harshly. Gorbachev's opponents feared that his reforms could lead to the breakup of the Soviet Union. Their fears were justified. By August 1990, thirteen of the fifteen Soviet republics were demanding greater autonomy if not outright independence.

The Conflict Begins

The demonstrations that began in Nagorno-Karabakh in February 1988 turned violent, and one result was a dramatic increase in the number of refugees. Armenians in Azerbaijan fled to Nagorno-Karabakh or to Armenia. The Muslims in Nagorno-Karabakh or Armenia fled to Azerbaijan. More than one million people became refugees. This contributed to the growing violence. Those that fled and lost their homes demanded vengeance.

With the breakup of the Soviet Union in 1991, Azerbaijan and Armenia became independent. The battle for control of Nagorno-Karabakh continued. Initially, the Azerbaijan government proved unable to cope with the insurrection. The Armenians won complete control of Nagorno-Karabakh and succeeded in establishing a corridor from Nagorno-Karabakh to Armenia. By 1994, the Armenians controlled about 20 percent of Azeri territory.

Numerous efforts were made to resolve the problem of Nagorno-Karabakh, but none succeeded. In 1992, the Organization for Security and Cooperation in Europe (OSCE), formerly the Conference for Security and Cooperation in Europe, tried to mediate the conflict, but its members could not reach a consensus on how best to deal with the issue. For a time, the Russian Federation wanted to play the dominant role in the Caucasus to prevent Western nations from encroaching on what the Russians believed to be their sphere of influence The Caucasus consists of three former Soviet republics: Azerbaijan, Armenia, and Georgia. The Azeris do not trust Russia and the distrust was deepened by Russia's support of Armenia in the Nagorno-Karabakh dispute.

In 1994, the OSCE did succeed in establishing a cease-fire, but that was all that could be accomplished. It was difficult to accomplish more because the Armenians and the Azeris approached negotiations from a different perspective. The Armenians were unwilling to accept a step-by-step approach to negotiations. They insisted that the final status of Nagorno-Karabakh must be on the agenda. The Armenians wanted the Azeris to agree to incorporate Nagorno-Karabakh into Armenia. The Azeris were willing to try step-by-step negotiations. They wanted to find some formula to grant Nagorno-Karabakh autonomy while remaining a part of Azer-

Armenian soldiers from Nagorno-Karabakh, 1993. *(Associated Press/Wide World)*

baijan. Negotiations were also difficult because the war lasted six years and many people died in the fighting, instilling much bitterness on both sides.

Consequences of the Conflict

Since gaining independence, Armenia and Russia have enjoyed a good relationship. Relations between Azerbaijan and Russia have been strained. The Azeris are determined, now that they are independent, to remain free of Russia's influence. The government in Baku, the capital of Azerbaijan, will not allow Russian troops or military bases in Azerbaijan. Armenia welcomes the presence of Russian troops. Russian military aid to Armenia was a major factor in defeating the Azeris in Nagorno-Karabakh. In February 1997, Russian officials confirmed that be-

tween 1992 and 1996, there was an unauthorized shipment of $1 billion in arms to Armenia. The arms included tanks, machine guns, and anti-aircraft missiles. Russia also supports Armenia because Azerbaijan is closely aligned with Turkey. In the nineteenth century, Russia and Turkey fought three wars. In 1945, the Soviets made territorial demands on Turkey that were not abandoned until after the death of Stalin in March 1953.

There is one factor that could contribute to a resolution of the conflict between Azerbaijan and Armenia. Azerbaijan has an abundance of oil and natural gas. If Azerbaijan does not politically implode, its economy should eventually prosper. The Azeris have to decide how their oil will reach markets. The least expensive and most efficient way to transport the oil is to build a pipeline from

Azerbaijan through Armenia to Turkey's Mediterranean coast. The possibility of building such a pipeline depends on political conditions in the region. A settlement of the Nagorno-Karabakh dispute would be a major factor in the final decision. The only alternative is to build a pipeline from the Caspian Sea through Georgia rather than Armenia. The Azeris are reluctant to build a pipeline through Georgia in part because of Russia's influence there. Russia has troops stationed in Georgia, and there is a good deal of political unrest.

Armenia has theoretically won the war because Azerbaijan no longer controls Nagorno-Karabakh. The victory has been costly. Armenia's economy is stagnant, and it cannot attract foreign capital because of actual or potential political instability. Turkey has closed its border with Armenia, and so has Azerbaijan. These actions have had a devastating impact on the Armenian economy. Like other ethnic and religious disputes, emotions play a more important role than logic. Any Armenian leader proposing a compromise solution with Azerbaijan would quickly lose political support. Armenian president Levon Ter-Petrossian had to resign in 1998 because he supported a compromise solution. Economic conditions are such that Armenia's population is declining. People are leaving in search of better economic opportunities.

There is no solution to the Nagorno-Karabakh problem that is acceptable to all the parties involved. One factor that makes a solution difficult to achieve is that many actors are involved. A solution to the Nagorno-Karabakh problem would impact Turkey, Georgia, Azerbaijan, Iran, Russia, international banks, and oil companies. The United States and other Western nations have an interest in the region because of oil and the possibility that a conflict could easily escalate. The region remains volatile.

The ethnic, religious, and territorial conflicts in the Caucasus combined with oil may keep this region in turmoil for years to come. On the other hand, a resolution of the conflict could bring prosperity and stability to the whole area.

Kenneth L. Hill

See also: Georgia: Civil War, 1990s.

Bibliography

Curtis, Glen, ed. *Armenia, Azerbaijan, and Georgia: Country Studies.* Washington, DC: Library of Congress, 1995.

Swietochowski, Tadeusz. *Russia and Azerbaijan: A Borderland in Transition.* New York: Columbia University Press, 1995.

BOLIVIA: Revolution, 1952

TYPE OF CONFLICT: Coups, left and right

Bolivia is a landlocked Andean country with an area of 424,164 square miles and a current population of approximately 8 million. Less than 10 percent of the population is white, the rest are mestizos, known in Bolivia as *cholos*, and Indians, which are divided into two main groups, Aymaras and Quechuas. The national territory is divided between the *altiplano*, the Andean highlands where the majority of the population still lives, and the *montana*, forested tropical lowlands leading down into the Amazon. The valleys of the montana, known as *yungas*, are warm and humid and increasingly important to the Bolivian economy for the production of tropical crops and the coca

leaf, used both legally and illegally. The *yungas* increasingly attract settlement from the overcrowded highlands. A third region in far southeastern Bolivia is the *Chaco*, a scrub forest area that Bolivia shares with Paraguay. Bolivia is unusual in having two capital cities. Sucre, the ceremonial capital, is home to the nation's supreme court. The administrative capital, seat of government, is La Paz, which has a population of about 1 million.

Historical Background

In pre-Columbian times a part of the Incan Empire, Bolivia, known as Upper Peru during the colonial period, was ruled from Lima as part of the Spanish vice royalty of Peru. The native Indian highland population, the Aymaras, only recently conquered by the Incas, put up little resistance initially and were soon converted into what was practically a slave labor force to work the silver mines that made Bolivia—at least for the non-Indians—one of the richest places on earth well into the eighteenth century. Those Indians not drafted for labor in the mines held their communal lands in a form of serfdom.

With independence in 1823, won by one of Simon Bolivar's generals, Antonio Jose de Sucre, Bolivia became separated from Peru. Although Sucre originally proposed to liberate the Indians, he soon found that the new nation's economy, with silver mining in decline and the colonial trade disrupted, could not survive without the traditional head tax collected from the Indian communities; so little changed.

The nineteenth century was a series of unrelieved political and economic disasters for the country. The silver mines became exhausted, and the once great cities of Potosi and Oruro dwindled to villages. The country was ruled by a series of feckless dictators, mostly drawn from the handful of Spanish residents, who, desperate for revenue, sought foreign loans on ruinous terms. In the 1880s, the economy recovered as huge tin mines were opened, and foreign entrepreneurs came in to build railroads. Another source of wealth was nitrates, natural fertilizer plentiful in the deserts on Bolivia's then Pacific Coast. Unfortunately, Bolivia was caught on the losing Peruvian side in the war with Chile in the 1880s and lost its coastal territories to Chile. A few years later, during the natural rubber boom of the early twentieth century, Bolivia's Amazon territories produced great wealth. However, Bolivia again lost a war, this time to Brazil, and handed over more land.

In the twentieth century Bolivia took on more of the attributes of a modern country. A multiparty electoral system was established, although voting was restricted to only a few. Indians were denied the vote. The tin mines—almost all owned by three Bolivian families, the Patinos, Aramayos, and Hochschilds—required a large skilled labor force, and a significant union movement grew up. To counter the political threat posed by the unions and by a growing educated urban population, the old political elites created a professional army and brought in a German general to train it.

The Chaco War

In 1932, in the midst of the world depression which reduced the demand for tin and all but wrecked the Bolivian economy, President Daniel Salamanca was fearful of a genuine social revolution led by the unemployed tin miners and urban radicals. His solution was to rouse patriotic fervor by fighting a war with a neighboring country in which he was certain that for once Bolivia would prevail. The neighbor, Paraguay, with which Bolivia shared the Chaco, was also poor and mainly Indian. Making the adventure even more tempting was that the Chaco held Bolivia's oil reserves, and Salamanca believed that he could capture even more oil fields in Paraguay. Yet another benefit was that he could conscript all his potential radical opponents and send them to the front

The Chaco War, which lasted for three years, was an unmitigated disaster for Bolivia. At first all went well. On July 18, 1932, Salamanca announced that Paraguay had attacked a Bolivian border fort. It was, in fact, a Paraguayan fort that Bolivian troops had seized a few weeks earlier. However, the Paraguayan attack was denounced, and, as planned, patriotic fervor gripped the nation. Then victory was proclaimed; Bolivian troops had captured three Paraguayan forts.

Paraguay, assuming this was nothing more than relatively minor border skirmishing, appealed to the United States to arrange a cease-fire and mediate an end to it. However, Salamanca, seeking a major triumph, sent reinforcements and ordered an offensive. The Paraguayans, fighting on their own terrain, were more than equal to the occasion. In late September they retook the fortress of Boqueron, capturing over 1,500 Bolivian troops and pressed on. Within days they had retaken all the territory Bolivia had captured and invaded Bolivia itself, taking the fortress of Arze and routing the Bolivians.

Panic gripped La Paz. Rioters demanded that Salamanca resign. Instead, he brought back the German general, Hans Kundt, and declared a state of siege, outlawing all labor unions. Kundt, for all his Prussian efficiency, proved a wretched combat leader. By January he had organized a new army of 77,000 men and led it against the Paraguayan fortress of Nanawa. The campaign lasted until July 1933. The Paraguayans held Nanawa and carried out successful attacks of their own on other Bolivian positions. By the time it was over, 14,000 Bolivian soldiers had been killed; 10,000 had been captured; 6,000 had deserted or were missing; and an astonishing 32,000 had been evacuated because of wounds or sickness. Anger at Kundt was so great he had to be smuggled out of Bolivia dressed in women's clothes to save him from lynch mobs.

Two relatively junior officers, Enrique Penaranda and David Toro, took command and raised a new army of 55,000 men and succeeded in stemming the Paraguayan advance for six months. Then the Paraguayan general, Estigarribia, broke through to the Andean foothills, into Bolivia's oil fields where he captured the departmental capitals of Santa Cruz and Tarija. At this point, Penaranda and Toro arrested Salamanca. Vice President Jose Luis Tejada Sorzano took office, and the war dragged on. The overextended Paraguayans could not take the main Bolivian headquarters, and a young officer, Major German Busch, led a counter-offensive that drove the Paraguayans out of the oil fields. Both sides were ready to make peace.

Bolivian losses were extraordinary; at least 65,000 were dead or missing in a country whose population was then only about 2 million. The trauma went deeper than mere loss of life, however. The old Bolivian elite had been totally discredited. The cowardice and ineptitude of the officer corps was the subject of numerous post-war novels. Ironically, the war that Salamanca had begun in an effort to destroy the minuscule left-wing opposition resulted in the growth of a powerful radical movement demanding that the big estates be broken up, that the land be given to the Indians, and that the tin mines and oil fields—especially those of Standard Oil—be nationalized. A general strike in May 1936 paralyzed the country, and the authorities did not dare try to interfere. Tejada resigned, and the two officers who had come out of the war with any credit, David Toro and German Busch, took power.

The Road to Revolution

Toro and Busch proclaimed a regime of "military socialism." Their first major act in 1937 was to nationalize Standard Oil. A ministry of labor was established. A new constitution written in 1938 created the framework for a rudimentary welfare state, even though it attempted no real land reform and did not give Indians the vote. Busch, though, was impatient with the constitutional political system. In April 1939 he pushed Toro aside and declared himself dictator, abolishing all political parties, canceling scheduled congressional elections, and suspending the just-adopted constitution. He introduced an advanced labor law, giving previously unheard of protection to workers, and defied the tin barons by imposing new production taxes. Frustrated by the magnitude of his self-imposed task of remaking the nation and the slow pace at which things changed, Busch committed suicide in August 1939, and it looked as though the old elites—the mine owners, the *hacendados* (major ranchers), and the conservative generals—would take over again.

Although the conservatives tried, and in 1940 indeed elected their candidate, General Enrique Penaranda—a relatively unstained Chaco War veteran—they were unable to rig the polls, and three radical parties—the fascist National Revolutionary Movement (MNR), the Leninist Left Revolutionary Party (PIR), and the Trotskyite Workers Revolutionary Party (POR)—joined in the Bolivian Leftist Front (FIB) to dominate the new congress.

Washington was cool to the Bolivian government, partly because of the pro-Axis stance of the MNR but mostly because of the nationalization of Standard Oil. It was not until after Pearl Harbor, when the need for Bolivia's tin became pressing that the United States relented and, after token Bolivian compensation, recognized the legality of the takeover.

The war, and the prosperity it brought, aided Bolivia's leftist reformers in their program. Increasingly, nationalist middle-class and upper-class Bolivians supported the left wing, if only because it was a way to strike at the United States and the traditional elites they saw as following Washington's orders. Hence, they approved of the growing strength of the miners' union led by Juan Lechin, a Trotskyite and leader of the POR, and were outraged by the Penaranda government's massacre of hundreds of strikers and their families at the Patino-owned Catavi mine in 1942. This event led to the overthrow of Penaranda in 1943 by the MNR allied with a group of junior officers and the installation of one of these officers, Gualberto Villaroel.

Villaroel turned out to be a tyrant. Lechin and the miners stood behind him as he executed most of the leaders of the PIR (who were orthodox communists) and did the same to many of the traditional politicians. Oppression became so bad that on July 14, 1946, the citizens of La Paz stormed the presidential palace, dragged out Villaroel and hanged him from a lamp post. Whatever hopes had been raised by Busch for transformation of Bolivia seemed over, and it appeared that the nation was heading for anarchy.

The Revolution of 1952

Strange alliances were formed. The PIR joined with the traditional parties in the post-Villaroel government. That government's policy was suppression of the miners' union, headed by Lechin, which had called for a worker–peasant alliance and worker control of government. Specifically, it demanded arming of the workers and peasants, abolition of the army, and worker participation in management. In early 1947 it was a PIR labor minister who ordered troops into Catavi to carry out another massacre of miners and their families.

The originally fascist MNR now found itself relying on the miners and the POR for organized support, even as it attracted more middle-class voters disgusted by the repressive measures of the traditional parties that made up the governing Democratic Alliance. Despite its past links with the army, it now broke with the military—which itself had completely rejected the Busch and Toro reform program—and committed itself to the miners' revolutionary platform. The MNR task was made easier by the post-war depression and the drop in tin prices that resulted in widespread economic hardship and discontent.

Supporters of the revolution on the streets of La Paz, April 10, 1952. *(Associated Press/Wide World)*

In September 1949, the MNR made its move. Under the leadership of Hernan Siles Zuazo it organized an entirely civilian armed revolt. Miners, students, and middle-class professionals fought the army for three bloody months before surrendering. Defeat, though, was not final.

In May 1950, the factory workers of La Paz, once adherents of the PIR, revolted under the MNR banner. This time the military used aircraft and artillery on working-class neighborhoods before the fighting stopped. Afterward, many army officers quietly arranged for posting abroad. The handwriting was on the wall.

Presidential elections were held again in 1951. The MNR vote was so overwhelming that the government could not disguise the fact that Victor Paz Estenssoro and Hernan

Silas Zuazo, both running from exile, had been the winners. Outgoing president Mamerto Urriolagotia resigned and illegally handed the office over to General Hugo Ballivian who annulled the election and outlawed the MNR as a communist organization.

The army remained united, and the MNR once again resorted to arms. This time though, unlike the 1949 insurrection when only party militants were armed, the MNR broke into government armories and armed the whole population. After three days of heavy fighting, and at a cost of at least 600 men, the army was totally defeated, and the MNR, which only six years before had been a moderately reformist party with a fascist ideology, now represented a full-blown popular revolution. In fact, one reason the

United States, at that time covertly intervening in Guatemala to overthrow a much less radical regime, did not move to oppose the MNR or assist the government, or even express disapproval, was because it still associated the MNR and Paz Estenssoro with its old ideology.

Moreover, all the competing parties and institutions had been destroyed, and the MNR had no need to compromise or make deals. The workers and peasants—both cholos and Indians—were armed. The police and army were disorganized, and it became possible to begin carrying out the most thorough social and economic revolution in the history of the hemisphere.

The Revolution in Power

Paz Estenssoro and Siles Zuazo were somewhat cautious about proceeding, but they were forced to respond to the demands of their followers, or they would soon have found themselves replaced. The first moves were political. The literacy requirement for the franchise was abolished, quintupling the voting rolls and enfranchising the Indians. The army was reduced to a bare minimum, and 500 officers were dismissed. A remnant remained, though, the source of future trouble. Temporarily the armed MNR cadres took over the tasks of both the army and the police.

The miners, while retaining their old union, set up a new Bolivian Workers Central (COB) of which Juan Lechin, who also became Minister of Mines and Petroleum, was the head. Immediately the COB demanded nationalization of all mines without compensation to the owners, total liquidation of the army and its replacement by militias, and agrarian reform abolishing the latifundia system and the traditional unpaid obligatory work demanded of Indians.

In the fall of 1952, COB practically became the government. In October a state-run enterprise, the Mining Corporation of Bolivia (COMIBOL) was set up and the Patino, Aramayo, and Hochschild mines were nationalized. Fearful of U.S. intervention, Paz Estenssoro and Siles Zuazo promised compensation and left U.S.-owned mines alone. The miners' union effectively controlled COMIBOL, getting veto power over any decision that affected the workers, and set up a system of state-subsidized stores at the mines.

At the same time, the revolution was proceeding even more rapidly in the rural areas. Armed peasants, cholo and Indian, took matters into their own hands. They seized the haciendas, driving off, and in some cases killing, the old owners and their overseers, and destroyed the hated compulsory work records. They organized their own militias, taking over police functions, and created a system of peasant unions, called *sindicatos.*

The government had no choice but to accept the situation. In August 1953 it passed an agrarian reform law that essentially recognized what the peasants had done, although it provided compensation for the old landowners in the form of bonds that were to be paid for by those who now had title to the lands. In the event, the peasants simply refused to pay, ignoring all aspects of the agrarian law with which they did not agree. The Aymara and Quechua Indian communities rapidly organized themselves politically, becoming a powerful force, independent of the MNR, POR, or PIR, all of which tried to control them. In fact, over the following years the peasant sindicatos and their political arms became, as landholding peasants usually do, an essentially conservative element. Their concerns were security in their land titles and the extension of health and education services to rural areas.

The Revolution Cools Down

While the miners and peasants were consolidating their revolutionary gains, the urban areas, where the traditional MNR political base was located, were suffering. Inflation had reached enormous levels and urban property values were destroyed. In order to carry out its ambitious industrial modernization and infrastructural investment programs, Paz Estenssoro was forced to turn to the United States.

Surprisingly, at a time when the United States was intervening militarily and politically to overthrow what it saw as dangerously leftist regimes in Guatemala and Guyana, the Eisenhower administration responded with large-scale economic assistance. It still saw Paz Estenssoro and the MNR, correctly, as anti-communist, something like the Peronist movement in Argentina, but in danger of being ousted by the marxist elements in the ruling coalition.

When Siles Zuazo succeeded Paz Estenssoro as president in 1956, however, the United States demanded Bolivia accept an International Monetary Fund stabilization plan, which required a balanced budget, ending food subsidization of the miners, freezing wages, and permission for private investment in the petroleum industry. Otherwise Washington would terminate the minerals purchase agreement, effectively stopping Bolivian international tin sales. Even more importantly, as another condition of U.S. aid, Siles agreed to allow a U.S. mil-

itary mission to rebuild the army. Gradually, the power of Lechin and the COB was reduced.

In 1960, Paz Estenssoro was re-elected with Lechin as vice president. Lechin, trying to overcome U.S. hostility, went to Washington to meet with the Kennedy administration, pledged support for the United States in the cold war, and even agreed to end worker co-government in the mines as the price for major U.S. and German investment in modernization of the tin industry.

By this time, it was too late. The army had been rebuilt and re-armed and was totally under U.S. control. The worker militias had been disarmed, and the peasants, now secure in their lands, were no longer supportive of the miners or workers. With support from the new army, Paz Estenssoro was easily able to crush miner and worker uprisings in 1963. In 1964 he was re-elected as president, this time with General Rene Barrientos as his vice president, a symbol of how much things had changed.

Paz Estenssoro, however great his concessions, had unfortunately made one mistake that Washington would not forgive. He had voted against Cuba's expulsion from the Organization of American States and continued to maintain diplomatic relations with Havana. He also had made one egregious domestic political mistake in naming Barrientos his vice president. Shortly after the election, Barrientos offered Paz Estenssoro the choice of leaving office alive or dead. Paz Estenssoro chose to leave alive, and Barrientos, effectively a U.S. agent under the control of Colonel Edward Fox, the senior U.S. military advisor, promptly moved against the unions. COB was dismantled, and Lechin sent into exile. Fifty percent pay cuts were ordered, and when the miners resisted, the Barrientos army crushed them in a series of bloody battles.

The revolution was over. Bolivia was back to normal—except for the fact that the peasant land reform could not be undone—and was to have twenty years of unbroken military rule until the restoration of a much older and much chastened Paz Estenssoro in 1985.

David MacMichael

See also: Cuba: Communist Revolution, 1956–1959; Guatemala: Coup Against Arbenz, 1954.

Bibliography

Blaisier, Cole. *The Hovering Giant: U.S. Responses to Revolutionary Change in Latin America.* Pittsburgh: University of Pittsburgh Press, 1976.

Blum, William. *The CIA: A Forgotten History.* London: Zed Books, 1986.

Klein, Herbert S. *Bolivia: The Evolution of a Multi-Ethnic Society.* New York: Oxford University Press, 1982.

BOSNIA: Civil War, 1992–1995

TYPE OF CONFLICT: Ethnic and religious **PARTICIPANTS:** Croatia; NATO; Serbia

Of the four republics that broke away from Yugoslavia in 1991, Bosnia-Herzegovina was the last and most reluctant to declare its independence. Trapped between the eager-to-leave republics of Croatia and Slovenia on one side and the Serb-dominated Yugoslavia on the other, Bosnia was forced by accelerating events to make a hasty break. The result was three years of war and brutality.

Historical Background

Bosnia-Herzegovina's 1991 declaration of independence was not motivated by the driving desire of the Bosnian people to have their own country but was rather a reaction to outside events. For most of Yugoslavia's history, most Bosnians had been happy to be a part of the larger entity. Bosnia was a multi-ethnic republic within multi-ethnic Yugoslavia. In the other breakaway republics, one ethnic group was dominant—Croatia had a majority of Croatians, Slovenia of Slovenes, and Macedonia of Macedonians—but in Bosnia, no ethnic group claimed a majority of the population. If Yugoslavia fell apart, Bosnia had the potential to do so also.

After the end of World War II, the possibility of a breakup of Yugoslavia was prevented by the strong arm of Marshal Josip Broz Tito's Communist dictatorship. With Tito's death in 1980, the whole country began to slowly fall apart. By the middle 1980s, the Communist party had lost most of its prestige, and nationalists leaders were able to gather support and demand greater rights for their particular ethnic group.

The first to be successful at this was Slobodan Milošević, a Serbian Communist politician. Milošević rose to power by playing on the fears of Serbs, who made up about 40 percent of Yugoslavia's pre-breakup population. Many Serbs felt that they did not have the power in Yugoslavia equivalent to their numbers. Since 1987, Milošević, the leader of the Republic of Serbia, had been agitating for greater power for the Serbs within Yugoslavia. Claiming that Serbs were being mistreated, Milošević was able to put friendly governments into power in Serbia, Montenegro, Vojvodina, and Kosovo.

With Milošević and the Serbs controlling four of the eight Yugoslav state governments, the rest of the republics felt the need to pull away and gain more freedom of action. As the Communist party lost support throughout Yugoslavia, nationalist movements advocating independence rose up in Croatia, Slovenia, and Macedonia. In June 1991, those republics declared their independence. (This initiated a series of wars with the Serbs, who, at first, were unwilling to let them go.) These declarations put Bosnia-Herzegovina in a difficult position. With three republics opting out of the Yugoslav federation, Bosnia was left alone in a Yugoslavia completely dominated by Milošević and his allies. Bosnia could either break away from Yugoslavia, and risk the ethnic conflict that might ensue inside Bosnia, or they could stay within a federal system that would then be completely dominated by Serb nationalists.

In December 1991, the Bosnian government decided on independence, and the different ethnic groups within Bosnia began to splinter into hostile factions.

Ethnicity and Religion in Bosnia-Herzegovina

More than any other of the old Yugoslavian republics, Bosnia-Herzegovina was a truly multi-ethnic state. The population was divided between Muslims (44 percent), Serbs (31 percent), Croats (17 percent), and a mix of other nationalities, including Hungarians and Albanians. Moreover, the various groups were not as segregated as they were elsewhere in Yugoslavia. Croats, Muslims, and Serbs often lived in neighboring villages, and sometimes even in the same village. Sarajevo, the capital of Bosnia, had about the same ethnic mix as the rest of Bosnia. And the ethnic barriers were not barriers to social intercourse: 18.6 percent of all Bosnian marriages between 1981 and 1991 were between people of different ethnicity.

Bosnians were also the people most attached to the idea of a unified Yugoslavia. In polls taken in 1992, Bosnia was the only republic to have a significant percentage of its inhabitants define themselves as "Yugoslavs," rather than "Croats" or "Muslims."

The labels "Muslim," "Serb," or "Croat" were deceptive. All three peoples belonged to the same ethnic group, South Slav, and all three spoke Serbo-Croatian (although Serbs used the Cyrillic alphabet, while Muslims and Croats used the Latin alphabet). The major difference between them was religious. Centuries ago, the northern South Slavs (Croats) had been converted to Catholicism. Those in the south (Serbs) had accepted Eastern Orthodox Christianity. The arrival of the Turks in the fourteenth century had convinced some Slavs to convert to Islam, and the Bosnian Muslims were born.

But to define Bosnians by religion would be a mistake—most Yugoslavians were not faithful attendees at their local churches or mosques. A Croat was a Croat because he considered himself to be a Croat. The Catholic faith of his ancestors might help to make this definition more clear, but it was no more important than the fact that he used Latin instead of Cyrillic letters. Croats and Serbs saw themselves as separate races, and therefore they were.

Of the three, Muslims were the least attached to a separate identity. Bosnia's Muslims were more urbanized than their neighbors. As city dwellers, they saw themselves as cosmopolitan, above ethnic differences. As Muslims, they were not great successes: many ate pork, drank wine, and the younger generation liked to dance at the discos in Sarajevo. A 1989 survey found that only 34 percent of Bosnia's Muslims were active believers.

Bosnia's Muslims were also forced to be more accepting in their ethnic attitudes: they were stuck in a state in which they were not a majority. Bosnian Croats could look north toward Croatia, while Bosnian Serbs could look south at Serbia, but Bosnian Muslims had only Bosnia.

In general, Bosnians who lived in the bigger cities—Sarajevo or Tuzla—valued their ethnic differences the least. It was the Muslims, Serbs, and Croats who lived in the small villages of the countryside who were more likely to view their neighbors with suspicion and distrust. It was from the countryside that the war in Bosnia drew its most dedicated fighters.

Independence

Even before Bosnia declared its independence, its various ethnic groups had begun to form political parties based upon their ethnic identities. In May 1990, the Muslims, led by Alija Izetbegovic, formed the Party of Democratic Action (SDA). A few months later the Bosnian Serbs established a branch of the Serbian Democratic Party (SDS), led by Radovan Karadzic, and the Croats created a branch of the Croatian Democratic Union (HDZ). (The Serb and Croat parties both had their roots in ethnic parties that had been created in neighboring Croatia.) Although some Bosnians, particularly in Sarajevo, deplored this rush toward identity politics, the majority of the republic's voters declared their loyalty to one or the other ethnic party. In the November 1990 elections, these nationalist parties won 90 percent of the vote and created an uneasy coalition government, with Izetbegovic as its president.

Throughout 1991, the SDA, SDS, and HDZ debated whether or not Bosnia should declare itself independent. The Muslims and Croats favored independence; the Serbs, wanting to stay connected to Serbia, opposed it. Tensions rose. Serbs claimed that Izetbegovic wanted to create an Islamic state (which was false), while Muslims accused Serbia and Croatia of cutting a deal to divide Bosnia between them (a possibility that had been discussed by Milošević and Franjo Tudjman, Croatia's president). To add to their worries, Bosnians could look across the border into Croatia, where Croats and Croatian Serbs were engaged in a nasty ethnic shooting war.

As Bosnia moved closer to declaring itself independent, Bosnian Serbs declared that parts of Bosnia were Serbian Autonomous Regions (SAOs), which would stay connected to Yugoslavia if Bosnia tried to secede. As Bosnia prepared to leave Yugoslavia, Serbs in Bosnia were preparing to leave Bosnia itself. In October 1991, they even declared their own separate parliament.

In December 1991, Izetbegovic, with the support of the Muslims and Croats, declared Bosnia to be an independent nation.

Civil War

On January 9, 1992, the Bosnian Serbs, led by Karadzic, declared themselves to be an independent Serb republic within Yugoslavia (the Republika Srpska). The borders of this new republic, as defined by Karadzic, included 65 percent of Bosnia's territory, even though Serbs were only 31 percent of the population. It also included many Muslim and Croat villages.

The Serbs, knowing that the Muslims and Croats would not accept this division, began to prepare to fight for their territory. With the help of Milošević and neighboring Serbia, the Bosnian Serbs were able to create a sizable and well-equipped army. Many Serbs in the Yugoslav army were allowed to transfer to Bosnia, where they became the nucleus of the Bosnian Serb militias. (Although the Yugoslavian federal army had theoretically represented all the Yugoslav republics, by 1992, it had become almost completely Serb dominated and was fully under Milošević's control.)

The first skirmishes occurred in March 1992, and open fighting began in April. Serbian militias, backed by elements of the Yugoslavian army that had stayed behind in Bosnia, began to attack selected Muslim villages in eastern Bosnia.

The attacks were designed to remove Muslims and Croats from the parts of Bosnia that were claimed by the Republika Srpska. Serb militias moved into villages inhabited by Muslims and terrorized the population into leaving. Muslim community leaders who showed signs of resistance were executed (along with many who did not resist at all). The rest of the population would be intimidated into fleeing for their lives. Those who stayed behind would be killed. The whole process was the beginning of what would eventually be called "ethnic cleansing." The Serb militias were attempting to carve out a Serb-only area of Bosnia on which they could build their own republic.

On April 4, 1992, Izetbegovic, after hearing of the first attacks on Muslim villages, mobilized Bosnia's territorial defense forces (a kind of national guard). Bosnia was at war.

The fighting in Sarajevo began on the following day. Sarajevo, more than any other city, had symbolized the possibility of ethnic cooperation in Yugoslavia. The different ethnic groups had been friendliest in this city, and the nationalist parties had garnered the least votes here. So, on April 5, the citizens of Sarajevo spontaneously organized a march through their city to protest the approaching violence. The unarmed crowd—made up of Serbs, Croats, and Muslims—was fired upon by Serb militiamen and forced to run for cover. From then until the end of the Bosnian Civil War, Sarajevo was in a state of siege.

The Bosnian Territorials, the progovernment militias, were caught off guard and had allowed the Serb militias—helped by the Yugoslavian army—to seize the hills around the city. (Although Muslims dominated Sarajevo, the hills to the east were filled with Serb villages. Bigoted and parochial, they were a fertile recruiting area for the Serb militias.) From these hills, the Serbs were able to drop a steady rain of artillery and mortar shells into Sarajevo. Serb snipers stationed in the heights surrounding the city waited until a target came into view, and then fired. As the siege wore on, the citizens of Sarajevo became used to going about their daily activities under the threat of random death. Men, women, and children were all possible sniper targets, and the mortar shells killed indiscriminately. Gradually Sarajevo was turned into a city of rubble.

Even though most of the fighting took place elsewhere in Bosnia, the world's attention focused on Sarajevo. Television and newspaper journalists sent their correspondents to stay at the city's shell-pocked Holiday Inn (one side of the hotel was left unoccupied because it could be, and was, fired upon by Serb snipers). From this surreal hotel they reported on the steady destruction of a once beautiful city.

Ethnic Cleansing

In Sarajevo, the Bosnian Territorials and irregular troops were able to hold off the Serbs in the surrounding hills, but elsewhere in Bosnia the Serb militias made steady progress. Under international pressure, Milošević had ordered the Yugoslavian army to leave Bosnia in May 1992; however, the army did not evacuate the pro-Serbian native Bosnian soldiers, along with abundant supplies of weapons and ammunition. In effect, therefore, Milošević had given the Bosnian Serb militias a well-equipped army of 80,000 men. To fight these militias, the Muslims and Croats had only poorly organized Territorials and irregular troops. For the first year of the fighting, the Serbs were almost always victorious. (Because of the settlement patterns in Bosnia, Muslim villages tended to be the main targets of Serb aggression.)

The Serb militias continued and escalated their policy of ethnic cleansing. One by one, Muslim villages were surrounded, the men rounded up, the leaders shot (whether they resisted or not), and the entire population forced to take to the roads, looking for a safe haven. Heavily armed thugs would wander the empty streets, beating up any Muslims who had been foolish enough to stay behind. Using these methods, northern and eastern Bosnia was steadily digested and incorporated into the Republika Srpska.

Sometimes the takeover of villages was much more violent, with Serb militiamen rounding up and shooting as many inhabitants as they could catch. Even when the takeover was peaceful, the Muslim men often were not allowed to leave, but were instead forced to relocate to Serb controlled detention centers. These centers resembled the concentration camps of Nazi Germany. In the camps, men were beaten, starved, and then often killed. Serb soldiers also practiced systematic rape of Muslim women. These rapes were both an attempt to further terrorize the Muslim population into leaving, as well as being an expression of the growing hatred within Bosnia.

The net result of these terror tactics was to make ethnic cleansing that much more effective. When Muslim villagers heard of the militia's approach, they often would quickly gather their possessions and depart without a fight. A steady stream of refugees moved from east to west. By the end of 1992, more than 2 million Bosnians—mostly Muslims, but also Croats and Serbs—had lost their homes.

Radovan Karadzic and other Serb leaders defended their actions in two ways. First, they denied that ethnic cleansing of any kind was occurring. The movement of Muslim civilians, they said, was entirely voluntary. When proof of the contrary became too overwhelming, the Serbs responded by arguing they were simply pre-empting a Muslim jihad. The Muslims, they claimed, had been planning to slaughter the Serbs, and so the Serbs were merely defending themselves. Few in the international community believed this, but they were still unsure what could be done about the Bosnian Civil War.

International Inaction

The international community was unhappy at the turmoil in Bosnia, particularly once refugees started streaming north into some European countries. They were unwilling, however, to use the only method that was likely to convince the Serbs to stop their offensives: military force. Using foreign troops to stop the fighting might result in casualties, and no nation's leadership wished to risk the political fallout that soldiers returning in body bags might cause. After returning from a visit to Serbia, James Baker, President George Bush's Secretary of State, said, "We got no dog in this fight." As the United States was the leader of the North Atlantic Treaty Organization (NATO), the region's most powerful military alliance, this made the use of combat troops unlikely.

Instead of NATO, the European Community and the United Nations took on the job of trying to end the Bosnian Civil War. But neither of these organizations was designed to (or desired to) threaten military force. United Nations peacekeeping troops were usually only sent to a region if all the parties in a conflict wished peace, which was not the case in Bosnia.

So, while the Serbs cleared eastern Bosnia of Muslims, the international community did little to intervene. The United Nations had imposed an arms embargo against all of former Yugoslavia, but this hurt the Muslims and Croats much more than the Serbs. The Serbs had the weapons inherited from the Yugoslavian army; the Muslims and Croats had much more limited supplies.

As early as May 1992, reports of Serbian atrocities began reaching the world, but reaction was still limited until television cameras were able to film one of the detention centers where Muslim men were being held. The pictures of skeleton-thin Muslims were too reminiscent of the pictures of Jews in World War II concentration camps, and public opinion in Western countries began to push for some kind of action to help the Muslims of Bosnia.

Izetbegovic and the Muslims wanted an end to the arms embargo, which would allow them to find arms to defend themselves, and Western air strikes against Serb troop positions. Together, these actions were called "lift and strike." In 1992, the West was willing to do neither of these things. Either action would seem to be promoting the war, whereas the Western powers wished to convince the combatants to sign a peace agreement. What they did not realize was that Radovan Karadzic and the Republika Srpska had no desire to make peace as long as their armies continued to be successful in expelling Muslims and Croats from their homes. So, instead of lift and strike, the West offered a series of limited, and inadequate, measures designed to discourage further fighting.

U.N. Action

In May 1992, the United Nations imposed an economic embargo on Serbia, in an attempt to force Milošević to rein in his Bosnian Serb allies. Eventually this would have an effect on Milošević's policies, but in the short run, it did nothing to stop the advance of the Bosnian Serb forces (which continued to receive some support from Serbia).

In June 1992, the Bosnian Serbs agreed to allow U.N. troops to take control of Sarajevo's airport (which they had captured in April). This provided a means of bringing food into a city that was rapidly filling up with hungry Muslim refugees, but did nothing to stop the fighting that was causing the refugee problem.

The airport was soon bringing in tons of food, and the United Nations felt able to expand its role. In 1992 and 1993, the United Nations moved more troops into other areas of Bosnia. The U.N. forces (known as UNPROFOR or United Nations Protection Force) were under orders not to interfere in the fighting; their job was just to protect food supply lines. Eventually the United Nations would put almost 30,000 troops into Bosnia. However, as their job was merely to protect food supplies, not Bosnians, they had little effect on the war.

The Enclaves

By December 1992, the Bosnian Serbs had taken most of the east and south of Bosnia, with the exception of four enclaves: Sarajevo itself, Zepa, Gorazde, and Srebrenica. Serb efforts in 1993 focused on conquering the last three, which were entirely behind Serb lines, while maintaining the pressure on Sarajevo.

Srebrenica was one of the most dangerous of the enclaves for the Serbs. It had been captured by the Serbs in 1992, but then retaken by a Muslim militia led by a former policeman, Naser Oric (who, before the war, had been one of Milošević's bodyguards). From April 1992 to January 1993, Oric organized raids on surrounding Serb villages, treating the Serbs with the same brutality that had been visited on the Muslims. But in January, the Serbs began a counter-offensive that slowly closed a noose around Srebrenica. This large city, with some 40,000 Muslims within its boundaries, looked in danger of being cleansed.

In March 1993, Srebrenica received a brief respite when U.N. Commander Phillipe Morillon brought a couple of U.N. armored cars into Srebrenica. Morillon had only planned to investigate the situation, but once he had arrived, the Muslims refused to let him leave. They assumed that with the U.N. commander in the town, the Serbs would hesitate to attack. Finally, the Muslims let Morillon leave, and the Serb attacks escalated. Although Morillon's gesture had not worked, it had attracted the world's attention to the situation in Srebrenica.

The United States, impatient with the slow pace of peace talks and shocked by the pictures appearing on its television sets, had been putting increasing pressure on the United Nations to do something about Srebrenica and the other endangered enclaves. On April 15, the United Nations Security Council declared Srebrenica to be a "United Nations safe area." What this meant was unclear, but it seemed to commit the United Nations to protect the Muslims from Serb attacks. Later, Tuzla, Bihac, Zepa, and Gorazde would also be declared "safe areas." The Serb offensive was temporarily halted.

Vance-Owen Peace Plan

The creation of safe areas allowed the U.N. negotiators to push forward a peace plan that had been worked out in January 1993. This plan, designed by European Community representative Lord David Owen and U.N. representative Cyrus Vance, would have divided Bosnia into ten separate provinces. Three of these provinces would have had a Serb majority, two a Croat majority, three a Muslim majority, one a mixed Croat and Muslim population, and Sarajevo, the tenth province, would have been left as a city shared by all three ethnic groups.

The Bosnians reluctantly accepted the Vance-Owen plan as the best they could hope for. The Croats also supported Vance-Owen because it would have given them large pieces of Bosnia that they might not otherwise have won. However, Karadzic and the Republika Srpska rejected it because it would have forced them to give back some of the land they had already cleansed of Muslims, and so Vance-Owen seemed to have failed.

However, the near-fall of Srebrenica had

A mass grave in Vlakovo, ten miles from Sarajevo, where Bosnian Serbs buried Bosnian Croats and Muslims they allegedly executed. *(Associated Press/Wide World)*

put more pressure on Milošević and Serbia. Late in April 1993, the United Nations had passed additional economic sanctions against Serbia that virtually isolated it from the rest of Europe. Responding to this renewed pressure, Milošević agreed to accept the Vance-Owen Peace Plan. Karadzic was browbeaten into agreeing. The Bosnia Serb hard-liners, however, including Vice President Biljana Plavsic and military Commander in Chief General Ratko Mladic, argued against Vance-Owen, and the Bosnian Serb parliament followed their advice. By May 1993, Vance-Owen was again dead in the water.

This was the first time Milošević had lost control of the Bosnian Serbs. The defeat showed that although Milošević had helped

to create the problems in Bosnia, he might not be able to stop them.

Croats and Muslims

At first the Muslims and Croats of Bosnia-Herzegovina had been allied in the face of Bosnian Serb attacks. In the north, the Croats and Muslims had a tradition of reasonably good relations, and here the alliance prospered. In Herzegovina (the southwest corner of Bosnia-Herzegovina), however, the Croats were more interested in carving out a Bosnian Croat state than they were in working with the Muslims.

Skirmishes occurred between Croats and Muslims troops in late 1992 and broke into open war in April 1993. Croat militias began ethnic cleansing operations against Muslim villages in Herzegovina. Muslims were murdered, raped, and forced to flee. Muslims responded by counter-attacking Croat villages, which created more refugees. Gradually, southwestern Bosnia became largely Croat, while central Bosnia was made mostly Muslim. In the less-heated north, Muslims and Croats continued to cooperate against the Bosnian Serbs.

The fighting continued throughout 1993, with Croatian army troops providing some help to the Bosnian Croat militias. Croatia's leader, Franjo Tudjman, seemed interested in slicing off the Croatian portion of Bosnia and merging it with Croatia.

By summer 1993, the Bosnian Muslims had begun to organize effective military units. Brigades were formed out of men who had been cleansed from other areas. Some of these units had an explicitly Islamic outlook. Their troops greeted each other in Arabic, banned the sale of liquor in areas they controlled, and advocated the creation of some kind of Islamic state in Bosnia. Many Bosnian Muslims, particularly those from the cities, felt uncomfortable with these attitudes, but were willing to accept support from wherever they could get it, including from their more religious-minded country cousins.

The Bosnian Muslims also started to receive help from the rest of the Islamic world. Weapons and supplies were smuggled past the U.N. embargo, and experienced fighters from around the world trickled into Bosnia to help support the government. Some of these were *mujahideen,* veterans of the wars in Afghanistan. Iran, in particular, sent tons of weapons along with men to train Bosnians in their use. These outsiders increased the Islamization of the Bosnian Muslim government. With their improved army, Izetbegovic

and the Bosnian government were able to stabilize the situation in central and northern Bosnia, but they could do little to help the isolated enclaves in the southeast.

On March 2, 1994, the military situation in Bosnia changed when the Croats and Muslims agreed to rebuild the Muslim-Croat alliance and create a Muslim-Croat Federation in Bosnia. The negotiations between the two sides had been pushed forward by American mediators, who saw a Muslim-Croat alliance as the only hope for Bosnia. Tudjman was threatened with economic sanctions if he did not withdraw Croatia's regular army from Bosnia and convince the Croats of Bosnia that a federation was necessary. Tudjman, wanting to keep Croatia linked to the West, agreed. With Tudjman behind the plan, the recalcitrant Croats of Herzegovina were forced to go along (the Croats of the north were already willing to work with the Muslims).

Change in International Opinion

Throughout 1993 and into 1994, the United States and Europe had offered up a series of peace plans that were turned down by one or another of the participants. The United States increasingly favored air strikes against the Bosnian Serbs, but these were opposed by the Europeans, particularly those with U.N. troops stationed in the U.N.-designated safe areas. These nations were afraid that any bombing attacks on the Serbs would elicit retaliatory attacks on U.N. troops on the ground. The Europeans were still hoping to convince the Bosnian Muslims to accept a plan that left them with only a small fraction of the country. The alternative was to continue the war and risk further European involvement.

The beginning of a strong shift in world opinion came on February 5, 1994, when a mortar shell landed in the middle of a Sarajevo market square, killing sixty-nine and wounding more than 200. Many of those killed were women and children. Karadzic and other Serbs claimed that the shell had been fired by Muslims who wished to attract international sympathy, but few believed them.

Pictures of the market square attack shocked the world, and the United States again pressed for NATO air strikes against the Serbs. This was still resisted by many within the United Nations. The Soviet Union, a traditional friend to Serbia, had always opposed the idea of NATO intervention in Bosnia. However, other European countries, including France and Britain, agreed with the Americans. NATO air strikes were threatened if the Serbs did not agree to pull back their artillery from around Sarajevo. Under this pressure, the Bosnian Serbs backed down and withdrew their artillery. The heavy bombardment of Sarajevo, which had gone on for two years, was over. But Sarajevo was still almost completely surrounded by Serb forces, and occasional attacks, as well as sniper fire, against the city continued.

In April 1994, in cooperation with the U.N. peacekeeping forces, NATO actually mounted some air strikes to defend the U.N. safe area in Gorazde. The strikes destroyed a few vehicles and may have convinced the Bosnian Serbs to halt an ongoing offensive. The West was becoming more aggressive but was still unwilling to envision more than token action against the Bosnian Serb forces.

By June 1994, the five countries most involved in the peace negotiations—Britain, France, Germany, the Soviet Union, and the United States—had formed a Contact Group to help coordinate the peace process. The Contact Group came up with another Bosnian peace plan, which would have divided the country between the Muslim-Croat Federation and the Bosnian Serb Republika Srpska, with the Serbs getting somewhat more than half the territory. The Muslim-Croat alliance reluctantly accepted the plan. Milošević, still hurting under U.N. sanctions, also accepted the plan. The Bosnian Serbs, however, again rejected the plan. The war drifted on.

On July 6, 1995, the Serbs attacked the U.N. declared safe area of Srebrenica. Surrounded and cut off from supplies, the Muslim defenders were overwhelmed in a few days. The Dutch U.N. peacekeepers located in Srebrenica were too few to do anything but watch. Forty thousand people were living in Srebrenica when it fell. The Serbs rounded up thousands of the men and drove them off to be executed. The women and children were allowed to flee to Muslim-controlled territory; some of the men managed to do so as well. The death toll was impossible to calculate, but as many as 8,000 Muslim men may have been murdered. Žepa, a smaller safe area, was taken two weeks later. Again, many were killed; again, U.N. troops watched helplessly.

The slaughter of Srebrenica was the deciding moment for the West concerning the Bosnian Civil War. President Clinton of the United States and President Jacques Chirac of France, reluctantly supported by Great Britain's Prime Minister John Major, pushed through a plan that called for immediate air strikes in defense of the remaining major safe area of Gorazde. They also committed themselves to indirectly supporting a Muslim-Croat offensive against the Republika Srpska.

Muslim-Croat Offensive

The Muslim-Croat counter-attack began in Croatia, in August 1995, when Franjo Tudjman ordered his armies to attack and seize the Croatian Serb territories known as the Krajina (which local Serbs had seized in 1991). This assault was coordinated with an attack against Bosnian Serb forces surrounding the Muslim-controlled town of Bihac. Aided by this Croatian attack, the Muslim army in Bihac was able to break out and push the Serbs back to the east. While these attacks went on, NATO warplanes attacked Bosnian Serb positions. The NATO attacks were supposedly retaliatory—Serb radar had been detected locking onto NATO planes but seemed too well timed to be anything other than preplanned.

On August 31, 1995, again supposedly responding to another mortar shell dropped near a Sarajevo market square (which killed thirty-seven people), NATO warplanes escalated their level of support and began attacking Serb positions all across Bosnia. The attacks continued for days and hit many Serb military and communications targets.

At the same time, Muslim-Croat troops were advancing all across the north of Bosnia. By September 1995, the Muslim-Croat Federation had gone from controlling 30 percent of Bosnia to controlling about 50 percent.

In October, the Bosnian Serbs, again pressured by Milošević, finally agreed to a cease-fire in Bosnia.

Dayton and Its Aftermath

In November 1995, the Americans organized talks between the three sides—Muslims, Croats, and Serbs—to discuss peace terms. The talks, which took place in Dayton, Ohio, resulted in a peace agreement that was signed on November 22, 1995. The three presidents—Izetbegovic of Bosnia, Milošević of Serbia, and Tudjman of Croatia—agreed to a peace that gave the Muslim-Croat federation 51 percent of Bosnia, including all of Sarajevo and a thin lifeline road to Gorazde, the last Muslim enclave in the southeast.

To make sure that all parties to the Dayton Agreement kept their word, the Contact Group promised to send 60,000 combat soldiers to Bosnia. This army was dominated by NATO troops; the United States, Great Britain, and France provided the largest contingents, but soldiers from many other countries, including the Soviet Union, were also included. The troops moved in over the next two months, and the two sides in Bosnia moved their forces apart.

The Bosnian Civil War had ended. It had killed at least 200,000 Bosnians and forced more than 2 million to leave their homes.

The Dayton Agreement created a two-tiered government in Bosnia. The Muslim-Croat Federation and the Republika Srpska each had their own presidents and parliaments. In addition, Bosnia as a whole had a government, which included a parliament and a presidency, which was supposed to be annually rotated between the Muslims, Croats, and Serbs. This complex system preserved the illusion of a unified Bosnia, but it was unclear whether it could function effectively. In practice, the Republika Srpska and the Muslim-Croat Federation operated as separate entities. Even within the Federation, the Muslims and Croats largely kept control of their own territories, with only limited cooperation between the two groups.

The peace allowed Izetbegovic's Muslim troops to arm themselves with international support. Weapons and equipment were given by the United States and other countries; the United States also committed to supervise the training of a new Federation army. Eventually, this army was supposed to allow the Bosnians to defend themselves without outside assistance.

Dayton was also supposed to allow citizens of different ethnicity to return to their old homes, but it had only limited success in this area. Elections were held in which refugees were allowed to vote for mayors and city officials in their old homes, but few refugees chose to risk actually returning home. Many of the newly elected officials who did return were attacked by mobs who didn't wish to see their work of ethnic cleansing undone. For the most part, the successes of ethnic cleansing remained unreversed.

Some work was made toward punishing those responsible for the worst crimes committed during the war. Radovan Karadzic, General Ratko Mladic, and numerous minor figures—mostly Bosnian Serbs—were all indicted by a war-crimes tribunal in the Hague. A few of them were captured, but most, including Karadzic and Mladic, remained at large as of April 1998.

The work of normalizing the situation was all supervised by the NATO forces in Bosnia. These troops, including a large U.S. contingent, remained in the country as of April 1998.

Analysis

The Bosnian Civil War was caused by the inability of Bosnians of slightly differing backgrounds to see one another as anything except enemies. The Bosnian Serbs, led by Karadzic and encouraged by Milošević, bear the lions share of responsibility for the start of violence; but Muslims and Croats were quick to respond in kind. Once the fighting began, even the moderates in Sarajevo were eventually forced to take ethnic sides.

The international community had at first failed to recognize that the essential problem in Bosnia was military, not humanitarian. As long as any side within Bosnia could advance its aims by fighting, it would do so. Because they believed that Bosnia's problems were largely solvable by food supplies and peace negotiations, the United States and Europe were unwilling to do more than watch as Bosnians killed each other. The U.N. peacekeepers were in some ways actually counter-productive. They gave the illusion of helping, while the reality was that their presence could discourage serious military action: NATO nations were often reluctant to initiate air strikes for fear that the Serbs would react by attacking the lightly armed U.N. troops on the ground.

Once NATO showed itself willing to use real military force, the fighting was brought to a halt, and the Dayton Agreement was signed. However, it remained unclear whether the agreement could last once NATO troops had left Bosnia. Contact Group representatives were working to put an end to the animosities that led to the horror of ethnic cleansing, but it would be difficult to erase the hatreds raised by three years of killing. When the NATO troops finally leave, it is possible that the fighting may begin again.

Carl Skutsch

See also: Croatia: War with Serbia, 1991–1995; Yugoslavia: Disintegration, 1990s.

Bibliography

Glenny, Misha. *The Fall of Yugoslavia: The Third Balkan War.* New York: Penguin Books, 1996.
Maass, Peter. *Love Thy Neighbor: A Story of War.* New York: Alfred A. Knopf, 1996.

Owen, David. *Balkan Odyssey.* Orlando: Harcourt Brace, 1995.

Pavkovic, Aleksandar. *The Fragmentation of Yugoslavia: Nationalism in a Multinational State.* New York: St. Martin's Press, 1997.

Rogel, Carole. *The Breakup of Yugoslavia and the War in Bosnia.* Westport, CT: Greenwood, 1998.

Rohde, David. *Endgame: The Betrayal and Fall of Srebrenica, Europe's Worst Massacre Since World War II.* New York: Farrar, Straus and Giroux, 1997.

Silber, Laura, and Allan Little. *Yugoslavia: Death of a Nation.* New York: Penguin, 1997.

Vulliamy, Ed. *Seasons in Hell: Understanding Bosnia's War.* New York: St. Martin's Press, 1994.

BRAZIL:
General's Coup, 1964

TYPE OF CONFLICT: Coup

Brazil is the largest country in South America and the fifth largest country in the world. With a population of 165 million, it is the only Portuguese-speaking country in the western hemisphere. The capital is Brasilia, a federal city in the interior state of Goias, which was constructed after World War II and which replaced the former capital, Rio de Janeiro.

Brazil has the world's tenth largest economy. However, wealth is poorly distributed, with the top 10 percent of the population controlling the majority of the national income. Wealth is also maldistributed regionally. The coffee-growing and manufacturing

states of São Paulo, Minas Gerais, and Guanabara and the cattle-raising and wheat-growing regions of the south have modern economies, while the old sugar-growing regions of the northeast are infamous for their poverty and their social and political distortions, as are the interior frontier states of Amazonia. The major cities, especially Rio de Janeiro, are notorious for their impoverished slums (favelas).

Most of Brazil's population is a mixture of Portuguese, Indian, and African. This mixture extends through all social classes, and while class and regional tensions are major factors in Brazilian political life, race carries little political weight.

In 1964, as now, Brazil was classed as a developing nation. While the modern sector was dynamic, it was still a minor part of the overall Brazilian economy, which was largely dependent on commodity exports. Brazil's international balance-of-payments problem was exacerbated by its need to import fuel for its economic development programs.

Historical Background

After establishment of the republic in the 1880s, Brazil's leaders sought to establish a special partnership with the United States. Seeing Brazil as separate from the rest of Latin America, but yet an intrinsic part of it, they believed that it would eventually equal the North American country in power and economic development. They felt it should not only influence Washington's hemispheric policies but interpret and help sell them to its Spanish-speaking neighbors. In return, Brazil expected special consideration of its views and needs. As evidence of the special relationship, Brazil was the only Latin American country to send troops to fight the Axis in World War II. The close military contacts continued after the war. The United States kept its largest Latin American military mission in Brazil, some 300 officers and men, and helped establish and run the Brazilian War College (ESG), where ranking officers and civilian elites were exposed to U.S. military doctrines and strategic policy views.

The 1964 coup had its roots in Brazil's complicated and tension-filled political situation, a function of deep disagreement among the elites over how to reach the state's goals of economic development and international stature, and over the reasons for the failure of its presumed special relationship with the United States during the post–World War II era. Far from growing toward co-equal status, Brazil's leaders felt themselves ignored by North American leaders, who were preoccupied by cold war problems with the Soviet Union and China. As the Brazilian leaders saw it, their economic development plans were dismissed as impractical and were denied financial support, and their suggestions for hemispheric policies were disregarded. What rankled especially was America's reneging on Franklin Roosevelt's promise to Brazil's wartime leader, Getulio Vargas, that Brazil would have a permanent seat on the U.N. Security Council. Roosevelt had also promised Vargas massive post-war U.S. economic assistance, and this too did not materialize.

Brazilian resentment was expressed, particularly during the Dwight D. Eisenhower years, in increasingly open opposition to North American initiatives in the Organization of American States (OAS), as well as, on a global scale, in taking a neutralist position in the cold war and in seeking expanded trade and economic ties with the Soviet Union and China. During the early 1960s the Soviet Union regularly bought up Brazil's coffee surplus, while China became its largest sugar buyer. Eisenhower's secretary of state, John Foster Dulles, equated Brazil's neutralism with communism. Secretary of the Treasury George Humphrey, an ardent free marketeer, found Brazil's state economic planning intolerable.

U.S. disagreement with Brazil's foreign and economic policies was compounded by understandable frustration in dealing with its complicated politics, which were intensely personal and involved rapidly shifting alliances and frequent crises, many of which were incomprehensible to outsiders. Vargas, who had returned to power as elected president in 1950, refused to send Brazilian troops to Korea and, to Washington's alarm, sought to normalize relations with the Soviet Union and China and to nationalize oil and mineral extraction. In 1954, beset by scandals in his administration, Vargas killed himself rather than resign as demanded by army leaders.

However, in death Vargas became a martyr to democracy in the popular mind. His designated political heir, Juscelino Kubitschek, was elected in 1955, with a supposed communist sympathizer, former Minister of Labor João (Jango) Goulart, as vice president. (Goulart was, in fact, a very wealthy cattle rancher and a strong Catholic.)

Kubitschek had as little luck as Vargas in getting financial aid from a U.S. government outraged by, among other things, the seizure by the state of Sao Paulo of a U.S.-owned electric generating plant. He had even less luck with the International Monetary Fund (IMF), which insisted on economic reforms that were opposed by rich and poor alike. Finally, Kubitschek reversed the traditional Brazilian hemispheric policy and sought, not to broker U.S. policies for the rest of Latin America, but to lead Latin America in attempts at altering U.S. policies.

The 1960 Election

The election of 1960 pitted the strongly anti-communist war minister, Army Marshal Henrique Lott, against the governor of São Paulo, Janio Quadros, a neutralist who had praised and visited Fidel Castro. Paradoxically, Lott was a strong supporter of Kubitschek's economic policies, anathema to the United States, while Quadros, like Goulart a wealthy cattleman and candidate of the "conservative" National Democratic Union (UDN) party, pledged to exercise fiscal restraint and to clean up corruption. What further perplexed observers was that Lott had the support of the outlawed but still active Brazilian Communist Party (PCB). The two parties that nominated him, the Social Democratic Party (PSD) and the Brazilian Workers Party (PTB), also nominated the supposedly communist-leaning João (Jango) Goulart for vice president. The United States favored Quadros, who won in a landslide, but Goulart, under the Brazilian system, was elected vice president.

Quadros took office just as John F. Kennedy assumed power in Washington, and there was a brief easing of tension between the two countries as the new U.S. administration sought a fresh approach. Quadros, however, even while pronouncing against corruption and communism, committed the cardinal sin of refusing to endorse the U.S.-backed invasion of Cuba at the Bay of Pigs. Further, he completely puzzled Washington when, after only seven months in office, unable to get support in the faction-ridden Brazilian congress, he resigned, possibly hoping to return to office after a plebiscite that would grant him emergency powers. In any event, his constitutional successor was Goulart, who was en route back home from an official visit to China at the time.

Right-wing elements in the military and civilian conservatives threatened a coup if Goulart were to become president. A split in the military prevented the coup, and the crisis was temporarily resolved by allowing Goulart to take office, after the constitution had been amended to create a parliamentary government with a prime minister assuming much of the presidential power. This lasted only until January 1963 when, in a plebiscite, Brazilians voted overwhelmingly to restore full presidential powers to Goulart. Although Goulart backed the United States during the 1962 Cuban missile crisis, he outraged Washington by joining with the other major Latin American states in refusing to vote for the ouster of Cuba from the OAS at the second Punta del Este conference in January 1962. It was clear his days were numbered.

The United States Opposes Goulart

In the meantime, the United States had sent a new ambassador to Brazil. Lincoln Gordon had been a Harvard economics professor and a Marshall Plan administrator. Just as important, the United States also sent a new head of the military mission, Colonel Vernon Walters. Walters was a former liaison with Brazilian forces in Italy, and a staunch conservative who would later become deputy director of the Central Intelligence Agency (CIA). Working closely with the CIA and the U.S. military mission, Gordon and Walters labored first to deny Goulart a majority in the congressional elections of October 1962 and a victory in the 1963 plebiscite. Though they failed partially, they admitted spending $5 million in covert funds. The actual amount has been estimated at $12 to $20 million, and this does not count substantial Agency for International Development (USAID) money doled out to state governors considered anti-Goulart.

The only reliable element in the country, as the State Department and the Pentagon saw it, was the Brazilian military—"an island of sanity." In 1958, Eisenhower had appointed retired Army Major General William Draper to study the U.S. Military Assistance Program (MAP). With regard to Latin America in general and Brazil in particular, Draper recommended abandoning the old rationale for military assistance—defense of the hemisphere against outside attack—and urged preparing the Latin armed forces for suppression of subversion and revolution. In addition, the CIA began covert activities funded through a political front called the Brazilian Institute for Democratic Action (IBAD) to organize business groups, women's organizations, labor unions, and peasant leagues responsive to U.S. direction. The CIA's major propaganda effort was to create a "red scare," a belief that Brazil was facing imminent communist revolution. The effort was directed principally at the military, especially younger officers.

Political tensions remained high in Brazil even after the 1963 plebiscite. The "red scare" propaganda had done its work well. Goulart, although he had won at the polls,

was as incapable as his predecessors of carrying out effective social and economic programs. He was not helped by the fact that the U.S. Embassy was now working closely with political groups seeking his ouster. Armed bands funded by the CIA and claiming to be communist revolutionaries staged raids on *latifundias* (plantations) in the northeast to increase the tension. The police were thoroughly infiltrated by USAID's Public Safety Office, a CIA front. Labor unions, penetrated by another CIA front, the American Institute for Free Labor Development (AIFLD) added to the confusion. Especially effective were middle-class women, organized through IBAD as Women for Democracy (CAMDE), who used their telephones to spread rumors and, with the backing of Cardinal Jaime Camara de Barros, held meetings to denounce the atheist Goulart.

What tipped the balance, though, was Goulart's tolerance for the organization of unions among naval and military enlisted men. This thoroughly frightened the officer corps and turned it against him. (Ironically, the leader of the navy enlisted union was a CIA agent and provocateur.) Rumors spread that Goulart was going to replace the military with a Castro-style popular militia. Indeed, by agreeing to address a mass rally of the military union on March 13, 1964, he sealed his fate.

The Coup

The army chief of staff, General Adhemar Castelo Branco—who had been promoted to general and appointed chief of staff by Goulart in 1963—was a frequent lecturer on the danger of communist subversion and takeover. He was also known as an opponent of coups. However, in January 1964 he had al-

Government troops loyal to Brazilian President João Goulart deploy in front of the War Ministry in Rio de Janeiro, March 31, 1964. The next day, however, a successful coup against Goulart began. *(Associated Press/Wide World)*

ready joined the coup-plotting group headed by retired general Golbery de Couto e Silva, convinced that the only way to save the constitution was to overthrow the elected government that was subverting it. Golbery was a leading figure at the War College (ESG) and also a member of the CIA-funded think tank, the Institute for Social Research and Studies (IPES).

On March 19 a mass anti-Goulart rally, organized by CAMDE, was held in Rio. On March 20 Castelo sent a memo to all army commanders saying that Goulart's policies were leading to subjugation to Moscow and that if the military defended him it would be betraying the country. However, Goulart, although aware of Castelo's memo, took no ac-

tion, told advisors he was certain of the army's loyalty, and interrupted his Easter holiday to come to Rio to address an enlisted men's rally.

Latin American policy had also changed drastically in Washington with the accession to office of Lyndon Johnson. Johnson, preoccupied by concerns for the Great Society and already having to deal with Vietnam, was not prepared to spend much time on Latin America. His appointee as Assistant Secretary of State for Inter-American Affairs, Thomas Mann, had little tolerance for Latin leaders who were unresponsive to U.S. wishes and was a firm adherent of the views of General Draper that the military represented an island of sanity in Brazil.

On March 13 Ambassador Gordon flew to Washington to consult with Mann and President Johnson, who advised him that the United States would not only not object to a military coup but would support it. A U.S. naval task force was ready to steam for Rio in Operation Brother Sam to support the anti-Goulart forces. An inter-agency task force was set up at the State Department to plan for provision of post-coup aid to whatever Brazilian government was established.

As it turned out, the Brother Sam task force was not needed. The military forces on whose loyalty Goulart counted did not act. Nor did Goulart, who had no stomach for civil war, order out loyal state militias or call for the arming of the masses. For several days after the coup began on April 1, 1964, he flew aimlessly from one of his ranches to another before going into Uruguayan exile.

Meanwhile, General Artur da Costa e Silva, who had been running a separate net of coup conspirators, had the head of the Chamber of Deputies, Ranieri Mazzilli, sworn in as president at two o'clock in the morning, and Lyndon Johnson officially recognized him within less than twenty-four hours.

There was no organized resistance to the coup. Officers strapped on their sidearms and waited for assaults by the red mobs, but the best they could do was fire on unarmed student demonstrators outside the military club, killing three. The fanatically anti-Goulart governor of Guanabara (Rio), Carlos Lacerda, armed with a submachine gun, barricaded himself in the governor's palace, screaming defiance against non-existent attackers over a loudspeaker for several hours.

Aftermath

The fact that, in the aftermath, the supposed arms caches and trained communist and Castroite forces were found not to exist, did not keep the Brazilian generals nor their American supporters, including Ambassador Gordon, from proclaiming that they had saved the nation from communist revolt in the very nick of time. Now the task was to make sure the danger did not arise again. Hastily organized military investigation forces, sent into the field as part of "Operation Cleanup," arrested thousands, including numerous office holders. Reports of torture and execution of suspects soon circulated. However, as Cardinal Adhemar de Barros commented, "without punishment of the guilty, we risk . . . the salvation of the fatherland. . . . [T]o punish those who were [guilty] is an act of mercy also."

The politicians who had hoped to lead the post-Goulart regime were soon disabused. Mazzilli was pushed aside. At a meeting in early April, the military informed the politicos that da Costa e Silva would exercise power until Castelo e Branco was installed as president by the Congress on April 15, with the CAMDE women's groups and IPES applying pressure for the move.

Once in office, Castelo e Branco issued Institutional Act Number One, annulling the constitution. This granted the executive power a ten-year mandate to restore economic and financial order, eliminate communist infiltration, and purge corrupt and subversive elements; to cancel the mandates of elected officials; to dismiss civil servants at will; and to revoke, on his own authority, the political rights of anyone found guilty of subversion or misuse of public funds. Former presidents Kubitschek, Quadros, and Goulart were among those found guilty.

Lyndon Johnson was also repaid. Brazil broke diplomatic relations with the Soviet Union and sent troops to support the U.S. invasion of the Dominican Republic in April

1965, even taking command of the OAS occupying force that gave an inter-American cover to Washington's unilateral action.

New state elections were held in October 1965, but the victories of anti-coup parties caused Castelo e Branco to annul them. The Second Institutional Act of that month suspended all existing political parties and decreed two official new parties, the only ones allowed to compete in future elections. Branco ruled by emergency decree for the remainder of his term.

As candidate of one of the official parties, General da Costa e Silva took his turn as president in 1967 under a new constitution which called for indirect election of the president and vice president on a single ticket, trial by court martial for civilians charged with national security offenses, and presidential power to rule by emergency decree without consulting congress. Not content with this, in December 1968, da Costa e Silva issued the Fifth Institutional Act, suspending all legislative bodies indefinitely, authorizing rule by decree, and prohibiting public political criticism.

David MacMichael

See also: Cuba: Bay of Pigs Invasion, 1961; Dominican Republic: Coup and U.S. Invasion, 1965.

Bibliography

Black, Jan Knippers. *United States Penetration of Brazil.* Philadelphia: University of Pennsylvania Press, 1977.

Dulles, John F. *Castello Branco: The Making of a Brazilian President.* College Station: Texas A&M University Press, 1978.

———. *Unrest in Brazil: Political-Military Crises, 1955 1964.* Austin: University of Texas Press, 1970.

Leacock, Ruth. *Requiem for Revolutions: The United States and Brazil, 1961–1969.* Kent, OH: Kent State University Press, 1990.

Schneider, Ronald M. *The Political System of Brazil: Emergence of a "Modernizing" Authoritarian Regime, 1964–1970.* New York: Columbia University Press, 1971.

BURKINA FASO:
Coups, 1966–1987

TYPE OF CONFLICT: Coups, left and right

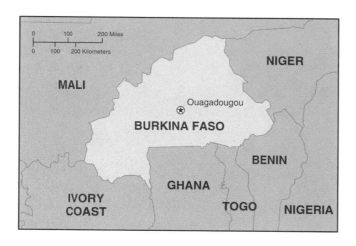

Burkina Faso, originally known as Upper Volta, until 1960 was a part of French West Africa. It is a land-locked nation of 105,870 square miles with a population estimated at 10,500,000 in 1995. The capital, Ouagadougou has about 650,000 people. Burkina Faso is bordered on the north and west by Mali, on the east by Niger, and on the south by, from east to west, Benin, Togo, Ghana, and Côte d'Ivoire. Desperately poor, with an estimated per capita national income of only about $170 a year, the country's economy is largely dependent on remittances from migrant workers.

About 85 percent of the people practice subsistence agriculture. National policy has been to encourage food self-sufficiency, and the main crops are maize, sorghum, millet, with some rice and sugar. Some cotton is grown and exported. The northern and

northeastern parts of the country are typical Sahel semi-desert suitable only for very limited cattle grazing. Further south are savannas, also subject to frequent drought and creeping desertification. Commercial agriculture is only possible in the country's three river valleys. There is some mining, principally for gold. Manufacturing employs less than 1.5 percent of the labor force.

The official language is French, although a great number of tribal languages are in common use. The majority of people practice animist (traditional) religions; about one-quarter of the population is Muslim and 10 percent Christian, principally Roman Catholic. The literacy rate is not much more than 10 percent. Life expectancy is only about forty-two years for men and forty-eight for women.

Historical Background

During the colonial era, France used Burkina Faso chiefly as a labor reserve. Beginning in 1919, the French authorities instituted a system of forced labor—which lasted until 1946—under which village chiefs were required to provide a quota of men to work for specific periods to ensure a flow of workers to other parts of France's African empire. While the majority of the population was used as semi-slave labor, France did, after 1946, educate a small elite, groomed to take over government after independence and to be amenable to continuing informal French control.

Upper Volta became independent on August 5, 1960. The first president, Maurice Yameogo, was surrounded by French advisors. Widespread dissatisfaction with government corruption and the obvious enrichment of Yameogo and his cronies served as the excuse for a military coup in 1966 headed by Colonel Sangoule Lamizana. Lamizana held power for fourteen years, periodically allowing limited political activity and then clamping down when he deemed things to be getting out of hand. Notably, in a country with almost no industry or industrial workers, labor unions headed by French-educated left-wing intellectuals were the most active of Lamizana's opponents. In fact, the overwhelming majority of union members were civil servants.

Nevertheless, it was not workers or bureaucrats but another military coup led by Colonel Saye Zerbo that ousted Lamizana in November 1980. Zerbo ruled through a thirty-one-member Military Committee for Recovering National Progress (CMRPN), among whose members were reform-minded, even radical, young officers including future presidents Thomas Sankara and Blaise Compaore. Sankara acted as minister of information and gained local fame for such populist gestures as riding his bicycle to work and refusing the usual ministerial perks.

In November 1982, Zerbo, in turn, was ousted and replaced by Major Jean-Baptiste Ouedraogo, who named Sankara prime minister. Sankara dissolved the CMRPN and brought civilians, notably the Marxist-Leninist union leader Souman Toure, into the government. Evidently this turn to the left disturbed French security officials. In May 1983, French president François Mitterand's advisor on African affairs, Guy Penne, ar-

rived unannounced in Ouagadougou. Shortly afterward, allies of Zerbo seized Sankara and two other revolutionary officers. Compaore escaped, succeeded in gaining control of the country's major military base, and freed Sankara and the other two officers. In August, Sankara and Compaore led yet another coup and forced Ouedraogo's resignation.

The Sankara Years

Sankara, although pronouncing himself a Marxist-Leninist on taking power at the head of the National Revolutionary Council (CNR), was basically a populist reformer with a genuine hatred of corruption. He considered it wrong, in a country where the vast majority were desperately poor, that anyone, no matter how the wealth was gained, could be rich. He assumed, in most cases correctly, that the wealthy of Upper Volta had not earned their wealth honestly. His anti-corruption campaign took particular aim at civil servants. He was determined that they not set themselves up as a well-remunerated educated elite, lording it over the illiterate masses. To show he meant business, he organized Popular Revolutionary Tribunals (TPR) to conduct show trials of the corrupt. Zerbo and other high officials were subsequently convicted by these courts. He cracked down on the bureaucracy; for example, in 1984, Sankara prohibited the wearing of expensive foreign clothing by civil servants, making them wear clothing made of Burkinade cotton, woven and tailored locally. He also prohibited any civil servant, regardless of rank, from using any automobile larger than a Renault 5. These restrictions resulted in bitter enmity from that quarter, something that contributed to his eventual downfall.

A brilliant public speaker and self-publicist, Sankara endeared himself not only

Crowds cheer the coup led by Thomas Sankara that overthrew the government of Jean-Baptiste Ouedraogo in August 1983. *(Gamma)*

to the masses of Upper Volta, which he re-named Burkina Faso (Land of Incorruptible Men) in August 1984, but quickly became something of a cult figure among national-istic young people throughout Africa. At the same time, he was feared and loathed by Af-rica's "big men," the post-colonial dictators who flaunted their new wealth while their countries remained impoverished.

His economic policy stressed food self-sufficiency. Key to this was developing new water resources, and a system of reservoirs was begun. More immediately, and again he made important enemies here, he ordered cutbacks on cotton production, ending the government incentives paid to cotton grow-ers and requiring that more of the fertile land along the country's rivers be turned over to food production. He also, again to the out-rage of the wealthy classes, severely limited imports of luxury foods. Real progress was made against tremendous odds as Burkina Faso was almost able to eliminate food imports in 1985. Since then, however, popu-lation growth, desertification, and a resump-tion of cotton exporting have resulted in huge food deficits.

Another Sankara economic objective was to develop major manganese deposits in the north. However, the only rail line in the country runs south from Ouagadougou to Côte d'Ivoire, and the investment required to reach the deposits has caused foreign inves-tors to shy away.

His social programs emphasized health care and education. Here again he was frus-trated. It proved easy to build schools and clinics in the villages but almost impossible to staff them with qualified teachers and health care workers. A number of Cuban doctors provided assistance but it was far from enough.

Throughout, Sankara preached self-sufficiency. He was outspoken in his denunciations of foreign aid missions. Typically, he was offended by the contrast between the living standards of foreign aid mission employees and those of the people they were ostensibly assisting. He believed that far too great a percentage of foreign aid benefited the aid workers and the local elites they employed. In an address to the U.N. General Assembly shortly after taking power, he said: "Few other countries have been inundated with all types of aid as mine has been. This aid is supposed to favor development. You will look in vain for any signs of anything connected with development."

In turning to countries such as Cuba, China, and Libya for guidance and assistance while publicly denouncing French imperialism, Sankara made numerous foreign enemies. The United States drastically reduced its economic assistance to show its displeasure.

By 1987, although most observers emphasize that Sankara's personal popularity was still high—his initiation of tax relief for peasants and his granting women the right to own property had been enthusiastically received in rural areas—he had clearly lost support in the military and the bureaucracy. His puritanical intolerance for corruption offended the ambitious; his populism outraged local Marxist-Leninists who wanted to act as a revolutionary vanguard, not to be sent off to work on village construction projects. In May 1987, a major tax fraud investigation led to the closure of many small businesses. In the same month, civil service trade union officials who had led protests against job cutbacks and

other austerity measures were arrested for "counter-revolutionary activities."

On October 15, 1987, Sankara, aged thirty-seven, was murdered, probably by order of Blaise Compaore, his one-time comrade. Thirteen members of the CNR died with him.

After Sankara

Compaore, announcing establishment of a new Popular Front (FP), dissolved the CNR and denounced Sankara, even while declaring he would continue to pursue his revolutionary objectives. It soon became clear, however, that the age of reform was over. Among Compaore's first acts was to accept a gift of a fleet of armored Alfa Romeo cars from Libya's Muammar Qaddafi.

The traditional left was pacified by emphasizing top-down control of local development work instead of Sankara's insistence on local control and involvement. The traditional right—village chiefs in the rural areas and businessmen in the cities—were quietly notified that their freedom of action had been restored. Foreign powers, offended by Sankara's often strident anti-imperialist rhetoric, also found Compaore much friendlier. Although retaining ties to Libya, Burkina Faso re-established relations with Israel and broke relations with China to recognize Taiwan. Finally, in a gesture to the memory of Sankara, in 1991, Compaore raised a memorial tomb to the former leader in Ouagadougou.

David MacMichael

Bibliography

Baxter, Joan, and Keith Somerville. "Burkina Faso." In *Benin, the Congo, Burkina Faso*, ed. Bogdan Szajkowski. London and New York: Pinter, 1989.

BURUNDI: Ethnic Strife Since 1962

TYPE OF CONFLICT: Ethnic and religious

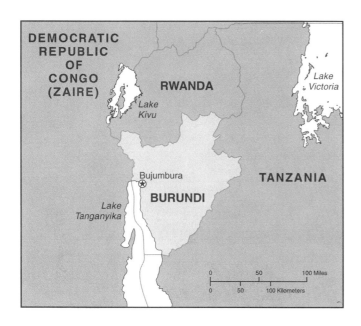

Burundi, like its next door neighbor Rwanda, has been wracked by genocidal conflict between the two dominant ethnic groups, the Tutsi and the Hutu. In Rwanda, at least half a million Tutsi died in a genocidal slaughter in 1994. Burundi's mass killings came earlier: one in 1972, in which over 100,000 Hutu were killed, and another in 1988, in which tens of thousands of Hutu were killed. Since 1988, ethnic warfare has smoldered on, with the death toll approaching 200,000.

Journalists blamed the killings on inevitable ethnic strife between "ancestral enemies," but this was overly facile. Most African countries have ethnic mixtures as complex as or more complex than that of Burundi, yet they have managed to avoid the internecine murders that plagued both Burundi and Rwanda. Furthermore, it was impossible to accurately characterize Hutu and Tutsi as ancestral enemies. The roots of their animosity did lie in the past, but they were tangled.

Historical Background

In the 1930s, about 14 percent of the indigenous population were Tutsi; 85 percent were Hutu; and Twa pygmies made up the remaining 1 percent. These figures take into account neither the sizable immigrant community in Burundi, nor the percent changes caused by the ethnic killings, and it is possible that Tutsi made up as much as 20 percent of the population by 1998.

The origins of these two ethnic groups was unclear, but what little evidence there was suggested that the Hutu may have arrived first, displacing the original Twa pygmies, and were in turn followed by the Tutsi immigrants from the north. The evidence for this history, however, was oral legend, and was therefore highly suspect. The first reliable historical accounts come only with the arrival of European invaders in the nineteenth century. The Europeans found that the Tutsis in Rwanda had clearly forced the Hutu into a subsidiary economic and political position, with Tutsi kings, chiefs, and their families dominating a Hutu peasant class; in Burundi, the situation was more complex. Tutsi tended to dominate, but Hutu chiefs still survived, and a powerful Hutu clan might have substantially more prestige and wealth than a poor Tutsi clan. Furthermore, a third class of princes, Ganwa, arose, who were viewed as separate from both Hutu and Tutsi.

Despite the ethnic and class divisions between Tutsi and Hutu, their history saw substantial intermingling; Hutu and Tutsi married, merged languages and culture, and became something other than entirely separate, without ever quite merging into one ethnic group. The Tutsi remained dominant, but it was possible for a Hutu through marriage or clan membership to be accepted as Tutsi and for a Tutsi who had suffered misfortune to sink down to Hutu status. The designations "Tutsi" and "Hutu" became as much caste or class categories as ethnic labels. They were also complicated by the Ganwa princely caste. The Ganwa appealed to both Tutsi and Hutu for support, and political conflict was based on Ganwa rivalries, not ethnic divisions. With the arrival of the Europeans this changed.

The Germans who ruled Burundi and Rwanda from 1897 to 1916 accentuated the existing differences between Tutsi and Hutu. The Germans, viewing Rwanda through the lens of nineteenth-century racial prejudices, saw the Tutsi, who tended to be taller and more "European" in appearance than their Hutu neighbors, as obviously superior and deserving of their higher status. The Germans ignored the reality that intermarriage and class mobility had already blurred what physical differences had ever existed between the two groups, making it very difficult to reliably identify a Tutsi or a Hutu from physical appearance alone. Prompted by their racial misreading of Rwandan society, the Germans favored the Tutsi ruling class, using them as their colonial puppets

and proxies. The Tutsi were labeled a superior race descended from Ethiopian invaders, while the Hutu were categorized as an inferior Bantu people.

The Belgians, who took over Rwanda after World War I, went even further and issued identity cards that engraved in bureaucratic stone the ethnicity of each Rwandan as either Tutsi or Hutu. Tensions between the two groups were exacerbated by this treatment, with some Tutsis using their status to oppress Hutus, which naturally increased Hutu resentment.

Independence

Under pressure from the United Nations, the Belgians agreed to grant Burundi and Rwanda their independence in 1962. The government was to be a constitutional monarchy, with the traditional Burundi royal clan providing the kings. In the years leading up to independence, two main political parties were created. The first was the Union pour le progrès national (UPRONA). UPRONA, led by Prince Louis Rwagasore—a member of the Ganwa class and the eldest son of Burundi's king, Mwambutsa IV—was a progressive nationalist party that advocated uniting all sections of society under a single banner. Its rival was the Parti démocrate chrétien (PDC), a more conservative party with strong ties to the Belgian administration.

In the elections before independence, the Belgians favored the PDC over the UPRONA, but Rwagasore was extremely popular among both Hutu and Tutsi, and his party won 58 out of 64 seats in the vote for a new assembly held in September 1961. Two weeks later, on October 13, Rwagasore was shot by a Greek assassin who had been hired by the PDC. There was also strong evidence that the Belgian colonial authorities had some connection to the assassination; the Belgians had thought that Rwagasore and the UPRONA were too radical and suspected that they had Communist sympathies—a completely erroneous belief.

On July 1, 1962, Burundi achieved a peaceful transition to independence. But without the unifying force of Rwagasore, politics in Burundi became increasingly polarized. King Mwambutsa IV attempted to give both Tutsis and Hutus positions in his government, but both resented what they felt was favoritism for the other.

Polarization between the Hutu and Tutsi of Burundi was increased by a revolution in neighboring Rwanda. In Rwanda ethnic divisions had always been much more important than in Burundi. Chaffing under Tutsi domination the Hutus of Rwanda had created an avowedly ethnic party, the Parti du Mouvement de l'Emancipation du Peuple Hutu (PARMEHUTU). PARMEHUTU led a 1961 revolution that ended the Tutsi control of the country and went on to eliminate Tutsis from almost all positions of importance.

In Burundi, many Hutus looked at events in Rwanda with envy. Hutu politicians began to campaign on a populist platform that advocated an end to Tutsi control in Burundi. Similarly, Tutsis in Burundi saw the Rwanda revolution as a sign that their own power might be in danger—their fears fanned by an influx of Tutsi refugees from Rwanda. Tutsis reacted by attacking all Hutu parties that they perceived as ethnically based. Thus, although Burundi had not had the same kind of ethnic polarization as Rwanda, events in Rwanda pushed Hutu and Tutsis into becoming more like their neighbors, thereby helping to fulfill their own prophecies of ethnic conflict. UPRONA,

the party that had unified Burundi, began to lose its Hutu supporters and become a Tutsi-dominated party.

Martin Ndayahoze, a moderate Hutu army officer, described the way in which unscrupulous politicians used ethnicity to gain power: "If they are Tutsi they denounce a Hutu peril which must be countered. If they are Hutu they unveil a Tutsi apartheid which must be combated." Ndayahoze was killed by Tutsis in 1972.

Tutsis Take Control

In January 1965 tensions were increased in Burundi when a Tutsi refugee from Rwanda assassinated the Hutu prime minister. In new elections held in May 1965, the Hutu won a victory, but then were incensed when King Mwambutsa IV chose a Tutsi prime minister. Hutu officers within the army and police reacted in October by attempting to overthrow the government. Their attempt was suppressed, and the Tutsi victors took advantage of their success to seize many of the leading Hutu politicians and military officers and have them executed.

The attempted coup and its suppression led to upheaval in Burundi's countryside. Through October and November, roving bands of Hutus attacked Tutsi homes and in turn were targeted by Tutsi troops and paramilitary political gangs, who also attacked innocent Hutu civilians. The Hutus, their leadership gone, received the worst of the violence; thousands were killed, many of them soldiers in the army slaughtered by their own commanders.

The following year (1966) the now completely Tutsi-controlled army overthrew the monarchy—King Mwambutsa IV had fled the country during the failed October 1965 coup—and declared Burundi a republic. The new government was completely dominated by Tutsi officers and politicians, one of whom, Michel Micombero, was chosen to be president. The monarchy, which had given Hutu and Tutsi a shared symbol of unity and authority, was gone.

1972 Massacre

From 1966 to 1972, Tutsi officers steadily purged the Hutu from the army. Some Hutu were included in the National Revolutionary Council (NRC), which ruled the country, and although the NRC denied that it was an ethnically based party, it was clear that part of their agenda was to make sure that Hutu had no more than a token presence at the highest levels of government. This Tutsi elitism inspired unrest among most Hutu, who felt that they were living under a system of ethnic apartheid.

The animosities between Tutsi and Hutu fed off of each other. When Hutu radicals accused the Tutsi of ethnic elitism, the Tutsis denounced the Hutus for practicing ethnic politics and then further tightened their grip on power. Extremists on both sides gained support by becoming even more extreme. Tutsi-Hutu hatreds, while having some historical roots, were largely manufactured by opportunistic politicians.

Hutu fear and hatred escalated into violence in late April 1972 with an uprising in the southern part of Burundi. The south had been, before the arrival of the Germans, traditionally dominated by the Hutu, even after the arrival of Tutsi kings, and many southerners resented their loss of influence. Hutus, in what was probably a planned rising, seized armories in several southern towns—including Rumonge and Nyanza-Lac—and

started killing any Tutsis they could find (as well as some Hutu who refused to join their rebellion). Two or three thousand Tutsis died during the week-long revolt.

The Tutsi government, led by President Micombero, responded to the Hutu rebellion by orchestrating a mass attack on the entire Hutu elite. In May, while Tutsi troops were crushing the rebels, Hutus elsewhere, who had not taken part in the uprising, were rounded up and executed. Even Hutus who had helped fight against the rebels, as many had, were arrested and killed.

The Tutsi carrying out these attacks came from the army and the Jeunesse Nationaliste Rwagasore (JNR), a Tutsi UPRONA youth group (by this time UPRONA was an exclusively Tutsi party). The murders were carried out with guns, clubs, and machetes. Those Tutsi who protested against the killings risked being killed themselves.

Although any Hutu was vulnerable during the massacres, the Tutsis particularly targeted the educated classes. Teachers at all levels were killed, as were their students, including those in primary school. Tutsi students helped the executioners find their victims by making lists of their Hutu classmates. A U.S. embassy report read, "Trucks ply the road to the airport every night with a fresh contribution [of bodies] to the mass grave."

Over the course of May and June at least 100,000 Hutu were killed by the Tutsi. This amounted to about 2 percent of the Hutu population, but included almost every educated Hutu. The Tutsi extremists of President Micombero's government had succeeded in wiping out those Hutu who would have been best able to resist Tutsi control. The massacres left behind a legacy of hatred that would haunt Burundi.

A Burundi army armored vehicle patrols the streets of the capital, Bujumbura, after the overthrow of President Melchior Ndadaye, October 24, 1993. *(Associated Press/Wide World)*

The Tutsi State

In 1976, Micombero was overthrown by Jean-Baptiste Bagaza, another Tutsi officer and a cousin of Micombero's. Bagaza attempted to maintain Tutsi power through strict bureaucratic controls placed on society. Education was restricted so that Hutu, still the vast majority of the population, were only a minority in secondary schools. Churches and missionaries were restricted because Bagaza and the Tutsi suspected them of being sources of dangerous ideas among the Hutu. Bagaza also attempted, with limited success, to force farmers to live in villages so that a closer watch could be kept upon them. In an attempt to eradicate Hutu "tribalism," Bagaza also forbade all mention of ethnicity, in public or in private.

This policy maintained Tutsi control without ever admitting that there were any such groups as Tutsi or Hutu.

Officially, anyone was allowed to be a part of Burundi's government, but in practice it was almost completely managed by Tutsis. Most government ministers were Tutsi and the thirty-member military council that ran the country was entirely Tutsi.

Bagaza's policies were unpopular among both Hutu and Tutsi. His regime was handicapped by its nature: It was difficult to lead a system that enforced apartheid while never admitting that apartheid existed. Extremist Tutsis wanted more limitations put on the Hutu; Hutus and moderate Tutsis wanted the government to attempt reconciliation and reintegration of the two ethnicities.

In 1987, Bagaza was overthrown by another coup led by a Tutsi army officer, Pierre Buyoya.

Buyoya's Regime

Buyoya, who ruled from 1987 to 1993, attempted to institute a more flexible approach to the problem of Hutu-Tutsi relations. He permitted greater freedom of speech and allowed ethnic terms to be discussed openly again. Many political prisoners, mostly Hutus, were also released. Buyoya argued that Tutsi and Hutu had to cooperate for Burundi to prosper. Finally, Buyoya ended the restrictions on religion that the previous regime had imposed.

However, beyond a few superficialities, Buyoya's regime was not substantially different from that of Bagaza before him. Tutsi still dominated the army, the civil service, and the judiciary.

In August 1988, frustrated by what they perceived as a lack of change—especially after their hopes had been raised by Buyoya's promises—Hutus in the northern provinces of Ngozi and Kirundo rose up and killed hundreds of Tutsi. This uprising, unlike 1972, seemed to have been completely unplanned; the Hutus who revolted suspected that extremist Tutsi were planning another massacre and staged a pre-emptive strike. The Hutu fears were not completely groundless, many ethnic clashes had occurred in the early part of 1988, often initiated by Tutsi extremists, and Tutsi army units had seemed suspiciously active in the two provinces.

The murders of the Tutsis were carried out with great brutality, and the Tutsi reaction was even more brutal. Some 15,000 Hutu were killed in the reprisals that followed. Unlike 1972, this Tutsi response did not seem to be organized from the center; rather, it was the combined responses of individual Tutsi commanders.

Buyoya's response to the 1988 massacres was unusual for Burundi. Rather than clamp down harder on the Hutu, Buyoya accelerated his liberalization policies. Buyoya brought a number of Hutus into his government and appointed a Hutu as prime minister. He also created a commission to investigate the massacres, which was composed of an equal number of Hutu and Tutsi members. It was probable that Buyoya's decision to open his government was caused in part by foreign pressure: international opinion was extremely critical of the Tutsi policies, and Buyoya risked a loss in foreign aid payments if he did not moderate Tutsi practices.

Ethnic friction continued in the early 1990s, with the occasional flare-up of violence. Buyoya, however, continued to move Burundi toward more openness. Under his guidance, Hutu gradually took over a majority of cabinet posts in the government. Finally, in June 1993, Buyoya allowed an open presidential election to be held. It was won by the Hutu candidate, Melchior Ndadaye, with 65 percent of the vote (Buyoya had received 33 percent). Ndadaye's party, the Front pour la démocratie au Burundi (FRODEBU) also won a majority of the seats in Burundi's legislature.

Chaos in Rwanda and Burundi

Ndadaye served as president for four months. Although the Hutu dominated the government, the Tutsi still controlled the army, and extremist officers resented Ndadaye's attempts to bring Hutus into the army. In October 1993, Tutsi army units seized the presidential palace and executed Ndadaye and other government leaders. The leaders of this coup were not backed by the rest of the army and were either put under arrest or forced to flee the country, but the damage caused by the coup was severe.

Ethnic violence by fearful Hutu and extremist Tutsi continued through 1993 and into 1994. The government was put back together with the ministers who were still alive. Moderates in the two major parties, the Hutu-dominated FRODEBU and the Tutsi-controlled UPRONA, put together a governing coalition in an effort to restore order. The coalition government picked a Hutu president, Cyprien Ntaryamira, and a Tutsi prime minister, Anatole Kanyenkiko. Their attempts to end the violence were handicapped by the Tutsi-controlled army's reluctance to search for those within its ranks who had helped the October 1993 attempted coup. Hutus suspected, probably correctly, that the army was protecting some of its own commanders who had been involved in the coup attempt. Hutus in the countryside remained afraid of another Tutsi-led genocidal slaughter. The reaction of peasants in the villages was to target each other. Hundreds were killed every week.

In a further attempt to calm the situation, the president of Rwanda, Juvenal Habyarimana, and Burundi's president, Ntaryamira, both Hutus, met in an international summit in Tanzania. On their return, their plane was shot down above the Kigali airport in Rwanda. Who assassinated the two presidents was never discovered. It was assumed by many that Hutu extremists in Rwanda had decided that the two men must die in order to prevent further reconciliation between Hutu and Tutsi. If the assassins had been the Hutus, where they acquired the equipment to shoot down a jet airliner was unknown. An April 6, 1994, report by the French paper *Le Figaro* claimed that French

officers admitted having sold the missiles to the Hutus as part of a general policy of supporting Rwanda's Hutu-controlled government. A retired French minister responded by suggesting that the United States had been responsible. This seemed unlikely, particularly as other sources had proved that France continued to supply the Hutus with arms even after some of their anti-Tutsi intentions had become clear.

In Rwanda, the double assassination was the trigger for a wave of violence that killed at least half a million Tutsi. In Burundi, the government, now shared between Tutsi and Hutu, was able to prevent any large-scale violence from breaking out. Small-scale violence, however, continued.

Violence and Breakdown

In October 1994, the government—again a coalition between FRODEBU and UPRONA—appointed another Hutu, Sylvestre Ntibantunganya, as president; the Tutsi Kanyenkiko continued on as prime minister. Although it was clear that some elements among both Tutsi and Hutu desired an end to the bloodshed between the two ethnic groups, extremists on both sides remained eager to undercut their efforts.

Particularly troublesome was the influx of some 200,000 Hutu refugees from Rwanda. In July 1994 a Tutsi-led army defeated the Hutu government of Rwanda, and hundreds of thousands of Hutus fled fearing reprisals. The violence in Rwanda had been greater than that in Burundi, and the refugees helped to raise Burundi Hutu fears—and may have contributed directly to violence in Burundi. Assassinations of government officials and murders of civilians of both ethnicities continued, with women and children being prime targets.

Hutus in exile in Zaire organized an armed militia to fight against the Tutsi army. The guerrilla group, Force pour la défense de la démocratie (FDD), which was the military wing of the extremist Hutu Conseil national pour la défense de la démocratie (CNDD), slipped its men across the border to attack Tutsi villagers. The Tutsi army responded with campaigns against the Hutu-occupied suburbs of Bujumbura, Burundi's capital. By 1996, Burundi was becoming segregated, with the larger towns and Bujumbura becoming all Tutsi, while the countryside was transformed into Hutu-only territory.

In July 1996, the Tutsi army toppled Ntibantunganya's government (Ntibantunganya fled to the American embassy) and replaced it with a military dictatorship led, again, by Pierre Buyoya. The world, tired of the killing in Burundi, responded with economic sanctions against the country, but Buyoya refused to step down. FRODEBU, now excluded from the government, became more radical and militant. Some of its members joined the CNDD in calling for an armed struggle against the Tutsi.

As of May 1998, the situation remained the same. Buyoya and the Tutsi army were still in charge but the Hutu rebels of the FDD were growing more bold in their attacks, even briefly seizing an airport outside the capital in January 1998.

Analysis

The ethnic war in Burundi was a tragedy that need not have happened. Class and ethnic differences existed, and they were exacerbated by colonial interference, but the cause of the conflict was the rise of an ide-

ology that created a new kind of ethnic polarization. Certain leaders among the Hutu and Tutsi found it to their advantage to push extremist politics. Violence led to violence, and the myth of age-old hatred between Tutsi and Hutu was turned into a reality.

A brief possibility of peace came with Buyoya's reforms and the 1993 coalition between UPRONA and FRODEBU. It was then ended by the extremist Tutsis who assassinated President Ndadaye.

When the violence will stop has been unclear. Hutu leaders have refused to end their guerrilla war as long as the Tutsi remain in charge of the government and the army, and the Tutsi, while they might agree to share power within the government, are unlikely to let the Hutu gain any substantial representation in the army. Even if Buyoya agreed to such a plan, his own Tutsi supporters would probably react by staging another coup against the government.

International pressure might have had some effect on Burundi, but events in neighboring countries have actually helped the Tutsis in Burundi. The victory of the Tutsi backed Rwandan Patriotic Front (RPF) in July 1994 secured Burundi's northern border from interference, while the May 1997 victory of Lauren Kabila's Tutsi-supported army in Zaire (which was renamed Congo) made it more difficult for Hutu rebels to continue to operate out of bases in that country.

The likelihood is that the violence will continue beyond 1998, and that the 200,000 who have been killed since 1993 (as well as the 200,000 who were probably killed between 1965 and 1993) will have more company.

Carl Skutsch

See also: Congo (Zaire), Democratic Republic of: Kabila Uprising, 1996–1997; Rwanda: Civil War and Genocide Since 1991.

Bibliography

Eggers, Ellen K. *Historical Dictionary of Burundi*. Lanham, MD: Scarecrow Press, 1997.

Lemarchand, René. *Burundi: Ethnic Conflict and Genocide*. Washington, DC: Woodrow Wilson Center Press, 1996.

Wolbers, Marian. *Burundi*. Broomall, PA: Chelsea House, 1989.